Captain of Her Soul

The publisher and the University of California Press Foundation gratefully acknowledge the generous support of the Kenneth Turan and Patricia Williams Endowment Fund in American Film.

Captain of Her Soul

THE LIFE OF MARION DAVIES

Lara Gabrielle

UNIVERSITY OF CALIFORNIA PRESS

University of California Press
Oakland, California

Library of Congress Cataloging-in-Publication Data
Names: Gabrielle, Lara, author.
Title: Captain of her soul : the life of Marion Davies / Lara Gabrielle.
Description: Oakland, California : University of California Press, [2022] |
    Includes bibliographical references and index.
Identifiers: LCCN 2021062368 (print) | LCCN 2021062369 (ebook) |
    ISBN 9780520384200 (cloth) | ISBN 9780520384217 (epub)
Subjects: LCSH: Davies, Marion, 1897–1961. | Motion picture actors and
    actresses—United States—Biography. | Motion picture producers and
    directors—United States—Biography.
Classification: LCC PN2287.D315 G33 2022 (print) | LCC PN2287.D315
    (ebook) | DDC 791.4302/8092 [B]—dc23/eng20220526
LC record available at https://lccn.loc.gov/2021062368
LC ebook record available at https://lccn.loc.gov/2021062369

Manufactured in the United States of America

31 30 29 28 27 26 25 24 23 22
10 9 8 7 6 5 4 3 2

Without the following people, the book you hold in your hands would never have come to fruition. I am forever grateful for their wisdom in all its varied forms, and I thank them from the bottom of my heart.

To my mother, Lynn Polon, whose loving support and meticulous eye as a reader has helped mold this story.

To Cari Beauchamp, for always keeping me laughing and whose sage advice, dedication, and steadfast belief in me and in Marion's story have been a guiding light.

To Marion Lake Canessa, whose family letters, photographs, and memories were so graciously shared. Her friendship and generosity mean the world to me.

To Taylor Coffman, who read every word of the manuscript for a clarity and accuracy that no one else in the world could have given it.

To Stanley Flink, whose unfaltering memory of every moment has helped breathe the breath of life into this book.

Out of the night that covers me,
  Black as the pit from pole to pole,
I thank whatever gods may be
  For my unconquerable soul.

In the fell clutch of circumstance
  I have not winced nor cried aloud.
Under the bludgeonings of chance
  My head is bloody, but unbowed.

Beyond this place of wrath and tears
  Looms but the Horror of the shade,
And yet the menace of the years
  Finds and shall find me unafraid.

It matters not how strait the gate,
  How charged with punishments the scroll,
I am the master of my fate,
  I am the captain of my soul.

WILLIAM ERNEST HENLEY,
"Invictus"

CONTENTS

Photographs Follow Pages 76 and 180

ACKNOWLEDGMENTS

Over the course of my research, the following people have gone to extraordinary lengths to help ensure that Marion Davies's story is told fully, fairly, and accurately. To them, I express my deepest gratitude.

Kay Pattison, Ruthann Lehrer, and the entire docent community of the Annenberg Community Beach House, who have guided and supported me with their knowledge and positivity from the very beginning.

Elaina Friedrichsen, producer of the documentary *Captured on Film*, who has been an ardent supporter of this project and gave me many of the autobiographical tapes that were so essential to the crafting of Marion's story.

Ned Comstock, a researcher's dream, at the USC Cinematic Arts Library, for his diligence and always thinking of me when he saw a Marion Davies item.

Hugh Munro Neely, who graciously gave me access to the interviews conducted by Fred Lawrence Guiles for his 1972 book, *Marion Davies*. The interviews allowed me to hear the people who knew Marion best, those who have long since passed away, speak about her in their own words. He also gave me access to the illuminating interviews he conducted, with Elaina Friedrichsen, for the *Captured on Film* documentary.

Kevin Brownlow, for his unmatched expertise and enthusiasm. He has been a great gift to this project, as have his photos and his willingness to let me explore them at his office in London.

Ty Smith, the curator at Hearst Castle, gave me a tour of the grounds early on in my project, from which I learned a great deal.

Jill Urquhardt, the librarian at Hearst Castle, has been a great friend to this project and to me personally, with her expert knowledge and diligent research.

The staff at the Library of Congress, for their dedication and effort in helping me to see all of Marion's extant films. I also thank them for their grace and top-notch sense of humor in the wake of some interesting film switches at Culpeper.

The staff at the UCLA Film and TV Archive, for accommodating me and letting me use the big rooms.

Jeanine Basinger of Wesleyan University provided much encouragement and support. Her respect for Marion's work shines through in her writing and interviews.

Ziegfeld historian Ann van der Merwe was instrumental in chronologizing Marion's stories from her Ziegfeld days.

David Silverman, the foremost expert on 1011 N. Beverly Drive, for helping me with the most intricate details of the home.

Kimberly and Victoria Lake, for being so generous with their memories of their father and grandparents.

Dr. Gerald Maguire and Dr. Barry Guitar, who helped me to understand Marion's stuttering, and answered my questions with patience and thoughtful care. I was so lucky that two of the world's leading experts on stuttering were willing to help me.

Dr. Nina Ghiselli, for expanding my understanding of stuttering in women, and for her continued interest and support.

Mrs. S. Williams, at PS 93 in Brooklyn, went far beyond the call of duty, digging through the archives for Marion's school records. Her dedication was so fierce that I think she missed a calling as a professional researcher.

Gary Jaskula and Nancy Okada of the New York Buddhist Church at 331 Riverside Drive. I arrived on a cleaning day, and as we cleaned the grounds, Gary talked passionately with me about the history of the home, which has barely changed since Marion lived there. 331 Riverside Drive is in good hands.

Larry Russell, who knew Marion in childhood, shared with me several laugh-out-loud stories and anecdotes.

The late Russell Brown, Marion's stepson and a lovely human being, who helped me to understand his father in new and important ways.

Professor Daniel Cano, who graciously allowed me to use his interviews with Lupe and Peaches Herrera.

Nick Langdon, for visiting with me and showing me his home-movie footage.

Michael Yakaitis, for his gorgeous photos and footage, his memories, and for his support from the beginning.

Marc Wanamaker, for his kindness and allowing me to go through his photos.

Lea Sullivan, for always being sunny and positive about life and this project.

Belinda Vidor Holliday, for sharing her time and her memories with me.

Andrea McCarty, cinema archivist at Wesleyan University, for her help with Marion Davies's tapes.

Dr. Kathleen Nadeau, for helping me get a sense of Marion's mind.

The late Julie Payne, Charlie Lederer's stepdaughter, for her dedication in helping me understand the family dynamics.

The late, ever-fabulous Mary Carlisle. I met Mary when she was 100 years old, and though blind and hard of hearing, she was eager to show me that she was in good health and did a high kick to prove it. A pistol to the very end, she gave me firsthand stories about the 1936 trip to Europe and what Marion was like when she was still working.

The entire staff at the Margaret Herrick Library, for their patience and accommodation over these past many years. I would like to mention Howard Prouty and Louise Hilton in particular, who were especially accommodating during the COVID lockdown, and Faye Thompson, who went above and beyond the call of duty to help me obtain the photos I needed.

Kristine Krueger, for helping me navigate the library's vast digital collection, and for her excellent communication and eagerness to help.

My wonderful friends: Kendra Bean, for inspiring me to start this process; and Carley Hildebrand, for supporting me when this idea was nothing more than a seed.

A sheynem dank to my Yiddishist friends, who helped push me to the finish line through our Zoom coworking group. Ri J. Turner, Karo Wegner, Lies Lanckman, Jenny Blair, freygl gertsovski, Sandra Chiritescu, Tamara Gleason-Friedberg, Elena Luchina, Sarah Biskowitz, and everyone else who has joined the "Coshmerking" Zoom room during COVID.

Lisa and David Kruse, for their care and support throughout this project. Burt, Joyce, and Zakai Arnowitz, for all their affection, advice, and laughs.

The expert staff at Montclair Photo, for patiently addressing all my questions and scanning the photos for this book.

My father, John Fowler, for his love and writing advice through the years.

My sister, Kayla Simone Fowler, for always seeing the funny side of things.

My aunt, J. P. Novic, for her unconditional support of me always.

L. Wayne Alexander, for his meticulous and expert support whenever I had a question about copyright or anything legal.

The entire production team at University of California Press, and especially my editor, Raina Polivka, for believing in me and in this project.

Editorial assistant Madison Wetzell, for helping with the art and for her patience with all my varied questions.

Julie Van Pelt, for overseeing the beautiful editing, design, and production of the book.

David Peattie at BookMatters, for being so communicative with me during "post-production."

Copy editor extraordinaire Paul Tyler, for his expert editorial eye and for giving the manuscript his devoted attention.

Publicists Katryce Lassle, Emily Grandstaff, and Teresa Iafolla, for their enthusiasm and for helping get the book off the ground.

As Marion would say, "millions of thanks" to everyone.

A NOTE ON SOURCES

This project is the culmination of a decade of intensive research in archives around the world. Interviews I conducted with those who knew Marion Davies have added depth and nuance to that research, and their revelations about the complexity and details of her life have helped me immeasurably. In addition to the myriad sources I reference from archival materials, early in this project I was granted access to Marion's extant autobiographical tapes, used to create *The Times We Had* (1975). The book, edited by Pamela Pfau and Kenneth Marx, was marketed as Marion Davies's memoir and released over a decade after her death. Listening to the tapes and reading the book are two very different experiences. Because the reminiscences are conversational, the tapes follow a thematic train of thought rather than a chronological one. Pfau and Marx spliced quotes together from various tapes to create a chronological version of what Marion might have written, had an autobiography been completed. Because of the nature of the work, *The Times We Had* is not a completely accurate record of what Marion Davies thought and felt.

Unfortunately, several of the original tapes have been lost for decades. A complete transcript exists, which has served as a backup for the lost tapes. On that transcript, there are many words indiscernible to the transcriber. Wherever possible, I use Marion's own words as I heard them on the extant tapes, citing my own transcription of the audio (with my best guess of what Marion said) if I was unable to discern a word. If I used a quote from one of the "lost" tapes that included an indiscernible word for that transcriber, I went to *The Times We Had* to find what that word was. In that case, I cite *The Times We Had* in the endnotes.

Marion began work on her autobiography at a difficult time in her life, and these experiences color what she says about certain people and affect the trustworthiness of some of her statements. In addition, she was often remembering events that occurred up to fifty years earlier. For each statement that I use from the tapes or *The Times We Had*, I have done my best to back up the statement with a second, independent source. If the statement cannot be verified with a second source, that is made clear in the text.

Research by Fred Lawrence Guiles for his biography *Marion Davies* (1972) has also provided me with a great amount of physical media. Guiles, who died in 2000, spoke to dozens of Marion Davies's friends and family, and his taped interviews have been of great value to this project. Because Guiles's published biography itself lacks citations, I use *Marion Davies* in a way similar to *The Times We Had*. I was able to find most of Guiles's assertions in the interviews that he conducted. If something could not be verified directly through the interview tapes, I tried to find a second, independent source. If one could not be found, there appears an "According to..." disclaimer in the text.

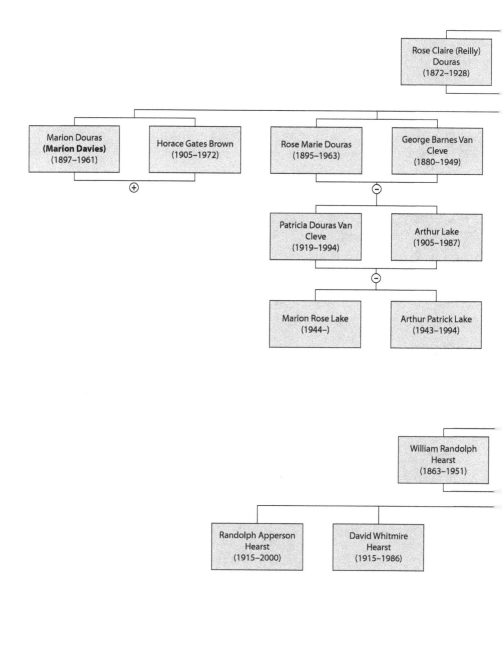

Rose Claire (Reilly) Douras (1872–1928)

Marion Douras (**Marion Davies**) (1897–1961)

Horace Gates Brown (1905–1972)

Rose Marie Douras (1895–1963)

George Barnes Van Cleve (1880–1949)

Patricia Douras Van Cleve (1919–1994)

Arthur Lake (1905–1987)

Marion Rose Lake (1944–)

Arthur Patrick Lake (1943–1994)

William Randolph Hearst (1863–1951)

Randolph Apperson Hearst (1915–2000)

David Whitmire Hearst (1915–1986)

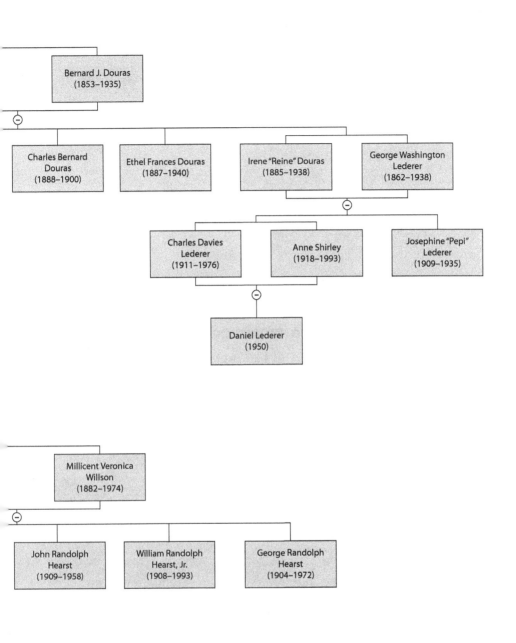

Introduction

In early 1953, Marion Davies began recording her autobiographical tapes. Twice a week, she met with *Life* magazine correspondent Stanley Flink in the library of her Beverly Hills home.

Although she had been in California for nearly thirty years, she still spoke with a gentle New York accent. Every now and then, a stutter halted her speech. Her limpid blue eyes were exceptionally large and round, and a wide, kind smile accentuated her naturally rosy cheeks. It was easy to see how the camera had loved Marion Davies. Hers was a face seemingly made for the silent screen. She wore a blouse and simple slacks, with house slippers on her feet, and no jewelry. Her demeanor was affectionate and loving, addressing Stanley Flink as "Stan" and referring to him as "sweetie" and "honey" throughout their talks. He had long since abandoned the formal "Miss Davies," addressing her warmly as "Marion," which she preferred.

A serious illness a decade before had left Marion with weak legs, and as she reminisced about her life, she rested her feet on a small footstool under the table. She tended to veer off topic, straying from her own experiences into current events, such as the recent death of Joseph Stalin or a minor news item she had read in the paper. Flink engaged with her in these diversions, but always steered her back to the topic at hand with masterful ease.

For decades, publicity departments wrote her life story for her. Public myths and legends had grown around her life, inspiring characters in both literature and film. The mistress of millionaire Jo Stoyte in Aldous Huxley's *After Many a Summer Dies the Swan* was thought to be based on her. Marion claimed never to have met Huxley, and she never read the book. Perhaps most significantly, she was closely associated with *Citizen Kane*, and with the film's untalented opera singer, Susan Alexander. The redeeming qualities of

Orson Welles's groundbreaking film are nearly undisputed, and many consider it the greatest ever made. But *Citizen Kane* and the character of Susan Alexander have contributed to public misconception of who Marion was, something Orson Welles himself publicly regretted. Marion's own avoidance of interviews allowed these ideas to propagate and recycle, resulting in a life shrouded in mystery, rumor, and half-truths. Finally, now, in the library with Stanley Flink, Marion was going to tell her own story.

Flink sensed that despite her purported happiness, there was an underlying sadness that gave her life a certain melody that was hidden from most who knew her. Eileen Percy, one of Marion's oldest and most trusted friends, agreed with his assessment. Flink had been the first to capture the essence of Marion Davies in a *Life* piece following William Randolph Hearst's death in 1951, though he was by no means the first journalist to realize what a story it was. For more than thirty years, Marion was the companion of press baron Hearst who, as Flink's feature on his life put it, was the "inventor, purveyor, prolificator and practitioner" of a type of controversial journalism that dominated nearly every part of American politics and culture for over fifty years. Theirs was one of the great love stories of the twentieth century and comprised almost all of Marion's adult life. With him, she had entertained the likes of George Bernard Shaw and Calvin Coolidge, but she found their greatest moments together to be those intimate moments when no one else was around. When Hearst was near death, she kept a three-day vigil by his bedside.

Following publication of the article, Stan Flink received a call from gossip columnist Hedda Hopper. "You sonofabitch," said Hedda, "you wrote my story, and damn well."

In my ten years of research for this project, I have come to know the real Marion Davies intimately. She had a gentle demeanor, and a wit that could send listeners into peals of laughter. She was a loyal friend, liked tapioca pudding, and was mildly allergic to shellfish. Early access to her autobiographical tapes taught me a great deal about Marion that could not be captured in descriptors—I heard her melodic intonations, and her quiet giggle when something struck her as funny. Some of the most captivating things were her whimsical phrases or her use of unusual words. "I swear it on twenty thousand stacks of Bibles," she would say to emphasize a point. Marion's mind worked quickly, and sometimes she became impatient when someone couldn't keep up. She might briefly show a flash of exasperation, before catching herself and returning to her naturally gentle temperament. Her stutter did not seem to faze her, though it was frequent and sometimes slowed the conversation significantly.

Marion lived life on a scale beyond most people's comprehension, but her group of true friends was small. Anxiety was a debilitating problem, and her use of alcohol to dull it had long worried her friends. Former chorus girls Eileen Percy, China Harris, and Justine Johnstone were regular guests at 1011 North Beverly Drive, the sprawling 18,000-square-foot home of twenty-two bedrooms that she bought to share with Hearst. The address then was 1007, but the city had grown around her and the address had changed. Though modest from the front, the property extended far back almost to Laurel Lane, with a grand pool and palatial backyard. In subsequent years, the home has been used for exteriors in such films as *The Godfather* and *The Bodyguard*. The Goldwyn family, of Metro-Goldwyn-Mayer fame, lived just behind her home on Laurel Lane. Frances, Samuel Goldwyn's wife, often worried about Marion and sometimes she would walk over and knock on the door, just to check on her.

These were steadfast confidantes, friends with whom Marion could be completely herself. Composed mostly of people from her early days as a lower-middle-class chorus girl in Brooklyn, they were evidence of the fact that she remained close to her roots, never fully at home in the lavish environment in which she lived. Nor was she comfortable with the sense of self-importance that many in her circles displayed. Flink, referring to her social distance from her surroundings, called her "a cork in the ocean."

When sound came to the movies, Marion worked tirelessly with coaches to overcome her stutter, and as a result she was one of only a handful of actresses to survive the transition. She is the matriarch of a certain type of comedic family, and laid the groundwork for future comediennes Carole Lombard, Lucille Ball, and Carol Burnett. Much like her comedic descendants, Marion's outward demeanor belied a steely grit and strong work ethic, essential for the successes she achieved in her career. She negotiated her own contracts, earning an astonishing $10,000 per week in the 1920s and investing wisely. Despite Hearst's influence over her career, Marion made all her own decisions. "I'm the captain of my soul," she told Stan Flink. "Therefore, what I want to do I want to do myself, regardless of what people think that I should do."

One of the inherent difficulties of this project is that Marion gave few interviews. Aside from the issues with her speech, I find that she was wary of strangers and reluctant to share her story. She had a persistent fear of revealing too much, aware of what others might think of her and the way she lived. Her reluctance to speak on the record about certain issues rendered an honest autobiography a difficult challenge, one that Flink and Marion ultimately abandoned. After her death, the fragmented reminiscences were molded into a makeshift memoir entitled *The Times We Had*. Flink did not participate in its creation.

Flink knew that she feared revealing too much, as she hedged around important points and spoke in veiled references. But when she was feeling confident, Marion would comment articulately about the momentous highs and deep lows of her life, especially the joyous moments with Hearst and the heartbreak at the end. Despite the many difficulties of her life, she remained a vibrant and energetic soul who loved life, loved to dance, and loved children. The rosiness in her cheeks remained until her very last moments on Earth.

Preparation for this book has taken me all over the world for interviews and archival research. I was struck by how eager people have been to talk about her. A recurring theme quickly emerged: "Marion was the most wonderful human being I ever knew." Not a single person declined to speak about her. This alone says a great deal about Marion, and the profound influence that she had on the lives of the people around her.

Marion was sophisticated in her knowledge of literature and poetry, and when she told Stan Flink "I am the captain of my soul," she quoted William Ernest Henley's poem "Invictus," evoking the strength to overcome difficult circumstances. Despite the challenges that Marion had in her life, she faced them straight on and fought to overcome them.

This is the story of the woman she was.

Beginnings

The winter of 1896–97 was a warm one in New York City, one of the warmest of the decade. The price of a ladies' heavyweight jacket was slashed from $6.90 to $3.97 in early January due to decreased demand for winter clothes. William McKinley had recently won the election of 1896, ushering in a new era that would shape the coming century. Brooklyn was still a separate city on the outskirts of a rapidly developing New York City. And at 289 89th Street in that suburb of Brooklyn, 29-year-old Rose Douras was at home expecting her fifth child.

Marion Davies spoke of her family history with pride. Both sides were prominent in New York City politics, contributing to efforts to better the city during a time of extreme corruption. Marion's maternal grandfather, Charles Reilly, had come to New York from his native Connecticut in young adulthood. He became active in New York politics, quickly rising to the upper echelons of the New York City Democratic Party. He helped to create the County Democracy, one of the few organizations to pose a threat to the Tammany Hall establishment, and was a well-known and much-beloved figure around the city. He married Mary Cushing, and the couple owned two blocks of Manhattan apartments from which they earned income.

His daughter Rose, Marion's mother, was a soft-spoken, caring woman who loved sunshine and solitude. She enjoyed sitting back and simply observing her surroundings, engaging friends in topics she found interesting, such as cooking and her family. When she had children, she gave herself completely to them and thought of little else. She and Marion developed a particularly close bond, and in return Marion was devoted to "Mama Rose."

Rose met Bernard J. Douras, a managing clerk at the law firm Vanderpoel, Green & Cuming, in the early 1880s and took an interest in him. The son of immigrants Daniel and Catherine Douras, Bernard had gone to Columbia Law School and showed a promising future. Although his parents had come from Ireland, the unusual name of Douras is French Huguenot in origin, the result of a branch of a family that fled France to escape persecution by the Catholic majority. The Dourases had settled in County Tyrone and County Mayo in the north of the country, where they worked as laborers until the onslaught of the potato famine in 1845. Daniel and Catherine came to the United States through Liverpool and made their home in New York City, where Bernard was born and educated.

The Reillys enthusiastically approved of Rose's choice in a match, and Rose and Bernard married in 1884. Rose soon became pregnant with her first child and gave birth to a girl named Irene in 1885. Nicknamed "Reine" (pronounced to rhyme with "Queenie"), she was docile, proper, and eager to please. Ethel, born in 1887, was significantly more spirited with a penchant for shocking people. She was a force of nature and delighted in letting loose with various off-color expressions such as "Oh, my ass for a banjo string!" Although she was devoted to all her siblings, Marion would later whisper to friends that Ethel was secretly her favorite sister.

The Dourases' third child, Charles, was born in October 1888. Childhood photos show him with the same lithe body that Marion had, the same big, expressive eyes, and, according to family legend, the same spirited and affectionate demeanor. Named after Rose's father, Charles was the long-awaited boy and the darling of his parents. His sweet nature and charming stutter allowed him to get away with almost anything. Charles's unremitting energy and constant troublemaking put his parents in a quandary regarding what to do with him. Rose and Bernard, by this time known by the nicknames "Mama Rose" and "Papa Ben," ultimately did little to curb his behavior, and Charles ran wild.

The fourth child, Rose, was born in 1895. Nicknamed "Rosie" as a child, she was stunningly pretty, with dark brown hair, a cherubic mouth, and a long, regal neck. Even at a young age, it was clear that Rosie had a magnificent singing voice and a prodigious talent for musical performance and composition. She started violin lessons at five years old with a local music teacher, and soon was giving concerts in the area. Throughout her life, she composed elaborate symphonies and other musical works that were performed publicly and well received by critics. However, it was also discovered that Rosie was having problems with her legs and, according to her own explanation, she was diagnosed as a toddler with a congenital hip dislocation. For the rest of her life, she walked with a limp or with the aid of a cane.

In the spring of 1896, Rose was pregnant again and on January 3, 1897, at 6:00 in the morning, the Dourases' fifth child was born in her parents' bedroom. The name on her birth certificate reads "Marion Douras," with no middle name. When Marion had her first communion, the name "Cecilia" was chosen for her, and it became her de facto middle name, despite her protests. "Can't I change my name?" she would beg her mother. "I don't like the name Cecilia. I like the name Violet instead." But her mother held firm, and whenever Marion couldn't avoid it, she was Marion Cecilia Douras.

From the very beginning, Marion was exceptionally loving and good-natured. Covered in freckles from head to toe, she had reddish brown hair and big blue eyes that sparkled with life. Affectionately nicknamed "Mardie" within the family, she charmed her parents and siblings with a winning combination of sweetness and mischief. According to biographer Fred Lawrence Guiles, adoring older brother Charles would cart Marion and Rosie around in his toy wagon, warning everyone, "D-d-don't touch my ba-ba-babies," as he rolled them proudly down the street, showing them off to anyone who would pay attention.

With the addition of their fifth child, the family was overwhelmed. Bernard tended to take cases he couldn't win because he believed in the cause. He devoted himself to overthrowing the corrupt political machine of Tammany Hall, at the expense of his practice. Rose began to wring her hands over money, and the fear that her husband was spreading himself too thin. But Marion was exceedingly loving toward her mother, and any stress Rose felt was inevitably relieved by her youngest daughter's devotion.

Marion remembered that her mother always smelled like gardenias and doted on her children. Recounting the proud tall tales her mother told about her babyhood, Marion remembered her mother telling people that she had stood up while still in the cradle. "How can a baby stand in bed?" Marion said, recalling the ridiculousness of the story. But the bond between mother and daughter was one of the most important of Marion's life. She described herself as having a "mother complex" as a child, never wanting to leave her mother's side, becoming distraught if she walked ahead of her or left her alone for a moment. "Don't run so fast!" Marion would implore her mother when they were shopping downtown. "Carry me, carry me, carry me!" This need for her mother's love was all-encompassing, to the point that for a long period during her childhood, Marion was unable to sleep in her own bed. She would remember this insecurity as an adult. "I would crawl out [of bed] and put my arms around [my mother's] neck—and now I know she must have thought: 'Oh, what a pest this one is!'"

When Marion was a toddler, the Douras family moved to a home at 352 47th Street, where they stayed for several years. The family was short on money, but Rose and Ben made travel and excursions outside of New York a priority for the children. Whenever Ben had a moment away from work, they would go to Montclair, New Jersey, where Rose's parents lived, or to Lake Saratoga near where Charles Reilly had a stable. Late in their marriage, Rose's parents had decided to separate and maintained separate residences, with her father Charles spending much of his time at Lake Saratoga with his horses.

Marion disliked the family's trips outside the city. In Montclair, she found her grandmother strict and unforgiving. A common disciplinary tactic at the Reilly house was being locked in the closet, which terrified Marion. As she was energetic and lively, Marion found herself locked there on many occasions while visiting her grandmother. At home, Rose disciplined her daughter for misbehavior, but Marion found her grandmother's "closet treatment" the worst punishment she ever received. She begged her mother not to take her back to her grandmother's house, and when bribes and coercion didn't make Marion feel any better about going back to Montclair, Rose never made her return. At Lake Saratoga, Marion had a series of bad experiences and accidents with her grandfather's horses. The most serious of these occurred at the age of 12, when Marion had a bad fall from one of the horses, landed on a pile of logs, and broke her tailbone. The healing process was long, and she emerged from it with a lifelong phobia of horses.

Despite her problems with her grandparents, Marion's childhood was generally a happy one. She was a sunny child surrounded by the care of her parents and siblings, and she loved and was loved deeply. But tragedy rocked the Douras family when they went to Lake Saratoga to get away from the city over Labor Day weekend in 1900. A few days after their arrival, 11-year-old Charles decided to go rowing on the lake, while Marion and Rosie, aged three and five, stayed with their mother. Charles was gone all day, and by the time darkness fell, he still had not returned from the lake. Believing that he had lost track of time, the family went out to the lake to call for him. There was no response. The police were summoned, and when Charles still could not be located, the family began to fear the worst. The police poled the lake while continuing to call for Charles, to no avail, for two days. Finally, on September 7, they found a body near the Boston and Maine Railroad bridge close to the north end of the lake. Charles's boat had capsized and he had drowned.

Charles's death was the beginning of a downward spiral for the Douras parents, and their relationship changed irreversibly. Overcome with emotion during the first Christmas season without Charles, Ben checked into the Clarendon Hotel on December 29, isolating himself from Rose and the rest of the family. Rose didn't know how to explain to her youngest daughter what had happened to her brother, and Marion was only aware that her brother was gone and her parents were despondent.

Rose and Ben spoke often of Charles during Marion's childhood, their stories of him keeping his memory alive in the minds of their children, who were too young to remember him. In the days before World War I, it was common practice to keep the memory of the deceased alive in the minds of survivors—a practice that changed with the mass wave of war deaths from World War I. But Marion and the rest of the family benefitted from this particular Victorian custom, as Charles remained in their minds symbolically long after he had died. When Rosie approached Marion in later years to make a documentary about their childhood together, she made a point to let her know that "I shall not forget Charles." For the rest of her life, however, Marion would have an agonizing fear of death, and coped poorly with the deaths of friends and loved ones. The deaths provoked extreme reactions that unnerved those around her, and as a result Marion was not often immediately informed of deaths, which only served to exacerbate her fear.

As Rose and Ben grew more distant over the course of the next several years, Ben's drinking escalated. One day, after receiving $1,500 in payment (likely from a client), he returned home from a day at the pub, having spent a considerable amount of it on liquor. Rose was so angry she refused to speak to him, and the children determined it was time to interfere. If Papa Ben were allowed to keep the rest of the money, Reine figured, it would never be seen again. Reine devised a scheme to pick his pockets while family friend Marie Glendinning distracted Ben. Reine managed to free $250 from her father's pocket, and gave the money to her mother.

While the Dourases were not religious to the same degree as many Catholic families of the era, their background and concerns with public perceptions were too important to allow for an official divorce or even an official separation, but they began to live apart much of the time. The children lived primarily at 47th Street with their mother while their father floated back and forth between his new and old homes. Ben's influence in his children's lives diminished, but Marion remained close to him.

Watching her own parents grow indifferent toward each other shaped Marion's views on marriage, instilling in her a wariness and bitterness that would stay with her. During her years with William Randolph Hearst, when it became clear that she couldn't marry him, Marion doubled down on this thought, as if to convince herself of the futility of marriage. "I used to see these things when I was a kid, and I used to say, 'What is marriage? Just a wedding ring. It means nothing.'" This would inform her ultimate acceptance of her relationship with Hearst, at least outwardly. "I'd say, 'Forget it. I don't want it that way. We're fine, we have great companionship'... and let it stay that way. Don't worry about it. It doesn't mean anything to me, I'm not the type to say, 'I want to be Mrs. So-and-so,' I was never that type." But was this something of which Marion was trying to convince herself, or something she truly thought? On the one hand, she often referenced how the marriages in her family never worked out, so she was sparing herself heartbreak by not marrying. On the other hand, throughout her relationship with Hearst, Marion retained the belief that she would somehow redeem herself by becoming a married woman, and this public denigration of marriage was a mask she frequently wore to hide her true feelings.

Around the time of Charles's death, Rose and Ben noticed that like her older brother, Marion was beginning to stutter. For the most part, her parents didn't call attention to Marion's increasingly halting speech, encouraging her to talk as she always did. But the effects of Marion's stutter soon began to make many aspects of life frustrating. The problem worsened under stress, and when she became frightened, Marion sometimes lost the ability to speak entirely. At varying times, her stutter was a mild inconvenience, a source of humor, and a huge detriment. It affected the course of her career and became a large part of her identity.

Marion recalled that very little intervention was done for her stutter as a child. Speech therapy was a relatively rare practice, mostly involving tactics such as putting marbles in a child's mouth for the child to talk around. Marion's parents did not do this with her. The only thing Marion recalled being told to do as a child was to breathe between words, which helped but was cumbersome. "I'm not going to go around going HOW [breath] DO [breath] YOU [breath] DO all the time," she said. So she had to find her own ways around her speech problems, which included, much of the time, substituting easier words for difficult ones. "Marion had great intelligence," remembered nephew Charlie Lederer's wife, Anne Shirley, in later years. But many times, Anne noted, her struggle with words made it hard for others to see it, and sometimes for Marion herself to see it.

When her parents enrolled Marion in school at PS 93, she proved to be an extremely bright child and a talented athlete, excelling especially in basketball and eventually becoming the captain of her school's basketball team. But in the classroom, she was flustered and frustrated. She continued to be an affectionate child to her family, and had no trouble making friends, but the classroom was torture. In the days of being called up in front of the room to recite, teachers humiliated Marion, knowing she couldn't get through the recitation. Marion would freeze with fear in front of her classmates, inevitably beginning to stutter. The children laughed as she was ordered back to her seat, dejected. After a long day dealing with the cruelty of her classmates and teachers, Marion would cuddle up to her mother and ask to have her head rubbed, which relaxed her muscles and her spirits.

Marion also turned to the comfort of books during her school days and became a voracious reader. She lost herself in the world of classic literature, devouring the complete works of Charles Dickens as a young child. Throughout her life, she would maintain a loyalty to Dickens as her favorite author, possessing nearly all his works in her libraries full of Shakespeare, Thackeray, Shaw, and Molière. She took joy in collecting the books she loved, her enthusiasm often keeping her too busy to actually read them. "I'll read them all when I'm an old woman," she told an interviewer in 1919, while showing her the hundreds of books in her collection. It was a passion that she shared with Hearst, and their combined libraries rivaled the greatest in the world.

In addition to seeking refuge at her mother's side, Marion had a secondary outlet for her energy and frustration. She spent much of her time outside of school playing alongside the Irish immigrant children of the neighborhood. Marion became a regular, rough-and-tumble playmate and had an excellent ear, quickly picking up the children's accents that she used later as the basis for her Irish brogue in *Peg O' My Heart*. While both of her parents had been born in the United States, her interactions with these children gave her a sense of "being Irish," a heritage that many of her friends later associated with Marion.

The Dourases were firmly in the working class and Rose wanted better for her girls. In the era before women's suffrage, there were very few avenues for women to improve their station outside of marrying into wealth. According to writer Anita Loos, who knew the family from the New York theatrical scene, the only way Rose saw for women to get ahead in life and lead a comfortable and financially secure existence was to become involved with a man who could provide for them financially. In what Loos called the "Gigi tradition," the modes by which a woman could attract and please a man, Marion's mother put little emphasis on the emotional entanglements of love. She pushed her daughters to accept the courtships of the older, wealthy men who came their way, regardless of whether there was love in the relationship. The ultimate goal was to marry those men and secure a comfortable life outside of Brooklyn.

Rose had been diligent about teaching her girls what she considered to be essential household skills, including cooking, washing, and sewing. Marion happily cooperated, and she took a special interest in needlework, for which she showed a natural gift. Before she reached her teens, Marion was a sewing prodigy, making her own clothes to pass the time, and knitting, crocheting, and embroidering tiny clothes for her dolls. As an adult, Marion kept up her needlework as a calming hobby, sewing many of her own clothes and becoming known among her friends for the elaborate and lavish dresses that she would make for them as gifts. In 1941, Marion would win a prize for three quilts that she entered into the Los Angeles County Fair.

Rose knew that Reine was a talented singer and actress, and she saw the chorus as a way for her eldest daughter to attract the attention of a wealthy man. Reine made her Broadway debut at the age of 16. She disliked the look of "Douras" on a marquee. Changing names in the theatrical profession was something of a rite of passage, if the performer had an unusual or difficult to pronounce name, and Reine decided to follow in the footsteps of such stars as Fanny Brice (born Fania Borach) and Al Jolson (born Asa Yoelson), changing her last name to make it more palatable to the public. When she saw a sign advertising a real estate agent by the name of "Davies," Reine chose it as her surname. The rest of the sisters officially adopted Davies when they went into the theatrical profession. Although Marion enjoyed the sound of "Davies" alongside her first name, it felt foreign to her, and she rarely used it outside of work. Marion never legally changed her name, using Davies only professionally.

Reine soon moved to Chicago under the mentorship of George Lederer, a prominent theatrical impresario in that city. Aware of Lederer's romantic intentions, Rose encouraged Reine to accept his advances to secure her financial stability. Ethel followed Reine to Chicago shortly thereafter. Rosie and Marion, still school age, stayed in New York with their mother, but in

1906, the three of them headed west to be near Reine and Ethel. Papa Ben stayed behind.

Marion spent the majority of the years between 1906 and 1910 in Chicago, with trips back to New York every few months with Rosie to see their father. It was during this time when Marion became enamored with dance. As she watched her sisters in the wings as they worked, Marion longed to be like them. Reine's connections with George Lederer meant that her shows were of the highest quality, and she starred alongside cowboy star Will Rogers and beloved vaudeville singer Sophie Tucker, known for her booming alto. Marion delighted in the intricate and colorful dance sequences in her sisters' shows, and she developed a particular enthusiasm for ballet. When asked what she would like to be when she grew up, Marion was adamant. "I would like to be a toe-dancer," she told her mother decisively. When Reine and Ethel were out of the house, Marion would try on their costumes and pretend to be a professional dancer like her older sisters.

Reine and George Lederer married in 1907, and George brought to the family his 11-year-old son, Maitland, from a previous marriage. Marion and Maitland were just one year apart in age, and they got along well. Marion was glad to have a friend in Chicago, coming to regard Maitland almost as a brother. Reine became pregnant herself shortly after the wedding, and in March 1909, gave birth to a girl named Josephine Rose Lederer. The baby was nicknamed "Pepi," a name that seemed to suit her bubbly personality. Marion was thrilled with her new niece and wrote to her mother's aunt Kate in her preteen cursive scrawl about how "lovely" new baby Josephine was. Marion was a natural caregiver, devoted to dolls and animals, and she was attentive and loving to her baby niece right from the beginning.

After four years in Chicago, Rose, Marion, and Rosie moved back to New York. Marion's stutter continued to plague her, and she compensated for her speech problems by clowning, invoking the ire of the teachers, who would continue to punish her by making her recite in front of the class. Marion knew that she was not living up to expectations, and longed to be more like Hazel Hart, a girl in her class whom she considered to be perfect. "She had all the things, all of the characteristics I didn't have," wrote Marion in an autobiographical newspaper column in 1925. Coddling as they could be with Marion as a young child, her parents felt that something had to be done to improve Marion's conduct as she approached adulthood. They hoped that enrolling her in Sacred Heart, a small convent school outside of the city, would give her the discipline that they could not. However well intentioned their efforts, and however Marion felt that a convent school would make her more like Hazel Hart, her time there was miserable. She resented the nuns when they hit her on the knuckles for playing the piano without permission, and Marion used this treatment as an excuse to convince her mother to remove her from Sacred Heart.

Marion was growing frustrated with her reputation as a wild child, yet she felt that her efforts to improve met with failure. Marion's self-esteem suffered, and she longed to follow her sisters into the theatre as a dancer, where she wouldn't have to recite or endure the taunts of her schoolmates. Marion talked to her mother, who at first resisted the idea of Marion's going on the stage at the age of 15. She wanted the same for Marion that she had wanted for Reine, but was hesitant about her youngest daughter being the object of men's glances at such a young age. However, when Rose asked Marion what she wanted to do, her response was insistent and unfaltering. "I would like to be a dancer," Marion replied. Finally, Rose gave in to her desires. By the next year, at the age of 16, Marion was out of school and on the stage.

"One of the Most Popular Girls in Town"

Marion would look back on her chorus girl years as the most enjoyable time of her life. The chorus put her schoolgirl insecurities behind her, opening a new world of fun and boundless freedom, as well as new friends and positive attention. She seemed happiest discussing those days, reminiscing about "whom her sister was going with, whom she went out with, who spilled champagne on whom." She rarely spoke about her film sets, but when she heard something that reminded her of the New York stage, she would brighten and recount the story with glee. The theater was a vital part of who she was, and she looked back on it with fondness for the rest of her life.

One of the theatrical customs that stayed with Marion was the chorus girls' unusual sleeping habits. Due to late nights at the theater, followed often by social events, Marion returned home in the early morning hours, as late as 6 a.m., and sometimes slept until 4 p.m. When she started in movies, this routine was impossible, but it remained her preferred sleep schedule. Following her retirement, she reverted to it.

When Marion left school to go into the theatre, her sister Rose, having dropped her childhood nickname of Rosie, managed to convince her mother that she, too, should follow in the family tradition. Despite the disability that might have limited her dancing, Rose's musical abilities were so advanced that she could easily make a living playing the piano in vaudeville musical acts. The two girls found support from Reine and Marie Glendinning, a British actress who had become a good family friend years before. Marie had always loved both Marion and Rose, but she had a special fondness for Marion's kind and affectionate demeanor.

When Marie heard that Marion and Rose wanted to begin stage careers, she advised them to call Lee Herrick, a theatrical agent she knew in New

York. The girls did what Marie suggested, and upon meeting them, Herrick was impressed with their potential. He agreed to take them on as clients. Although Rose had originally thought she would play music, Herrick believed she could dance, and he found roles for both girls in an upcoming production, *The Sunshine Girl*. In it, they would appear in the chorus line alongside the famous dance team Vernon and Irene Castle, known for their innovative techniques and popularization of the tango and the turkey trot. Marion adored Irene Castle, and after rehearsals she practiced Castle's routines in front of her mirror at home. She latched on to Irene Castle as someone to look up to, in much the same way that she looked up to Hazel Hart in school. In turn, Castle was gentle and kind with the young chorus girl. "My ambition at that time was to be precisely like her in every way," Marion later wrote. "She was more than wonderful to me." Despite Rose's issues with her legs, she seems not to have been held back and enjoyed her time as a chorus girl as well.

The Sunshine Girl had a test run in Washington, DC, before opening at the Knickerbocker Theater in New York, where it played for several months to good reviews. Reine, George Lederer, four-year-old Pepi, and a newborn son, Charles, visited New York to see Marion and Rose perform in *The Sunshine Girl*, and the group stayed at the Claridge Hotel on 44th and Broadway. Marion was happy to have the family reunited again, to see Pepi and to dote on her new nephew.

Backstage at the Knickerbocker one evening, Marion and Rose were handed a stack of congratulatory telegrams. When they opened them, the girls saw the names of President Woodrow Wilson, Calvin Coolidge, and Andrew Mellon in the signature section of the telegrams. Excited though they were at first glance, they were also puzzled and then skeptical that such prominent personalities were sending them telegrams. As soon as they saw the sending address, The Claridge Hotel, New York, they discovered the prankster—Reine.

Instead of touring with the company when the show went on the road, Marion and Rose left the cast and tried their luck in other New York–based productions. Following *The Sunshine Girl* came a small but moderately successful play called *The Little Cafe*, in which older sister Ethel (who had since moved back to New York from Chicago) had a role. In order to be closer to the theater and save money, Mama Rose, Ethel, Rose, and Marion moved in together at 920 West End Avenue along with Reine and her family, who had decided to return to New York permanently. Marion and Rose were each earning a respectable $15 per week, and they contributed to the rent and overall functioning of the house. When Marion came home after getting her weekly salary on Saturday nights, she crept into her mother's room and placed her share of that week's household bills on Mama Rose's night table. "Here it is, Mama," she said, crawling into bed with her mother for a few moments, as she had when she was a child, before going to bed herself.

Despite her new financial independence, Marion continued to rely on her mother for emotional support. Mama Rose, for her part, took joy in the fact that Marion was still her "baby," as she referred to her in public. She often visited Marion backstage to act as a buffer for protection from men with ulterior motives, and between scenes, Marion relaxed by sitting quietly with Mama Rose, her head resting on her mother's chest.

Marion had always been generous by nature, and she learned much about giving from the chorus girls. She believed chorus people to be "the most generous in the world," and she thrived in a milieu that put much emphasis on benefits for the poor, that actively reached out to improve the lives of people in the community. She recalled that when a benefit was put on, there was never anyone missing from the whole show, and Marion took these values to heart. When she received her first week's pay, she began to save every extra penny after bills until she had earned enough to buy a new car. With this money she went out and bought one—not for herself, but for Mama Rose, who had never owned a car and was overwhelmed by Marion's gift. Others took note as well, including Marie Glendinning, who realized that Marion was a rare soul. "I've never met such an unselfish girl in my life," she said later.

While Marion's name had not yet appeared in the program, she was already being noticed. "Marion was an incredible beauty," Mary Anita Loos, the niece of New York friend Anita Loos, remembered. "The kind of beauty that you could look at across the room." She was popular among "stage-door johnnies," rich men who frequented New York shows to woo chorus girls backstage with flowers and gifts. Marion was, in fact, "one of the most popular girls in town," according to headliner Elsie Janis, as evidenced by the "coffin-like boxes of flowers that crowded the stage entrance nightly." Marion's sunny personality and extreme generosity endeared her to the chorus girls as well, contributing to close friendships that Marion cherished throughout her life. Marion bought gifts for her friends in the chorus and took special pride in sewing elaborate dresses with intricate designs. The holiday season was a particular favorite time of year, and she became known as "the Christmas lady" for her desire to give presents to everyone she knew. For Marion, gifts were the currency of affection, and she gave freely and generously.

Marion saw her name in the theatrical program for the first time in 1914, at the age of 17. *Chin-Chin* was a vehicle by theatrical impresario Charles Dillingham, subtitled "A Modern Aladdin." It told the story of Aladdin set in modern China, broken up by a smorgasbord of modern American musical numbers alongside dancer Fred Stone's signature stunts. The production was staged at the Globe Theatre at Broadway and 46th, and images of Marion in *Chin-Chin* show a radiant, youthful beauty with dark hair and an adolescent face that still had not lost its baby fat. She wears three different costumes— including one that looks vaguely sailor-like alongside several other ensemble girls, and a dark, sleeveless dress with tights and ballet shoes. The third costume looks to be part of a dream sequence, as she is pictured alongside co-star Eleanor St. Clair as St. Clair emerges from a white cloth bubble.

The October 1914 opening of *Chin-Chin* was a spectacular affair, and critics were ebullient in their praise, calling it a "dazzling show, with a world of fun in it," one "sure to please everybody." Nonetheless, it was not without its technical problems. During one scene, the chorus girls appeared stacked on top of each other, poking their heads through holes in the backdrop around which flower petals were painted. Marion was on the top tier, standing on a platform above another girl. Suddenly, her platform gave way and she crashed into the girl below her, who had to be taken to the hospital. "It left me chinning myself on the backdrop," Marion said. "The audience must have thought me a most unhappy-looking blossom." Despite accidents involving the scenery, Marion's ensemble roles up to this point served to bolster her stamina and confidence as a stage performer, enough to give her the courage to audition for the Ziegfeld Follies the following year.

The Ziegfeld Follies were a New York institution, symbolizing escapist entertainment at its best. Fanny Brice, the beloved vaudeville comedienne who would later find posthumous fame as the subject of *Funny Girl*, got her start in the Follies. Billie Burke, best known as Glinda in *The Wizard of Oz*, was a Follies performer and the wife of producer Florenz Ziegfeld.

Ziegfeld is considered today to be among the most important producers in theatrical history, having become a household name by the time his first Ziegfeld Follies show premiered in 1907. A role in the Follies was a sign that one's career was about to skyrocket, and if Ziegfeld liked a showgirl, that showgirl was destined for immediate success, sometimes culminating in an affair with the notorious womanizer himself. The lavish costumes and luxurious atmosphere distracted audiences from the many social ills that plagued New York, and the world, during the 1910s. World War I was turning Europe to a mass of shattered alliances and gruesome deaths. As waves of immigrants came through Ellis Island to find refuge in New York, tenements sprang up to house them, often in squalid and unsanitary conditions. Amid these ills, the Ziegfeld Follies transported audiences to a time of beauty and high living.

In the days before women's suffrage, political discussions were considered unladylike. Marion, like most women, was discouraged from learning about the events of the day. Nonetheless, this era contributed to a fierce interest in current events on Marion's part. George Lederer's son, Maitland, went off to war when the United States joined World War I in 1917 and returned home alive, but with a bad case of Addison's disease. He died of Addison's-related heart failure at the age of 37. In response to what she had seen in her own family, Marion became an avid consumer of current events after the passage of the Nineteenth Amendment in 1919. She familiarized herself with intricate details of political positions and platforms, and became an educated voter who never missed an election.

As the world outside imploded into war, the New York stage was beginning to recognize the unique qualities of Marion Davies. Her reputation grew within the industry, and Charles Dillingham had been so impressed with her during the New York run of *Chin-Chin* that he hired her again for *Miss Information* and *Stop! Look! Listen!* Her co-stars delighted in Marion's positive energy. "She used to keep everyone giggling all the time," remembered *Stop! Look! Listen!* chorus girl Ina Claire, and it was her high spirits and wit that secured her a prominent spot in the showstopping number "The Girl on the Magazine Cover." "Just through her infectious humor," Ina Claire recalled, "Marion made that girl different from the other three in it."

During the run of *Miss Information*, Marion became acquainted with a good friend of Elsie Janis by the name of Frances Marion, an up-and-coming writer who had written several Mary Pickford films. When they met, Frances was struck by the exuberant, blue-eyed beauty and thought she would be an intriguing character to write for, seeing that Marion was, in her eyes, a natural-born comedienne. Although it would be several years before they met again under different circumstances, Frances had an image in her mind of Marion Davies that influenced their later personal and business relationship.

As *Stop! Look! Listen!* neared its end, Marion went to the New Amsterdam Theater on West 42nd to try out for the Ziegfeld Follies. She was expecting to audition for Florenz Ziegfeld himself, but instead found herself in front of Ned Wayburn, the *maître de ballet* of the show. Wayburn had revolutionized the Follies productions the previous year. He took the job of staging a Ziegfeld show very seriously, and in an industry where chorus girls were largely treated as objects, Wayburn respected them as artists and as people. "Mr. Wayburn is the only professor who regards the training of chorus girls as strictly as science," noted a 1916 profile in the *New York Tribune*. He demanded a great deal from the dancers, and respected their intelligence, acknowledging and lauding the fine memory required to be a showgirl. Wayburn equated those who thought little of showgirls' importance with those "who imagine that theatrical folk go into hotels and steal towels and silver spoons." At her audition, Wayburn recognized Marion's talent immediately. He saw that she had the intelligence, stamina, and endurance needed to be successful in the demanding role of a chorus girl in the Ziegfeld Follies and cast the 18-year-old in the show that same day.

The 1916 cast remains among the most illustrious of all the Follies ensembles. When Marion reported to rehearsal in the fall of 1915, she found herself working alongside veterans Fanny Brice and W.C. Fields, as well as famed vaudevillian Bert Williams, who two years earlier was credited as the first Black man to play a lead role in a feature film. Marion was among the youngest performers in the cast, and one of the least experienced. Working among such vaudeville superstars, it would have been easy for Marion to retreat into the background. But Marion was extroverted and made several lifelong friends in the cast of the Ziegfeld Follies, becoming especially close to another young cast member, Justine Johnstone.

There were few people in her life whom Marion actively disliked, but she found Ziegfeld's mistress Lillian Lorraine haughty, pretentious, and downright cruel in her one-upmanship. The entire cast felt the same way. Being around theatrical people liberally seasoned Marion's vocabulary with salty language, and one day, Marion called her "a real sh-sh-shit." Lillian laughed in Marion's face at her stutter, which made Marion even more indignant. Shortly afterward, she summoned up all her courage and marched into the luxurious dressing room that Ziegfeld had given Lillian. Without missing a beat, Marion looked her in the eye, took a deep breath, and yelled "Sassafras up your ass!" before running out. Nearly in stitches recalling this event decades later, she wondered out loud how she could have had so much gall. "How did I do that?" she said through tears of laughter.

To commemorate the three hundredth anniversary of William Shakespeare's death, the Follies of 1916 had a Shakespearean theme. Marion appeared as Juliet in a number entitled "My Shakespeare Girls," and also played the role of Anne of Cleves in "Six Little Wives of the King." Marion had a small, throwaway speaking line in "Six Little Wives of the King," in which she was to say, "He sure was a hell of a king!" Marion had never spoken onstage before, and "H" sounds tended to trigger her stutter. At the dress rehearsal, she stuttered "H-h-h-h…" Lyricist Gene Buck rooted her on. "You gotta do it! You gotta do it!" Marion stopped and addressed him calmly: "Let me sing it." As is typical with people who stutter, Marion sang fluently. She started over and sang the line straight through without any trouble. When demonstrating this for Stanley Flink in 1953 on her autobiographical tapes, despite stuttering through the rest of the tapes, she sang the line without a stutter.

When not working, Marion's evenings were filled with the fun and excitement that befitted her new life as a Ziegfeld girl. Tuesday evenings consisted of what she called "cat parties," wherein she would join Anita Loos, Marilyn Miller, her new friend Justine Johnstone, and others for games and merriment after that evening's show. She delighted in creating mischief, but always in fun, stopping short before any harm was done. "It's all right until it hurts somebody," was the motto by which Marion lived. According to Anita Loos, during one of these sessions at Anita's house, the women went searching through her closet and found a Dictaphone with cylinders in it. Upon inspection, they found that the cylinders contained sermons recorded by Anita's landlord, who had made an unwelcome pass at Anita not long before. This gave Marion an idea. The friends would record over the cylinders with their own voices, replacing the sermons with dirty jokes and suggestive song lyrics. One song, sung by Marion, was a parody on "The Merry Widow Waltz," with the lyrics:

She wears a chiffon nightie,
In the summers when it's hot.
She wears her wooly panties,
In the winter when it's not.
But often in the springtime,
And sometimes in the fall,
She slips between the sheets
With nothing on at all.

"Even though mild," wrote Anita Loos, "it must have provided something of a shock in anyone who ran the cylinder expecting to hear the voice of my landlord come out with 'Dearly beloved, I come before you on this Sabbath day with the warning against a sin of…'"

Anita Loos remembered that even as early as these chorus girl days, Marion was rare among the girls in more ways than one. Her bubbly, vivacious demeanor made her stand out as one of the most popular people at these parties, but she also had an unusual tolerance for alcohol. Anita noticed that Marion drank substantially more than others, and despite her lithe frame, never appeared intoxicated and didn't seem to realize how much she was drinking. "We didn't know what alcoholism was in those days," remembered Anita Loos, "but she was a chronic alcoholic." Alcohol never made her sad or angry—if anything, it made her even more affectionate and loving than she was without it. At this point in time, her drinking served to dissolve any inhibitions and bring out an increased sense of confidence, in a theatrical world in which these traits were necessary for success.

Marion's first taste of alcohol had not been at one of these parties but had in fact been provided by Mama Rose. Marion told this story at varying points in her life, each time with the same foundation—that around 1916, during a Ziegfeld show, she had to say a line onstage and was not allowed to sing it. She was petrified at the thought and turned to Mama Rose for help.

"I don't think I can say that line," she told her mother, "because I stutter."

"It's all right," Mama Rose told her. "I think you can do it."

On opening night, Marion's mother arrived backstage with a bottle of champagne. "It will relax you," she told her daughter. Marion took a sip and grimaced, but at Mama Rose's continued encouragement, Marion drank the whole glass. Her confidence increased, and when she walked onstage to play her scene, she felt much more relaxed. As she opened her mouth to speak her first line onstage that evening, she prayed that her stutter would stay at bay. Although it didn't keep her stutter from interrupting her line that night, this newfound vehicle for relaxation was a revelation—and ultimately a curse.

Marion's mother had never discouraged her from speaking, nor made her feel self-conscious about her speech. She raised Marion to be comfortable speaking in any necessary circumstance, and as a result, Marion did not normally shy away from expressing herself. She had no fear of speaking on the telephone (a common trigger for stuttering), nor did she stay silent solely out of fear of her repetitions and blocks. Now, though, her mother felt that the stakes were high. Marion would need to speak fluently onstage in order to advance the career that would bring her a better life. Mama Rose's advice would stay with her, and alcohol remained a lifelong crutch to soothe anxiety and keep her speech fluent.

The older wealthy men continued to woo chorus girls backstage at the Follies. Marion was still a teenager, giggly and childlike, reminding Anita Loos of a playful kitten. Despite the attention she was receiving, she remained naive, modest, very much the teenager she still was. But at 19 years old, she was now at an age where she could have flirtations and romances with men, or so her mother felt. Although she had been protective when Marion was younger, she now accepted that her daughter was attractive and desirable to the men who crowded the stage door every night, and she even encouraged Marion to accept their advances. One of those men was advertising giant and future newspaper publisher Paul Block.

In 1916, Paul Block was the director of advertising at the *Pictorial Review* and an up-and-coming powerhouse in the world of publishing and newspaper acquisition. In the late 1920s, he bought the *Pittsburgh Post-Gazette* and became the founder of Block Communications, Inc., the Toledo-based advertising firm that owns the paper to this day. With a special affinity for Ziegfeld productions in his after-work hours, Block would attend the theater with William Randolph Hearst, sitting in the second row of the New Amsterdam Theater and going backstage to meet the chorus girls afterward. Block's introduction to Marion was made by Ziegfeld himself, and the married Block felt himself falling for the girl with the big blue eyes that brimmed with a zest for life.

He brought Marion gifts and took her out to dinner at Delmonico's restaurant on Fifth Avenue and 44th Street, where Block would gather with other men of his social set. At Delmonico's, she chatted easily with powerful men about the stock market and the New York Yankees. In addition to her beauty and engaging personality, Block was enraptured by Marion's ability to discuss many subjects, unshaken by the status of the men of his circle. He was so taken with Marion that he began to believe that the chorus was a waste of her talent, and he wanted to get involved with the advancement of her career. Block landed on the rising art of motion pictures, a medium that was experiencing a maelstrom of changes in the mid-1910s, as a perfect milieu for Marion. She seemed to him to have the ideal combination of qualities that had proven to be star-making attributes, as the concept of stardom grew from its infancy. In the days before sound on film, Marion's huge, expressive eyes would be an asset to her in creating the big, magnified expressions necessary in the silent era to convey meaning. Unable to shake his fantasy, Block began to brainstorm ideas to get Marion out of the chorus and into the movies.

Stardom was a novel concept in the 1910s, and an exciting one. Fan letters rolled in for stars, whose names the public sometimes didn't even know. While Florence Turner hadn't been credited in any of her films and audiences didn't know her name, fan letters came in addressed to "The Girl with the Big Eyes." At the *Pictorial Review*, Block observed that the public was starting to take an interest in the stars they saw onscreen, what they did, who they were, and how they spent their time. Paul Block felt that Marion had a quality not unlike Mary Pickford, the perennial "Girl with the Curls," and since Pickford was making huge amounts of money as a star, he saw potential for this to be a very lucrative career change for Marion.

This new phenomenon spurred a new kind of journalism, celebrity journalism, where magazines and newspapers made entire columns out of celebrity news, which helped to increase sales. For the *Pictorial Review*, Block had commissioned producer Sam Goldwyn to write "Behind the Screen," a series of articles that detailed life in the motion picture industry, and those articles thrilled readers looking for a taste of what this new industry was like. Feeding off this new interest in stars and their lives, feature-length film productions were made in increasing numbers in the 1910s, featuring the people the public had come to know and love. By 1915, feature films were on the brink of becoming an industry standard, and by 1917, short subjects were in the minority. It was in the domain of feature films where Block felt that Marion's natural star power would thrive and succeed.

Still, many producers were hesitant about the costs and risks involved in feature-length productions. Block lacked the artistry and experience to create a motion picture himself, especially a high-risk feature-length production that he envisioned for Marion. He went to his friend William Randolph Hearst, who had been involved in motion picture production for several years and had recently signed a partnership with Pathé. Having made several successful serials by this time with the Pathé studio, Hearst was growing more confident, but remained risk averse. He knew Marion from Block's parties at Delmonico's and had flirted playfully with her, but their connection remained unserious. Hearst had done Block favors by promoting Marion in his papers, but in his shy, high-pitched voice, politely declined Block's request to create a movie for her.

Fueled by Hearst's rejection, Block took matters into his own hands. He asked newspaper reporters from the *Newark Star-Eagle*, which Block had just acquired as a publisher, to create a screenplay scenario for Marion. The reporters met Block on a Sunday afternoon at the Ritz Carlton Hotel, and by ten o'clock that night, having been paid $25 each plus beer and sandwiches, the reporters had cobbled together the outline of a screenplay. The plot involves a young Roma girl named Romany who escapes from her family compound to avoid an unwanted marriage. She is adopted by a man who himself had been stolen by "gypsies" when he was a child, but when she is suspected of stealing money from him, complications ensue. All works out in the end, and Romany's name is cleared.

To direct the movie, Block hired George Lederer, who by this time had separated from Reine but remained on good terms with the family. Marion loved the idea. Now 20 years old and eager to try new things, she decided to take an extended vacation from her current show, *Oh, Boy!*, which she had begun in February of 1917, in order to try her luck on the screen, pledging to return to the show if it didn't work out.

The filming of *Runaway Romany* is a testament to the ragtag, resourceful method of filmmaking of the 1910s. The film was shot in Westchester County, New York, and rural New Jersey, with interior work done at Pathé, likely a favor from Hearst. The production was fraught with mishaps and problems, but Marion proved herself to be a hard and dedicated worker. She subjected herself to difficult and sometimes painful stunts time and again until Lederer was satisfied. During one scene, Romany was to be rescued from an ocean liner, requiring that Marion dive from the boat into the water of the freezing Hudson River. To make it as realistic as possible, Lederer chartered a boat, and the cast and crew sailed out into the middle of the river. Marion took her dive without hesitation. She emerged to raucous, panicked shouting that Lederer had gotten a cramp in his camera hand and was not turning the crank when she went over the edge of the boat. Without a word, Marion got out, dried off, changed clothes, and dove into the water again.

Laws in Westchester County regarding "decent dress" proved to be an issue while shooting an outdoor scene that required Marion to be dressed in masculine clothing. In a white suit and jockey hat, Marion stood at the train station in Dunwoodie, Yonkers, with the rest of the crew. They were preparing for a moment where Marion's character escapes from her home and jumps onto a train. In order to shoot it, the crew had to wait for a real passenger train to come by for Marion to jump onto a train car, while George Lederer captured the scene on camera. As they waited, two police officers happened to walk by, noticing that this "boy" on the platform was not a boy at all.

"There is a law against young women masquerading in men's clothing," one said. The crew tried to reason with the officers to no avail, and they were still reasoning when the train came and went, without any film being shot. Finally, exasperated, George Lederer handed the officers a slip of paper entitling them to two free tickets at the movie's premiere, as well as cameos on the train platform. This excited them and they agreed to their debut, allowing the film to be shot when the next train came by.

Paul Block was on the set constantly, to oversee the production but also to monitor what was said about his involvement with Marion. In order to protect them both from suspicion, the story given to the press was that Marion herself had written the scenario, and that she had presented it to George Lederer for approval.

Runaway Romany finished production and had its first public showing in July 1917. Block was riveted by Marion's performance, but the film itself was seen as poor. Despite Hearst's initial hesitations he was supportive of his friend, and at Block's insistence he attended an advance screening of *Runaway Romany*. As the theater darkened, Marion's image appeared on the screen. Hearst was overcome and filled with emotion. He sat in silence, and a wave of softness washed over him. Mesmerized by the youthful, angelic figure he saw on the screen, he fell in love over the course of the film's sixty-three minutes. Hearst walked out speechless, only able to articulate to Paul Block was that he would like to be formally introduced to Marion Davies.

. . .

From the beginning, Hearst was an entertainer, his newspapers built on fact mixed with fantasy, exaggeration, and showy headlines. For the small price of a newspaper, readers were treated to the best theatre money could buy. An editor at the *San Francisco Examiner*, Arthur McEwen, summed up the Hearst papers in the following way: "We run our paper so that when the reader opens it he says 'Gee-whiz!' An issue is a failure when it doesn't say any of that." Hearst was a man with two distinct sides to his personality. He could be magnanimous with his employees, and in the next moment a demanding disciplinarian. His cousin Anne Apperson Flint considered him "a great failure," his selfishness and aloofness destroying the potential he had. "He had so much promise, so many delightful things about him—he was a tragedy. If he could have developed normally, he might have become an important man." Frances Marion recalled that he was "a sad man, who really walked alone." William Randolph Hearst was such a paradoxical and complex figure that to this day, historians struggle to make sense of him. "There's nobody in the world like him," Marion said in remembering the man she called "W.R." "I don't know anybody who could ever supplant him."

Born into wealth in 1863 San Francisco, Hearst had been raised on culture, refinement, and artistic endeavors, cultivated during lavish European vacations with his mother, Phoebe Apperson Hearst. Phoebe doted on her son, and "Willie," as he was called, was accustomed to getting everything his heart desired.

Since her own childhood, Phoebe had possessed an insatiable curiosity and thirst for knowledge. She was largely self-taught, having come from a poor Missouri family that, despite their economic limitations, encouraged Phoebe to become fluent in French and expert in English grammar. By the age of 16, Phoebe's education was so advanced that she was offered a three-month teaching position at a school forty miles from her St. Clair home. William Randolph Hearst's father, George, had made a great fortune mining the silver boom of the Comstock Lode as well as gold in California. With that money, he acquired the *San Francisco Examiner* and became influential in politics, ultimately becoming a U.S. senator representing California. He also bought huge parcels of land, including a large stretch of mountainous terrain just above the ocean at San Simeon, California. Following the marriage of Phoebe and George Hearst in 1862, Phoebe devoted her life to philanthropy, often coupling it with her interest in education. She founded the National Cathedral School for girls in Washington, DC, served as director of the Golden Gate Kindergarten Association, and became the first female regent of the University of California at Berkeley, where she founded the Museum of Anthropology in 1901. Hearst Avenue, which runs through the city of Berkeley today, is named for Phoebe.

From his mother, William Randolph Hearst inherited a fascination with knowledge for its own sake, and an appreciation for history and culture. From his father, he inherited a salt-of-the-earth, gutsy demeanor. "Willie" grew into a large man, reaching a height of six feet, three inches, and possessing a strikingly thin, high voice that seemed incongruous to his size. But as his biographers Oliver Carlson and Ernest Sutherland Bates put it: "From neither father nor mother came the son's mysterious eyes that were his most striking physical feature, large, pale blue eyes peculiarly his own, cold as steel, inhuman, remote, revealing nothing."

As "Willie" grew, he shed his childish nickname and became known to those close to him as "W.R." He enrolled at Harvard in 1882, but at the *San Francisco Examiner*, George Hearst enlisted his son as a consultant and assistant editor. W.R.'s passion for publishing quickly outweighed his interest in his studies, and his academics faltered. In addition, he had become involved with a young waitress named Tessie Powers, whom he took on vacations to New York and New Haven. When W.R. was with Powers, the upstanding Phoebe was not happy with the fact that her son was "keeping" a woman, and made her feelings known regarding her disappointment with what W.R. had become. Although Phoebe supported women's issues as far as they went to improve the lives of children and families, she was not so progressive as to approve of this arrangement. W.R. had good intentions but hated disappointing his mother. An old family friend, Orrin Peck, who was devoted to Phoebe, tried his best to calm her. "Nastiness is not born in him," Peck wrote, "and I would hate him if he didn't possess a mixture of boyishness and devilishness—neatly spiced with a college wittiness surging here and there onto wickedness."

With his one-track mind on the publishing industry, W.R. failed several classes, was "rusticated" (suspended indefinitely) from Harvard just before his senior year, and dove headfirst into the lucrative business of newspaper publishing and acquisition. W.R. bought the *New York Journal*, and soon became part of the growing industry of sensational "yellow" papers, so named likely because they ran the cartoon "The Yellow Kid." Through heavy use of illustrations and cartoons as well as simple language, the "yellow" papers eschewed established journalistic norms and told bold stories in terms the average reader could understand. Everything was carefully arranged on the page, to make the paper come alive visually. Those who saw Hearst working at home recalled that he looked at early versions of his papers from a distance, and moved photos and text with his toes to make them more visually appealing.

Possessing the resources to buy and maintain just about anything he wanted, Hearst spent wildly not only on newspaper acquisition but also on expensive art whose history he admired. "It wasn't idle buying, only," said his cousin Anne Apperson Flint. "But it was a sense of *acquiring* things."

In early 1897, he met Millicent Willson, a spirited chorus girl from the cast of *The Girl from Paris*. Millicent and her younger sister, Anita, were part of a dance troupe called "The Merry Maidens" and had received excellent notices in the *New York Journal* for their run in the play (which, in a twist of irony, is about a rich man who keeps one house for his wife and one for his mistress).

W.R. was taken by Millicent's energy and charm, the same qualities he would later see in Marion. According to the accounts of those who knew them both, Millicent and Marion were very similar in demeanor and temperament. Millicent was a beautiful and smart chorus girl, who was generous and caring. Phoebe, the matriarch of the family, was unimpressed. A simple chorus girl, "so common" in Phoebe's words, would simply not suffice for her son, and Phoebe made her disapproval of Millicent quite clear.

Despite Phoebe's feelings, the couple married in 1903. The Hearsts' first child, George Randolph, was born the year after their marriage, followed by William Randolph Jr. in 1908, John Randolph in 1909, and finally a set of twins in 1915, Randolph Apperson and Elbert Whitmire, the latter of whom would rename himself David in the 1930s.

From the beginning, there were signs of irreconcilable differences in the marriage. Millicent enjoyed high society, W.R. found it stifling. Before long, they began to grow apart. W.R. started spending more time away from home, at the theater with Paul Block and others who shared his appetite for fun and frivolity. "He was a great showman," Millicent recalled. "I suppose he had his faults like everybody else. He thought he could do what he liked. But a man in his position couldn't do what he liked and escape criticism."

W.R. saw the new medium of motion pictures as a means to increase his newspaper circulation, and as a natural extension of his own unique style of storytelling. Between 1895 and 1898, as the United States prepared to go to war with Spain over its control of Cuba, he used his papers to drum up support for the Cuban cause, extolling the virtues of an independent Cuba. Recognizing the power of new media to attract the public's attention, when the battleship *Maine* exploded in Havana Harbor on February 15, 1898, Hearst sent divers to the shipwreck to take photographs of the wreckage, only to be blocked from the site by Spanish officials. Calling the conflict with Cuba "our war," the Hearst papers were the first to send fully equipped ships to Cuba to cover the ensuing conflict. "Remember the *Maine*!" became an American rallying cry, and Hearst's reporters arrived complete with movie cameras on deck to film what became the Spanish-American War in real time, the first war to have been documented on film as it happened.

Hearst's newspapers were outwardly progressive, pro-labor, and pro-working class, and he won as many critics from the right as he did champions from the left. When progressive causes such as the newsboys' strike of 1899 threatened his own bottom line, Hearst was able to quickly change direction, demonstrating that his own politics were often directly tied to their profitability.

The partisan nature of W.R.'s reporting and his growing influence on the general public made him a natural to seek public office as a Democrat, eventually being elected to the United States Congress representing New York's 11th District in 1902, taking office in 1903 and serving until 1907. He was defeated in a bid for the presidency in 1904, and subsequently ran a brutal yet unsuccessful campaign for the governor of New York in 1906. The failure of his political career was a shadow that would haunt him for the rest of his life.

In the years following the war, he continued to produce short film versions of news items to go along with the printed word. With the increasing popularity of moving pictures, he signed a deal with the Selig studio to produce newsreels in 1913, followed soon afterward by a contract with Pathé. The stories of Pathé films would run in Hearst papers on the day the films were released, and Hearst and Pathé co-produced a twenty-episode movie serial, *The Perils of Pauline*, in 1914. *The Perils of Pauline* was such a hit that a second series was made, *The Exploits of Elaine*, and the following year the Hearst International Film Service was created to capitalize on the success. By the time Hearst began his association with Marion, his name had become synonymous with both publishing and film production.

. . .

The story of Marion's first meeting with William Randolph Hearst has taken on almost mythological proportions, with nearly everyone who knew them telling a different version. Marion herself claimed that in childhood, she had gone trick-or-treating at his home on Lexington Avenue in Manhattan, only to be chased away by the police. Anita Loos said that as chorus girls, Marion and Justine Johnstone were invited to a party at Hearst's flat in the West Forties and Marion was so nervous that she downed champagne to calm her nerves and promptly vomited on the couch cushions. The most commonly retold tale seems to be that Hearst fell in love with Marion as he watched her in the chorus, sitting by himself in the front row having bought two seats, one for himself and one for his hat.

The precise date when they first met is unknown, but starting around 1915, they saw each other regularly at Delmonico's. Marion recalled Hearst sending her little gifts when she was in the chorus; candies, flowers, and other trinkets were typical of stage-door johnnies looking for a bit of fun, but one of those gifts from Hearst included a poem:

I love a girl named Marion, she holds me in the thrall,
Her blue eyes and golden hair and figure lithe and tall.
She loves me too, she tells me so, alas that isn't all,
She also loves Flo, Charlie, Henry, Nealie, Joe, and Paul.

With her distaste for people who took themselves too seriously, her earthy humor, and her infectious joy, Marion was the ideal person to come into W.R.'s life at this point, as she represented the opposite of Millicent's increasingly high society circle. In spite of his initial hesitations, after the screening of *Runaway Romany*, W.R. saw that Paul Block had been right. Marion Davies had enormous potential. W.R.'s attraction to Marion's charismatic personality, combined with his dogged determination to make everything he touched a success, led to an insatiable desire to make Marion Davies the brightest star in the business. His obsessive drive would settle for nothing less.

Paul Block had long been wringing his hands over his attraction to Marion. He felt that he was falling in love with her, and this relationship had the potential to break up his marriage. As a man with a growing family, this was not something he was willing to risk, and when Hearst came into the picture, there was some sense of relief that someone else was taking over watch of Marion's career. Though Paul Block's relationship with Marion would fade, he would never lose the love he had for her. Block would remain such a close and loyal friend that he was considered almost a member of the family. Block also became a trusted advisor to Hearst in his business dealings, and his death in 1941 came as a great shock and sorrow.

In 1918, Hearst signed a new contract with Select Pictures, run by producer Lewis J. Selznick. Selznick had fallen into motion picture production after the failure of his jewelry business, and perhaps his biggest mark on the film industry was made with the later success of his two sons, David and Myron. Both sons had learned the business at a young age. Myron became a noted talent agent, and under the name of David O. Selznick, David's career as a producer skyrocketed with his production company, Selznick International, which produced *Gone with the Wind* and *Rebecca*.

Under his new contract with Select, Hearst created the Marion Davies Film Company and pre-production began on *Cecilia of the Pink Roses* in March of 1918. It began shooting in April, at Biograph Studio on 176th Street, under the direction of Viennese director Julius Steger, who had signed a contract with Hearst for several movies over the course of the year. As in *Run-*

away Romany, Marion was the highlight of the film and shone as the spunky Cecilia. When the production wrapped in late May, a massive publicity campaign began in the Hearst papers. The story, written by popular romance writer Katherine Haviland Taylor, was told in installments in the *New York Evening Journal* in the week preceding the film's release, complete with stills from the film featuring Marion in the role of Cecilia.

The allure of Hearst publicity for the studios served to give Marion opportunities that other actresses in her position had to work years for. Selznick was impressed with Hearst's publicity campaign on *Cecilia of the Pink Roses*, and, despite Marion's inexperience, he signed her to a six-picture deal for the studio even before the film's premiere.

The attraction for Lewis J. Selznick was clear. With this partnership, Marion Davies films would be advertised in the Hearst press, with the Select logo prominently featured. He had never met Marion and had no idea of her acting abilities, but free publicity for the company in such important papers as the *New York Evening Journal* and *New York American* was far too good to pass up. Marion was keenly aware of her privilege with this opportunity, and in keeping with the generosity that others associated with her, she frequently used it to help others who didn't have such luck—campaigning for down-on-their-luck actors and new talent to be cast in her films.

When *Cecilia of the Pink Roses* premiered, all the publicity came to a head and Hearst was determined to stage the most breathtaking evening possible. Gargantuan advertisements featuring the face of Marion Davies appeared all over New York City, and garlands of lilies were hung in the streets to herald the opening of what Hearst was convinced would be the greatest event of the year. On the stifling day of the premiere at the Grand Theatre on June 2, 1918, Hearst ordered electric fans to cool the theater. He bought thousands of pink roses, laying them below the screen as an altar. When the audience arrived, the theater darkened and the giant image of Marion Davies appeared flickering on the silver screen, cradled by the sea of thousands of fragrant roses whose sweet scent flooded the room.

"Unusual Box Office Attraction"

The morning after the spectacular premiere of *Cecilia of the Pink Roses*, the Hearst papers were effusive in their praise. The *New York American* reported that "only a marble heart could withstand the charms of Marion Davies." Nell Brinkley of the *New York Journal* described Marion's "clear-cut face, haloed with a cloud of fair hair, [that] looks out, unaffected, childishly cool, easily read, like a clear little sheet of blue water lying in the sun that every breeze stirs and rumples and dimples." This was the beginning of Marion Davies's rise to stardom.

W.R. was willing to spend huge amounts of money on Marion Davies productions. His control over Marion's surroundings was all-encompassing. Filled with antiques from Europe, many acquired by W.R. himself, her sets were designed to highlight what he perceived to be her angelic, ethereal qualities. She wore lavish and heavy costumes, reflecting W.R.'s idea of perfection. "The whole trouble was that W.R. was ahead of the times," remembered his general manager George d'Utassy many years later. "He made 'super' pictures several years too soon."

Lewis J. Selznick wanted to ride the wave of W.R.'s spending on his rising star. In an effort to funnel the remarkable Hearst publicity into Select Pictures, Selznick wrote in his exchanges, "Have signed up Marion Davies, greatest advertised star in America, for six pictures a year.... We believe publicity will be unusual box office attraction."

Marion was noticed outside the Hearst press as well. An up-and-coming writer with the *New York Morning Telegraph* named Louella Parsons was scheduled to meet Marion for an interview to be run in her column. Given what she had heard, Louella expected to see "a gorgeous creature in a sable coat." "Instead," wrote Louella, "I saw a slender little girl with big eyes and a rather wistful expression waiting to meet me."

Almost always called by her first name, or by her nickname "Lolly," Louella had begun her career as a part-time writer at the *Dixon Star*. For her column, "Society Doings," she reported on local gossip and stories of community interest in small-town Dixon, Illinois. Louella married John Parsons in 1905 and had a daughter, Harriet, the following year, but her husband soon abandoned the family for another woman. With a daughter to support, Louella moved to Chicago with Harriet in tow and secured a low-paying typing position at the *Chicago Tribune*, followed by a job as scenario editor for Essanay, the Chicago-based studio of Gilbert "Broncho Billy" Anderson. At Essanay, Louella sorted scripts and wrote several of her own, which were successful and demonstrated her skill as a writer. The *Herald*, a failing Chicago paper, thought an investment in Louella's talents might pay off for them. Louella was hired at the *Herald*, and she began her weekly column, "Seen on the Screen," consisting of screenwriting tips accompanied by bits of movie gossip. In 1918, the paper, which had continued its downward spiral, was acquired by Hearst. He let Louella go, seeing little value in her column, but through a friend who felt pity for her, Louella heard of a position at the *Morning Telegraph* in New York. She decided to make the trip East to take the job.

When Louella interviewed Marion for the *Telegraph*, she was lonely and was looking for companionship. Sensing this, Marion befriended her immediately and began to bring her to the cat parties with her chorus girl friends. In turn, Louella always wrote kindly about Marion in the *Telegraph*. Marion considered her a sincere friend, and the connection between Marion Davies and Louella Parsons would remain one of the most lasting and complex in the industry. Although Louella had a secure and high-paying job at the *Telegraph*, she had been trying to move up in the world of journalism and felt she could do better than her column at the *Telegraph*. Despite having been let go by Hearst at the *Herald*, she nonetheless wanted the coveted position of a Hearst society columnist. Marion Davies would be Louella's way of working herself into the Hearst-Davies circle. Marion's honed sense of loyalty and devotion contributed in no small way to the great successes that Louella was able to accomplish in her very illustrious journalistic career. And because of Louella's influence with the *Telegraph*, Marion's positive publicity expanded beyond the Hearst press in these important early days, ironically doing so in tandem with Louella's increasing desire to join the Hearst papers.

Meanwhile, the personal relationship between Marion and W.R. grew stronger. In February 1918, W.R. went down to Florida to participate in a wartime benefit for the Red Cross. Marion and her family went too, as Marion was performing with a Follies crew assembled by Florenz Ziegfeld. After the benefit, several Follies figures including Marion and her family were houseguests at the home of James Deering, who had been the vice president of International Harvester. Deering's Miami home, known as Villa Vizcaya, was "a shimmering white palace on the shores of a lagoon," built as a retreat for Deering to recover from pernicious anemia. It had been featured in the July 1917 edition of *Architectural Review*, which marveled at the villa's state-of-the-art engineering and mechanics. It was a bit staid and formal for Marion's sensibilities, and she recalled trying to escape out the back to find a more fun environment. But she delighted in the frequent calls from W.R., who took the name of "Carl Fisher" to disguise his identity over the telephone. As W.R. and Millicent's marriage became more distant, and W.R.'s attraction to Marion intensified, he was unable to keep Marion out of his sight or mind. He kept up appearances with Millicent, whose sphere of influence in his life was waning, while thinking constantly about Marion.

During this time, Millicent lived primarily at the Hearst family home, in the Clarendon building at 137 Riverside Drive. The house had plenty of space for W.R. to do his work, and an expansive dining room and ballroom, ideal for Millicent's entertaining. At the Clarendon, Millicent hosted the elite of New York's high society, who were eager to socialize with Mrs. Hearst. Whispers circulated about W.R. and Marion, and while many of Millicent's New York society friends tried to disparage Marion or W.R. to her, she remained steadfast in her public protection of W.R. Millicent did not speak badly of either W.R. or Marion, and she seemed to have a sense of inevitability surrounding W.R.'s having an affair. Still, privately, she was hurt at the way things turned out and confided to her family members how she felt. She enjoyed being Mrs. William Randolph Hearst and relished in the social standing her position brought her. She could not fathom a divorce. Millicent still felt the utmost respect for her husband—if not marital love.

Keeping up appearances with Millicent was not meant solely for W.R.'s public image. His friends and extended family, who knew and liked Marion very much, felt that his mother, Phoebe, should not be told of this new relationship. Despite W.R.'s almost worshipful adoration of his mother, her expectations of her son were impossibly high. Phoebe had tried since W.R.'s childhood to make him a gentleman, and though she had done groundbreaking work on women's rights, she remained a very traditional woman, proper and strait-laced. Phoebe's relationship with Millicent was already fractured, as she had always felt that her son deserved better than a common chorus girl. If she knew about Marion, her disappointment with her son would have been profound.

Back in New York, W.R. discovered Marion's keen interest in literature. Her ability to speak at length on the works of Dickens and the classics fascinated him. Dickens was W.R.'s "first literary hero," as his biographer Cora Older put it, and he was developing an interest in collecting Victorian authors himself. He sent valuable, first edition books he bought at the Anderson Galleries to West End Avenue for Marion. They began speaking on the phone nearly every day, and those phone calls turned into regular visits. Mama Rose and Papa Ben (who was still in and out of the house) both liked him tremendously. For Mama Rose, W.R. represented the rich man that she had dreamed of for her girls, and Marion seemed to be truly happy when she was with him. W.R. spoke with Papa Ben about his feelings for Marion, and Papa Ben left the relationship up to her. "Whatever my daughter decides," he said, "it's all right with me."

Up to this point, Marion had only had one semi-serious relationship, with Paul Block, but even he was more a dalliance than a true romantic partnership. Marion found herself in a quandary. While Mama Rose had quietly encouraged Marion to accept the advances of the men who crowded the stage door, the goal was always for her girls to get married. W.R. was gentle and kind with Marion and appreciated her for who she was. If this relationship continued, Mama Rose's marriage plans for Marion might be derailed. For now, though, Marion and the family were content to watch and see what happened.

With the nearly thirty-four-year age difference, this relationship was complex for Marion, who simultaneously felt romantic love for W.R. and sought a sense of gentle, fatherly protection from him. She had longed for an attentive father figure since Charles's death drove her parents apart, and in W.R. she seemed to have filled the paternal void in her life.

W.R. utilized his significant influence in New York politics to boost the status of Marion's family. Using his relationship with Mayor Hylan as leverage, he helped secure Papa Ben a position as a city magistrate, where he stayed for twelve years. Marion's father became a well-respected public servant, aligning himself with liberal ideals in his public comments and rulings, and upon his retirement in 1930, he made a plea for retiring magistrates to receive a pension, though he himself would not get one.

W.R. bought for the Douras family a large home not far from West End Avenue, previously the property of William Ahnelt, founder and publisher of the *Pictorial Review*. The new house, at 331 Riverside Drive, would be far less cramped. Space was desperately needed, as nearly the entire family was living under the same roof. "It always sounded like the biggest family in the world," Anne Shirley, future wife of Marion's nephew Charlie, mused. "It would have been so terribly easy to go off with Mr. Hearst and say goodbye, Mama Rose. But the family was all together all the time." 331 Riverside Drive was a marvel for the Dourases, and it was truly a marvel by any standard. "When the cat party met at Marion's," Anita Loos said, "we were all very impressed with this house." Complete with a spacious kitchen, a staircase for servants, a large library, and a stellar location just across from Riverside Park, the Dourases had risen from middling poverty to being firmly entrenched in the lifestyle of the elite New York set. Servants used a dumbwaiter to move food to the upper floors with ease. Marion and the family received guests on the second floor, overlooking Riverside Park, and ate in a wood-paneled dining room beneath colorful stained-glass windows. Papa Ben took up occupancy next door and every Sunday he would come over to visit with his family but never stay long.

Such lavish living was still very foreign to 21-year-old Marion, and indeed to the whole family. Nine-year-old Pepi had become a veritable force in the upscale neighborhood, with a penchant for beating up neighborhood children who made fun of her boyish demeanor. One day, she walked through the paneled doors with bruises and dirt covering her entire body. "Well, I got him," she announced.

"Who?" Marion asked.

"The boy who made a face at me the other day when he was with his nurse. I saw him today without his nurse!"

Over the years, Marion gradually acclimated to a luxurious lifestyle that was far from her modest Brooklyn roots. Marion found herself among opulent possessions that she cared very little for, except that they pleased W.R. "She never could be brought to care about clothes, she couldn't have cared less about jewels," Anita Loos remarked. "It never was grandiose. She kept it from being grandiose." Because she was down-to-earth by nature and had an instinct for phoniness and insincerity in people, Marion was wary of many who passed through her world because of W.R. Louella Parsons later wrote in her column, "She is like a child who has suddenly found herself in a golden palace surrounded by every luxury money can buy."

Marion's sister Rose was the only sibling who did not live at 331 Riverside Drive with the family. During this period of Marion's ascent to stardom, Rose grappled with issues related to her own sense of identity and self-worth. Her younger sister was on the brink of obtaining wealth and stardom, and Rose faded into the background, her musical talents overshadowed by Marion's success. She moved out of the house, having fallen in love with a composer named William Kernell, and they married quickly. At first, this seemed to be a way for Rose to affirm her own identity as a gifted musician, but the marriage was annulled only a few months thereafter due to incompatibility. Rose married again in 1918, this time to a newspaper reporter by the name of George Van Cleve, and promptly became pregnant. In June 1919, Rose gave birth to Marion's second niece, Patricia Van Cleve.

Even in utero, Patricia was a big personality. Marie Glendinning recalled her husband, Ernest, placing his hand on Rose's belly and Patricia kicking him so hard that his hand flew off. Patricia's birth was difficult, and Rose, often inclined to dramatics, would recount the intense labor she endured. "I felt like I was going to die, but I didn't care…as long as my daughter lived!" Rose exclaimed dramatically whenever recounting the day of Patricia's birth.

The maternal instincts of Reine and Rose were not strong, and Marion functioned more as a parent than an aunt. She delighted in Pepi's boyish energy, seeing something of herself in her eldest niece. Charlie was an entirely different brand, a prodigious student, wise beyond his years, with a flair for the written word. Charlie felt more at home with the adults of the family than the children, and in turn it was easy to forget that he was still a young child. The family doted on him, providing him with as much room for exploration as they could, and Marion devoted her time and financial resources to Charlie's development. At the age of 13, Charlie was admitted to UC Berkeley as a freshman, but like many profoundly gifted children, he found college life dull and dropped out to take a position on the Hearst papers. In 1931, at 19 years old, he teamed with Ben Hecht, Charles MacArthur, and Bartlett Cormack to write the screenplay for *The Front Page*. With the playwrights' blessing, Charlie later adapted *The Front Page* himself to create the 1940 film *His Girl Friday*.

To Marion, Charlie was the epitome of everything that she felt she wasn't. "She worshiped him," remembered Charlie's wife, Anne Shirley. Possibly out of insecurity about her own lack of formal education, Marion often leaned on Charlie. "She really looked upon him as 'Charlie knows how to do it, Charlie knows how to fix it, Charlie knows how to talk.'" Shirley believed that the last part was particularly admired by Marion, who deferred to Charlie as the one who had "the big words." "Perhaps Marion had many more words inside of her that she really knew," Shirley remembered. But because of her stutter, she was not able to get them out.

Pepi was also a talented writer. Because of Charlie's extreme gifts, she never got the attention she desired. Marion, perhaps feeling a yearning for the education that she never had, took Charlie under her wing and he in turn gave her a devoted love that would last all of Marion's life. She loved Pepi but took less seriously Pepi's efforts to be a writer and put her energy into nurturing Charlie. Whether it was because Marion saw more potential in Charlie, or that the traditional "favoring of the boy" had taken hold in Marion, Pepi was not given the support Charlie received, and this affected her greatly. She was the elder sister, and to see her younger brother succeed where she hadn't caused her great pain and embarrassment. Compounding these challenges, Pepi discovered early on that she was a lesbian, and preferred traditionally masculine clothing. That difference made her feel further isolated from her family and society.

In the days following World War I, the Spanish flu ripped across the United States and the rest of the world. Government-mandated quarantines closed businesses, and mask-wearing requirements became standard as the flu affected every part of American life. By the time it was over, the flu had claimed the lives of 50 million people worldwide, and 675,000 of them were Americans. One of those 675,000 killed in the 1918 flu pandemic was W.R.'s beloved mother, Phoebe. It caused him great pain to learn that in her will, Phoebe had written him out of both her Pleasanton estate and Wyntoon, her rural wonderland on the McCloud River. He vowed to fight the estate's bequeathment of Wyntoon to his cousin, Anne Apperson. At the same time, however, he learned that he was to inherit the sprawling tract of land above San Simeon, California, that had belonged to his father, on which they had spent memorable camping trips on the mountains above the Pacific Ocean.

Marion told Eleanor Boardman that as a young boy W.R. had big dreams for the vast expanse of land in the hills above San Simeon that his father had called Camp Hill. When asked by his mother what he would like to do with it, he told her, "I'm going to build a castle." The quiet isolation of the rolling hills, green in winter and spring, golden in summer and fall, offered him the perfect location for a magnificent house of dreams. When the land became his in 1919, he immediately began looking for an architect who could help him make this dream a reality.

The architect who came to W.R.'s mind was Julia Morgan, whose San Francisco firm had been in high demand since it first opened in 1904. Between 1903 and 1910, Morgan had remodeled Phoebe Hearst's Hacienda del Pozo in Pleasanton, in the San Francisco Bay Area southeast of Berkeley and Oakland. It is likely that Phoebe Hearst first introduced Morgan to W.R. in 1903 or soon thereafter, since Morgan was working with John Galen Howard on the Greek Theatre at Berkeley, and that building was a gift to the university from W.R.

Her resume was fitting to be the architect for W.R., who was above all else quality-minded (and equality-minded, if the most talented person for the job was a woman), and when he told her that he was looking to build "a little something" at San Simeon, she set to work right away.

A tiny force of nature at just five feet tall, Julia Morgan standing beside W.R., at six feet, three inches, was almost a comical sight. But Morgan held her own, and W.R. had immense respect for her talent. She had been the first woman to enter the architecture program at the École des Beaux-Arts in Paris. By the time W.R. contacted her for this project in 1919, she had already co-designed the Greek Theatre in Berkeley, and several buildings at Mills College in Oakland. To create the castle that W.R. had dreamed of since childhood, Julia Morgan used fireplaces, pillars, and anything that struck W.R.'s fancy, purchased primarily from New York auction houses.

She soon learned that working with W.R. was no easy task. At one point, Morgan found a fireplace that she thought he would love. Initially impressed, W.R. quickly changed his mind, forcing Morgan to put the fireplace in storage in San Francisco and search for another one like it. The quest for the right fireplace took two years, with Morgan becoming increasingly convinced that what W.R. was looking for was, in fact, the exact fireplace they had put in storage. Finally, Morgan burst out in exasperation that they *had* this fireplace already. As though there were no issue, W.R. calmly asked Julia Morgan to bring it to San Simeon.

Building on the ranch at San Simeon gave W.R. so much joy that the ranch was never to be finished, nor did he have any intention of doing so. "When do you plan to complete this?" an assistant asked him. "I hope never," was the reply.

In New York, Marion kept busy in early 1919, filming *The Belle of New*

York and *Getting Mary Married* under her contract with Select Pictures. The latter was directed by the great silent director Allan Dwan, who noticed Marion's childlike naughtiness right away. During the filming of *Getting Mary Married*, Marion reverted to her chorus girl days and made some mischief on the set. One day, she showed up on the set with pillows in her costume, making it look like she had suddenly become pregnant. On another day, during a love scene with co-star Norman Kerry, Marion smiled to reveal a blacked-out tooth and sent Kerry into laughing hysterics, rendering both of them useless for the scene. This three-day binge of hijinks ended up costing the studio several thousand dollars in wasted film and lost time, but Marion had her fun.

In an industry that took itself too seriously in Marion's mind, her penchant for fun and games endeared her to crews and co-stars alike. Allan Dwan, who became one of Marion's great advocates, said that despite all the wasted time and footage that she had cost him, Marion "had a sense of humor, and if you gave her anything funny to do, she'd do it funny. She had a great smile. Half the time they didn't pick stories for her with enough humor in them."

"She was more like Mabel Normand than anybody," said Anita Loos, recalling the physical comedy of the actress of the 1910s known for starring alongside Roscoe "Fatty" Arbuckle. "That's what Marion should have done and should have been." Once when Marion was with Anita on a set without W.R. present, Marion began leading the cast in high-spirited fun, ad-libbing dialogue and sending the cast and crew into hysterics. "We must have wasted maybe $12,000 or $15,000 that day, just cutting up when there was nobody around in authority," Anita remembered.

After years of partnering with other companies, W.R. had been trying to create a distribution arm of his own that could capitalize on the stories coming out of his papers and magazines. After having been rejected by United Artists, he collaborated with Adolph Zukor of Famous Players-Lasky (later Paramount) to build his own studio in Manhattan, where he would create films for distribution by Zukor. This was the birth of Cosmopolitan Productions, the name coming from Hearst's beloved *Cosmopolitan* magazine. It was an exciting deal for both Hearst and Zukor—Hearst could join the ranks of established film producers, and Zukor could take advantage of the stories coming out of the Hearst presses. Cosmopolitan Productions would become the center of Hearst's film interests over the next two decades, and the medium through which Marion Davies's career was built.

W.R. was looking to find Cosmopolitan its own studio, and through the fate of a popular beer garden at 127th Street in Harlem, W.R. saw an opportunity. The building had been called Sulzer's Harlem River Park and Casino, and had operated as an amusement park through 1917, then as an event hall until it closed indefinitely after Prohibition passed in 1919. As alcohol sales were now illegal under the Constitution, it forced many businesses to either close or sell alcohol underground, and the business model of Sulzer's Harlem River Park and Casino could not survive. The space covered an entire city block between 126th and 127th Streets, and 1st and 2nd Avenues, and seemed to W.R. to be perfect for a studio. For $6,000 a month, W.R. decided to rent the space. It would serve as Cosmopolitan's home until production moved to California in 1924.

The location was perfect for an amusement park and beer hall, but it was an unusual spot for a film studio. The surroundings were noisy, with elevator ("el") trains going by frequently and household noise from the tenements across the street threatening to distract the filmmakers and actors. Though the films were silent, the crew found it difficult to stay focused. As many potential distractions as there were on 127th Street, however, the camaraderie was strong. Like several film studios of the era, W.R. organized a Cosmopolitan baseball team (known as the Marion Davies Baseball Team) that competed against other studios, and was remarkably good. Marion, always the athlete, was the catcher on the team, and helped lead them to a shutout against Paramount Studios in June 1921.

Due to all the building at San Simeon, W.R. was in California much of the time during 1919 and 1920. In addition, in the middle months of 1920, he attended the 1920 Democratic National Convention in San Francisco, because the Massachusetts delegation had allotted him one vote for president. He missed Marion dearly. Unable to take the separation much longer, he decided to bring her to California to film the next movie on her schedule, *The Bride's Play*. Along with Ethel, Mama Rose, and baby Patricia, Marion boarded a train west, arriving in Santa Barbara and then heading east to Montecito. Rose was away on vacation with her husband, George Van Cleve, and had left Patricia in Mama Rose's care. W.R. had arranged for the family to stay at La Paz Hotel for the summer, while the filming of exteriors for *The Bride's Play* took place in nearby Santa Barbara. Booked under the name of R.C. Douras, in order to avoid gossip, their accommodations at La Paz were idyllic, surrounded by a seventeen-acre lemon grove. After their hotel stay ended, they moved to a small cottage called Mon Desir, and Mama Rose was overwhelmed by its beauty. "This new place is a gem," she wrote to Rose one day.

By November the Dourases had left Mon Desir to return to New York by train, for the interior scenes that Marion had to complete at the studio. W.R. worked from California until business called him back to New York. He was interested in securing Marion's old friend Frances Marion to write for Marion at Cosmopolitan. Frances had written several pictures for Mary Pickford, and with his desire to turn Marion Davies into the next Mary Pickford, W.R. found Frances a natural choice to write the scenarios for Marion's movies. He also knew her writing firsthand, as she had been an employee of his at the *San Francisco Examiner*, though they had never met. While working in California for Mary Pickford, Frances received a telegram: "Would you consider contract as writer and director at Cosmopolitan Studio, New York? Salary two thousand dollars a week. W.R. Hearst."

In addition to the pay raise, Frances's friend Adela Rogers St. Johns always spoke highly of Hearst and the perks of being a high-ranking employee. The women working on the Hearst papers were among the highest paid in the industry, and W.R. encouraged male editors to assign newspaperwomen important stories, considering them "essential to every paper." "Everyone in his employ showed him the most awed respect," Frances wrote. "Everyone talked about the enormous office, the formidable figure of a man sitting at a huge desk, his glacial eyes on the poor insignificant soul in front of him."

Frances Marion was a remarkably impressive woman, having served as a war correspondent during World War I. She became the first woman to cross the Rhine and set herself up as a journalist in the area where the United States was to put its base during occupation. By 1918, several years after Marion had first met her through Elsie Janis, Frances had made a name for herself on her own terms as a writer, war correspondent, director, model, and actress. At the *Examiner*, she was paid $15 a week, though her father objected to Hearst's politics and lifestyle. "He wrote, 'Hear you've gone from bad to Hearst,'" Frances recalled. Regardless, she would become a frequent Cosmopolitan writer, one of W.R.'s most trusted film advisors, and one of Marion's greatest advocates.

Frances began writing for Mary Pickford vehicles in 1915 and had become inextricably linked with Pickford, and offscreen, the two were best friends. In late 1918, Frances was recently back from France, where she had been sent to cover women's activities during the war, but after the Armistice was signed, she returned to California just as Mary Pickford was about to establish United Artists. While biding her time as she waited for Mary, Frances received W.R.'s telegram to come work for Cosmopolitan. She contacted the Hearst office the morning she arrived in New York, and was told that she was to be at the Beaux-Arts building that afternoon.

W.R. and Marion met at the building, one of Hearst's favorite properties in Manhattan, the afternoon of Frances's arrival from California. Marion had brought a few chorus girl friends along, and while they waited for Frances in a large suite, the girls decided that it would be fun to teach W.R. how to shimmy. They put on a wild, loud jazz record and proceeded to instruct the newspaper mogul, now 55 years old, in the popular dance, giggling and delighting in his fruitless attempts to keep up. When Frances arrived and knocked on the door, she was greeted by a flood of lively music and an overly excited Marion. "Come in, Fran-Frances," she said, her stutter triggered due to all the excitement. "We're just tea-teaching W.R. how to shim-shimmy." Frances entered and saw W.R. in the middle of a shimmy, exhausted and just as delighted as the rest of the girls were by his new trick. He panted a welcome to Frances.

Marion turned off the music and addressed the other chorus girls. "Frances wrote the Pick-Pickford stories W.R. and I are so cra-crazy about."

W.R. nodded. "That's why we were anxious to have her with us."

Frances was dejected. She had dreams of working with Marion on comedies, not the overproduced costume spectacles that Marion had starred in up to now. She found them dull and restrictive of actors' abilities. But it looked as though her attempts to change Marion's image would be more difficult than she imagined. She had always liked Marion very much, since they had first met briefly when Marion was a chorus girl. She wanted to help her, and thought about how to tell Mr. Hearst.

When they began to talk, Frances was direct—she did not want to write for Marion if it meant doing a story similar to the ones Marion had done before.

"Why not? Don't you like her?" W.R. asked Frances. Frances replied that she did. "That's why I don't want to do anything which could jeopardize her career."

W.R. was puzzled. "I'm willing to spend a million on each picture!"

"Lavishness doesn't guarantee a good picture, Mr. Hearst," she said.

Frances shared Allan Dwan's opinion that Marion's talent was not being properly utilized. "Marion is a natural-born comedienne and she is being smothered under pretentious stories and such exaggerated backgrounds that you can't see the diamond for the setting," she told W.R.

He suggested that she find some stories in the Hearst magazine holdings. Perhaps she would find some better material for Marion there, Frances thought, and she agreed to sign with Cosmopolitan. Frances began writing *The Restless Sex*, in which Marion played a young woman in love with two men. That was followed by scenarios for *The Dark Star* and *The Cinema Murder*. By the time Frances had finished *The Restless Sex*, the new Cosmopolitan studio in Harlem was ready and *The Restless Sex* was shot there. Now, Frances thought, they could focus on getting Marion into comedies.

Going through the stories available to be filmed by Cosmopolitan, Frances and Marion together agreed on several light comedies that might work well for Marion's talents. But W.R. quickly vetoed each, saying "the background was too colorless."

Through the years, Frances tried to get through to W.R., but in spite of the respect he had for her, he almost always continued with another loaded-down production. Whenever she felt she might have gotten through to him, he would start daydreaming. "Wouldn't it be nice if Marion could be out in a wheat field, with a beautiful bonnet on?"

Although she often lost these arguments, there were few in the industry willing to stand up to W.R. Frances possessed a self-assurance and confidence that was rare in W.R.'s circles, and she used it to push against a vision she considered shortsighted. She picked her battles, sometimes simply shrugging her shoulders, knowing that she could do nothing. Other times, she fought hard for Marion, sticking up for Marion's reputation and talent in the face of the great adversity that was the conviction and stubbornness of William Randolph Hearst.

There was a part of W.R. that never grew up; a part of him was almost childlike in his obliviousness to the needs and desires of other people. One night, after Cosmopolitan had moved production to California in the mid-1920s, Frances got a phone call from an editor at the *San Francisco Examiner*. He told her that W.R. was in San Francisco with Marion on business, and he needed Frances to be there by morning. Frances drove all night on the rocky road to San Francisco, thinking there was a business-related emergency, and arrived in the city in the early morning. She met W.R. and Marion at the St. Francis Hotel. Bleary-eyed and sleep-deprived, she was anxious to hear what the matter was. "We heard it was going to be a beautiful day," W.R. told her with a cheery smile. "We wanted you to come on a picnic with us at Mount Tamalpais."

Frances couldn't believe that she had been summoned from Los Angeles for a picnic. But there was no arguing with W.R. She went to Mount Tamalpais with W.R. and Marion, all the while shaking her head and ruminating on the idea that this was the nature of her boss. She loved his impulsivity, his friendliness and openness. But the lives of other people simply didn't factor into the equation. His desire for Marion to be the most respected actress on the screen was all-encompassing, but the consensus was near universal—his blindness to other perspectives, and to Marion's natural gifts, was limiting her possibilities.

"If You Stutter,
They Find You Guilty Right Away"

Marion's next film, *Enchantment,* was filmed at the new 127th Street studio in early 1921. Correspondence with screenwriters from the early stages of *Enchantment* shows how much W.R. tried to control Marion's persona and image. In a letter to the screenwriter Luther Reed, W.R. essentially rewrites the entire script, scene by scene, negating what Reed envisioned for the film and instead creating his own story and narrative for Marion. He controls aspects as minute as what the first intertitle should be, and how Marion's costar should "sink down on his knees—not knee, but plural—KNEES."

To design the "super pictures" that Cosmopolitan general manager George d'Utassy described, W.R. hired Joseph Urban, the former designer of Ziegfeld's sets, to work on the Marion Davies pictures. Concurrently under contract to the Metropolitan Opera Company, Urban designed some of the most lavish productions of the 1920s, evoking the aura of grand, theatrical operas.

Born in Vienna in 1872, Urban came of age in a milieu where art and intellect intersected. This influenced the way he approached his craft, guided by the principle of *Gesamtkunstwerk,* creating a unified artistic experience for the audience through a confluence of stage design, costumes, lighting, and music. When Urban was hired at Cosmopolitan, one of the first things he did was to redesign the interior lighting system for the studio. With strategic lighting, and analysis of how the colors of the sets and costumes worked with the light, "the mind of the spectator can be made to think in colors even when they are not shown." Urban's lighting techniques were a revolution for the industry and benefitted Marion greatly. With Urban's redesigned system, shadows and contours were accentuated with discrete rather than diffuse lighting—allowing the set designer or director to choose the type of lighting that was right for a certain scene. Urban designed Marion's sets and lighting to highlight W.R.'s perception of Marion as a saintly, angelic figure.

Urban's first year at Cosmopolitan was not easy, as he, too, ran into difficulties with W.R. Urban was very particular about historical accuracy, and this posed a problem when it came to W.R.'s antiques. Frequently, the artworks that W.R. placed in the scene were somewhat anachronistic, and Urban balked at them. But W.R. was insistent about keeping them, and he was the ultimate authority. Once during an argument, W.R. backed up a large truck of antiques and instructed Urban in no uncertain terms to "put them on the set." Raging mad, Urban packed his bags and left for Vienna to visit his mother, swearing that he would never return to work at Cosmopolitan again. His impromptu resignation was short-lived, however, when W.R. wrote and offered him a significant pay raise to return. He sailed back to New York, grudgingly, and continued to work with Cosmopolitan for many more years.

After *Enchantment* was finished, Marion and W.R. boarded his yacht the *Oneida* for a cruise around New York Harbor. The plan was to celebrate and watch the rushes with a group of family and friends, then go on to Mexico for an extended vacation. This would be Marion's first trip out of the country. When applying for her passport, to avoid any questions about her relationship to W.R., she listed her reasons for the trip as an intention to "produce a motion picture...particularly in and around the City of Guadalajara." Her sister Ethel was in on the ruse, saying that she would also be working on the picture, and Mama Rose would be their chaperone.

Docking at Galveston, Texas, they took a private railroad car to San Antonio where they then crossed the border into Tampico. This impromptu Mexican vacation was the first in a series of international trips that W.R. and Marion took together. Between 1921 and 1936, they brought large groups of friends and family on long, memorable vacations, where they would meet international political figures and soak in the sophisticated culture that W.R. loved.

While in Mexico, Marion and W.R. took the opportunity to have a private audience with the newly-elected president of Mexico, Álvaro Obregón. The government officials from Obregón's office offered to take the group to a traditional Mexican bullfight, to which most of the guests reacted with enthusiasm, but Marion and W.R. refused to go. From childhood, Marion had an extraordinary concern for animals and children, which she shared with W.R. This strong ethical stance stayed with her even when faced with backlash for her views on such issues as vivisection and capital punishment. Marion remained unapologetic in her defense of those she felt were wronged, or who needed protection. Nearly every photo from the trip to Mexico shows Marion interacting with the local children, playing and smiling with them as she tries to communicate in her extremely limited Spanish.

Marion's life with W.R. was frequently shadowed by worries about scandal or unwanted attention from the press. While in Mexico, Marion was often absent from group outings, for fear of inviting gossip and whispers. In W.R.'s absence, Millicent had been talking with Joseph Moore, editor of the *New York American*, expressing her displeasure with the paper's focus on Marion Davies rather than the film as a whole. On October 19, Moore wrote W.R. a telegram asking for advice. "Have talked with Millicent regarding publicity for *Enchantment* in your papers," it read. "She insists all advertising be distinctly on picture and not on star. Do you want this." W.R. wrote back to Moore two days later: "Advertising in our paper different from other papers would cause unpleasant comment in Shandal [*sic*] sheets."

The *American* was fearful of a backlash from Millicent, and the editors ordered that Millicent's request be followed. When W.R. saw that his directions had been discarded, he was furious. "I note advertisement of *Enchantment* without any mention of star. This is ridiculous and wrong. I thought I made clear that advertisement in our paper were [*sic*] to be the same as in other paper advertising, star and photoplay as usual. Has this been done or not? Please proceed promptly to do so now." Still raging two days later, he wrote again, "Also…ask papers to give same news and pictorial attention to *Enchantment* and star and other star pictures of ours, and if don't comply, replace dramatic staff necessary. Take full advantage our publicity [*sic*] to secure success in this difficult business." This was a period of intense polarization between W.R. and Millicent, affecting their relationship as well as Marion's with W.R. Despite the growing distance between husband and wife with each passing decade, Millicent held tight to her unique position as Mrs. Hearst.

The 1920s was a decade of contradictions. After suffering a recession following World War I, the American economy bounced back and was headed for an economic boom in the early 1920s. Warren G. Harding had been elected president in 1920, and while the economy rose steadily under Secretary of the Treasury Andrew Mellon, Warren G. Harding's presidency was beset by corruption. Secretary of the Interior Albert B. Fall secretly granted private companies access to public oil reserves, shocking the nation in a political crime dubbed Teapot Dome. It threatened to derail Americans' trust in their elected president and eroded their faith in governmental systems.

Prohibition was a symptom of a growing social divide in the United States, one that separated the religious and nonreligious, the old and the young. The adoption of the Nineteenth Amendment saw new and increased support for the rights of women, but social conservatives cracked down on immigrants with the National Origins Act of 1924. Governmental policies that restricted immigration, favoring those of Western European descent, shaped the decade alongside the high living that came with the era's economic abundance.

Marion's first movie of 1922, *Beauty's Worth*, illustrates this growing divide. It tells the story of Prudence, an adolescent from a strict Quaker family who breaks with religious traditions to live her own, liberated life. For *Beauty's Worth*, Marion cut her long, auburn hair and had it bobbed short for the first time in her life. It remained this way for the remainder of her career, and though she frequently played with the color and style of her hair, she enjoyed what was then a novelty. It was, also, a symbol of her individuality, and a glimmer of defiance against the roles that were already starting to define her. *Beauty's Worth* offered Marion a chance to play a modern girl, a welcome break from the angelic characterizations that Hearst so adored.

Beauty's Worth was released in May 1922, and Marion received a good deal of praise for her performance. Marion's approach to complex characters like the one she played in *Beauty's Worth* was a testament to her capacity for nuanced portrayals. The whimsical scene in which Prudence participates in a performance of charades especially caught the critics' attention, marking the first time that Marion danced onscreen. It was something she had longed to do since her chorus girl days. "Dancing and singing are two of the things I miss in pictures," Marion said, giving rare voice to disappointment with the onscreen persona that had been created for her.

Newspapers, too, were beginning to tire of Marion's weighty roles. The *New York Times*, a leading competitor and no fan of the Hearst papers, wrote: "She has had more in the way of rich settings, fine costumes and careful direction thrust upon her than almost any other screen player has enjoyed....Her role...doesn't mean anything, except that Marion Davies is in another movie."

Beauty's Worth was followed by *The Young Diana*, where she played two parts—an old woman, and the woman's younger self. In the 1920s, dual roles became something of a trend, offering actors a chance to show off their versatility. It was a formula used time and again in Marion Davies films, and whether it was intentional or not on the part of the scenario writers, this ability to play two different characters offered Marion a chance to show her dramatic skill and gave her some relief from the pressure of W.R.'s laser focus. "Miss Davies appears in two extremes of characterizations—first as a young girl, then as a gray-haired woman twenty years older," wrote the *Motion Picture News* about *The Young Diana*. "Miss Davies in this picture has been given her opportunity."

After *The Young Diana*, she immediately started preparing for her next project, a million-dollar epic of Tudor England, taken from the 1898 novel by Charles Major entitled *When Knighthood Was in Flower*. Filming began in March 1922 with Robert G. Vignola directing, and it was slated for a September release. Although the shoot itself only took 160 days, nearly eighteen months of detailed research and planning had preceded it, including securing the highly desirable screen rights and creating elaborate Tudor costumes. *When Knighthood Was in Flower* told a romanticized story of Mary Tudor, a sister of King Henry VIII who fell in love with a commoner. It was a popular and acclaimed novel, and in 1904 it became a play starring Julia Marlowe. Marlowe maintained the rights to the property, and Mary Pickford tried several times to get the rights for herself. Hearst and Cosmopolitan negotiated with Marlowe for months to secure the rights, and finally after offering a large sum of money, she allowed Cosmopolitan to buy them outright.

The sheer scale of *When Knighthood Was in Flower* is staggering, and the twelve parts that encompass it reflect the energy, finances, and dedication that went into creating an epic of these proportions. In the time that it took to make the three-hour film, Cosmopolitan spent over $1.2 million and employed more than 3,000 actors, all wearing elaborate medieval costumes sewn at Giddings & Co., an upscale Fifth Avenue boutique. A theater program of 1922 released by the newly formed Cosmopolitan Corporation claims that *Knighthood* boasted "the largest set ever constructed, covering over two city blocks." The set in question, a model of the streets surrounding Notre Dame on the day of Mary's wedding in Paris, occupied 28,800 feet of floor space and cost $41,721 to construct. It was a process right out of W.R.'s playbook.

Marion learned to fence for a scene in the film where, disguised as a boy, Mary Tudor engages in a swordfight with people who question her "manhood." She displays quite a bit of skill, and her natural athleticism and physicality shine through. This is an early example of Marion cross-dressing for a role, a frequent occurrence in her early career. It is fascinating to watch. In drag, she never tries to make the audience believe in her as a male; she is always herself, simply in different clothes. Marion was ahead of her time in this way, very naturally implying a sort of gender fluidity in herself. As Jeanine Basinger notes in her essay on Marion in the 1999 collection *Silent Stars*, Marion's approach to drag is unique. In contrast to someone like Katharine Hepburn, who completely inhabits the body of a male, Marion is nonchalant in her cross-dressing characterizations. She is always her feminine self, even in drag, suggesting that this same gender ambiguity can be achieved by any girl who so desires.

When Knighthood Was in Flower is mostly a serious movie, but not without its moments of comic relief. At home, W.R. found Marion's joyful, comic demeanor amusing and attractive. Onscreen, he felt it a distraction. But Marion knew who she was, she knew her limitations and her personality. Despite his best efforts to place her in costume dramas and historical epics that would characterize her as the world's most perfect woman, Marion allowed her comic personality to shine through. At one point, a courtier stares at Mary Tudor, and she responds by mimicking his gaze, bug-eyed and lemon-mouthed, as she squishes her face together to glare at him. It is a remarkable moment, more like a scene from *I Love Lucy* than one from a 1922 Tudor drama. Marion, in her medieval costume surrounded by lavish antiques, was clowning for the camera in the same way that she clowned with her friends offscreen.

In the early 1920s, freedom of individuality and expression was countered by a return to religious conservatism, especially by the older generation. The religious fervor that swept the country in the early 1920s also fueled distrust of the film industry. Over Labor Day weekend in 1921, Roscoe "Fatty" Arbuckle was accused of the rape and murder of young film extra Virginia Rappe at a St. Francis Hotel party in San Francisco. Although the evidence against him was minimal and he was ultimately acquitted on all counts, the ensuing three trials and press coverage surrounding them resulted in the destruction of Arbuckle's onscreen career.

Much of the attention on the Arbuckle case was led by Hearst's *San Francisco Examiner*. The Hearst papers knew that keeping Arbuckle and the trial in the news would increase circulation, and salacious headlines such as "LAST WORDS OF ACTRESS ACCUSED ARBUCKLE, NURSE SAYS" were designed to keep the reader saying "Gee, whiz!" as had been the practice since the nineteenth century.

Marion was opinionated on current events, and W.R. valued her take on a wide range of topics, especially when it came to the film industry. Along with many in the industry, Marion was steadfast in her belief that Arbuckle was innocent. But in this case, W.R. did not instruct his editors to change their reporting.

Just months after the Arbuckle trials, Hollywood was again rocked by the murder of the director William Desmond Taylor, under mysterious circumstances that involved the actresses Mabel Normand and Mary Miles Minter. The scandals gave moviemaking a reputation of indecency, and repercussions in the industry were enormous. The studio heads, fearing their own futures, formed the Motion Picture Producers and Distributors Association (the MPPDA) in January 1922 to preserve the image of motion pictures. They appointed Will Hays, who at that point was the postmaster general in the Harding administration, to head it. For $100,000 a year, Hays would be in charge of regulating morality in motion pictures and preserving the careers of the studio bosses. A week after his acquittal, Arbuckle was banned from the screen by the MPPDA.

As evidenced by the precautions taken in Mexico, even before these scandals broke, W.R. and Marion were careful about their own relationship in public. Any negativity toward Marion was met with W.R.'s swift rage. "I want to protect you," he would tell Marion. But soon, she would be the center of a scandal that threatened to derail her career.

In the spring of 1922, shortly after Marion finished *When Knighthood Was in Flower*, W.R. and Millicent, along with their five sons, embarked on a trip to Europe. While the American economy was booming in 1922, the European economy was still reeling from the effects of World War I. The Treaty of Versailles had left Germany financially decimated, wracked by inflation and unable to pay its war debts. On subsequent travels to Europe over the next decade, Marion would see this firsthand.

W.R. wanted to keep up appearances as much as possible with Millicent, while keeping a close eye on Marion, out of fear that she would be susceptible to other men. With that in mind, W.R. paid for Marion, Mama Rose, and her sisters Ethel and Rose to go to Europe at the same time. It is unclear how much Marion and W.R. saw each other during the trip, but Marion went to Paris in early June, where she met with her old friend Justine Johnstone. Justine had married the producer Walter Wanger and was living in London, and the two chorus girls were happy to have a reunion.

The Dourases left for New York on June 17 aboard the *Mauretania*. Mama

Rose was violently seasick and was still ill when they arrived at the port. Reine had planned to throw a welcome-home party for the family upon their return at her home in Freeport, Long Island, to which Papa Ben was also invited, but Mama Rose was not able to attend due to her illness. Marion decided to stay home to take care of her mother, while Ethel and Rose went to Reine's for the party. In the wee hours of the morning, as the party was winding down, Oscar Hirsch, a neighbor, came bolting out of his house and onto Reine's lawn, chased by his screaming wife. Mrs. Hirsch, seething with rage, suddenly drew a gun and fired a shot at him. The bullet hit her husband in the cheek, then ricocheted and lodged near his heart.

Papa Ben rushed to Hirsch, who was delirious and losing blood, then took him to the hospital in critical condition. Marion's father then went to the police station with the rest of the attendees, where they presented their affidavits as witnesses. Everyone was on edge, and Reine complained about how long it was taking. Her father snapped at her, telling her to be quiet.

The incident was reported widely in the papers. Prominently mentioned in the *New York Herald* and the *Evening Telegram*, as well as several other papers that rivaled Hearst's, was that the shooting occurred at the home of the sister of Marion Davies. They also erroneously claimed that Marion herself was there.

The reporting of Marion's presence at a party where a crime had occurred caused the incident to blow up in Hearst's circles and on Riverside Drive. By attacking Marion Davies in the press, the *New York Herald* and the *Evening Telegram* attacked Hearst by proxy, and Marion was all too aware of their motivations. Giving these accusations attention would fan the flames of the lies, but leaving the accusations unaddressed could potentially cause them to blow up further. Filing a lawsuit herself would likely bring about negative publicity and had the potential to reveal her relationship with W.R. to the public. This would almost certainly jeopardize her career under the auspices of the zealous Will Hays of the MPPDA. In order to remedy this, Rose's husband, George Van Cleve, stepped in and filed a lawsuit for libel on Marion's behalf.

The court hearings, overseen by New York judge George W. Simpson, occurred in late July. By 1922, the relationship between W.R. and Marion was an open secret in film and social circles. Many of the questions from the defense focused on hinting at Marion's relationship with W.R. and outing it as a scandal, with the goal of threatening Marion's career and ruining the credibility of the libel suit. Reine gave testimony about the party and its attendees, and she also actively avoided questions from the defense about her sister, according to the *New York Times*:

> "You know Mr. Hearst employs Marion Davies as a star, don't you?" pressed defense lawyer Macdonald De Witt to Reine.
>
> "I know my sister works for the International Films," Reine answered.
>
> "You know that Mr. Hearst owns the film company and productions in which Marion Davies appears before the public and that Hearst is her employer?" persisted De Witt.
>
> "I consider her employer the Cosmopolitan Films," replied the witness.
>
> "Isn't Hearst her boss?" De Witt demanded.
>
> The court sustained an objection on the motion of William Harmon Black, attorney for Van Cleve on the ground that the question called for a conclusion.

The account of this exchange in the *New York Times* is one of the earliest public insinuations that Marion and W.R. were romantically involved. Newspapers, even papers that rivaled Hearst's, had an unspoken rule about printing their names together. Journalism of the 1920s did not publish scurrilous rumors about celebrities, unless they ended up in court (as in the case of Roscoe Arbuckle). But here, in this *New York Times* piece, the defense questions were reported as they happened, blurring a journalistic line that the defense would use to attack Hearst via Marion and get the suit thrown out.

In addition, the questions from the defense showed that the lawyers knew the house on Riverside Drive was bought by Hearst for Marion. Reine dodged the question, saying that she knew of no "transaction" by which Marion acquired 331 Riverside Drive.

Marion was petrified as she sat in the courtroom waiting to testify on the stand. She had nothing to hide in terms of facts, since she wasn't at the party, but she feared that her speech would incriminate her. "If you stutter," she said later, recalling the events of that day, "they find you guilty right away."

Overcome with fear at the prospect, and too worked up to think about legal implications, Marion suddenly leapt to her feet and ran out of the courtroom. She got in the car and drove herself home, leaving an empty witness stand when it was her turn to testify. She cloistered herself inside the house, and a short while later, her father stormed through the door, furious. His daughter, the child of a magistrate, had not only embarrassed him, but she had endangered herself legally. "You've certainly upset the apple cart now," he railed at her. "What are you afraid of?" Fortunately for Marion, her father was able to explain to Judge Simpson why Marion had run from the courtroom before giving her testimony. In the end, Marion did not have to testify after all, as the libel suit was soon thrown out. Judge Simpson stated that though there was no merit to the accusations of libel, "it has been conclusively established that Marion Davies…was not at the home of her sister in Freeport, L.I."

Marion was still young, and she was finding herself under increasing strain due to her relationship with W.R. and the social mores of the time. She had an underlying sense of propriety and knew that the societal implications regarding relations outside of marriage, especially with a figure as important as William Randolph Hearst, had the potential to destroy her. Marion's fear of speaking in court and running away was a manifestation of all the emotions that were coming to the forefront in these early years with Hearst, feelings that she did not yet know how to manage.

"A Good Actress, a Beauty, and a Comedy Starring Bet"

The Hirsch incident had blown over by the time *When Knighthood Was in Flower* opened on September 14, 1922. The film had its premiere at the Criterion Theatre, and in true Hearst fashion, the ad campaign was almost as lavish as the film itself. Nearly seven hundred billboards heralded the opening of the film, accompanied by three hundred subway ads and special *When Knighthood Was in Flower* souvenirs sold in stores all over the city. Spectacular electric lights illuminated Times Square in anticipation, leading humorist Will Rogers to quip that Marion's next film would be called "When Electric Light Was in Power." Beginning the week before, Hearst's papers almost spoon-fed the film to their readers, giving *When Knighthood Was in Flower* full-page ads in the morning *American* and the afternoon *Journal*, and praising it with over-the-top headlines like "WHEN KNIGHTHOOD WAS IN FLOWER, THE GREATEST PICTURE EVER FILMED, MASTERPIECE OF THE SCREEN, MOST COSTLY AND GORGEOUS PRODUCTION."

In preparation for the premiere, W.R. rented the Criterion and sponsored a complete remodel. To reflect the Tudor setting of *When Knighthood Was in Flower* and the grand scale of the production, he renovated the theater to appear in the style of King Henry VIII, installing twelve extra loges in the balcony to accommodate the large crowds that W.R. expected. The orchestra pit was expanded to fit the fifty-two musicians who would play a score written for the film by William Fred Peters. In addition to the Peters score, Victor Herbert had written two songs to be played as an overture—"The *When Knighthood Was in Flower* Waltz" and "The Marion Davies March."

The Hearst press crafted marvelous opening-night reviews. "Marion Davies wiggles her toes at King Henry VIII," began the review in the morning *American*. That review referred to a comical scene in which Mary Tudor threatens to do a striptease when her brother Henry VIII walks in, and she wiggles her toes in defiance of the king's prudishness.

But perhaps the loudest voice praising Marion in the role of Mary Tudor was that of Louella Parsons. The film was "rich in educational and artistic merit," wrote Louella, and "one of the best films ever made." In a separate editorial, she lambasted Hearst for focusing on the costumes and the magnitude of the film rather than on the talent of Marion Davies. "Why don't you give Marion Davies a chance?" she wrote. "She is a good actress, a beauty, and a comedy starring bet. Why talk about how much was spent on the lovely costumes and the production cost?"

When Knighthood Was in Flower propelled Marion Davies into the consciousness of the 1920s, due to Louella's praise and the Hearst papers' extensive publicity. W.R. was starting to notice Louella's journalistic influence, and the appropriate time finally came for Louella to approach Marion about a position with the Hearst papers. Marion jumped at the opportunity to help a friend, and convinced W.R. to see Louella.

Marion called Louella in early 1923 to ask if she could come to a ball that Louella was attending at the Hotel Astor. She did not mention that she was bringing W.R. When Marion showed up at the door with W.R. in tow, Louella brightened. The two began talking, and in casual conversation, she made it clear that she wished to leave the *Telegraph* and join the Hearst papers. W.R, smiled and said nothing. Louella was dejected. But when he invited her to lunch the next week to discuss a position (no doubt at Marion's urging), Louella became hopeful once more. Again, though, her optimism was short-lived when she discovered that W.R.'s suggested salary was below what she wanted and felt she deserved. Louella asked for $250 per week, where Hearst drew the line at $150. Neither gave in and the contract stalled.

Meanwhile, Marion was preparing for her next movie, *Little Old New York*, originally slated to be directed by veteran director Frank Borzage. Borzage preferred to work on the West Coast, conflicting with Marion's desire to remain in New York to be close to her family. Borzage was ultimately replaced with Sidney Olcott, a New York–based director. *Little Old New York* was another lavish costume drama, and another dual role of sorts for Marion. It was a nostalgic look at New York of the early 1800s, telling the story of a young Irish woman who comes to America disguised as her own deceased brother, to collect on his inheritance.

There are several interesting social issues brought to light in the subtext of *Little Old New York*. For most of the film, Marion's character masquerades as her own brother, once again dressing in drag and convincing everyone around her that she is a boy. There is a thought-provoking twist in the plot when a male cousin becomes enamored with the "brother," and spends the rest of the movie trying to come to terms with his attraction to a man.

Little Old New York's nineteenth-century atmosphere attracted many guests to the set, among them the writer W. Somerset Maugham, author of *Of Human Bondage* and the envy of the writers on the lot. On the day he came to visit, the scenarists sneaked out of their offices to see him. As Maugham chatted with designer Joseph Urban, the writers strained to hear the conversation—and they discovered that, like Marion, he had a severe stutter. As he finished his conversation with Urban and made his way toward Marion, the writers shifted uncomfortably and glanced at each other with unease. Maugham arrived at Marion's side and took her hand.

"I'm cha-charmed to m-meet you, M-iss Davies."

Marion panicked. "Stuttering is contagious," Marion said later, "from one stutterer to another stutterer." She was unaware that Somerset Maugham shared her speech disorder and was sure he was mimicking her. Nonetheless, she dove into the conversation and did the best she could.

"Th-ank you, Mis-mis-ter Mau-mau-Maugham, I'm de-de-delight-lighted to me-me-meet you, too-too-too."

He turned purple, managed to squeak out a "Thanks," and turned back to Urban, his eyes blazing. "Fr-fr-fresh b-b-b-bitch!" he growled, and walked out.

Marion turned to her friends, tears in her eyes. She began to cry. "He was p-p-poking f-f-fun at me," she sobbed.

Urban ran to comfort her. "Mr. Maugham thought you were mimicking him. It's all a mistake. Let's clear this up before Mr. Hearst arrives." The author was nowhere to be found. Distraught though Marion was at first, as she often did when her stutter flared, she ultimately found the humor in the situation and laughed it off.

On the evening of February 18, 1923, as *Little Old New York* neared completion, a raging fire engulfed the 127th Street studio. A staggering $600,000 worth of sets, antique pieces of art, furniture, and costumes were destroyed. It was an especially cold night, and the next morning icicles hung from the ceiling where the fire crew had extinguished the flames, over the charred remains of the Cosmopolitan studio. Fortunately for everyone, the fire was contained in the main building and firefighters managed to save the nitrate film reels containing *Little Old New York*. Nothing had to be reshot.

The fire marked a turning point for Cosmopolitan Productions. For the past few years, the movie industry had been shifting its primary focus from New York to California. By 1923, fifty-three studios were producing films in Los Angeles, accounting for 80 percent of the world's output. Movie star hopefuls flocked to Los Angeles, gradually changing the shape of the city from a largely agricultural area to a bustling metropolis. It was clear that the future of film was in California, and it was only a matter of time before Cosmopolitan moved west to join it.

Cosmopolitan estimated that the studio would take three months to rebuild, and reconstruction began almost immediately. In the meantime, executives scrambled to find a temporary studio in New York to continue shooting so as not to lose any more money. *Little Old New York* had a deadline to be finished by August 1. Cosmopolitan rented the small Tec-Art studio on Jackson Avenue in the Bronx, where production was completed. *Little Old New York* managed to meet the deadline, and the movie was released to the general public in November at the Capitol Theatre to great acclaim. The publicity paled in comparison to the massive campaign launched for *When Knighthood Was in Flower*, but turnout was good and the reviews were positive in both the Hearst and non-Hearst press. Upon the film's success, one of the first congratulatory telegrams was from Marion's mother, who was overjoyed at her daughter's achievement. The telegram read:

JUST LEFT MATINEE AT CAPITOL AM DELIGHTED AT HUGE SUCCESS CAPACITY AT PERFORMANCE LINE OUTSIDE FOR TWO BLOCKS LONG WAITING TO GET IN ALSO HAS EXCEPTIONALLY FINE PROLOGUE WITH SINGING CONGRATULATIONS AND LOVE MOTHER

Over at the *Morning Telegraph*, Louella heartily praised Marion's performance in her column. It "has done a great deal to add to the glories of Marion Davies as well as to pin new laurels on William Randolph Hearst as film producer," Louella wrote, and the movie "is the true blood-sister of *When Knighthood Was in Flower*." By this time, several months had passed since Marion's introduction of W.R. to Louella Parsons at the Hotel Astor. But Louella was still contemplating the contract, never giving up hope on her $250 a week. Louella was persistent, and Hearst could not very well ignore Louella's journalistic influence. He agreed to Louella's terms, and in November 1923, Louella Parsons signed to work for Hearst, for $250 a week.

Marion was relieved, not only for Louella's sake but for her own. She knew that too many of these heavy costume dramas were bad for her career, and that the constant inundation of "Marion Davies news" was making the public tire of her. Louella could help, by shaping the publicity in the Hearst papers to reflect what Marion felt she needed, and perhaps convince W.R. of the same.

As Louella formally joined the Hearst circle, other Hearst companies were undergoing drastic changes. In May of 1923, Cosmopolitan made the decision to break with Adolph Zukor and develop a partnership with Goldwyn Pictures in Culver City, California, a studio that would provide an extensive filming space on the West Coast. Although W.R. "vowed to rebuild" the fire-damaged studio in Harlem, and the work was eventually completed, Cosmopolitan gradually shifted production to California.

During this period of transition to the West Coast, Marion was responsible for helping others in the industry. In mid-February, she read a report in the *Los Angeles Record* that Florence Turner, the early film star who had received fan mail addressed to "The Girl with the Big Eyes," had fallen into poverty in London. Marion had been a fan of Turner's since childhood, when she spent her pocket money going to the movies near her homes in Chicago and New York. According to the report, Turner had gone to London to work, but was now out of a job without any further prospects.

Without delay, Marion wrote to George Allison, a Hearst liaison in London, asking him to find Turner and immediately offer her a part in Marion's upcoming film, *Janice Meredith*. Overwhelmed with gratitude, Turner agreed. Marion arranged to bring her and her mother back to the United States, and paid for their hotel room in New York. Production on *Janice Meredith* began in early 1924, and Turner was cast as a maid. After its completion, Turner was signed by Cosmopolitan. When the studio moved to California permanently, Turner went with them, and enjoyed a revival of her career that lasted well into the 1930s. She remained grateful to Marion for the rest of her life. "She's a beautiful character," Florence later said about Marion, "as many broken down actor or actress [*sic*] could testify."

Janice Meredith bridged the gap between New York and California production. Although filmed in New York, Cosmopolitan brought E. Mason Hopper from California to produce the Revolutionary War epic. Once again, W.R.'s influence is evident in the production. Marion wears heavy, overbearing costumes, the sets loaded down with lavish antiques and ornate decorations, to Joseph Urban's chagrin. It was a beguiling drama, but due to the exorbitant cost, *Janice Meredith* failed to make a profit.

W.R. was already in California by the time *Janice Meredith* was finished. He wanted Marion to be close to him, but Marion was initially hesitant to make the move. She had never been particularly attached to New York, but she wanted to be near her family. They would not be willing to leave, she felt. To her surprise, when she tentatively suggested the idea to them, they accepted it happily. The Dourases wanted to be where Marion was, and if that meant moving to California, they would go. With the confidence that her family would join her, Marion packed up and joined W.R. in California. Her mother, Rose, came along, and Marion's sisters and their families would all be in California before the end of 1924. The only member of the Douras family who stayed behind was Papa Ben, who continued his work there as a magistrate. They lived temporarily at the Ambassador Hotel, before renting actor Norman Kerry's home at 910 Bedford Drive in Beverly Hills.

Marion warmed to Los Angeles immediately. The growing culture of cars was slightly foreign at first, and Marion found herself badly shaken after she was involved in a minor car crash as she turned onto Hollywood Boulevard one day in September 1924. Most of the damage was to the fender, and Marion was unhurt except for a few bruises. Aside from the cars, Marion found that her love of people was nurtured in Los Angeles. She was exposed to a vast landscape of artists, directors, crewmembers, and intellectuals, finding her circle much more diverse than the one she had back home. In the summer of 1924, W.R. bought a white stucco house for Marion and her family, at 1700 Lexington Road in Beverly Hills. The property was deeded under the name of Rose Douras, to keep Marion's name out of the transaction. It was a spacious home, with a large, kidney-shaped swimming pool as its central feature. Marion began hosting large parties centered around the pool and constructed a large ballroom for indoor entertaining. There was a sense of warmth and community at 1700 Lexington, due to the constant coming and going of friends and family. Marion affectionately remembered the atmosphere as "like the Sanger circus," bringing to mind the chaotic fun of the late nineteenth-century entertainment spectacle.

Interest in Hearst's private life intensified in California, as Marion's name was brought into yet another unlikely court case. The prominent lawyer William J. Fallon was the object of an investigation covered heavily by the Hearst papers at the time of Marion and W.R.'s move to California. Fallon was on trial for fixing the juries in a high-profile, Tammany Hall–backed stock swindling case, and went into hiding. A former associate of his agreed to testify that Fallon had fixed the juries. When found, Fallon was swiftly brought to court. At his trial, to throw off the jury and to plant distrust in media coverage of the trial, the names of William Randolph Hearst and Marion Davies came up.

Fallon came before the court on July 22, 1924. At the outset of the trial, Fallon's lawyer, R.J. Shanahan, and the prosecution's attorney, William J. Millard, questioned potential jurors for bias during jury selection. Shanahan's questions to the jurors included: "Are you acquainted with William Randolph Hearst?" When the juror Charles Rosenzweig answered that he was not, Shanahan followed up, "Are you familiar with Marion Davies?"

Before he could answer, Millard jumped to his feet. "Objection!" he shouted. "May I be impertinent enough to ask why you asked that question?"

As it turned out, a key part of Fallon's red herring defense centered on the assertion that he had in his possession incriminating documents regarding the private life of Hearst. When Fallon's associate, Eddie Eidlitz, took the stand, he was questioned by Shanahan about a talk Eidlitz allegedly had with Victor Watson, assistant publisher of the *New York American*.

> "In that talk that you had with him you told him, didn't you, in words or in substance, to say that Mr. Fallon had birth certificates of a certain moving picture actress in connection with Mr. Hearst?"
> "I object to that!" shouted Millard again.
> "We will show," continued Shanahan, "that the acts of the witness and the reason for testifying the way he has is certainly evidence of bias on the part of that witness. We can show a motive for this man testifying the way he is and we will prove the accuracy of the things I am saying right now."

Fallon later confessed to inventing the story to impugn the motives of the media. No birth certificates were ever found. Although the false claims were debunked, news coverage of the trial threatened to damage Marion and W.R.'s reputations and expose their life together.

Throughout their relationship, rumors swirled about a possible child between Marion and W.R. In the late 1920s, one of Marion's cooks, a Mrs. Grace, died suddenly. Marion took over the financial care of Mrs. Grace's teenage daughter, Mary, who was now an orphan without financial support. Mary was often at San Simeon, and some mistakenly believed that Mary was Marion's child, since she had the lithe figure and light features that Marion did. The same was thought for a time about Charlie Lederer, due to his closeness with his aunt. Both rumors are demonstrably false.

While no rumors about Patricia's parentage seem to have existed during Marion's life, some believe today that she was Marion's biological daughter with W.R., possibly born in secret in France. The stories are fueled by those of Patricia herself in later life when she was ill. Claimants assert that Patricia resembled W.R., with her long face, prominent nose, and tall stature. However, Patricia's birth in mid-June of 1919 (when Marion was filming *April Folly*) is confirmed by birthday telegrams, as well as a February 1920 article announcing Rose's trip to Florida with Patricia. Photos from that trip show Patricia as a baby, and one is captioned with a verification of her age— "8 months old." Family friend Marie Glendinning recounted stories about Rose's pregnancy with Patricia, remembering that the baby kicked her husband's hand so hard he was startled. Marion's filmmaking schedule in 1919 was very busy, and her films show no visible signs of pregnancy.

Marion knew the rumors, laughed them off, and enjoyed riffing on them. Those close to Marion scoffed at the idea of secret children. "If she had one child with Hearst," said Marion's close friend Evelyn Wells, "she would have worn it around her neck."

Janice Meredith premiered in New York on August 5, but Hearst and Marion decided that it was best to stay on the West Coast and not return east for the premiere. W.R. conducted most of his business from San Simeon, keeping a relative distance from Marion. A great deal of building was going on there in 1924, including the first installment of the outdoor pool. He would come down to Los Angeles from time to time, to see Marion at home and to finish negotiations on a partnership with the newly formed Metro-Goldwyn Studios that would give Cosmopolitan a permanent home on the West Coast. Cosmopolitan's deal with Goldwyn Pictures would be automatically incorporated into the merger between Metro Pictures Corporation and Goldwyn Pictures, and when Louis B. Mayer was named general manager and vice president, the studio became known as Metro-Goldwyn-Mayer.

Marion would have a new contract under the agreement, which would give her major oversight of her roles as well as a third of the box office receipts, and an astronomical salary of $10,000 per week (nearly $150,000 per week in today's money). The publicity generated by the Hearst papers was a priceless commodity for MGM, and with Cosmopolitan as part of the company, the studio's films had guaranteed press and visibility.

In 1930, an article in *Picture Play* magazine expressed what reporters had known for years about Marion's unique circumstances. Marion's career had risen "up from the top," and her star power had been "foisted upon the public ready made." It was then her task to live up to it. From the beginning, Marion had been billed as a star, bypassing the work that most people had to put in to get there. Marion was aware of this unusual situation, and it was a source of insecurity. She felt that others had more talent, had worked harder, and were more deserving. "I think Marion had more talent than she knew," said Anne Shirley, Charlie Lederer's future wife, who saw Marion's natural abilities even long after she had retired, though Marion always downplayed them. This feeling of inadequacy in Marion translated to a need or desire to give back, and to use her position to build up others who needed support. "She will give the clothes off her back to anyone she thinks needs them, and has to be forcibly restrained from distributing most of her possessions," wrote Alice Head, the managing director of Hearst's British publishing company The National Magazine Company, who knew Marion in the 1920s. Frances Marion also thought Marion's generosity was due to some sort of insecurity. To keep her friends, Marion felt that she had to give her possessions away. "I'm so happy to see you, Frances," Marion would say, "you've been gone so long. Here, I want you to have these pearls."

"Marion, I don't want anything from you," Frances would tell her. "Just your friendship."

Frances was part of a group of friends who made it a rule never to accept anything from Marion. In later years, Eleanor Boardman, Hedda Hopper, and Doris Kenyon were among those who refused Marion's gifts for her own sake. Once, Marion tried to give Eleanor Boardman a gigantic ring right off her own finger. "It would look lovely on your hand," Marion told her.

Eleanor refused. "Marion," she said to her, gently but sternly, "you've got to learn that there are many of us who love you for yourself, and not for what you give us."

"It's Very Convenient to Have a Double"

The atmosphere of 1920s Los Angeles was described by journalist Don Ryan in his novel *Angel's Flight*. It was a "city with aspirations for the Los Angelicizing of the world...the optimistic, the positive, the vociferous... Jazz Baby of the Golden West." In 1924, six thousand cars a day zoomed along the throughways connecting downtown Los Angeles with the growing suburbs. On Sundays, those cars were seen parked next to the shores of Venice and Santa Monica beaches, as throngs of tourists and residents alike enjoyed the sunshine. The opening of Grauman's Egyptian Theatre the previous year had been a sensation, and drew visitors from all over the country. Designed to look and feel like an authentic Egyptian temple, Grauman's spectacular movie palace took full advantage of the American public's fascination with ancient Egypt, following the recent discovery of King Tut's tomb. The increase in religiosity in the country at large was reflected in Aimee Semple McPherson's Foursquare Gospel Church at the Angelus Temple in Echo Park. By 1924, thirty-five film studios were in operation in the greater Los Angeles area, with the newly formed MGM establishing itself as one of the top three.

The outward urban growth of Los Angeles reached westward toward the ocean, and a trend grew among the Hollywood elite to buy or build homes on the Santa Monica beach. Despite a cooler and foggier climate than is generally expected in the Los Angeles area, Santa Monica was otherwise the ideal location—urbanized enough to benefit from the newly minted electric plants that powered Los Angeles and its immediate suburbs, and isolated enough to ensure much needed privacy in a tranquil and picturesque setting.

Marion's lucrative new contract cemented her work in California, and she put 331 Riverside Drive on the market. The home was bought by George

S. Jephson, head of a food manufacturing firm in Hoboken, and with the sale, Marion officially cut ties with her hometown. Her first film to be made solely in California was *Zander the Great*, another project with written supervision by Frances Marion. *Zander the Great* is a unique film, in that it flows from genre to genre, from comedy to stark drama to western, and Marion gets the opportunity to showcase her versatility. The film tells the story of a young orphan, abused in a Dickensian orphanage and adopted by a woman with a baby named Alexander. She begins calling him "Zander," and when his mother dies, she sees to it that Zander will not be sent to the same orphanage where she was mistreated, embarking on a trip to find Zander's father.

After a prologue where she pratfalls and is chased on a bicycle, Marion shifts immediately to drama, pleading with the orphanage director with real tears in her eyes. Co-starring with Marion in the film was an actress named Hedda Hopper, with whom Marion struck up a friendship. Hedda had so much fun on *Zander* that she later wrote that working on a Marion Davies picture was "like inheriting an annuity without knowing beforehand." She expressed great respect for Marion and how she handled her fame. "Marion Davies held in her hands the greatest power of any woman on earth," Hopper later recalled. "She had something royalty never had, the power of the press. She never misused it." Later, Marion would be instrumental in helping Hedda pursue an alternate career—that of Hollywood gossip columnist, as a rival to Louella Parsons.

Due to space constraints at the new MGM studio, the bulk of *Zander the Great* was filmed on the United lot. Norma Talmadge invited Marion to stay in her bungalow dressing room, which was shared with Norma's sister Constance. The Talmadge sisters were already well-known to Marion, and were frequent guests at Marion's parties. The sharing of a dressing room was a pleasant experience for all three women. Constance Talmadge was known to Marion as "Connie" or "Dutch," and to the Talmadge sisters, Marion was "Daisy." It was a nickname that she kept for the rest of her life, and the Hearst sons affectionately used it. In later years, when her young relatives would ask Marion to divulge information from adult conversations, Marion winked at them and said, "Daisies never tell."

A climactic scene toward the end of *Zander the Great* required several dangerous horseback-riding stunts. Marion's fear of horses, stemming from her riding accident at age 12, made this scene impossible for her to do on her own and she needed a stunt double. Vera Burnett, a stunt actress under contract to the studio, came to the set of *Zander the Great* to see if she might be a good fit. The physical resemblance was close, and Vera's horseback riding was impressive. Cameraman George Barnes approached her after the day's work was done. "Would you like to do this some more?" he asked her. Vera said she was eager to, and she was hired as Marion's stunt and camera double. The working conditions were good, she remembered—Vera was paid $10 a day whether she worked or not. Marion frequently bought lunch for everyone on the set, cast and crew alike, and though Vera's professionalism precluded her from talking to Marion while they were filming, Marion would often strike up a conversation with her. Vera stayed with Marion throughout her career at MGM.

Another friend with whom Marion was spending more time was Charlie Chaplin. Chaplin first met Marion at a dinner given by Elinor Glyn at the Ambassador Hotel, while he was in production on *The Gold Rush*. A telegram from Glyn read: "My dear Charlie, you must meet Marion Davies; she really is a dear, and would adore meeting you, so will you dine with us at the Ambassador Hotel and afterwards come with us to Pasadena to see your picture *The Idle Class*?"

He went to the dinner and was charmed by Marion's gregarious nature and kindness. Marion enjoyed Chaplin's company too, and they became fast friends. Chaplin had first become aware of Marion through the publicity machine of the Hearst papers and magazines, and he found the publicity "bizarre." This publicity turned Chaplin off from Marion Davies films, but one night at Mary Pickford's home they screened a print of *When Knighthood Was in Flower*. "To my surprise she was quite a comedienne, with charm and appeal, and would have been a star in her own right without the Hearst cyclonic publicity," he wrote in his autobiography.

They started to spend more time together, and papers took note. At a party at the Café Montmartre in November, Grace Kingsley of the *New York Daily News* noticed the smitten Chaplin as the two danced together. "He never took his eyes off Marion's blonde beauty," she wrote. Vera Burnett remembered that Chaplin was also frequently on the set of *Zander the Great*.

Chaplin had known Millicent Hearst since the 1910s. When he met W.R. for the first time at lunch with Millicent, he accidentally alluded to W.R.'s relationship with Marion. "The first time I saw you, Mr. Hearst," he began, "you were at the Beaux Arts restaurant with two ladies. You were pointed out to me by a friend." The *Variety* editor who had invited him kicked him under the table as W.R.'s eyes twinkled. "Oh!" said W.R. with a laugh. Chaplin tried to walk it back. "Well, if it wasn't you, it was someone very much like you—of course my friend was not quite sure." But W.R. laughed it off. "Well, it's very convenient to have a double."

Millicent also defused the situation, and saved Chaplin in the moment. "Yes," she laughed, "it's very convenient."

This anecdote emphasizes the *entente* that existed between W.R., Millicent, and Marion. Millicent often confided in Chaplin about the relationship between W.R. and Marion. Millicent told Chaplin that when she came to California to visit, the routine was always the same—W.R. stayed with her for a few hours, then the butler would hand W.R. a note. After reading it, Millicent said, W.R. would say that he had urgent business in Los Angeles that he had to attend to, and "we all pretend to believe him. And of course we all know he returns to join Marion."

W.R. was not happy with the initial rushes of *Zander the Great*, and decided to redesign the entire production. He brought in George Hill (Frances Marion's future husband) to replace original director Clarence Badger, and he also brought set designer Joseph Urban in from New York to work on the staging. Urban was also to design a large bungalow for Marion on the MGM lot, a two-story Spanish house of fourteen rooms, each filled with fine antiques, including a dressing room upstairs and dining room downstairs. It was unsurpassed by any other star's dressing room in Hollywood. There was an office there for W.R., and a bedroom for Marion in case she wanted to sleep at the studio after working late. When it was completed in 1925, the bungalow served as a meeting place at MGM, where stars got together during breaks on the sets of their various movies. At the bungalow, one could expect to see the biggest stars of the era, along with politicians, newspaper editors, and other celebrities gathered to meet with Hearst and Marion. When Marion was on the lot, the bungalow had a full kitchen staff that prepared luncheons and dinners for important guests, including studio executives, foreign dignitaries, and visiting artists. It also served as the West Coast headquarters of the Hearst International Film Service.

During much of the filming of *Zander the Great*, W.R. had been negotiating a deal with producer Thomas Ince, one of the other major production forces in Los Angeles. Ince wanted to obtain screen rights to a new Cosmopolitan story, *The Enchanted Isle*, and many in the industry predicted that this was a harbinger of a possible unification of the Cosmopolitan and Ince production forces.

In a letter during this time, W.R. asks Marion's opinion on how he should proceed with the financial aspects of the Ince deal. "The important question is what is to be charged to overhead, etcetera," he wrote. "If these charges are strictly legitimate and reduced to a minimum the profits would be considerable and my share of the profits would probably be more than I could sell the story for. There is a good profit for some stories however." This inclusion of Marion in financial dealings nurtured a business acumen that served her well later. She was often present for meetings with members of the Hearst business circle. Marion modestly downplayed the significance of her presence at these meetings, saying that she "always had a book" to read, but her mind absorbed the information, and she used it when becoming involved with business independently later.

On the weekend of Ince's forty-fourth birthday, W.R. invited him on a cruise on W.R.'s yacht the *Oneida*. "It was a beautiful boat," Marion remembered. "One of the most beautiful boats I've ever seen." To be invited aboard the *Oneida* was the experience of a lifetime—with a crew of thirty and state-of-the-art living quarters, the two-hundred-foot yacht had all the amenities a guest could ask for. That weekend, the *Oneida* was to leave San Pedro on November 15, arriving the next day in San Diego, with a large group of people onboard to toast Thomas Ince for his birthday.

Thomas Ince had been having problems with his health since at least 1916. He suffered from ulcers and "acute angina pectoris," chest pain due to heart trouble, which sometimes left him in such distress that he broke out in a sweat during meetings. When he consulted with doctors about this yacht trip with W.R., they approved, as long as he didn't drink or eat salted foods. Ince boarded the yacht on November 15, setting sail to San Diego to celebrate his birthday.

The group included Marion's sisters Ethel and Reine, as well as 15-year-old Pepi, Marion's stand-in Vera Burnett, actresses Seena Owen, Aileen Pringle, and Alma Rubens, and Rubens's husband, Dr. Daniel Carson Goodman. Goodman was a medical doctor who had not been practicing for some years, working instead as a screenwriter. Charlie Chaplin was also on board. Elinor Glyn and Hearst's secretary Joseph Willicombe joined the group as well.

Unaware of Ince's dietary restrictions, W.R. served finger foods that included salted almonds. Ince, not wanting to be impolite, had a few almonds. At dinner that evening, W.R. proposed a toast to his birthday and Ince drank some champagne. A legend about this evening says that Ince was about to drink the toast with water, so as to obey the advice of his doctor, when Elinor Glyn leaned over and whispered, "Don't drink the toast with water. It's bad luck."

Ince began to feel fatigued shortly thereafter, and retired to bed. Sometime during the night, he became violently ill. He decided that in the morning, he would leave the yacht and go ashore to San Diego, and from there he would return home. Ince consulted with Dr. Goodman, and though not a practicing doctor, Goodman felt it best for them to go together. They hailed a water taxi and went into San Diego, after which they caught a train north toward Los Angeles. On the train, Dr. Goodman noticed the signs of a heart attack. They got off the train in Del Mar to consult with doctors, and Ince told them that he had drunk "considerable liquor." Dr. Goodman called Nell to tell her what happened. She accompanied Ince's Los Angeles doctor down the coast to Del Mar, where the decision was made to transport Ince back to Los Angeles by train. At home, he seemed to be improving, until he had a second heart attack the following morning. He died at home with Nell and the rest of his family.

After Ince's death, rumors began to spread when the *New York Daily News* reported that there would be an investigation into Ince's death. "DYING MAN TOLD OF YACHT BOOZE," announced a headline in the December 10 edition of the paper. Prohibition was still the law, and the discovery of alcohol on the *Oneida* had the potential to snowball into a destructive scandal. From there, gossip evolved to the point where people believed that W.R. had shot Ince on the yacht. The motive: mistaking Ince for Chaplin when W.R. saw him with Marion. In later years, the gossip expanded to include a hush deal, giving Louella Parsons a job at the *American* in exchange for her silence. These rumors quickly unravel. Louella Parsons was already working for Hearst at the time of Ince's death, and remained in New York in November 1924. She did not come to California until the next year.

The only time that W.R. was known to shoot a gun at anything in particular was years later at San Simeon, when some pigeons were destroying a dovecote of rare shingles. He fired a BB gun in the pigeons' direction, more to scare them than anything, but the incident deeply upset Marion. "If I ever catch you doing that again," she fumed at him, "I'll never speak to you again." He never did.

"Who would shoot him?" Marion said later, recalling the Thomas Ince episode. "If anything of that sort had happened, everybody would have been in jail, wouldn't they?"

In recent years, this yacht trip has been revived with a series of spectacles of theater and film, with Steven Peros's fantasy play *The Cat's Meow* having been turned into a movie directed by Peter Bogdanovich. The plot of *The Cat's Meow* recounts the rumor that has permeated public perception of this yacht trip since the event, one that has been misinterpreted by many as fact.

In 1966, Nell Ince wrote to George Pratt, a historian at George Eastman House. Concerned about the rumors and false statements that had been perpetuated in the ensuing years, she wanted to set the record straight. In her letter she recounts exactly what happened in clear detail. "I, as his widow, am writing this letter to you in order that you may know the truth—the actual facts—in which there was no mystery whatsoever." Nell Ince concludes her letter to George Pratt with harsh words for those who tried to exploit Ince's death for gossip. "Why did 'they' have to make such a cruel, sensational story out of it? It was all so unnecessary and terribly unjust," she wrote. "That is my reason for wishing you to know the true facts in the matter."

As to Chaplin, Marion's nature was to be affectionate and demonstrative to everyone, which sometimes makes it difficult to gauge when Marion's attachments were legitimately romantic. Marion's free and uninhibited displays of affection were often misconstrued, which sometimes worried her friends. Marion may have begun the relationship with Chaplin as a good friend, but it quickly grew into an attachment from which it was difficult to extricate herself.

Chaplin said that he "had a visa to both establishments" due to his friendship with W.R., Marion, and Millicent, and that he was privy to the nuances of the relationship between Marion and W.R. Once when Chaplin was a guest at San Simeon, Marion asked his opinion on a script she was considering. When he spoke of it favorably, W.R. became upset, and contradicted him on its merit. Chaplin defended himself, and W.R. exploded. "When I say something is white, you say it's black!" he exclaimed, slamming his fist on the table. Chaplin calmly rose, and asked to have a taxi called to take him back down the hill before leaving the room.

Marion followed him. "What's wrong, Charlie?" she asked him.

"No man can shout at me like that. Who does he think he is? Nero? Napoleon?"

At that, Marion rushed out of the room. She went directly to W.R., and told him that his behavior was rude and he should go apologize to his guest.

W.R. went to Chaplin, and asked to talk it over. Chaplin followed him to a recess in the hall, where W.R. invited him to sit with him in a large antique chair. W.R. extended his hand, explaining to Chaplin that the reason he had exploded that way was because Marion respected Chaplin's opinion, and W.R. really didn't want Marion to do that script. When Chaplin spoke positively about it, W.R. felt frustrated.

"In his ugly mood," Marion explained to Chaplin later, "the storm comes up like thunder."

W.R. was often away from Marion in 1925, and he had an inkling about what was going on between Marion and Chaplin. "I wish I knew what you were doing in Los Angeles," he wrote to her in the fall of 1924. "Be a good girl, dearest. I hate to leave you alone so long. I am afraid you will wander along the primrose path....Be *good*, even if it is painful. Write often and make believe you miss me, anyhow."

In May 1925, Marion visited New York to attend the premiere of *Zander the Great*. Following the premiere, Marion was scheduled to go back to Los Angeles by train, and W.R. asked Louella Parsons to go with her. According to Louella Parsons's 2005 biography by Samantha Barbas, Louella didn't particularly want to follow Marion to Los Angeles. She had a great deal of work in New York and she felt the trip was unnecessary. "No," said W.R., "this is a mission." He wanted Louella to follow Marion to California and report back to W.R. with a rundown on Marion's comings and goings, particularly in regard to Charlie Chaplin. With this request, Hearst put Louella in a very precarious position. As Marion's friend, she was a trusted confidante and Louella knew that this had the potential to destroy their friendship. But she was also an employee of Hearst, and it didn't take her long to decide which was more important. She was too ambitious to let sentiment stand in her way, and despite her friendship with Marion, she complied with W.R.'s wishes.

Marion and Louella left for California on the Lake Shore Limited, departing Grand Central Station on May 15, 1925. They spent a week on the train, and after the weeklong ride to Los Angeles, Marion and Louella were greeted with sunny weather and a large throng of reporters, writers, friends, and admirers who had come to see Marion and witness Louella Parsons's first view of Los Angeles. "I felt as if I were in a dream," Louella wrote the next day, "seeing for the first time this town about which I have written so much." With barely any time to rest after the taxing transcontinental journey, both Marion and Louella were invited to be guests of honor at a party given by Florence Lawrence, dramatic editor of the *Los Angeles Examiner*. It was a magnificent affair with much of the Hollywood elite in attendance. In her position at the *New York American*, Louella had begun to write extensively on actors' offscreen lives, becoming a pioneer in the new culture of celebrity-focused American journalism. With Louella now in Hollywood, they would be obligated to watch themselves at all times, for fear of any transgression being written in her column.

The backstage world of the entertainment industry had been an appealing subject for papers since the nineteenth century, but much of the attention was on production rather than on stars. With the rise of celebrity culture in the 1910s and 1920s, Louella helped to pioneer a type of consumerist journalism focused on the personal details of stars' lives. It fit right in with the heightened consumerist culture of the 1920s and the easy availability of mass media. It paid off for Louella handsomely, and she became a veritable force in the film industry.

Upon her return from New York, Marion started almost immediately on her next film, based on a Broadway play entitled *The Merry Wives of Gotham*, changed to *The Lights of Old Broadway* for the screen. Harkening back to the early days of electric light in New York, the climactic scene of *The Lights of Old Broadway* was a glorious lamplighting sequence in two-strip Technicolor, a relatively new technology that thrilled audiences. Other colorization processes such as hand-tinting and the Handschiegel process appear in the film as well, adding to its appeal. In the film, Marion plays twins separated at birth, one adopted by a poor Irish immigrant family and the other by aristocratic old money New Yorkers. In one scene where the twins appear together, Marion plays one twin, and stand-in Vera Burnett plays the other. Their physical similarity is evident, so much that if one were not aware of the trick, it would seem to be a split screen.

At the same time, Marion resumed the parties that were becoming legendary at 1700 Lexington Road. Marion was a charming hostess, and she delighted in having her Hollywood friends, or anyone in town whom she liked, over to her home for merriment and fun. As Marion acclimated to the scene in Los Angeles, her get-togethers were becoming increasingly large and often raucous. Mama Rose, who was living with her daughter on Lexington Road, was frequently awakened by the commotion, and would lean over the banister and let the guests know in no uncertain terms that they were making too much noise. Marion's mother still came first in her world, and Marion heeded her desires and told her guests to please quiet down.

Sometimes Mama Rose came downstairs to interact with Marion's guests.

She often situated herself in a corner, looking lost and a bit horrified at the wild living of her youngest daughter. Few people except Marion paid attention, but her presence was keenly felt. Frances Marion enjoyed sitting down next to Mama Rose, engaging her on her two favorite subjects, recipes and her daughters. Frances listened to this small, retiring woman talk about the olden days in New York when her daughters were little. It seemed a welcome distraction, and Frances recalled that Mama Rose would brighten as she approached.

Louella reported these parties to W.R., who still couldn't shake his fear that Marion was growing away from him. His jealousy became so severe that he soon hired a detective agency to watch Marion in California while he was away in New York. To ensure that no one found out exactly what he was doing, he asked his secretary, Joseph Willicombe, to contact Roy C. Fairchild of Cook County, Illinois, who then contacted the Harry Lubbock detective agency in San Francisco. Two investigators were vetted, and sent to the area around Marion's home.

The detectives wasted no time in sending reports to W.R. Huge volumes of observations were sent between May and June 1925, including physical descriptions of those coming and going, vehicle makes and models and license-plate numbers. One of the most frequent license-plate numbers that showed up at Marion's house was that of Rolls-Royce roadster 827-759 — Charlie Chaplin's car.

A typical report read like the one from June 6, 1925:

At 2 PM subject came out of her house and got into her Marmon sport touring car alone and drove to Charlie Chaplin's residence in Beverly Hills. She parked her car in the driveway so that it would not be seen from the road and entered Chaplin's house at 2:10 PM. There were no other cars parked in the vicinity of Chaplin's residence. She was evidently the only party there.

At 3:15 PM subject and Charlie Chaplin came out of Chaplin's residence and got into subject's Marmon car and drove to subject's residence and both entered subject's residence at 3:20 PM.

At 3:25 PM Charlie Chaplin's Rolls-Royce Roadster 827-759 was driven up to subject's residence by a Japanese driver.

At 3:40 PM Charlie Chaplin came out of subject's residence and got into the Rolls-Royce Roadster and drove away with the Japanese chauffeur.

When he was presented with these reports, W.R. wrote a scathing letter to Marion in mid-1925:

My dear Marion,

I just haven't got the courage to go to California and see you again. I am sending George [Van Cleve] out with the reports so you will know why. I had heard that things were going wrong so I hired some men to learn the truth. I got it in the reports and it's sickening—a dirty little ignorant cockney clown. Well you are welcome to him and he to you. I am getting off at Kansas City and going back. I will try to arrange your affairs with George Van Cleve. I have no doubt that you will be quite happy at Hollywood and I wish you nothing but happiness. I am sorry that you did not prefer the kind that comes from honest love and loyalty.

His anger did not last long. Marion was young and beautiful, in a city that was quickly becoming one of the most glamorous in the world. W.R. was threatened by the nearly thirty-four-year age difference between Marion and himself, knowing that Marion would naturally gravitate toward people her own age. With Marion's free-love mentality and affectionate nature, the problems were almost inevitable.

To this day, the full extent of Marion's involvement with Chaplin remains a mystery. In later years, Marion spoke of "Charlie" with tears in her eyes. After his exile to Europe in 1952 due to government hostility toward his left-ist political views, Chaplin rarely returned to the United States and Marion missed him terribly. Aside from W.R., Charlie Chaplin was perhaps the second great love of Marion's life and he remained close to her heart for the rest of her life.

FIGURE 1. Marion (left), around age three, with her sister Rose. Courtesy of Marion Lake Canessa.

FIGURE 2. Older brother Charles, shortly before he drowned in a boating accident on Lake Saratoga. Courtesy of Marion Lake Canessa.

FIGURE 3. With her father, Bernard J. Douras. Courtesy of Marion
Lake Canessa.

FIGURES 4–5.
Having fun with
her chorus girl
friends. Marion is
on the right.

FIGURE 6. (above)
Family portrait,
circa 1918. From left:
Marion, Reine, Rose,
Ethel. "Mama Rose"
is seated. Courtesy
of Marion Lake
Canessa.

FIGURE 7. (right)
In costume for
Runaway Romany
(1917). Photograph by
Ira Hill.

FIGURE 8. William Randolph Hearst with his new bride, the former Millicent Willson.

FIGURE 9. With Millicent and their first three sons: George (next to Millicent), William Randolph Hearst Jr., and John (in Millicent's arms).

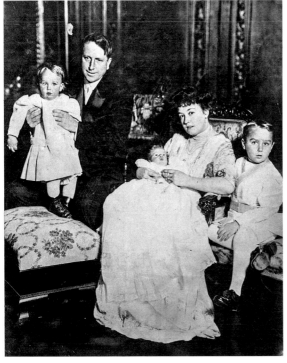

FIGURE 10. Lobby card for *When Knighthood Was in Flower* (1923).

FIGURE 11. 1700 Lexington Road.

FIGURE 12.
(left) Marion
reads on the
patio of her
home on
Lexington
Road. Courtesy
of The Academy
of Motion
Picture Arts and
Sciences.

FIGURE 13. Marion signs her contract with Metro-Goldwyn-Mayer, 1925. The new
contract guaranteed Marion oversight over her own roles, and $10,000 per week.

FIGURES 14–15. Scenes from *Zander the Great* (1925). The film was shot at the United Studio lot, because Metro-Goldwyn-Mayer did not yet have the space. Courtesy of Marion Lake Canessa.

FIGURE 16. Pepi Lederer, Marion's niece, whose dreams of being a writer were overshadowed by her younger brother's success. Courtesy of Marion Lake Canessa.

FIGURE 17. Pepi with her girlfriend, Betty Morrisey, in 1927. Courtesy of *Chicago Tribune* Photo Archive.

FIGURE 18. Behind the scenes of *Beverly of Graustark* (1926). Dressing in masculine clothes became a signature of Marion's early films. Courtesy of The Academy of Motion Picture Arts and Sciences, Margaret Herrick Library.

FIGURE 19. The ranch at San Simeon.

FIGURE 20. Exercising on the set of *The Fair Co-Ed* (1927).

FIGURE 21. Marion takes a short break between scenes of *The Red Mill* (1927). Courtesy of Kevin Brownlow.

FIGURE 22. Celebrity culture of the 1920s allowed for some interesting crossovers. Here, after an event for Sunkist, Babe Ruth signs an orange for Marion at her bungalow. Courtesy of the Los Angeles Public Library.

FIGURE 23. The palatial home built for Marion on the Santa Monica beach. Courtesy of the Santa Monica Public Library. Courtesy of the Santa Monica Public Library Image Archives, Carolyn Bartlett Farnham Collection. Photo by Adelbert Bartlett.

FIGURE 24. Feeding the pigeons in Venice, 1928. Courtesy of Marion Lake Canessa.

FIGURE 25. On the beach at the Lido di Venezia in 1928, Marion (in the floral robe) shares a laugh with friends. Courtesy of Marion Lake Canessa.

FIGURE 26. (right) Marion and Billy Haines in *Show People* (1928). Courtesy of The Academy of Motion Picture Arts and Sciences.

FIGURE 27. (below) "A mud-pie stunt." Marion puts her hands in cement at Grauman's Chinese Theatre, May 13, 1929. Courtesy John Kobal Foundation/Getty Images.

FIGURE 28. Holding hands with Charlie Chaplin at the premiere of *The Florodora Girl* (1930). Courtesy of the Los Angeles Public Library.

FIGURE 29. With her beloved dachshund, Gandhi, at San Simeon. Photo by Clarence Sinclair Bull.

FIGURE 30. Clowning around during a photo shoot for *Marianne* (1929). Photo by Clarence Sinclair Bull.

"Drinking Champagne Out of a Tin Cup"

In late 1925, Marion began filming *Beverly of Graustark*, her final production of the year. Directed by Sidney Franklin, a large part of *Beverly of Graustark* sees Marion cross-dressing as a prince, and Marion's gender transformation elicited a comment from writer Delight Evans of *Screenland*: "Ninety years from now," she wrote, "when all the war pictures and propaganda films are forgotten, some old white-beard is sure to mumble: 'There was a girl named Marion who looked awfully cute in boys' clothes.'" The fan magazines realized the appeal of the characterization, especially Marion's short, masculine haircut, and warned their female readers, "Don't try it unless you are very beautiful."

Marion caught a bad flu while filming *Beverly of Graustark* and spent her twenty-ninth birthday in bed. Production was suspended until mid-January while she recovered. By the end of the month, she was well enough to travel up the coast to San Simeon. The grand property was now ready for occupancy, and Marion planned to throw a costume party with a throng of guests, including Eleanor Boardman, King Vidor, Irving Thalberg, and Elinor Glyn. The party followed a Christmas when Millicent and the boys were in town, and Marion had left to spend the holidays with her mother and sisters.

Known as "the ranch" by regular guests, but often referred to as simply "San Simeon," it became a coveted Hollywood destination, an awe-inspiring "never-never land" of gargantuan proportions. Located five miles up from the main San Simeon throughway, on a lush hill that was verdant in the colder months, dry in the warmer months, Julia Morgan's sprawling design was to become a veritable Hollywood destination. It was punctuated by world-class gardens and another novelty—W.R.'s own private zoo. He was fascinated by exotic animals and searched the market for rare species that he purchased for the ranch, just as he bought his antiques. Most of the animals were bought from dealers in New York, with a few purchased from local California markets. Ostriches, zebras, lions, apes, and elephants roamed throughout the property, and many of the animals were uncaged. This caused frequent traffic problems with visitors, as W.R.'s rules stipulated that the animals were to always have the right-of-way.

On one visit, Louella Parsons and her husband became stranded on the hillside when a moose lay down in the middle of the road. As the rules of the ranch dictated that the animals were never to be disturbed, Louella didn't dare touch the moose or move the car for fear of hurting it. The moose refused to move, and they waited on the road for an hour before it got up and they could continue up the hill.

Alongside the exotic animals was a large kennel of dachshunds that W.R. bred. Some of the dogs went home with family and friends as gifts, but the kennel was a large one and most of them, it seemed, stayed on. Anita Loos remembered that "whenever they saw anyone, they nearly went out of their mind." Anita spent a great deal of time petting them and asked the handler what they were doing there. "Well, Mr. Hearst loves dachshunds," replied the handler. It pained Anita that the dachshunds that W.R. loved were all alone, except for the handler, in the kennel.

To be invited up to San Simeon was a tremendous honor and privilege. For those lucky enough to receive an invitation, the journey would start in downtown Los Angeles or Glendale, where the guests caught a train to San Luis Obispo. Often, Marion and W.R. were on the train as well, after finishing a week of work. On the journey, Marion moved around the train cars, finding people to sit with and engage in conversation. W.R. played solitaire.

When the train arrived at San Luis Obispo, cars waited to take them to San Simeon, about an hour's drive from the station. Once there, they drove up the windy road leading to the glorious castle at the top. The first building in sight was a towering Spanish-style main house that W.R. called Casa Grande. Anita Loos recalled that W.R. had the property wired for sound, and loud, jovial music greeted the guests as they approached the house. Instead of the majestic music that one might expect from such a grand place, W.R. went with whimsical modern choices that he played at a high enough volume to be heard all over the countryside. As Anita ascended the hill for the first time, her first glimpse of the ranch was accompanied by the 1920s novelty song "'Tain't No Sin (To Take Off Your Skin and Dance Around in Your Bones)." The music, combined with the larger-than-life surroundings, led to a contrast in imagery at the ranch that was, as Hollywood actor and frequent guest William Haines put it, "like drinking champagne out of a tin cup."

An array of servants showed guests to their rooms in one of the three spacious guest houses. "If you were lucky, you stayed there," remembered Anita, because the main house could be unbearably cold, while the cottages—Casa del Mar, Casa del Monte, and Casa del Sol (usually known as House A, House B, and House C)—were all outfitted with modern heating and were much more comfortable. The servants unpacked guests' bags, which would seem a nice service, but in reality, they were searching for any trace of alcohol. A guest caught breaking the iron rules of behavior, which included no alcohol brought from outside the ranch, had their bags repacked. They would find themselves sent down the hill and back on a train to Los Angeles in shame. Life at San Simeon was not that of a luxury vacation. Everyone was expected to dine together, at the set times for breakfast, lunch, and dinner, and to participate in the activities that W.R. planned. At dinner in the main dining room, only one cocktail was allowed. According to Evelyn Wells, these rules were implemented not because W.R. wanted to curb drinking in general, but because he felt that Marion's drinking needed to be controlled.

The employees of the ranch, such as the men who worked with the dachshunds at the kennel or with the zoo animals, would have liquor of their own that was unrestricted by W.R. The guests, likely spurred on by Marion, would sneak out and talk to the employees, who were often "corruptible" and would give the guests bottles of their own liquor. Then there was an elaborate, sneaky game of hiding the liquor around W.R., which was as much fun as it was risky. "Marion was like a naughty girl," remembered Anita. "W.R. was a big, important man, and we were all brats."

When Marion winked and nodded to her friends, they hurried away and tucked themselves in the bathroom. There, they opened the secret gin bottle that Marion kept behind the toilet and started drinking. W.R. pretended not to notice, but he always kept an eye on how long Marion and her friends stayed in the bathroom. One night, when they had been missing for a good half an hour, W.R. became furious. He stormed upstairs, grabbed Marion's nightgown, came back downstairs to the bathroom, and threw Marion's nightgown in. "Why don't you just stay in there all night?" he yelled. It was one of the only times W.R. ever expressed anger with Marion in front of others.

The dining room in the main house was a grand scene featuring long Italian refectory tables, choir stalls, and high-set windows, giving the room an air of Europe in the Middle Ages. It could have easily passed for a fourteenth-century Spanish monastery, aside from the anachronistic paper napkins and bottles of ketchup and mustard that W.R. placed on the refectory tables. This presentation was a throwback to when his father packed condiments, still in the bottle, for camping trips on the hill that had now become W.R.'s ranch.

Parties were filled with Marion's generous spirit. They were often costume parties, which Marion enjoyed organizing on a whim. If anyone arrived without the proper themed attire, clothes were provided, and the guest could usually keep them. On one occasion, at a party at which costumes were brought up from the studio, a guest decided that she didn't like the dress she was given. Marion took the dress and went upstairs to change. She gave her own dress to the guest and donned the offending garment herself. Marion gave away jewels to anyone who admired them, and fur coats were wrapped around any young actress trying to impress a producer.

When weather permitted, W.R. organized lavish western-style picnics down the coast from San Simeon. Riding horses over the long trail was very difficult for Marion due to the accident at her grandfather's stable, but she rode, sometimes long distances, trying to keep her fear of horses to herself. Sometimes these excursions would consist of dinner and overnights at the Mission San Antonio de Padua, where all guests were supplied with a small, individual tent and a cot to sleep on. When W.R. was feeling particularly in the mood for a daytime outing, they went to the harbor by San Simeon Bay, where servants and a portable kitchenette went before the guests to prepare a lunch of soup, squab, and potatoes, served by a butler on elaborate china paired with champagne served in glass flutes.

Friends invited to the picnics came from all different parts of Marion and W.R.'s lives, from Hearst newspapermen, to Hollywood actors, to former chorus girls whom Marion had befriended a decade before. There was no discrimination based on class or social standing at a Hearst picnic. Marion, still adjusting to California life, suddenly found herself in a world distant from her lower-middle-class life in Brooklyn. Surrounded by those far more educated than herself, Marion was both an insider and an outsider, part of the inner circle and yet isolated by her own lack of education and sophistication.

One of the guests who came to San Simeon often was William Haines, known in the industry as "Billy." He was seen as a heartthrob among teenage girls and had established himself as something of a superstar by the late

1920s. W.R. had been very impressed by Billy's keen eye for fine furniture. "I'd pick up a particular piece of furniture, not knowing a damn thing about it," Billy remembered, "and I'd ask Mr. Hearst questions. He was very knowledgeable. We had a rapport, and he was very patient with me. I learned a great deal from him."

Billy sometimes came to these parties with his partner, fellow actor Jimmy Shields. Billy was openly gay, one of the first actors in Hollywood to be out of the closet. He had been in a long-term relationship with Shields for many years by this time, and Marion was a loyal friend to them both. She felt, as other industry professionals did, that theirs was truly "the best marriage in Hollywood."

Other prominent guests at San Simeon were producer Joseph P. Kennedy and Gloria Swanson. Though they came as guests separately, Kennedy started making movies for Gloria Swanson in the late 1920s, and their relationship quickly evolved from a business endeavor to a full-blown romantic affair. Kennedy was married with eight children, but he was captivated by Gloria, and wanted to have total and complete control over her career.

Joseph P. Kennedy is a controversial figure in history, and in the life of Marion and W.R. Marion found him down-to-earth, practical, and affable. He quickly became the type of friend that Marion liked to refer to as a "pal." Kennedy would do a great deal to help Marion in the coming years, and Marion would become very close to his family. The extent and nature of their relationship is the subject of controversy among Marion's friends, with some believing him to be generally benevolent in her life, and others believing him to be someone who used Marion for her influence.

Gloria, by contrast, was happiest when she was having a romantic affair and took her career very seriously. Marion found her pretentious, arrogant, and self-involved. When Marion met someone whose persona was centered around the serious and dramatic, she usually found the humor in the situation and mischievously began crafting an imitation of them. She soon developed a devilish one of Gloria Swanson that delighted her friends.

Around this time, Marion made her first trip to Wyntoon, Phoebe Hearst's rural estate near Mount Shasta on the McCloud River. When W.R.'s mother had left Wyntoon to her niece Anne Apperson, it had driven a wedge between the cousins. From the time of Phoebe's death in 1919, W.R. had argued with Apperson over Wyntoon, and finally, in 1925, she agreed to sell it to him.

Under W.R.'s purview, Julia Morgan began to work on additional structures at Wyntoon in 1928, including a swimming pool and two tennis courts. In early 1930, Wyntoon suffered a major fire and much of the original architecture was damaged beyond repair. W.R. was heartbroken but saw this as an opportunity to rebuild Wyntoon in a new way. A quaint Bavarian village scene was begun in 1933, with Julia Morgan once again supervising, along with contractor Fred Stolte. Three main houses were added—Cinderella House, Bear House, and Angel House.

Among the picturesque, fairy tale–like buildings, Marion felt the stillness and silence of the rural forest and it made her slightly uneasy. The most time that Marion had spent away from the city, or from easy access to the city, was when she went to her grandfather's stable at Lake Saratoga as a child. At San Simeon, Marion was almost always with friends. But Wyntoon was too far for Marion's friends to reach easily, so it was lonely for the extroverted Marion, who felt the most joy when she was around lots of people. But in later years, after W.R.'s death, Marion would remember Wyntoon fondly, and the precious alone time she spent with W.R. there.

In stark contrast to Wyntoon, San Simeon buzzed with people coming and going, including Marion's nieces and nephews Pepi, Charlie, and Patricia. By this time, sister Rose and her husband, George Van Cleve, were having domestic problems. Marion was protective of Patricia, who was now nearly seven years old and increasingly aware of the problems between her parents. Marion wanted to shield her from the problems at Rose's, and frequently brought her to San Simeon for a respite. With her beloved Aunt Marion, Patricia could relax and be her free-spirited self. She often roamed the gardens on the hunt for "fairies," and delighted guests with her creative stories and wild imagination. "The ones without wings I can catch all right," she told writer Jane Tilton, "but the ones with wings I have a heck of a time getting."

Possessing a strong maternal instinct and an innate desire to have children of her own, Marion was drawn to young people, and in response to her own childlessness, took on even more of a mothering role to her nieces and nephews than her less maternally inclined sisters. Marion cared and provided for her nieces and nephews, while Reine and Rose, for whom having children was more of a social obligation than something they wanted, focused on their own lives. Marion ended up being the source of maternal warmth and comfort that Patricia, Charlie, and Pepi needed, as her sisters became more distant, and both ultimately devolved into alcoholism. Marion, despite her own problems with alcohol, provided both Pepi and Charlie with a refuge from Reine's emotional coldness, and Patricia from Rose's moods and family instability. In later years, Charlie's home was filled with photos of Marion, but there was not a single photo of his mother.

Additionally, Marion took a genuine interest in the lives of her friends' children, remembering their birthdays and giving them meaningful gifts. Elaine St. Johns, the daughter of columnist Adela Rogers St. Johns, remembered Marion inviting her to San Simeon alone, without her mother. Marion spent hour after hour with Elaine, teaching her how to put on makeup, letting her play among her clothes and giving her the attention that a 13-year-old girl craves. Marion seemed to gain as much joy from her time with Elaine as she did, reliving her girlhood in the most unlikely of milieux.

When it came to W.R.'s sons, Marion was attentive and maternal. W.R. was frequently harsh and judgmental with his children, taking them to task for the slightest perceived imperfection. Marion was horrified at this and let W.R. know. "When your sons come in, I want you to talk to them. After all, you know, they're your flesh and blood." She was only seven years older than W.R.'s eldest son, George, but she felt a responsibility to mitigate W.R.'s emotional attitude toward his sons. They, in turn, were devoted to Marion.

As Marion became more familiar with the social climate of her new home in California, she became increasingly aware of the poverty that pervaded the west side of Los Angeles. The second half of the 1920s was starting to look a great deal starker and grimmer than the comfortable and happy first half, especially for the already poor residents of Los Angeles. A group of concerned local women came to Marion shortly after her arrival in California, hoping that her financial wealth might be an asset to the community. A proper, low-cost pediatric medical clinic was lacking in the community, and parents were increasingly unable to afford care. They brought statistics to Marion, showing her that the need was dire, and after mulling over the figures and pondering what to do, Marion decided that she would help. She used her own money to purchase the land for a children's clinic in West Los Angeles for low-income children. Meanwhile, she underwrote the activities at the Neighborhood House Association on Beloit Avenue in the Sawtelle neighborhood, making the services free of charge for children and their mothers.

The concept of taking care of the myriad needs of disadvantaged children was especially dear to Marion's heart. Her own background as a lower-middle-class child, struggling with speech problems, and watching her sister Rose live with a congenital hip dislocation, was a great influence on Marion wanting to help other children in similar situations. The Marion Davies Children's Clinic became one of her proudest accomplishments, one that enabled her to help in the direst of times that befell the United States in the coming decades, and she always treated it with the utmost care. Doctors worked for free at the clinic, because no fee was charged to patients. In addition to the clinic being Marion's way of helping West Los Angeles, it was a way for her to feel connected to her adopted home, giving a piece of herself to the community.

In order to secure the future of the clinic, she pieced together the Marion Davies Foundation, a loosely formed entity that would oversee the monetary and logistical needs of the clinic. Although it would not become a legal organization until 1932, the Marion Davies Foundation completed its first quarter of active work in January 1927, serving several hundred children in its first year.

In view of the strain of the holiday season on low-income families, Marion put a system in place to help clinic families at Christmas time. In December 1927, Marion partnered with the Women's Club of Sawtelle to host seven hundred children at a grand party. In addition to those the clinic had helped, also included were children whose fathers were in government hospitals and whose mothers were struggling to make ends meet. At the Tivoli Theater in Sawtelle, the only place deemed large enough to house seven hundred children and their families, the young attendees received toys and dolls, and each family received a bag of Christmas groceries, which included potatoes, fresh vegetables, and a full turkey. The party became a yearly event for the Marion Davies Children's Clinic and was an important institution for West Los Angeles for as long as the clinic existed.

In the spring of 1926, Marion began work on a light comedy based on a Broadway play, *The Red Mill*, the story of a mistreated Dutch girl who plays matchmaker with her friends while searching for love herself. The original play was written by Victor Herbert and Henry Blossom, and Cosmopolitan Productions standby Frances Marion was brought onboard for the movie scenario.

According to what silent film comedian Buster Keaton told film historian Kevin Brownlow in the 1960s, as W.R. searched for a director, Keaton went to Marion to ask a favor. "You're going to make *The Red Mill*," he said to her. "Why don't you use Arbuckle? He would make a great comedy director for you."

Following Roscoe "Fatty" Arbuckle's scandalous trial, he had been banned from appearing on the screen by the MPPDA under the purview of Will Hays. Despite his acquittal, he was relegated to work behind the camera, hiding behind the name "William B. Goodrich" (Will B. Good) and directing several low-budget movies. This situation was especially heartbreaking to Keaton, who had worked with Arbuckle on the stage and considered him a mentor and a best friend.

Marion was enthusiastic and agreed. Despite the Hearst papers' role in staining Arbuckle's reputation, Marion was optimistic that W.R. would agree to support him. When she asked W.R., he agreed. The Arbuckle case had been fodder for the newspapers, and in W.R.'s mind this was an entirely different milieu. W.R. compartmentalized his various careers to the point that he considered each a separate entity, and his newspaper life did not overlap with his film life. W.R. invited Arbuckle to San Simeon as though nothing had happened. This was a clear showing of the two sides of W.R.—while he had helped to ruin Arbuckle publicly, he didn't appear able to comprehend why others might consider his invitation to Arbuckle an odd gesture. W.R. retained an aversion not only to the mixing of his public and private lives but also to the infiltration of either of his businesses into the other. He didn't see why Arbuckle might have held a grudge for destroying his career, and fortunately for Hearst, Arbuckle didn't seem to. He accepted the invitation, and came to spend a weekend at San Simeon to discuss the deal. Photos of Arbuckle at San Simeon show him clowning with other guests and clearly having a good time. In the five years that had passed since the scandal, Arbuckle seems to have moved on from any bad feelings toward Hearst.

Anxious about getting the results he wanted from Arbuckle, W.R. hired King Vidor to observe Arbuckle's work on the production. Vidor was a frequent guest at San Simeon, and both Hearst and Marion had greatly admired his work on the World War I epic of 1925, *The Big Parade*, which remained Marion's favorite movie for the rest of her life. Vidor was an amicable person and was a positive presence on the set, but Arbuckle knew he was being watched. The actress Colleen Moore remembered that the intrigue on the set would have made a good thriller.

Hiring Vidor to oversee *The Red Mill* was also an opportunity for W.R. to see how Vidor worked on a film set. He believed that Vidor would make a good director for Marion, because the grandiosity of *The Big Parade* was very much what W.R. desired for Marion's career, and he was very interested in hiring Vidor to direct Marion in a similar dramatic epic. Vidor recalled W.R.'s laser focus, and said that "Mr. Hearst never gave up until he had me directing Miss Davies." King Vidor had been a good friend of Marion's for several years. He had been at San Simeon for the party Marion gave at the beginning of 1926, and his romance with Eleanor Boardman is clear in the footage. The sparks between them had been flying for some time, and they married at Marion's Lexington Road home shortly thereafter.

Although it was supposed to take place in the winter, *The Red Mill* began production in May 1926. Exterior scenes were shot at nearby Verdugo Hills and interiors on the MGM lot in Culver City, complete with a large ice rink cooled by ammonia gas. Trade papers were amused by the timing of the winter-based production and noted that "owners of moist brows and wilted collars may be interested to know that a few hundred players are skating on ice (artificial) at the MGM Studios on the coast."

The production involved the casting of many children who were to play Marion's village playmates. When the casting of children was taking place, Marion thought immediately of a familiar face at MGM, an 11-year-old newspaper boy who sold his papers just outside the studio gate. The boy, Carl Roup, was energetic and friendly, and studio employees found him so charming that Carl was eventually invited to sell his papers inside the gate. Marion received free newspapers through her association with W.R., but she liked Carl so much that she often bought papers from him on her way into the studio.

The morning that they were casting the children for *The Red Mill*, Marion approached Carl and asked him if he would like to be in a movie. Of course, he did, so Marion took Carl by the hand, brought him to the set, and that morning Carl found himself cast as one of the village children in *The Red Mill*. The story that Marion Davies had handpicked him for the role assured him a certain amount of fame on the lot.

In talking with Carl in the years after filming, Marion learned that he aspired to attend the newly established Pacific Military Academy in Culver City. She wrote the school, and with the permission of his parents, Marion arranged for Carl to be enrolled there when the school opened in 1929. She paid for the entirety of his tuition, and he graduated in 1933. "Marion was a very great person," Carl remembered in later life. "A generous person." He returned to the film industry after military school, and grew up to be a respected cameraman, working on such high-profile television shows as *The Patty Duke Show* (1963–66) and *Trapper John, MD* (1979–86).

Despite Carl's presence and the novelty of ice skating during the summer months (on ice kept cold under the Klieg lights through the use of ammonia gas), the production exhausted Marion. One scene of the production called for her to cry on cue and then laugh. Crying on cue was normally easy for

Marion. But when they had to retake the crying scene multiple times over the course of twenty minutes, Marion became slightly exasperated and snapped at Arbuckle, "I thought you were a comedy director." Arbuckle's direction called for a great number of pratfalls, kicks, and tumbles, including a fall into a freezing pool of water during an ice-skating scene. The scene involved an ice-skating race, which Marion was to win, after she grabbed hold of a dog running to chase a cat. Marion's sensitivity toward animals made it very difficult for her to complete the scene. She remembered that the dog eventually caught the cat and injured it, and afterward she was so upset that she went back to her dressing room and called the Society for the Prevention of Cruelty to Animals.

A system of pipes had been installed under the pond, through which ammonia gas was pumped, pulling the heat from the water and freezing the ice. Naturally, this intricate process also rendered the water devastatingly cold. The racing scene had to be taken and retaken several times, with Marion required to fall into freezing cold water each time. She did it, without complaint, but her body suffered an immense shock.

Retakes of *The Red Mill* went on into the early months of 1927, and Marion was exhausted physically and emotionally. She later said that after seemingly endless retakes of the scene where she falls into the icy water, she became severely ill. At the end of her illness, she claimed, she had permanently stopped menstruating at the age of 30.

The true cause is unknown, but something did happen in Marion's body around this time, causing her to stop having menstrual periods and thus leaving her unable to conceive. Marion's desire to have children was deep, and the loss of her ability to have biological children was a deep wound in her life. In the wake of this loss, she threw herself even deeper into caring for the children at her clinic.

"Why Don't We Forget the Play That's Written and Let Marion Do What She Does?"

Over the course of 1927, demand for the Marion Davies Children's Clinic grew significantly. The early part of the 1920s had been punctuated by a strong economy and financial comfort for many, but the increase in patients at the clinic was a sign of troubled times to come. The large new hospital for the Marion Davies Children's Clinic was begun that year, on a large parcel of land bounded by Mississippi, Barry, Barrington, and Louisiana (soon to become part of Olympic) Avenues in West Los Angeles, about half a mile south of the original clinic site on Beloit Avenue. The new building was designed by Julia Morgan in a Spanish style, made of white stucco with a tile roof following the design of the early California missions. It would include a gymnasium and many specialty departments, such as ear/nose/throat and orthopedics units, to address the growing needs of the clinic's population. Doctors began seeing patients at the expanded five-acre building in the middle of July 1928.

The community surrounding the clinic largely comprised Mexican and Japanese immigrants. By the 1920s, most Mexican American families in West Los Angeles were no longer reliant on *curanderos* and herbs, and they brought their children to medical facilities for immunizations and doctor visits. The clinic served as a community resource as much as a medical center—a haven from the racism and economic disparity that families experienced all too frequently outside. Lupe Herrera, who grew up in the Mexican American community of West Los Angeles, was a regular patient at the clinic. Lupe's father, rejected by labor unions due to his Mexican heritage, struggled to find adequate work. Keeping Lupe and his siblings fed, housed, and clothed in these dire conditions "was really a miracle in itself," Lupe said. There was no money left to spend on doctors or medicine. "In those days, there was diphtheria and a lot of serious diseases [among poor people]," and the clinic played an important role in stopping the spread of illness among neighborhood families.

In June 1926, Marion and W.R. decided to build a house on the ocean in Santa Monica, in keeping with the growing trend among the Hollywood set to build beachfront homes. In these early years, the house would be kept in Marion's name but leased back to W.R. at $2,500 a month, to keep up appearances with Millicent and anyone else who might be apt to target them in the press. Marion and W.R. would make decisions for it together, and the home would be jointly theirs. Naturally, Julia Morgan was W.R.'s first choice to build it, but with her busy schedule, she was unable to commit the time and energy that was needed for a project of this scale.

The architect W.R. chose instead was William Flannery, a 27-year-old Hollywood designer who had also designed the 1700 Lexington Road house before Marion came to California and had worked with Julia Morgan on the new clinic building. Flannery's youth and relative inexperience made him a somewhat odd choice for such a huge project, but it was typical of both Marion and W.R. to favor the underdog in these situations. They also liked him personally, and it was also typical of them to favor people they knew rather than those that they didn't, especially if the person's work had real potential, as Flannery's did.

Julia Morgan supervised Flannery's work, though her busy calendar in the late 1920s prevented her from having much direct contact with Flannery and his team. She nonetheless kept an eye on the Beach House project and occasionally offered advice. In 1929, when Julia Morgan's schedule became freer, she would take over from Flannery and finish the house.

W.R. envisioned a grand property consisting of a main house flanked by several guest houses, much like San Simeon, directly on the sands of Santa Monica Beach. The main house had about twenty rooms, divided between the first and second floors, and thirteen rooms on the third. Sitting on a long stretch of beach between the addresses of 321 and 415 Ocean Front between the shore and the Pacific Coast Highway, the design included an impressive swimming pool with blue tiles speckled with gold, which later provided the inspiration for the indoor Roman Pool at San Simeon. Their neighbors up the beach soon included Norma Shearer and Irving Thalberg, Louis B. Mayer, and Anita Loos.

Similarly to San Simeon, W.R. conducted a massive search for amenities for the Beach House. Fireplaces were purchased from the New York market, dating from several hundred years back. Envisioning a beer cellar downstairs for entertaining, W.R. found and transported an entire inn from Surrey, England, dating from 1560. Lighting was provided by lamps from Tiffany & Co. in New York.

The news of Marion's new Beach House spread excitedly through Hollywood and by extension the Hollywood gossip columns. Louella Parsons wrote in her column on September 9, 1926:

> Marion Davies will soon move into her beach home at Santa Monica. It is the largest house on any southern California beach. While being shown around, I counted fifteen bathrooms, and even Marion doesn't know how many other rooms there are. When she tires of [the house], she plans to convert it into a beach club.

Marion set a move-in date for April 15, 1927. With so much work left to be done, she became impatient and decided to start occupying the home before it was finished. There were issues and complications that stalled the construction of the house, but she more or less managed to move in by the fifteenth and promptly began inviting friends over for parties.

The Beach House offered Marion a chance to let loose outside of W.R.'s watch. While at San Simeon, Marion had to abide by W.R.'s rules around deportment and alcohol consumption, but the Beach House was Marion's territory. It gave her an opportunity to socialize without having to worry about W.R., a place where Marion could be unguarded and unwatched. W.R.'s frequent absences allowed Marion to have parties that might total several hundred guests at once, taking advantage of the two antique bars that had been built into the Beach House. Marion and her guests were able to drink as much as they wished, sometimes culminating in wild raucousness and conga lines down the beach. Mama Rose was still living at 1700 Lexington Road and spent little time at the Beach House, so Marion didn't have to worry about her mother breaking up the party.

Despite what W.R. may have wanted, Marion held onto the notion that her life was hers to live and that she was an independent woman. In a sense, Marion was straddling two worlds—the new, independent consciousness of the 1920s that ignored societal constraints based on sex, and the traditional model of society that dictated her role. This created a gray area for Marion that was sometimes startling to friends like Anita Loos, who found it strange that there was nothing Marion loved more than inviting all her friends over for a huge party, but would very rarely go out to others' homes unless she was entirely sure of the guest list. One day Anita spoke of a party to Marion and just assumed she was going because "everyone will be there." She was surprised to learn that she wasn't. Anita asked her why. Marion said, "You see, N-N-Nita, when I get among strangers, I never know."

Marion's contract with MGM had come up for renewal in October 1926. Marion negotiated substantial gains, including producing rights for her films beginning with her next, *Tillie the Toiler*. From this point on, movies starring Marion Davies would be known as "Marion Davies productions," and would say so in the opening credits. There would be three Marion Davies productions out of MGM every year, and she would maintain her salary, guaranteed at $10,000 a week. In addition, she would receive a third of the box office receipts, and top or equal billing with any other star, male or female. There was a rumor around town that W.R. was going to dissolve his association with MGM and take Cosmopolitan Productions elsewhere, but the newspapers felt that Marion's renewed contract put that rumor to rest. It also showcased the power that Marion Davies had over the studio.

Up to 1927, Marion had played almost exclusively in costume or period pieces, but *Tillie the Toiler* was different. Based on the comic strip of the same name, Marion was joyous as she played a modern secretary. Her first scene in *Tillie the Toiler* is an expertly crafted bit of situational comedy, as Marion tries to blink a piece of dust out of her eye, leading all the men on the sidewalk to believe that she is winking at them. She continues to blink and wink as she walks, never aware of the parade of men following her. As in *When Knighthood Was in Flower*, it is reminiscent of a Lucille Ball routine.

Marion was scheduled to start *Quality Street* shortly after *Tillie the Toiler*, but she was in desperate need of rest and went to San Simeon for a vacation before starting production. "I have worked very hard for the past six weeks, days, nights, and Sundays, making *Tillie* in daytime and *The Red Mill* retakes at night," she wrote Irving Thalberg in February 1927. "I will come to Los Angeles whenever you think I must, but I must advise that all preliminaries be done here." She returned to Los Angeles rested and relaxed, ready to start another dramatic production.

Quality Street was set during the Napoleonic Wars, and Marion once again plays a dual role of sorts. She portrays Phoebe Throssel, a young, vibrant, Napoleonic War–era maiden who grows older while her love interest (played by Conrad Nagel) fights in the war. Marion's acting is nuanced, emotional, and raw. When her lover shuns her due to aging and she dresses up like a young girl again, posing as "Phoebe's niece, Miss Livvy," Marion's youthful radiance reappears, but this time with a worldly air about her. We can tell that this is a woman who has lived. With a weary gaze and restrained movements, Marion plays an older woman pretending to be a younger woman. The performance stands among Marion's greatest dramatic works. Upon its release, the *Exhibitor's Herald* said that "it has proven.... that Marion Davies can act." The critics were effusive. "Gentle and refreshing is the screen translation of... Quality Street, in which Marion Davies gives the most conscientious performance of her career," said the *New York Times*. The *New York Evening World* agreed. "She gives a performance whose quaint wistfulness, poignancy, and power make it the most surprising event of the season," wrote Gene Gerhard.

Despite the success of *Quality Street*, Marion was becoming restless. *Tillie the Toiler* had made it clear to her that she wanted to let loose and have fun onscreen. Wielding the power of her new contract, she began secret discussions with Irving Thalberg to try to shift her image. She was 30 years old in 1927, had been a film star for a decade—and she felt stifled and infantilized in the ingenue roles that W.R. wanted her to continue to play. Thalberg sympathized and vowed to help. In July 1927, he wrote to W.R. that he had been "encouraged by various talks with Marion who told me she wanted to play a modern girl." The tone of the letter to W.R. is gentle, as though softening the impact of disappointing news. He used the right approach. W.R. came around and agreed to try Marion in a different role—not as a historical maiden but as a modern-day woman. W.R. chose a George Ade play called *The Fair Co-Ed*, whose plot centered around a young woman trying to make it at an all-male college. The play had been written in 1909, but the story was updated by MGM scenarists to attract 1927 audiences.

The Fair Co-Ed went through several different incarnations from writers Agnes Christine Johnston, Frances Marion, and Byron Morgan before a final plot was set. The director was to be Sam Wood, and Marion's character's name was changed many times before the story department finally settled on the choice before them—"Marion." By this time, Marion had decided to dye her hair a light blond, which, paired with the bob that she had retained from *Beauty's Worth*, gave her a peppy quality that served her well in this role.

The Fair Co-Ed began filming in mid-1927, a time when commercial airplane travel was taking the world by storm. Innovations in airplane combat during the war years had led to technological advances for passenger planes. Charles Lindbergh, who had been a combat veteran in the war, became an aviation cause célèbre when he completed the first solo transatlantic flight in a passenger plane in May 1927. He was awarded several medals, achieving a cult of celebrity similar to that of the greatest stars in the movies. During the filming of *The Fair Co-Ed,* Marion hosted Lindbergh for breakfast at her bungalow before throwing him a large tea party at the Ambassador Hotel. The flyer had specifically requested that Norma Talmadge and Mary Pickford share hosting duties. Crowds gathered outside to catch a glimpse of the famed aviator, including Marion's former co-star from *Zander the Great,* Hedda Hopper, who was ushered in alongside her son, Bill. Lindbergh fell immediately under Marion's spell and spent the afternoon fascinated by her charm. Co-hostess Mary Pickford tried flirting to attract his attention, but was unsuccessful. Although Lindbergh had specifically requested that Pickford co-host the party, he was so taken with Marion that he could barely take his eyes off her.

When it came time for dancing, the crowd began whispering about who would be the first to dance with the guest of honor. W.R. walked over to the actress Marie Dressler, took her hand, and introduced her to Lindbergh for the first dance. Fifty-eight-year-old Marie Dressler, five feet, seven inches tall and weighing two hundred pounds, was often considered an outsider in beauty- and youth-centered Hollywood. The opportunity to dance with Lindbergh was likely something she was not expecting, but this generosity of spirit was typical of both Marion and W.R. The two of them danced together, as both Marion and Mary Pickford drifted into the background, understanding that this was a precious moment for Dressler.

Following the party, Lindbergh was treated to a day on a Marion Davies movie set, as Sam Wood shot the climactic basketball scene in *The Fair Co-Ed.* Years after her school years on the basketball team, Marion still plays very well. She guards passionately and with surprising aggression in the game, envisioned as a real and unstaged match. On several occasions, Marion fearlessly grabs the ball, drives toward the basket, and scores.

Once again, on set, Lindbergh couldn't take his eyes off Marion, squinting to see her better as she played. "Do the klieg lights hurt your eyes?" producer Harry Rapf asked. "It isn't the lights," Lindbergh replied.

In later years, when Lindbergh's America First agenda and antisemitic beliefs overshadowed his celebrity as a pilot, he became persona non grata in many Hollywood circles, and lost favor with Marion as well. She did, however, keep a photo of Lindbergh that was inscribed to her on that trip to Hollywood in 1927: "To Marion Davies. Best wishes and many thanks."

On July 4, 1927, just after Marion had moved into the Beach House, she threw a combination housewarming and July Fourth party at her new home. W.R. organized his own fireworks show for the occasion. Frances Marion remembered that W.R. had had trouble coercing people out to the deck to watch the show, so only Marion, Frances, and a handful of friends were there with him. They watched the fireworks "hiss upward and burst into a myriad of brilliant stars" in the sky over Santa Monica Beach. "Like our dreams," Frances recalled him saying. "They last for such a little while, in all their glory, and then they fade away."

At the same time, *The Jazz Singer* was being planned at Warner Bros. in Burbank. As the first feature film with synchronized dialogue, the effects of *The Jazz Singer* would revolutionize filmmaking and threaten careers in all corners of the industry. The primitive machinery ensured that voices too high-pitched or too low would not register well, speech impediments could not be hidden, and foreign or regional accents could destroy an already established screen persona. For many stars of the silent era, their established screen personas didn't match their voices. At first, the industry was not sure how much they should fear the film. *The Jazz Singer* was still a novelty, and novelties often wear off.

Marion was on her guard. Her soft New York accent didn't threaten to cause much of a problem, but her stutter could not be hidden. If sound became standard, Marion thought, her speech problems would ensure that her career would end.

For now, though, Marion's career was soaring. Critics praised *The Fair Co-Ed* upon its release, and they were especially effusive about Marion's performance. "Marion Davies is a natural born comedienne, no mistaking," wrote *Photoplay*. But before release, W.R. had made several recommendations for scenes to cut. "I do not see that it adds materially to the picture to have Marion kicked in the pants by the hero," he wrote. "I think that incident will offend quite a few people and not particularly please many." Nonetheless, he was starting to adopt a more flexible attitude toward Marion's portrayals, and conceded that the film was a solid achievement. "I will never be wholly enamored of this type of picture, as you know," he wrote Irving Thalberg, "but it is good of its type."

In the wake of the positive reviews for *The Fair Co-Ed* and Marion's performance, new comedic material was explored for Marion to build on the success of that film. *The Patsy* was one of these, a property that MGM had acquired for Marion based on a 1925 play by Barry Conners. It tells the story of a teenage girl, the odd duck of her family who always plays second fiddle to her older sister... until she finds her older sister two-timing her boyfriend and decides to take matters into her own hands. The play seemed written for Marion's manic energy, and the story allowed her ample room to display her bubbly persona and rough-and-tumble athleticism.

W.R. had approved of King Vidor's work supervising Roscoe Arbuckle on *The Red Mill*, and by this time W.R. was beginning to cautiously warm to the idea of Marion in comedies. Vidor had convinced W.R. to allow him to do comedy with her instead of a drama, and W.R. approved *The Patsy*. He was under the impression that the comedy was to be subtle and underplayed, and he trusted the direction of King Vidor.

When the movie was in discussion, Vidor, having seen Marion's persona at parties and get-togethers at San Simeon, felt that her gift for impressions needed to be introduced to the world. She was a phenomenal mimic, with an ability to do imitations of movie stars and the people in her life with a devilish accuracy that left friends rollicking with laughter. "Why don't we forget the play that's written and let Marion do as she does?" he asked W.R., who left the film in Vidor's hands. In *The Patsy*, Marion imitates Mae Murray, Lillian Gish, and Pola Negri with cutting accuracy. "We just put those things in the script," remembered King Vidor, years later. "A lot of that stuff, especially in silent pictures, you can sort of make up as you go along... particularly someone like she was.... And that's why that picture has such sheer delight. She wasn't pretending to be anybody. In both *The Patsy* and *Show People* she was just being herself all the time, kidding and laughing, and we put in all the things that she did." The results are hilarious, and *The Patsy* stands as one of Marion's greatest films.

The Patsy is vivacious and zany, animated and witty, and King Vidor found Marion "an absolute joy" to direct. She was "very, very easy and just playful all the time. It was not hard work," he later said. In addition, Vidor enjoyed the musical atmosphere on a Marion Davies set. During the silent era, most sets had musical accompaniment, in order to help the actors get into the mood. Often, it was a single instrument—a violin, piano, or miniature organ. But on Marion's sets, there was a full string quartet. Vidor made three movies with Marion, and when asked what drew him to continue working with her, he responded, half-jokingly, "Have you heard the music?"

Watching Marion in *The Patsy*, the audience is reminded of the kind of humor that Carole Lombard became famous for, comedy that later inspired Lucille Ball and then Carol Burnett. Lombard helped set the genre of screwball comedy in motion with her film *Twentieth Century*, where she uses a great deal of agility and body language to make the audience laugh. Her combination of witty banter and physical comedy created what came to be known as a "screwball comedienne." In *The Patsy*, pre-dating Lombard and *Twentieth Century* by six years, Marion acts out witty dialogue as she tumbles, dances, makes faces, and has an all-around wonderful time in front of the camera. In short, she is the essence of a screwball comedienne.

Assisted by a very funny scenario, as well as a magnificent supporting cast, Marion shines on the screen, and the press took note. Mordaunt Hall of the *New York Times* could barely contain his enthusiasm. "Of all the varied Cinderellas who have from time to time graced the screen," he wrote in his column, "Marion Davies...not only holds her own in the matter of vivacity and appearance, but she also elicits more fun than one would suppose could be generated from even a modern conception." *The Patsy* was also a box office success, grossing $617,000 and with a profit of $155,000.

By this time, the domestic problems of Marion's sister Rose and her husband, George Van Cleve, had reached a fever pitch. One night in late September 1927, Rose returned home to find Patricia missing. Panicked and frantic, she set Los Angeles police detectives on the case and the search soon turned into a nationwide hunt for the little girl. George Van Cleve had expressed a desire to leave Rose and go back to New York to set up a home. A search was taken up, and finally, after a month of painstaking search and anxiety, George Van Cleve was found in New York and Patricia with him. When reporters asked Marion about the case of Patricia's abduction, she answered through her secretary, Ella "Bill" Williams, that she had no knowledge of the domestic disputes between Rose and George Van Cleve. Ultimately, Rose regained custody of Patricia, but from then on Marion kept a close eye on her niece and was wary of George Van Cleve. Rose started divorce proceedings, which were finalized in mid-1928.

On January 25, 1928, Mama Rose had a heart attack at 1700 Lexington Road and could not be revived. She had been having heart trouble for some time, but the family was under the impression that her condition was improving. Marion was in the middle of a Beach House party at the time of Mama Rose's heart attack and had no knowledge of what was happening. Ethel was home with their mother, and held her in her arms as Mama Rose died. Ethel thought it better that Marion not be told over the phone. Marion's sensitivity to death was so great that no one knew how she would react, so Ethel sent the Beach House watchman, along with Rose for good measure, to let Marion know that her mother was ill and she should come to the house immediately. Rose and Marion made their way back to Lexington Road. As they approached Sawtelle Avenue, Marion remembered, her sensitive nose suddenly smelled gardenias, the unmistakable scent she associated with their mother. "Rose, that's Mother's perfume," she said.

"When we got to the house," she recalled, "my sister Ethel was there and my mother was dead. I had heard about self-control, but it doesn't always work. I just went crazy." Marion immediately broke down, screaming and crying at the loss of her beloved Mama Rose. This was Marion's first significant family loss since the death of her brother Charles, twenty-eight years earlier. Mama Rose had been Marion's everything, and despite her sometimes unconventional methods of raising her girls, Mama Rose took her responsibility as a mother very seriously. She had always been there to support her youngest daughter when Marion needed her.

During Marion's breakdown, the phone rang and on the other end was W.R. at the Beach House. Upon hearing the news, he told Marion, "I'm awfully sorry." Mama Rose had always accepted his role in her daughter's life with grace and dignity. She loved him as part of the family, and that meant a great deal to Marion and W.R.

W.R. continued his conversation with Marion on the phone, and in his effort to comfort her, he said, "May I be a mother to you?"

"It was the sweetest thing," Marion recalled. "He said 'I'll try my best.'"

"It was more like a father/daughter relationship than that of a sweetie," said Anita Loos. The easy, familial love that would be more fitting of two people of such disparate ages was the dominant factor in the relationship between Marion and W.R., and this conversation as recalled by Marion underscores her knowledge and acceptance of what their relationship was.

Marion's extreme sense of loss at Mama Rose's death was multifold. In addition to the normal sense of grief that anybody feels following the death of a parent, Mama Rose's death came just at the outset of talking pictures, during a time when Marion was feeling very vulnerable and unsure of her future. She would have to brave the coming of sound without the support on which she had always depended. Better than anyone, Marion's mother understood her fears and helped her conquer them with confidence and grace.

Mama Rose's funeral was held the following Saturday, January 28, 1928. She was interred in a large white-marble mausoleum that Marion had commissioned for her at Hollywood Cemetery. Marion and W.R. wanted the most beautiful mausoleum in the cemetery. Despite the training she had provided her daughters in their early lives, teaching them to accept the advantages of wealthy men to improve their standing in life, the level to which Marion's wealth rose surpassed even Mama Rose's expectations, to the point where Marion's mother became somewhat frightened and embarrassed by it. The woman who Frances Marion remembered sitting in the corner at parties, talking shyly about recipes and her daughters' childhoods, would be buried in a large marble mausoleum graced by bas-relief angels with the family name of "Douras" inscribed at the top, designed by Julia Morgan. Situated toward the back of the cemetery near a small duck pond, it would become the burial place for the entire Douras family, and remains one of the most eye-catching mausoleums at the cemetery to this day.

The funeral was a large affair. W.R. was an honorary pallbearer, as was Charlie Chaplin. Throngs of industry friends arrived, bringing with them piles of flowers. Marion's mother was now being interred in one of the grandest mausoleums in Hollywood. It was a paradox, but in a way, it was fitting— Mama Rose lived for her daughters, wanting to be near them and thriving on her role as the mother. Mama Rose's shy personality mixed into the background of the lavish life her daughter was providing for her, and she accepted it quietly, without any demands.

"I Cannot Do Sound Pictures"

The Patsy had wrapped in February and Marion rested as she waited on her next project. The respite was welcome, as she needed time to process Mama Rose's death and relax after a stressful few months. In addition to her grieving, Marion was ruminating on her career and its future, especially if sound were to make as big a splash as some were saying it would. She had saved and invested her money well, and her contract's guarantee of $10,000 per week ensured that she would not need to worry about financial matters if she were to retire now, at the age of 31. She spoke to W.R. about her fears of going into sound production, and W.R. assuaged them. He wanted her to continue making movies and would do whatever he could to make that a reality.

The script of a film called *Polly Preferred* had been a property of MGM for some time. There was a smattering of advertising in the fan magazines and trade papers in 1926, but it wasn't until early 1928 that production began. The scenario department had taken a full three years to get the story up to a standard that they felt was appropriate, and by the time it was ready to begin shooting, the title had changed from *Polly Preferred* to *Show World,* and then it would be changed again to *Show People.*

Show People is a meticulously crafted comedy, among the first films to poke fun at Hollywood from an insider's perspective and to mock the clichés that had already become commonplace. The storyline mirrored Gloria Swanson's rise in Hollywood from comedic player to serious dramatic actress, and Marion, as the character Peggy Pepper, does her not-so-subtle impression of Swanson throughout.

Gloria Swanson was, of course, a familiar figure to Marion. By 1928, Joseph P. Kennedy's affair with Swanson was in full swing, and Marion was thoroughly unimpressed with Swanson's too-serious demeanor. Swanson's reluctance to let go of her movie star persona irritated Marion, whose free and self-effacing personality was the antithesis of Swanson's haughtiness, and her parody of Swanson in *Show People* is brazen and cutting.

Marion's leading man in *Show People* was to be James Murray. King Vidor had spotted Murray while he was working as an extra, and he cast him in the lead role in the 1928 film *The Crowd*, a story of a man whose life spirals out of control following tragedy. The course of Murray's life was eerily similar to his character in *The Crowd*—he was a severe alcoholic and had difficulty getting work. King Vidor wanted to help him out by casting him alongside Marion in a film that was sure to be a hit, and Murray accepted the part.

The production started in early March, and the notes on Murray's first scheduled day of shooting read "Unable to locate Mr. Murray so had to switch sequence, and rearrange people." On the next day of production: "Company unable to locate Mr. Murray and not able to work until leading man is found…extras dismissed and call cancelled." After three days of shooting, still no one could locate Murray. Finally, Vidor made the executive decision to replace him.

His replacement was Marion's good friend Billy Haines. Due to his star status, Thalberg felt that Billy was a good choice to boost publicity in the non-Hearst papers. "I didn't need her," Billy remembered later, "she needed me."

Marion's chemistry with Billy shines through on the screen, as their scenes together have a sense of genuine closeness and friendship. In *Show People*, even when that closeness and friendship evolves into a romance, their comfort together is a high point of the movie. There are numerous industry gags in *Show People*—in addition to the references to Gloria Swanson, there is a scene where Peggy Pepper is supposed to be unable to cry on cue. Although this was never a problem for Marion herself, she is both magnificent and hilarious in this scene, pinching herself and banging her head against the wall to make herself cry. To help Peggy cry are on-set musicians who play sorrowful music to try to induce tears. They are played by the real-life set musicians that King Vidor loved so much, who played mood music for Marion during scenes.

Billy Haines also gives a delightful performance. He rollicks and jumps and looks to be having just as good a time as Marion. He squirts her gleefully with a siphon bottle and jokingly ribs Peggy Pepper when she becomes a snooty film star. The siphon bottle bit was an edit from the original scene where Marion was to have been hit in the face with a pie, an homage to the Keystone Kops and Mack Sennett's slapstick comedy. When W.R. heard about the planned gag, he was outraged. W.R. was beginning to warm to Marion in comedies, but a pie in the face was out of the question. It was the kind of lowbrow entertainment that he loathed, and he refused to let Marion engage in it.

King Vidor, still in his twenties and full of enthusiasm, was adamant about the pie-throwing scene being played as it was written. W.R.'s respect for Vidor was at odds with his desire for Marion to be seen as a proper and sophisticated woman. Despite this, nothing could defeat W.R. when he had his mind set on something. His was a "quiet determination," without raising his voice or getting upset. He merely stated his ideas, and what he felt needed to happen. He didn't feel it necessary to discredit Vidor's ideas. In fact, W.R. validated them, almost seeming to recognize that his demands were unusual. "King's right, and I'm right too," he would say, "but I'm not going to have Marion hit in the face with a pie."

Marion found the idea of being hit in the face with a pie great fun. But, as King Vidor put it, "She was too loyal to W.R. to object. She was a loyal person to her friends and to him and to everybody. She's not the kind of person that would split her loyalties, although she and I were good friends and we liked each other. Nevertheless... W.R. was the boss, no question about it."

Neither W.R. nor Vidor gave in, and Louis B. Mayer was brought in for advice. Vidor recalled that W.R.'s already high-pitched voice got even higher in times of stress. "I'm not going to have Marion hit in the face with a pie," he squeaked insistently to Mayer and Vidor. Even Louis B. Mayer felt powerless in the presence of Hearst. After all, if Hearst didn't get what he wanted, he held the fate of the studio in his hands. While Mayer had power over the inner workings of the studio, Hearst had the power of publicity. That kind of control intimidated even the formidable figure of Louis B. Mayer, and the support of the Hearst press and Louella Parsons was integral to the continued profitability of MGM.

Finally, it became clear that W.R. was not going to be convinced. Marion had always been on King Vidor's side when it came to this scene, though she never had the heart to tell W.R. He was always on the set, watching Marion like a hawk, so there was no chance of shooting the scene in secret. Instead, Marion came up with a plan. She would phone the *Los Angeles Examiner* and get the head bosses in on the scheme—then, at the right moment, the bosses would call W.R. out of the studio for a meeting. That would leave Marion and King Vidor free to shoot the scene without W.R. knowing about it. However, in order to keep some respect for W.R. and his wishes, they shot the scene with a siphon bottle instead of a pie. It worked beautifully.

Reviews of *Show People* were overwhelmingly positive, with the *New York Times* describing the comedy as "simmering in a delightful fashion" and occasionally "boiling over" into boisterous fun. The *Daily News* said that with *Show People*, Marion Davies "holds the position as filmdom's most hilarious comedienne." The studio wasted no time in getting Marion into another comedy. She began work on her next movie, a European-themed romantic comedy that had been taken from a French stage play called *Dans sa candeur naïve*, with the English title changed to *The Cardboard Lover*. The film co-stars Nils Asther and Jetta Goudal, and there is a brief moment with Marion's niece, Reine's daughter Pepi (playing a character aptly named "Peppy"). It tells the story of a young woman on a European vacation who stalks a tennis champion, only to have him hire her to double-cross his girlfriend, who is cheating on him.

The movie affords Marion the ultimate in theatrical entrances—as the camera pans the length of a car full of tourists, we see a window break, and Marion's elbow emerges. Then we see her face, at first with a puzzled expression, then lit up by a delighted smile. Her character is established—a young woman who causes trouble and laughs about it. It was the essence of Marion's real-life personality, and she relished it.

The scene with Pepi is delightful. They push and shove each other in play, then show that they are the best of friends as they enter the hotel at Monte Carlo. Despite having inherited her father's very dark hair, Pepi has Marion's unmistakable blue eyes and pixie mouth, and shares many of Marion's characteristic mannerisms.

After finishing *The Cardboard Lover* in early July 1928, Marion went up to San Simeon, where she rested for the first significant time since before the filming of *Show People*. But once again, she quickly became concerned about the well-being of nine-year-old Patricia, who was being bounced back and forth between Rose and George Van Cleve in New York. In June, Patricia had come back to the United States from France, where Rose had been on an extended vacation. She had been sent by Rose with a trusted governess and met up with George Van Cleve in Maryland, where he had rented a cottage. Without Rose's knowledge, George fired the governess. Marion wrote to Rose, expressing her concerns.

"I do not think it a good idea to let him have a strange governess for Pat," she wrote. "Especially one he engages. You might not like her, then you'd have to get another one, then he'd discharge her and get one, and Pat won't know which end she is on." Marion went on to say that she had spoken to Rose's lawyer, and the lawyer suggested a way for Rose to get full custody of Pat, if George had not been keeping up with his child-support payments. "Of course you can do what you want," Marion said, "but if I were you, I wouldn't be a softy with him."

Marion's tendency to give strong advice, and intervene in places where she didn't necessarily belong, was a combination of genuine care for her family and an involvement that sometimes bordered on intrusive. Rose's maternal instincts were not as honed as Marion's protective nature, and when Marion felt that Patricia was in real danger, either psychologically or physically, she intervened. Marion frequently worried about her sisters' children, feeling that Rose and Reine were not good parents and the children were suffering. Her intentions were genuine and in the right place, but from time to time her level of involvement angered both Rose and Reine.

Marion continued to bring Patricia to San Simeon frequently, and beginning in 1928 Patricia began to spend so much time there that it was necessary to hire a governess for her so that she could be watched on the palatial grounds when W.R. and Marion weren't able to tend to her. The actor Lee Tracy had hired a 21-year-old African American woman named Carrie Smith to be a housekeeper in his home, and had been impressed with her work. He thought she would be a good match for Patricia. On his recommendation, Marion brought Smith up to San Simeon to meet Patricia. She was kind and gentle, with a gift for working with young children. Patricia loved her immediately, and Smith was hired, taking an active role in the young girl's upbringing. She became one of the dominant figures in her life, giving her rare stability in a family that had been chaotic for so long.

As well as things were going for Marion professionally, there was a dark cloud above her. The previous October 6, *The Jazz Singer* had premiered to great acclaim in New York City. Using synchronized dialogue as the central feature, *The Jazz Singer* had the potential to revolutionize the very core of the industry. The prospect was terrifying, especially for those with vocal abnormalities like Marion's.

Synchronized dialogue on film had always been a theoretical possibility. In the early 1890s, Thomas Edison invented the Kinetophone, a primitive machine that featured both a record player and an individual film screening device. To test it, he made an experimental sound film at his Black Maria studio in West Orange, New Jersey. In the twenty-second film, two men dance as another plays a violin into a Dictaphone. The sound of the violin was imprinted on a record, which was to be played along with the film when it was shown on the Kinetophone. It was a cumbersome and difficult way to achieve sound on film, and the Kinetophone remained a novelty.

Further attempts to refine the concept of sound on film continued through the early part of the twentieth century. In 1926, the John Barrymore and Mary Astor epic *Don Juan* was the first feature-length film to make use of the technology that would later be used in *The Jazz Singer*. While *Don Juan* had no dialogue, it featured synchronized sound effects. Initially, *The Jazz Singer* was not supposed to have dialogue at all. Warner Bros. envisioned a synchronized musical score and synchronized sound effects, with the rest of the film shot as a silent. But New York vaudevillian Al Jolson improvised the words "Wait a minute, wait a minute, you ain't heard nothin' yet!" These would become the first words of dialogue to be heard in a feature film.

Marion was "appalled" at the idea of sound film. Without Mama Rose to encourage her, as she had in her chorus girl days when Marion had to speak lines onstage, Marion felt insecure and self-conscious about what her future held.

In the late 1920s, Marion kept a close eye on the stock market. Louis B. Mayer had purchased stock for Marion as an employee of MGM, and she now asked him to close it out. "I am leaving for Europe as you know," wrote Marion in July 1928, "and the market being weak, I would like to close out my stock interests now for the present at least. Therefore, if you will kindly dispose of the stocks which you were good enough to buy for me and put the money in my bank account, I will be greatly obliged."

Shortly after Marion finished work on *The Cardboard Lover*, she and W.R. took a trip to Europe, joined by a large party of friends and family. It was their first European vacation truly together. They still sailed on different ships to avoid media attention—Marion on the *Ile de France* and W.R. on the *Olympic*. It began in July of 1928, and from the *Olympic*, W.R. sent Marion messages cryptically signed "Joe." "If I don't get radios from you," read one telegram sent on July 22, "I am going to turn this boat around and go back to New York. I guess you are having too good a time. I hope it storms and you get sea sick and Pepi breaks a leg and Anita falls overboard and Maury [Maury Paul, a Hearst columnist] gets his hair mussed. Joe."

They arrived in Paris and cabled Alice Head, the managing director of Hearst's British publisher National Magazine Company, to join them at the Hotel Crillon. Head had packed a small bag, expecting to spend a weekend with the party. But she soon found out that this was a Hearst vacation, and she would be expected to join a motor tour across France. As a typical Hearst European vacation, all expenses would be paid, and any money that a guest might try to spend on their own account would be deeply offensive to W.R. Everything was covered for all guests, from meals to transportation to clothes to incidentals. Everyone had their own hotel room, paid for by W.R.

The day following their arrival in France, four large touring cars took the group, which included Pepi, Charlie, Ethel, W.R., Marion, and Alice Head, to Versailles. From there they headed to Rambouillet and Chartres, where they took in the magnificent Gallo-Roman cathedral with its legendary stained-glass windows.

European tours with W.R. were filled with art and architectural history. Having learned to appreciate the finer things in Europe as a young child on trips with his mother, W.R. tried to impart his love of all things historical to his traveling companions, some of whom were more receptive than others. W.R. repaid the favor when Marion and her friends wanted to take advantage of the other side of Europe, the world-class shopping experiences, from which Marion often came away with suitcases full of clothes.

Marion learned a great deal on these trips, becoming something of an art expert in her own right. In later years, a small group of friends came to San Simeon for a weekend, and Lord Duveen, one of W.R.'s art buyers and advisers, brought some paintings for W.R. to see. The columnist Adela Rogers St. Johns, who was also there for the weekend, was struck by the fact that Marion had a comment, "specific and sure," for each painting. Lord Duveen was similarly impressed. "It's quite amazing," he said. "I don't quite understand it. I know Miss Davies as a motion picture star and a—if you will pardon me—a most fine comedian, and the lady of this castle. But how is it, if I may ask Miss Davies, that you are likewise an authority on art, as it were?" Marion was amused by the compliment, but before she could get an answer out, Charlie Chaplin interjected, "But my dear fellow," he said, gesturing to W.R., "*he taught her.*"

Marion's presence in Europe caused a sensation. In addition to the novelty of a smartly dressed American woman appearing in some of the remote villages of France, many of the French people had seen Marion's movies. She was surprised by the warm and enthusiastic reception, and on the occasions when the press would stop to photograph Marion, W.R. took it in stride and joked to Alice Head, "We're *much* the most important people, but nobody wants to photograph us!" There was never a negative word spoken or written in the European press about her alliance with Hearst. "Never once a curse. Everything was adulation," Marion remembered.

Driving through Vichy, Grenoble, and Monte Carlo, the group passed the Italian border, arriving in Genoa. In Italy, the group was joined by Papa Ben, on his first European trip, and now most of Marion's family was together. Pepi's inclusion on this trip in 1928 may have stemmed from concern on Marion's part for her welfare. Pepi had become involved in the rampant drug scene of the 1920s, attending hardcore Hollywood parties and hosting some of her own when her aunt was away. Marion was aware of her involvement with cocaine and promiscuity. Pepi's gender presentation and attraction to women did not bother Marion, but her excessive partying and drug use did. Marion felt that Reine's lack of parental warmth had contributed to what was happening to her niece, and she kept a watchful eye on Pepi to establish strict boundaries and curb her destructive behavior.

Marion's communication with Pepi stands in stark contrast to the loving way she spoke with other members of the family. She adored her niece, but absent were the warm pet names and caring words that she used when corresponding with Charlie, Patricia, and her sisters. Instead, it was punctuated by an uncharacteristic air of distant strictness. Back in March 1927, when Pepi was staying with her girlfriend Betty Morrisey at the Algonquin Hotel, Marion sent Pepi a series of stern telegrams. On March 7, she wrote:

BE SURE TO PAY FOR ALL OF BETTY'S MEALS AND TRAVELING EXPENSES AND DO NOT PLAY CARDS WITH HER FOR MONEY. LOVE. M.D.

Then on March 20, she sent another:

YOU WILL RECEIVE TWO HUNDRED FIFTY EACH TOMORROW. BETTER GO EASY AS THIS WILL HAVE TO LAST UNTIL YOU RETURN HOME. M. DOURAS.

Although there was a great deal of tolerance for alternative lifestyles in the Hollywood of the 1920s, society did not take kindly to what was perceived as Pepi's "boyish" nature and style of dress. She gained a significant amount of weight and delved deeper into the drugs and hard partying that had become her escape.

In a sense, Marion may have felt that she had failed Pepi by including her in the lavish lifestyle that was now consuming Pepi's life and destroying her. This was a recurring theme in Marion's life, treating her family members with such magnanimous and unfaltering generosity that they never learned to fend for themselves, instead relying on the flow of money that came to them so easily from Marion, who seemed incapable of saying "no" to them.

W.R. was also concerned about Pepi. The families of Marion and W.R. had become more like one big family than two separate ones, and they all supported each other—financially as well as emotionally. Marion and W.R. disagreed on how to deal with Pepi. In contrast to Marion's tone, W.R.'s telegrams to Pepi when she was traveling are warm, loving, and paternal, asking her how much money she needed and immediately wiring it to her.

Marion and the rest of the group ventured down the Italian coast to Viareggio, then to Pisa, Florence, and Venice. They spent the first two weeks of August 1928 at the Lido, fifteen minutes off the coast of Venice, where they rested and relaxed at the picturesque Venetian beaches before saying goodbye to Alice Head, who needed to return to London. Marion and the rest of the group went on to Bad Nauheim, Germany, while Rose decided to return to Paris. After her split from George Van Cleve, she had struck up a love affair with Roland de Cassé, the Marquis de Brissac, whose ancestral home was in the Loire region. Rose was anxious to get back to him. This relationship was the most serious and romantic of Rose's life, but the Brissac family considered this relationship to be beneath the marquis's station in life. It was a tragic love affair, ending when his family would not allow him to marry "the sister of the actress." Rose never got over him, and when the marquis died under mysterious circumstances at the age of 37, she could not return to France without painful memories.

The group came back from Europe in early October, having stopped off in the United Kingdom to see St. Donat's, a relatively recent acquisition of W.R.'s, for the first time. St. Donat's, a medieval castle in Glamorganshire, Wales, had been continuously inhabited since the twelfth century. W.R. was fascinated with the castles in the area, and in 1925 he saw in *Country Living* magazine that St. Donat's was coming up for sale from its most recent owner, the diplomat Richard Pennoyer. W.R. instructed Alice Head to purchase it for £45,000. The property itself was smaller than the other castles in the area and, W.R. felt, more domestic. Still, the land comprised around a thousand acres, and included a small church at the bottom of the hill. The atmosphere of St. Donat's became similar to that of San Simeon whenever W.R., Marion, and company were vacationing there. The grandeur and storied history of the land provided the backdrop for the fun and merriment of a Hearst vacation. In 1930, W.R. planned an elaborate firework display for the July Fourth holiday and invited all the villagers around St. Donat's. The local residents enjoyed the fireworks, though many of them had no idea what the occasion was, and the display had to be cut short because the lights were disrupting the cargo ships' signals in the Bristol Channel.

Marion's warm welcome in Europe included several awards from the countries they visited. Among them was the "Office of Public Instruction" award from the French government, becoming the first female American film star to receive it. Marion was flattered by the attention, but she was much more content to explore with friends, shopping and chatting and buying presents for them. Shop she did, and upon her return sixteen trunks of clothes that Marion had bought were offloaded from the ship to New York. The group stayed at the Hotel Ritz for several days and Marion caught up with New York friends, before taking the train back to Los Angeles.

One evening while staying at the Ritz Towers in New York, she went to see the new Jolson film, *The Singing Fool*, with Hearst columnist Maury Paul. It was a talkie, and in it Jolson sang "Sonny Boy," which later became a standard. Listening to the song, Marion began to cry. Maury took her hand and patted it comfortingly, believing she was simply moved by the song. At this gesture, Marion leaned over to him and whispered, "I'm ruined... I'm ruined."

She returned to the Ritz distraught and would not speak to anyone. W.R. asked Maury what was the matter. "'Sonny Boy' got her down," he replied.

Meanwhile, MGM officials had called a meeting to decide who should be given a screen test for sound film, and who should be let go. They brought with them a list of MGM stars, and analyzed the way they sounded, their accents, the timbre of their voices. With a stroke of a pencil, careers of those with displeasing or problematic voices were ended. The actors who made the cut were allowed a screen test. The officials went down the list quickly, until they came to Marion's name. They looked at it for a long time.

"She stutters," one of the officials finally said.

After a discussion, it was decided the power that Marion carried with her was too valuable to the studio to jeopardize, so despite the concerns, Marion's name avoided the stroke of the pencil. She remained on the list of MGM stars who would be given a screen test to go into sound.

Marion's insecurity about the coming of sound is complex. Like most people who stutter, if Marion rehearsed the "choreography" of her lines, muscle memory would inhibit her stuttering. But she knew it would require a huge amount of work, and she would be constantly aware of her speech. "I didn't want to go back," Marion said, remembering those days. "I wished the earth would open up, because I said, 'I cannot do sound pictures.'" But she had a contract, and also felt a loyalty to W.R., who she knew wanted her to continue.

Upon her return to Los Angeles, dozens of Marion's friends threw her a welcome home party at the Cocoanut Grove at the Ambassador Hotel. They redecorated the room in the style of a French café, complete with an awning reading "Chez Marion." Charlie Chaplin, Gloria Swanson, Norma Shearer and Irving Thalberg, and Billy Haines and his partner Jimmy Shields all attended. It was a grand affair, and it helped Marion take her mind off her fears for an evening.

The distraction didn't last long. When the day came for Marion's screen test, she was numb and depressed. Thinking of Mama Rose and Marion's first time speaking a line onstage, she drank a bit of sherry to do what she could to keep her stutter at bay, then tossed away the script she was given. Feeling resigned to failure, she ad-libbed on the given dialogue that she saw as trite, and walked out convinced that she had been an abject disappointment.

At 1700 Lexington Road, the family was waiting on bated breath. Marion arrived dejected, and promptly went upstairs to bed. "Don't ask anything, don't talk to me, please," she said. "I'm going to sleep and I hope I never wake up." But the next day, she received a call from Irving Thalberg, asking her to come into the studio. Her voice registered exceptionally well, and she had passed the test.

The timbre of Marion's voice comes as a bit of a surprise. With her soft, ethereal beauty, audiences might expect a wispy, fragile voice. Instead, what comes from Marion's throat is a solid contralto, with a melodic lilt to her intonation. Her words are clear and carefully articulated, with just a hint of the Brooklyn accent of her childhood, in words like "walk" and "talk." To Thalberg's incredulity, she had not stuttered during her test. Improvisation was an ingenious method—it had allowed Marion to substitute troublesome words with similar ones that she could say, and projected an image of fluency to the camera. And so began Marion's transition to sound film, a long road that highlighted her determination and will to preserve her own career.

"A Butterfly with Glue on Her Wings"

Almost immediately, newspapers speculated about how successfully Marion would make the transition to sound. In January 1929, *Picture Play* posed a question to its readers regarding Marion: "Will she retain her stutter, expecting the world to like it, or will she decide to overcome it for production purposes?"

A series of voice coaches came from New York and Los Angeles to try to enhance Marion's confidence. The most influential of these was George Currie, the dramatic coach who had tutored Marion at the 127th Street studio for *When Knighthood Was in Flower* and *Little Old New York*. Currie and Marion had worked well together in New York, and he had great faith in her abilities. Currie was well-intentioned, but his expertise was in drama coaching. He worked with Marion as if she were the same dramatic student he had known in New York, rather than someone with a complex speech disorder that she needed to control in front of the sound camera. She would become extremely frustrated with the lessons and found Currie's advice useless. Adela Rogers St. Johns remembered that Marion would frequently end sessions in fits of rage, convinced of the futility of what she was doing. "Some days she would come roaring in," Adela remembered, "and say 'I'm not going to go any farther with this!...I'm not running around memorizing this kind of stuff, saying this stuff all the time.'"

Marion began production on what was to be her first talking picture, *The Five O'Clock Girl*, in late 1928. Slated for direction by Alfred E. Green, it would star Marion alongside Jane Winton, whom Marion adored and who was making a name as Marion's "nemesis" in movies such as *The Patsy* and *The Fair Co-Ed*. In addition, at Green's insistence, a young football player from Pomona College named Joel McCrea was to make his screen debut in the film. McCrea had started as an extra on the MGM lot in 1927, before his graduation from Pomona, and Alfred Green recognized his potential. Shortly after his graduation, he was signed to a contract and began working on *The Five O'Clock Girl*. But the film was permanently shelved, shortly after the newspaper articles questioning Marion's ability to speak. The reason seems to be multifold—in addition to Marion's fears, Hearst and Thalberg had artistic differences about the story, and the cancellation came as a disappointment to everyone involved.

Shortly thereafter, Marion tried her luck in *Buddies*, originally a Broadway play by George Hobart that had been a Cosmopolitan property since 1925. *Buddies* told the story of a French farm girl toward the end of World War I who falls in love with an American soldier stationed in her town. As a Broadway play, it bore some resemblance to *The Big Parade* of 1925, something very appealing to Marion and W.R. With the coming of sound, the musical numbers in the Broadway play could contribute to the appeal of the movie.

As was common in the early days of sound, *Buddies*, which would eventually become *Marianne*, was shot twice—once as a silent and once as a sound feature. To maximize profits, many studios chose to make two versions of major films like *Marianne*, which were expected to bring in large revenues. Shooting of the silent version of *Marianne* began in March 1929, with Oscar Shaw, a stage actor from Broadway, as Marion's leading man. It was completed on March 30 without a hitch, and preparations began for the sound version. But soon after completion of the silent film, Oscar Shaw was called back to New York. He was to film *The Cocoanuts* with the Marx Brothers and prepare for a new Broadway show, *Flying High*, and was unable to complete the sound version of *Marianne*.

Numerous screen tests were made for a new leading man who could sing. Marion recalled that she had heard Lawrence Gray, who had co-starred with her in *The Patsy*, sing at a party, and that he had an impressively good voice. She had enjoyed working with him, and suggested him as a possibility to Hearst and Thalberg. His singing test was successful, and on April 1 Marion began rehearsing the sound version with Lawrence Gray as the leading man. The movie opens as Marianne's boyfriend, a soldier going off to war, sings her a farewell song entitled "Marianne." The similarity between the character's name and Marion's real name is difficult to ignore as the character sings about her sweetness.

While Marion was filming the sound version of *Marianne*, she began work on *Hollywood Revue of 1929*, an onscreen vaudeville act starring some of the biggest studio names of 1929 including Norma Shearer, John Gilbert, Jack Benny, Laurel and Hardy, and the up-and-coming starlet Joan Crawford. Marion's number was an elaborately staged marching band routine, in which she sang "Tommy Atkins" along with a dozen extras dressed as soldiers. At the end of the number, Marion stands at the right end of the soldiers and is picked up and twirled in a complete circle by the closest soldier to her, who then passes her off to the second soldier who does the same, until Marion is picked up and flipped by each soldier in the line.

The scene had to be shot twice, and Marion's dizziness is visible after the second take, which made it into the final cut. That morning, Marion had awakened with a sore throat and spent the morning in consultation with a doctor, arriving an hour and a half late to the set of *Marianne*. By the time of the *Hollywood Revue* rehearsal at 6:00 p.m., her voice was still not back to normal. Singing was never Marion's strong suit, and having spent the day with a sore throat, her rendering of the Tommy Atkins number sounds vocally strained. It is nonetheless charming, and Marion fools around with the soldiers, blowing them down with her breath and back up again as she breathes in.

The finale of the film is a grand number, a reprise of an earlier rendition of "Singin' in the Rain" written by Arthur Freed. It includes all the stars who appeared in the movie assembled in front of a huge, painted Noah's Ark, wearing raincoats, with a few getting closeup treatment. Marion is situated between Joan Crawford and Buster Keaton, and as the camera passes her face, we see her singing the lyrics "Come on with the rain, I've a smile on my face … I walk down the lane … with a happy refrain … and singin' … just singin' in the rain."

Hollywood Revue of 1929 had a quick release, having its Los Angeles premiere on June 20, 1929, just days after the final scenes were shot. The first words that the public heard from Marion onscreen were sung, not spoken, just as she had requested from lyricist Gene Buck back when she was a young girl on the stage.

Out of necessity, Marion kept a tight schedule during these early years of sound so that she could devote the needed time to her speech. She woke at six, went the studio for makeup and costuming, and worked until the late evening. She then returned home, ate a hurried dinner, and spent two hours on her lines with George Currie. Her diligence paid off—she never once stuttered onscreen. This seemed a miracle for the girl who couldn't speak in front of the class at school, and the irony was not lost on her. In 1939, ten years after her talkie debut, Marion wrote a letter to Robert L. Ripley of the newspaper feature "Ripley's Believe It or Not":

Dear Mr. Ripley,
I stammered all my life.
  When I went into silent pictures, I thought they had happily been made for stammerers.
  Then talking pictures came in.
  And then I stopped stammering—I suppose because I had to.

Offscreen, she never lost her stutter. Despite her parents' support, the teasing that Marion endured as a child haunted her. She had internalized the feeling that her voice was inferior, and for that reason, Marion was never fully comfortable in talkies. The wild and liberated freedom that had been her trademark in silent films turned into a slightly stilted and stiff persona with the coming of sound, because of the strict control Marion had to maintain over her voice to make it through the scene.

The spring of 1929 was eventful for Marion. In late March, the old Rialto Theater at 936 Market Street in San Francisco was renamed for her when it converted to sound. While she was unable to come up to San Francisco for the ceremony due to her filming schedule on *Marianne* and *Hollywood Revue of 1929*, she was thrilled at the idea of having her "own playhouse." In a twist of irony, the film that opened the newly named theater was *Sonny Boy*, featuring the same song that had sent Marion into tears in New York during *The Singing Fool*.

On May 13, 1929, Marion was invited to put her handprints and footprints in the forecourt of Grauman's Chinese Theater in Hollywood. The practice was so unknown at the time that Hearst's *Examiner* called it a "mud pie stunt," carried out before a matinee performance of *Broadway Melody*. At that time there were only a select few people who had put their hands and feet there, so it was more of a novelty than the honor it is today. It had been several months since *Show People*, her most recent film, had come out, and the ceremony served to keep her in the public mind before her next movie. She inscribed her prints with a typical cheerful, playful phrase, scrawled alternately in cursive and capital lettering. Perhaps in a nod to her stutter, she placed a dash in between two words:

To Sid Grauman
Marion Davies

Marianne was released on August 24, 1929. The premiere at the Mayan Theater in downtown Los Angeles was a gala world event, according to the *Los Angeles Times*, since the theater was not only celebrating the release of *Marianne* but also the theater's official conversion from a stage theater to a film theater. Problems with the newly installed sound equipment were evident, as the sound failed in the first reel. Marion was already nervous and anxious about the public hearing her voice for the first time. The sound rattled her nerves to the point where, like a scene in *Show People* where Peggy Pepper watches herself onscreen, she began to cry. Through her tears, she noticed that the audience was having a marvelous time. They didn't seem to mind that the sound was out of sync, and they reacted to the funny spots with uproarious laughter. The critics loved it, the audiences loved it, and Marion's confidence was boosted to the point where she felt talkies might work for her.

With *Marianne*'s success, W.R. had finally admitted to Irving Thalberg in 1929 that he thought Marion had an unusual knack for comedy, and even said that she should do *only* comedy. In spite of his conscious admission that Marion was a gifted comedienne, he still retained a seemingly intractable cautiousness about Marion in comedy, fearing that his vision of Marion as an angelic woman of perfection would be ruined if she were seen as the comedienne that even he knew she was. Her friends continued to stick up for her and push for her right to these comedic roles that she so enjoyed and was so good at playing. But despite their efforts, Frances Marion would always see Marion as "a butterfly with glue on her wings."

In addition to the changes in the film industry, the late 1920s saw terrifying turns in the stock market amid a generally strong era. A fever of stock speculation swept the country, with hordes of inexperienced investors buying on margin and sellers making margin calls when the stocks began to fall. In June of 1928, the market suffered a startling setback. The economic downturn of the summer of 1928 was an easy scapegoat for what was to come in October of 1929, but a myriad of factors were responsible for the disastrous calamity that befell Wall Street. The country had a "vested interest in euphoria," in which people believed that because the market had been so strong for so long, nothing could truly bring it down. The corporate mergers and acquisitions that had dominated the 1920s, of which W.R. had been a large part, were symptoms of the country's economic overconfidence. It all came crashing down on October 29, 1929, when over 16 million shares were traded and $14 billion was lost, slamming investors and creating a domino effect that, over the next few years, affected every sector of the American economy. Many of the country's banks were no longer able to give customers their money. They folded, foreclosing on homes and leaving millions homeless and jobless. As an after-effect, the Marion Davies Children's Clinic saw increasing numbers in 1929 and this trend continued steadily through the Depression.

Marion's first movie of 1930 was her third pairing with King Vidor, a story originally called *Dumb Dora*, renamed *Not So Dumb*. Compared to *The Patsy* and *Show People*, *Not So Dumb* was a bit of a disappointment. But Marion always loved a chance to work with Vidor, and looked to be having a good deal of fun making it. Interestingly, *Not So Dumb* features Marion's longest continuous stretch of rapid-fire dialogue, occurring during a card game. It is fascinating to watch Marion rattle through these lines, articulating each word without the tiniest hesitation. Her friends were awed at Marion's fluency onscreen. "Marion stuttered like mad," remembered Dorothy Mackaill, who was often on the set, "but the minute that camera went [on], she never stuttered. The minute the scene was over, sh-sh-sh-she'd go like that. This was the most fantastic thing I'd ever seen." Billy Haines felt the same way. "Once Marion got before the camera, a funny thing happened to her. A transition took place. She lost her stuttering, but she became self-conscious."

In February 1930, former president Calvin Coolidge spent several days at San Simeon with his wife, Grace, while on a cross-country trip. The sheer size, immensity, and luxury of San Simeon was foreign even to the Coolidges. The former president, a quiet New Englander, spent a great deal of time just wandering through the gardens and rooms. He marveled at the landscape that was William Randolph Hearst's home, and the confluence of old and new that defined San Simeon. Grace Coolidge got an unexpected taste of the "new" when she decided to go up to bed early in the elevator on a stormy and blustery night, instead of taking the stairs. On her way up, the electricity went out and Grace found herself stuck halfway between the floors. There was no emergency button and thus no one could do anything about it, except to keep shouting up to Grace "All right! The lights will be on in a second!" Ever the lady, Grace responded calmly, "That's all right. I'm perfectly happy."

After about a half an hour, the lights came back on, and Grace managed to get up to bed.

Leading up to the Coolidges' visit, W.R. was in the midst of constructing a state-of-the-art movie theater at San Simeon. Prior to this, the movies were simply shown in one of the other rooms on the hilltop or sometimes outside, but W.R. thought Marion's movies deserved their own theater. From 1930 on, the movies that had become a staple of time spent at San Simeon played on the big screen, as they were meant to be, in the ornate theater designed in time for the Coolidges' visit. Marion, however, was never impressed by her own work. She would often use the comfortable new theater as an opportunity to take a nap while her movies were being shown, and her snoring reduced guests to laughter.

Coolidge represented an era in American politics that seemed eons away by 1930. In the wake of Harding's presidency, beset by scandal and Americans' lost faith in the political system, Coolidge had restored American trust in politics, presiding over an era of abundance. Hoover was failing to satisfy the American people with his actions after the stock market crash, and thus, even though Coolidge had left office just over a year earlier, his presidency was seen as nostalgic, a time of general American abundance and happiness.

Marion loved the Coolidges and Grace Coolidge, on her part, quickly took to Marion. The two women had a rapport that eradicated any prejudices that the Coolidges might have had against Marion and W.R. as a couple, and they ventured down to Los Angeles to visit Marion as she worked. A huge crowd of MGM stars came to the set of Marion's new movie, *The Florodora Girl*, to meet the former president. Filming stopped as Marion introduced Coolidge to some of Hollywood's most popular figures, including Mary Pickford and Louis B. Mayer.

The Florodora Girl is a fictionalized account of the backstage life of *Florodora*, a popular Broadway show at the turn of the century. *Florodora*'s popularity derived largely from its sextet of chorus girls performing dances considered risqué for the era. Marion plays a chorus girl in the show wooed by a rich stage-door johnnie who is already engaged to be married, and when she finds this out, their relationship falls apart.

Much of *The Florodora Girl* comes right from Marion's own life—from the stage-door johnnies that the main character encounters, to the fondness Marion's character has for having her head rubbed. The character's name is "Daisy," the nickname that so many of Marion's friends, and even the Hearst sons, called her. Adding to *The Florodora Girl*'s charm and appeal is a scene shot in two-strip Technicolor, still an experimental and expensive process in 1930.

The Technicolor process was invented in 1915 by the Technicolor Motion Picture Corporation, and though the technique initially proved too cumbersome for commercial use, by 1930 it had evolved to the point where it could be used with relative frequency. Technicolor filming involved shooting two black-and-white prints at the same time, dyeing one print red, one print green, then gluing them together to create one color print that would be threaded through the projector. There were still inherent problems with Technicolor in 1930, such as the difficulty of recreating true blues and yellows. This is evident in *The Florodora Girl* when we see a shot of Marion in Technicolor, singing "Tell Me, Pretty Maiden" from the original production of *Florodora*. Due to the Technicolor process, her bright blue eyes don't register on camera and instead appear green.

The Florodora Girl called for a swimming scene shot on a beach, and Marion offered the stretch of sand in front of her Santa Monica home for filming. The construction of the house had been beset by delays, which irritated W.R. and caused him to nearly fire William Flannery over his dissatisfaction with the slowness and quality. Whether Flannery was indeed fired remains unclear, but his work on the Beach House ceased in the second half of 1928. Julia Morgan took over from then on, and by 1930, the house was approaching completion, just in time for the filming of *The Florodora Girl*.

The Beach House had become a veritable center of Hollywood life. The size of the home and its myriad add-ons, such as a tennis court and two swimming pools, made it a prime destination for partygoers looking for a good time. "If you can get into the Marion Davies set," wrote *Screenland* magazine in November of 1929, "you're of the socially elect in Hollywood." But in reality, parties at Marion's Beach House were open to anyone who needed a meal or a friend. Over the next eighteen years, the vast expanse on the Santa Monica beach became etched in the cultural fabric of Los Angeles, synonymous with generosity and fun.

When *The Florodora Girl* was finished, it came time to pick a venue for its premiere. The theater chosen was the Pantages Theater on Hollywood Boulevard, which had not yet opened to the public. Having *The Florodora Girl* open the new Pantages Theatre was an idea that seemed mutually beneficial. The gala premiere of *The Florodora Girl*, and the grand opening of the Pantages Theater, took place on June 4, 1930. "Again the screen colony turned out," noted the *New York Times* the following week, "in all its brave panoply of white fur and orchids to make another Hollywood holiday, and once more the weaving shaft of lights called across the countryside for the faithful to come and do homage." Among the attendees were Walter Catlett, who co-starred with Marion in the movie, along with Fifi D'Orsay, Dolores Del Rio, Billy Haines, King Vidor, and Charlie Chaplin. So big was the event that the movie itself didn't start until 11:00 p.m., several hours after its advertised start time, because the stars kept arriving late into the night.

While the sparks between Marion and Chaplin had cooled somewhat by 1930, at the premiere they were inseparable and held hands through much of the ceremony. W.R. was not there, but the photos of Marion and Charlie together were publicized widely. Those photos did not do anything to quell the possessive suspicions W.R. continued to have, and in the wake of *The Florodora Girl* premiere, he began to feel threatened again.

Marion's second movie of 1930, *Five and Ten*, was taken from a Fanny Hurst story based on the life of the heiress Barbara Hutton. *Five and Ten* would be directed by Robert Z. Leonard, one of Marion's favorite directors, and her co-star was Leslie Howard, whom Marion liked immensely. With this movie, Marion would finally get the opportunity to play a nuanced, three-dimensional character, a human being with flaws and faults. As stubborn as W.R. was about Marion playing these parts, she attacked the role with vigor and enthusiasm. Playing an heiress who falls in love with an engaged man, it was the kind of role that Frances Marion had been begging W.R. to allow her to play for years. Although Marion was once again perhaps too old to be playing a youthful figure, it features some of her finest acting moments in sound film and it remained one of her favorite roles.

Five and Ten was also a typical "pre-Code." Amid the political and social turmoil that characterized the late 1920s and the early 1930s, the American public flocked to see movies that allowed them to immerse themselves in fantasy worlds, where they could laugh and forget about their often heavily burdened lives. In 1930, the Motion Picture Producers and Distributors of America had some success in its efforts to sanitize Hollywood in the face of what they felt was the continued degradation of the industry. With Will Hays at the helm, the Motion Picture Production Code provided guidelines as to what could be shown in movies, but the Code was weak with little real oversight. Between 1929 and 1934, audiences enjoyed a period that came to be known as the "pre-Code" era—a glorious time when sound had come to movies without any enforceable rules on what could be done with it. Steamy plots and strong, powerful female characters define pre-Code films, as well as quick, witty scripts filled with double entendre.

Another European holiday had been planned for the summer of 1930, so Marion's film production schedule that year was deliberately limited. She wasn't scheduled to start her productions for the 1931 releases until after their return, so she could maximize her time on vacation with W.R. and their large party of guests. They left for Europe in June 1930, and this time they traveled on the same ship, the *Olympic*. Their first weekend in London was spent shopping for antiques before the group left for St. Donat's at the end of the month.

The group mostly relaxed at St. Donat's, with a few trips to London, until July 26, when they went on to Paris for four days. There, W.R. encountered some problems. While resting in his room one day in early September, he was informed that there was a government representative downstairs. The representative met W.R. in the lobby, and handed him a slip of paper informing him that he would have to leave the country. The paper outlined the reasons for W.R.'s expulsion from France—that two years prior, W.R. had published a document related to the Anglo-French Naval Compromise in his newspapers, and for that he was being told to leave immediately.

Marion later claimed to have been responsible for the whole thing. In a tall-tale story that may or may not be true, Marion claimed that while in France in 1928, she and the rest of their traveling party had been at lunch at the American Embassy in Paris, alongside several other Hollywood and newspaper people vacationing there at the time. At one point, everyone got up and left the room, but Marion saw a small, half-open door, leading to what looked like a safe. She decided to look in, and saw a piece of paper in French that she didn't understand. Marion put it in what she called her "sissy britches," meant to put it back, but forgot about it until she was back at the hotel and ready to take a bath. Then, as Marion told the story, she went to W.R. and said, "Look, I stole something. You know what they say about curiosity..."

A few days prior to W.R.'s expulsion, however, he had given an interview with a German newspaper in which he criticized the terms of the Treaty of Versailles as excessive, which was likely the real motive for expelling W.R. This was not a new or novel viewpoint, but one that would peg W.R. as pro-German for the rest of his life. "If being a competent journalist and loyal American makes a man persona non grata in France, I think I can endure the situation without loss of sleep," he wrote in an editorial the next day.

W.R. would never go back to France. His defense of Germany in the years following World War I would be a blot on his reputation for the rest of his life. "He was never pro-German," Marion said after his death. "I'll tell you one thing—he was pro-American."

Following the debacle in France, W.R., Marion, and the group went to Bad Nauheim, Germany, before returning to London by plane. The group went to the Savoy Hotel for a dinner party, and to visit George Bernard Shaw, the notoriously curmudgeonly playwright and wit who was a semi-frequent contributor to the Hearst papers. At first, Shaw didn't want to go to the dinner. "I never heard of Marion Davies," he wrote on the invitation extended to him by a friend, "and would not go to a little dinner at the Savoy if she were all the 11,000 virgins of St. Ursula rolled into one." He was persuaded to change his mind, however, when the friend assured him that "Mr. Hearst has expressed more interest in your work than that of any other living writer." He reluctantly agreed to the dinner, and met Marion, Hearst, and company at the Savoy.

For all Shaw's reluctance, Marion was enthusiastic and seemed not to notice that Shaw really did not want to be there. Marion was very familiar with Shaw's work, and she was excited to meet him. She cozied up to the pouting playwright and asked him questions about his works.

"I didn't think you were smart enough to read them," muttered Shaw.

"I'm smart enough to read them," Marion answered, "but I'm not smart enough to understand them." She leaned in closer to him, ready to listen. "Now, explain them to me."

Such a candid, persistent, and unbothered response took Shaw by surprise. He was used to offending people with his insults, but Marion seemed beyond that. As Shaw spoke about his work, Marion listened and interacted with him with great interest. By the time dinner was over, Shaw had fallen under Marion's spell. It was the beginning of a great friendship—and when Shaw visited the United States two years later, their affection for each other as friends turned the visit into a cherished and beloved memory for Hollywood, avoiding a potential disaster due to Shaw's acerbic bitterness.

Five and Ten was released in July 1930 while Marion was in Europe. Upon her return to the United States, Rose was with yet another man, this time a married one named Ned McLean. While Marion was in Europe, McLean himself had been in Latvia, supposedly trying to get a divorce from his wife so he could marry Rose. Marion tried to warn Rose not to take any drastic steps. She didn't trust him, and advised Rose to hold off on any marriage until "we have some evidence of Ned's sincerity and his ability to carry out his promises." As it turned out, McLean never got the divorce that he had promised Rose, but that didn't seem to deter her. She lived with him for the next ten years and when he died, he left her a large inheritance, citing Rose as his "common law wife."

Marion's relationship with Rose was one of the most complicated of her life. She cared deeply for her sister, but in many ways, Rose required more energy than Marion was able to give her. She always supported Rose financially and emotionally, despite Rose's often difficult and erratic behavior. Marion felt somewhat responsible for her sister—whether it was taking over the raising of Patricia or guiding her through her questionable choices in men—the irony being that Marion, living a life that was considered by society to be unacceptable, was the stabilizing force in Rose's romantic life. Rose was married a total of six times. All the while, Marion remained with W.R.

Another trip to Europe occurred in the summer of 1931. When the group checked out of the hotel in Bad Nauheim, Germany, Marion learned that a customer, unable to pay his bill, had left his puppy at the hotel as collateral. Marion was heartbroken at the thought of someone being so callous to an animal and asked to see the dog. The hotel secretary obliged and brought Marion back to the office where the dog was kept. He was a dachshund. Upon seeing the dog's bony frame, Marion was reminded of the photos of Mahatma Gandhi, whose *satyagraha* campaign against British occupation of India continued to make world headlines. The dog was shaking in fear, but Marion got down and called him gently, "Here, Gandhi!" When he came over to her, she scooped him up and cuddled him in her arms. W.R. saw their bond immediately, paid the bill, and Gandhi began his new life at Marion's side.

Gandhi was an unusual-looking dachshund, with a downward-pointing nose and a solid build. Of all the many dachshunds that W.R. and Marion would have over the years, Gandhi is most identifiable in photos due to his unique features. He was a nervous and neurotic dog, only allowing Marion and W.R. to touch him and snapping at everyone else who came close. "I don't know why the nicest people always have the most horrible animals," remembered Billy Haines about Gandhi. Marion adored the grouchy dachshund, and he became an integral part of the Hearst-Davies circle. He accompanied Marion on all subsequent trips and became somewhat of an emotional support dog for her. During her years with Gandhi, when Marion was faced with anything she wanted to avoid, she would invoke Gandhi as the reason for her avoidance. "Gandhi doesn't like it," she would say, if there was a movie she didn't want to see, or a record she didn't want to put on. When Gandhi died thirteen years later in 1944, it was a blow from which she never fully recovered.

Upon the group's return from Europe, a party was given for Marion at the Ambassador Hotel, an event that the *Los Angeles Examiner* called "the opening of Hollywood's fall and winter social season." In a rare public appearance with Marion, W.R. also attended. Shortly after the party began, a group of newspaper boys broke through the doors of the Cocoanut Grove carrying copies of a mock *Los Angeles Examiner* issue. In place of the normal masthead was *The Front Page*, and the Hearst motto of "A Paper For People Who Think" was replaced by "A Paper For People Who Drink." It was exactly Marion's humor, a prank of the type in which she delighted. The practical joke had been organized by a creative group of Marion's friends, who had (likely with W.R.'s blessing) broken into the offices of the *Los Angeles Examiner* and changed the printing blocks. Everyone had a good laugh, but W.R.'s good humor changed to panic when, a few days later, it was discovered that the *Examiner* was still carrying the motto "A Paper For People Who Drink."

In late 1931, Marion prepared for Christmas and New Year's Eve costume parties, including an elaborate "kiddie party," where guests arrived in children's costumes. Activities were planned to go along with the theme, including spirited games of marbles and top-spinning. Joan Crawford, who had arrived with a hula hoop as an accessory, engaged the Talmadge sisters and actress Aileen Pringle in a round of jacks, while Buster Keaton organized a match of indoor football. That soon came to a close when Keaton sprained his ankle trying to run around the piano. Late in the evening, after all the fun had subsided, the guests began dancing to a local Los Angeles orchestra, whose harmonies mixed with the gentle sounds of the ocean just outside the door.

In an article for the *New Movie Magazine*, Eileen Percy wrote about her experience at the kiddie party, describing the event as "aglow with music and laughter," capturing the mood and tenor of the gathering, and of Marion Davies's parties in general.

As the end of the year approached, a strange package arrived at the Beach House. It was at first thought to be a Christmas present, until it was noticed that Marion's name was misspelled on the package and it was oddly wrapped for the season. Marion was cautious about her mail, and never opened packages or letters herself. Her staff would open them, give the appropriate items to her, and she would answer accordingly. This time, though, Marion's staff was suspicious. They decided to investigate and unwrap it themselves before giving it to Marion. When they opened the package, they found a small key sticking out of the side. It began to smoke, and Marion's chef, Carl Mueller, threw it out the window toward the beach. The police were called, and they took the box and submerged it in water to dismantle it. Upon examination, the police traced the bomb to a disgruntled MGM employee. They deduced that the bomb was crude and had Marion opened it, it wouldn't have done enough damage to kill her, but it had been sent to cause her serious harm. While Marion had been aware of the vulnerability that came with her public lifestyle, she had never felt threatened to the point of fearing for her life, and after this incident she was increasingly on her guard.

By 1932, the Depression was finally beginning to affect W.R.'s money supply. Construction on San Simeon had continued uninterrupted since 1920, but in 1932 money was running out. There would still be construction, but it would be less and cheaper than what W.R. was accustomed to. He sought to finish many projects quickly in 1932, so that he could stop spending money on them. This was the beginning of what turned out to be a very difficult decade for W.R.

The summer Olympics were held in Los Angeles in 1932. The Los Angeles Memorial Coliseum, which is today the home field of the USC Trojans and the Los Angeles Rams, served as one of the main competition venues for the Olympic Games. It was there, at the Olympic Coliseum, where Marion co-sponsored a massive benefit, jointly for the Marion Davies Foundation and the Motion Picture Relief Fund, in late September. The fund, founded by Mary Pickford at the same time as the Marion Davies Children's Clinic, provided financial assistance to members of the motion picture industry who needed help, with finances, health, or funerals.

The Marion Davies Foundation had been created to oversee the clinic only ten days earlier, and all of Hollywood turned out in support of the foundation and the relief fund. Contributing to the grandeur of the benefit were such show business names as Mary Pickford and Will Rogers, who put on a Wild West show. After some speculation over whether or not he would come, the event was attended by Franklin Delano Roosevelt, then governor of New York and running against Herbert Hoover for president of the United States in 1932, and he became the guest of honor. The event was a smashing success, with 105,000 people filling the stadium. As the representative from the Marion Davies Foundation, Marion addressed the stadium, braving her stutter to thank everyone involved in planning and executing this massive undertaking. The Olympic stadium event placed both the Marion Davies Foundation and the Motion Picture Relief Fund in a position to continue operating through the Depression, providing a vital lifeline to the neediest residents of Los Angeles.

"I Didn't Want a Part Where I Just Sit on My Tail and Recite Poetry"

Professionally, 1932 was shaping up to be one of Marion's best. Playing a circus performer who falls in love with a budding pastor, Marion acted alongside a young Clark Gable in *Polly of the Circus*, and the two got along well off-screen, too. It is one of Marion's finest acting performances of the sound era, and she found comfort in the idea that her career was going in a new direction. It was released on March 18, 1932, and Marion's acting received stellar reviews from critics. "Miss Davies...has never had a role that suited her talents as a comedienne more completely," wrote the *Brooklyn Times Union*, a non-Hearst paper, "and in spots where Polly is called upon to show dramatic talent the star measures right up to scratch."

The origin of Marion's next movie, *Blondie of the Follies*, was in a script originally called "Three Blondes," written by Frances Marion on her way home from Europe in 1931. It was the story of a young woman living in the New York tenements who dreams of going into the Ziegfeld Follies and who finds herself at odds with her best friend over a love interest, played by Robert Montgomery. W.R. was adamant that this be a romantic vehicle for Marion, and not a comedic one. "I want you to curb your inclination towards humor," he told Anita Loos, who had been assigned to adapt the story. Anita managed to do that to an extent, but Marion's natural humor came out in several key scenes, especially toward the end when she and Jimmy Durante perform something of a vaudeville act together that parodies the recent movie *Grand Hotel*—where Marion once again uses her honed skills of mimicry to do an impression of Greta Garbo.

A story conference in May of 1932 provides a glimpse into the planning that went into the production of *Blondie of the Follies*. At the conference, Anita Loos, Irving Thalberg, Paul Bern, and director Edmund Goulding debated the story, discussing and arguing about what would make the best script. Much of the talk at this conference referenced W.R. and his tastes, whether directly or indirectly, and worries were voiced around what W.R. would or would not accept. "It hasn't the feeling of life," Irving Thalberg said at one point, perhaps alluding to W.R.'s love for beauty and vibrance. "You see my point, don't you?" It is a testament to just how much power W.R. had over these productions, even when he wasn't in the room. Initially, Marion's character of Blondie was to contract a life-threatening illness at the end of the film. But it was decided to reduce the illness to a debilitating injury, for which Robert Montgomery's character could find specialists and put Blondie on the road to recovery. It was a "happily ever after" that W.R. could live with. Frances Marion, by contrast, had tolerated as much as she could from W.R. After the revisions he made to her story, making it unrecognizable and a regression for Marion, she vowed that she would never work with him again.

Blondie of the Follies was released in September, and both Blondie of the Follies and Polly of the Circus marked a new normal for Marion—complex dramatic roles, playing characters with faults and real personality. Blondie of the Follies and Polly of the Circus promised to open her up to the possibility of breaking through the confines of W.R.'s desires. Although W.R. was now tolerating Marion in comedies, he was slower to allow her to play a character with flaws. He still held to his desire for Marion to be portrayed as a perfect, angelic woman, and even with the altered endings, films like Blondie of the Follies and Polly of the Circus were difficult for him to accept. At the same time, however, he liked the fact that Blondie of the Follies reflected aspects of Marion's own life, and referred to it as "Marion's story."

Meanwhile, the government was on the verge of a turning point. Franklin D. Roosevelt was elected in November, and while Europe was in turmoil due to the after-effects of the Treaty of Versailles, Roosevelt was overflowing with ideas on how to make the United States more effective domestically and internationally—and many of them involved increased taxation.

When Franklin D. Roosevelt began his campaign for the presidency in 1932, W.R. was curious about his positions. He wired Edmond D. Coblentz, managing editor for the New York American, to research Roosevelt's campaign speeches when he ran for governor of New York in 1920. What he found turned him against Roosevelt for the Democratic nomination, but none of the other candidates seemed acceptable to W.R. either. He was concerned that they were all internationalists, and feared American involvement in another war. Finally, he supported the isolationist John Nance Garner, who benefitted from the support of the Hearst papers to win the California primary in a surprise victory.

Garner made a last-minute decision to release his delegates to Roosevelt to secure him the nomination, and Roosevelt went on to win the 1932 general election. Roosevelt remembered that W.R. had been an indirect force in helping him win the nomination, and they began a cooperative relationship. W.R. suggested policies, and Roosevelt considered them seriously.

Despite the overwhelmingly positive reviews afforded to Marion in 1932, with the success of *Polly of the Circus* and *Blondie of the Follies*, in 1933 Marion found herself back in unidimensional roles. *Going Hollywood*, in which she co-starred with Bing Crosby, would be something of a step backward in her quest for more substantial roles. *Going Hollywood* was originally written by Frances Marion as *Paid to Laugh* with Marie Dressler cast as Marion's mother. Frances was off-contract at the time, and MGM paid her $10,000 for the rights before handing the material over to Donald Ogden Stewart, who cut out the role of Marion's mother and retitled the project *Going Hollywood*. Raoul Walsh, a veteran director of dramas, signed on to be the director, and it would be his first musical.

The story is one of Marion's stranger films and more convoluted plot lines. In *Going Hollywood*, Marion plays a young boarding school teacher who yearns for freedom, deciding to follow her favorite singer (played by Bing Crosby) across the country. *Going Hollywood* is noteworthy for introducing the song "Temptation," which became a Crosby standard, and as one of the movies in which Marion was able to do her biting, spot-on impression of co-star Fifi D'Orsay. Marion's alcoholism was beginning to affect her health, and it is noticeable in *Going Hollywood*. Her face was slightly puffier, and she had gained weight. This increase in Marion's drinking was exacerbated by Crosby's, as the two of them clowned around on the set. Since W.R. was not watching Marion, they felt free to let the alcohol flow.

An adaptation of a turn-of-the-century Broadway hit, *Peg O' My Heart*, was an entirely different story. Marion was slated to play the spunky Irish teenager that Laurette Taylor had made famous on the stage and played in a 1919 film. Marion, at 36 years old in 1933, was far from the girl that Peg was supposed to be. The movie came at what was likely the last possible moment when she could have had any chance of pulling off the role of a teenager. While she was still beautiful, the effects of her drinking along with the fact of her age made playing Peg seem an improbable stretch for her. Frances Marion, who had thrown up her hands and given up on W.R. the previous year following *Blondie of the Follies*, had decided to give it another chance with *Peg O' My Heart*. She adapted it from the original play in order to suit Marion.

The original play on Broadway had been written by J. Hartley Manners, starring Manners's wife, Laurette Taylor. It had debuted on Broadway in 1912 and became a smash hit, with the role becoming indelibly linked with Taylor in the eyes of theatergoers. In the process of adapting the script, Frances Marion felt she had to add her two cents. "Let her be older," Frances pleaded with W.R. "Let her mature emotionally. Let her have children." But there was still no arguing with him and Marion ultimately conceded to W.R.'s wishes. She soon began playing two-dimensional roles again—where she was a young girl, beautiful, but lacking complexity. She couldn't bring herself to defy W.R. and threw herself into the role of the young Irish girl Peg O'Connell, sent to America to inherit a fortune, and the characterization is considered to be one of her best.

Peg O' My Heart began filming in February 1933. On March 10, in the middle of a scene when her co-star Onslow Stevens was in bed while Marion knelt by his side, the ground began to shake. Scenery fell, one of the orchestra members fainted, and the electricity went out, trapping many people inside the soundstage that was secured by an electric door. W.R., frantic about Marion's well-being, appeared with lit matches to look for Marion on the darkened and chaotic soundstage. "Marion!" he called. "Marion, where are you?" He ran up to someone he thought was Marion and spun her around. Marion's stand-in, Vera Burnett, took off her blond costume wig so that he would know she wasn't who he was looking for. "You're not Marion!" W.R. exclaimed when he saw Vera, and left to continue his search. W.R. managed to find Marion after several minutes, trapped inside the soundstage but unharmed.

The cast was safe, and no one was hurt, but soon, the damage done to downtown Los Angeles became clear. The 1933 Long Beach earthquake registered 6.4 on the Richter scale, and to this day it is the deadliest earthquake in Southern California history. Buildings collapsed between Santa Ana and Compton, trapping people under rubble and leading to the deaths of at least 120 people. The earthquake brought increased awareness to the need for better retrofitting of California buildings, and Congress authorized the Reconstruction Finance Corporation (RFC) to begin providing reconstruction relief to companies affected by the quake.

Peg O' My Heart wrapped in early April, and had its premiere in May at the Capitol Theatre in New York. The reviews were fantastic, even outside the Hearst press. "It is evidently a part to Miss Davies' liking," wrote Mordaunt Hall of the *New York Times*, "and she gives a whole-souled portrayal, always giving more thought to Peg than to any idea of making herself especially attractive." Marion appears in pigtails, barefoot, and with no makeup, wearing trousers as she played the role of a fisherman's daughter in Ireland.

In some ways, *Peg O' My Heart* signified a shift for Marion—in her career, but also in her relationship with W.R. It would be the last time that Marion would play a young girl, as W.R. finally took to heart the idea that his fresh-faced chorus girl of 18 was no more. From here on, Marion would play adults—still virginal and angelic, but adults nonetheless. Keeping Marion young, and in need of protection (at least in the movies), somehow put W.R.'s mind at ease, and Marion knew this. But after *Peg O' My Heart*, playing young girls would be in Marion's past.

Marion's next prospective film was The *Barretts of Wimpole Street*, a Broadway hit that had starred Katharine Cornell on the stage. It was originally meant to serve as a vehicle for Irving Thalberg's wife, Norma Shearer. But her schedule was too full, and W.R. appealed to Louis B. Mayer to have the production transferred to Cosmopolitan Productions as a vehicle for Marion instead. Thalberg protested vocally, but when W.R. wanted something, he fought tooth and nail for it.

W.R. was aware of the issues. Katharine Cornell had been such a hit in the stage version that Marion would have a hard time measuring up to expectations. In addition, she had been so established by 1933 as a comedienne that playing such a dramatic part would likely not be welcomed by audiences. But it was a risk W.R. was willing to take to secure this once-in-a-lifetime opportunity.

In the early 1930s, as the Depression wreaked havoc on the American economy, many American homeowners and business owners found themselves in precarious economic circumstances. Joseph P. Kennedy, who had supported FDR, was appointed the first chairman of the U.S. Securities and Exchange Commission upon its creation in 1934, which helped regulate investment practices, stabilizing economic circumstances for the long term. In the short term, foreclosures were rampant. In June of 1933, President Roosevelt signed into law the Home Owners' Loan Act, which protected certain Americans from banks foreclosing on their properties, providing a safety net for countless people in danger of ending up on the streets or out of business. The same month, Marion was elected president of the Motion Picture Relief

Fund. Much like the Marion Davies Children's Clinic for the children of West Los Angeles, the Motion Picture Relief Fund, originally founded by Mary Pickford, had become an important lifeline for struggling industry professionals during the Depression. In the years following its founding, the fund had adopted a streamlined paycheck deduction system, with 1.5 percent of an industry member's salary going to the fund if they chose to contribute. By 1933, 2,400 industry members contributed to the fund.

Marion's tasks as president were demanding during the Depression. A staggering number of people required help from the fund, and the following January 1934 alone, the fund helped 2,500 hungry industry professionals by fulfilling grocery orders amounting to $4,000 (nearly $76,000 in today's money). The fund also paid utility bills, covered medical expenses, and saved seventy-five families from eviction in that month alone.

In spite of the arduous nature of the work, Marion was a natural in the role of president. Her involvement with the Motion Picture Relief Fund was a testament to her financial savvy and acumen, reflecting her ability to direct the fund to provide help to those in need while still managing to stay well within the budget. Just as she did with the clinic, Marion gave struggling members of the industry Christmas baskets full of ingredients for a full turkey dinner. In all, 1,500 individuals received the baskets.

Meanwhile, the Marion Davies Children's Clinic was going through another period of growth. A large medical staff of ear-nose-throat doctors, ophthalmologists, and tonsil specialists provided high-end care. Clinic patient Lupe Herrera remembered that for children having their tonsils out, the clinic offered a luxury that few families could afford—an unlimited supply of ice cream. Children soon learned that if they had the surgery, part of the recovery process was to eat as much ice cream as possible. From then on, Lupe said, "Tonsils, boy, were coming out left and right."

Back in the studio, in the later part of 1933, trade papers announced Marion as having secured the role of Elizabeth Barrett in *The Barretts of Wimpole Street*. Almost immediately, letters from fans came pouring into the fan magazines, begging Marion not to play the nineteenth-century poet. One such letter appeared in *Picture Play* magazine in December of 1933, as an open letter to Marion from Bertram G. Knowles, a fan in New Jersey. "Please, Miss Davies, won't you reconsider before you undertake this role?" he wrote. "Stick to the parts we like you best in and leave heavy drama for those who can do it well. We need you as a light comedienne, for there is no one like you."

Support for Marion's comedic talents came from higher up as well—both

Louis B. Mayer and Irving Thalberg disapproved of Marion playing Elizabeth Barrett (though ulterior motives were certainly present with Irving Thalberg, who wanted the role for Norma Shearer, his wife), but one simply did not tell W.R. no. To appease him, Mayer and Thalberg let him cast Marion as Elizabeth Barrett, and Marion was once again relegated to playing a role in which she felt stifled. Marion was getting older, but W.R. still could not shake his desire for her to play the ethereal angels and historical maidens that he so loved. The announcement of Marion in this role would contribute to tensions between MGM and Cosmopolitan Productions over the course of the next year and would highlight the shifting power dynamic at the studio.

From 1924, W.R. had held the power of the Hearst press over Louis B. Mayer to get what he wanted and renewed the contract with MGM due to his ties and friendship with the studio head. But whispers of a possible Cosmopolitan move to Warner Bros. had been circulating since at least 1929, and it nearly happened several times over the years that followed between 1930 and 1933. Few thought that such a break would happen, but the changing dynamics made such a move possible once again in 1934.

Before moving ahead with *The Barretts of Wimpole Street*, Marion began production on the Civil War drama *Operator 13*. Future director George Sidney got his start as a boom boy on the set of the film. In the days of primitive sound equipment, there was only one microphone to register the voices of all the actors in the scene, held by a long handle called a "boom." One of the more experienced set workers told him, "If you hit Miss Davies with a microphone, you will never work in the film industry again." In his fear, he fumbled with the microphone and it started to swivel perilously close to her. Marion, seeing what was happening, turned her head and delivered her line over her shoulder, so as to avoid getting hit with the microphone and saving 17-year-old George Sidney from certain banishment from the set. When the scene was over, Marion turned and smiled at George, giving him a subtle wink. "Thank you, Miss Davies!" he whispered.

Operator 13 had its Los Angeles premiere in May 1934. Shortly after filming, Louella Parsons asked Marion to be a guest on her radio show on CBS. It would be Marion's first appearance on radio, focusing on promotion of *Operator 13* as well as on beauty and health tips, which were standard Louella Parsons subjects. The year 1934 was relatively late for a star as big as Marion to be making her debut on radio. She had avoided the medium due to fear of her stutter but didn't want to let it stand in her way. Marion said yes to Louella and made the decision to add radio to her repertoire.

The show was publicized widely. W.R. did everything he could to make Marion's radio debut a success, and he took special care to make sure that the non-Hearst papers picked up the story of Marion's radio debut first. "Mr. Hearst wants a break in the non-Hearst papers in the east," Louella wrote *Los Angeles Evening Herald Examiner* journalist Eugene Inge in the week before the program. By this point, W.R. had become aware of the detrimental effect of excessive Hearst publicity on everything Marion did, and he wanted to make sure that this radio program received as much positive press as possible.

In the days leading up to the broadcast, papers across the country heralded the radio debut of Marion Davies, and she braved the radio waves for the first time on May 16, 1934, on a nationwide hookup via CBS. Newspapers were quick to note that this was the first time that scenes from a film were broadcast over the radio, and the first time that a radio broadcast had been musically scored in the same way as in a film. It was a watershed moment for Marion, too. In spite of her vocal challenges, she had braved the new medium and would do so several more times throughout the 1930s. Her stutter was only noticeable when Marion broke character, speaking as herself. In a 1938 radio version of *Peg O' My Heart* for Lux Radio Theatre, Marion engages in a small, scripted interview afterward to discuss next steps in her career. Throughout the broadcast, Marion speaks fluently in character as Peg, without the slightest hint of her stutter. In the interview following the show with host Cecil B. DeMille, it is evident that she is trying to control her stutter as she reads her interview script, and several words give her trouble. On those words, she stumbles for a moment, then pauses, and continues confidently.

In late May 1934, just a few days after her successful radio debut, Marion and W.R. embarked on a trip to Europe, bringing along an entourage of family and friends. These included Hearst's three older sons—George, Bill Jr., and John—plus their wives, as well as Eileen Percy, Dorothy Mackaill, Harry Crocker, and Buster Collier. As usual, Marion's dachshund Gandhi was along as well. The trip included stops in nine European countries, plus a quick jaunt to Morocco. The group headed east from Los Angeles by train, to sail from New York. The Chicago World's Fair was underway when they were passing through the city, so the group stopped to enjoy the attractions before resuming their cross-country trek. Once in New York they stayed at the Ritz Tower, and sailed on the *Rex* a few days later, arriving first in Italy. While in Italy, W.R. had hoped to meet Mussolini, in order to gain a better understanding of the devolving European situation for the Hearst papers.

This didn't happen in 1934, but photo evidence of the trip is a chilling testament to a Europe on the brink of collapse.

The home movies from the 1934 trip to Europe show the lavish style in which the Hearst crew traveled. The films were shot by members of the party, likely with W.R.'s son George Hearst behind the camera much of the time. George had developed a great interest in amateur photography, and is often seen with a camera in his hand on this trip. Several cars were rented seemingly just for the luggage, and women dressed in new outfits almost each time they were photographed. The notable exception is Marion. Although she loved to shop and came home with suitcases full of clothes, she tended to have favorite outfits that she repeated, appearing on several legs of the trip in the same dress. Gandhi is frequently underfoot, and always by Marion's side.

The home movies also speak to the fondness that the Hearst sons felt for Marion, the woman they referred to as "Daisy." All the sons are frequently seen close to Marion, smiling and laughing with her. The atmosphere is joyful and fun, and even the normally ill-tempered Gandhi seems to tolerate being touched and played with. In one amusing moment, Bill Jr. models Marion's hat for the camera. In the shots where George Hearst is not in the frame (and thus is likely filming the group), Marion is photographed in tender moments with Gandhi, having fun posing and dancing, or waving to the camera.

The group changed cars in Germany, and Buster Collier rode with Marion in the rumble seat through the mountains to the restaurant where they were to have lunch. They met the rest of the group there and dined outdoors, which was reminiscent of the gourmet outdoor picnics at San Simeon. Marion was especially impressed with the wine. "This is the best Rhine wine I have ever tasted," she told Buster. "Let's take some for the road."

"How are we going to do that?" Buster asked her. They couldn't very well have a bottle of wine in the rumble seat of the car, and W.R. surely wouldn't approve of it.

Marion had an idea. They emptied out a Coca-Cola bottle, poured the wine in, and sneaked it into the car, giggling at their mischief. They giggled all the way to their hotel, much to W.R.'s puzzlement, and at one point he turned around and said, "What's so funny?" Buster finally told him of their prank.

"She was like a bad kid," Buster said of Marion. "She enjoyed the hiding of it."

The German leg of the 1934 trip is documented by Buster Collier in a fascinating and chilling scrapbook. The photos show that since Adolf Hitler's rise to power in 1933, the country had descended into a sea of swastikas and Nazi flags. The Nuremberg Laws were already firmly in place by 1934, stripping Germany's Jews of their citizenship and instituting curfews restricting their movement. The climate for Jews was becoming increasingly dangerous, and due to W.R.'s easy access to Hitler as a world leader, many in Hollywood's Jewish community saw him as someone who could help. Amid signs that read "Juden sind hier unerwünscht" ("Jews are unwanted here"), it was obvious that the Germany that W.R. knew as a child was quickly disappearing.

Before leaving the United States, W.R. had been urged by Louis B. Mayer, to whom he was still close, to meet with Hitler and implore him to change his antisemitic policies. "You may be able to accomplish some good," he said.

As early as 1932, W.R. was seen by Hollywood's Jewish community as a potential champion, as he had been a public supporter of Jewish causes since the early 1900s. After the National Socialist Party became Germany's second-largest party in the election of 1930, Hitler had been hired to write a column for the Hearst papers. The main draw for W.R. was his anger over the Treaty of Versailles that had ended World War I and demanded heavy reparations from Germany, but Hitler was ultimately fired from the paper when he continually failed to meet deadlines. Nonetheless, W.R. maintained a direct line to Hitler through Hitler's foreign press chief, Ernst Franz Sedgwick "Putzi" Hanfstaengl. Though Hitler's antisemitism was no secret—it had, after all, been the focus of his autobiography, *Mein Kampf*—by 1930 his public speeches were less overtly antisemitic and more anti-Marxist. In a sense, he was fooling the world, W.R. included—nothing had actually changed in Hitler's worldview, only the presentation of those views.

In 1932, president of Universal Pictures Carl Laemmle, who was Jewish, wrote to W.R. to beg him to meet with Hitler:

> I might be wrong, and I pray to God that I am, but I am almost certain that Hitler's rise to power, because of his obvious militant attitude toward the Jews, would be the signal for a general physical onslaught on many thousands of defenseless Jewish men, women, and children in Germany.... As a man so sincerely and consistently the champion of human rights, there is none whose voice would carry more effectively to the consciences of all races alike than your own.... there is none in America whose influence and opinions would command more respect and consideration from Mr. Hitler than your own.

In July of 1932, Laemmle's concerns came to fruition when the Nazis became the largest party in the Reichstag. In 1934, W.R. used his connections with Putzi Hanfstaengl to arrange a meeting with Hitler and, on Laemmle's and Mayer's urging, try to serve as a liaison to Hitler for America's Jewish community.

Marion wanted to come along. However, there were serious concerns, which likely involved Marion's Jewish family members. George Lederer, Reine's ex-husband and Charlie and Pepi's father, was Jewish, and Charlie especially identified strongly with his Jewish heritage. If that came out, they feared it could have disastrous consequences.

In order to placate Marion, W.R. and journalist Harry Crocker included her in the plan to meet Hitler. But when their private plane arrived in Berlin, Marion was sidetracked by a Hollywood friend, Ruth Selwyn, who (perhaps orchestrated by W.R. to get Marion out of the way) claimed she was out of money and asked Marion to pay her hotel bill. Marion went with the friend, paid her bill, and helped her pack. The meeting with Hitler occurred while Marion was occupied with Ruth at the hotel.

"W.R. was not impressed by him," Marion recalled about W.R.'s meeting with Hitler. "[W.R.] wanted to talk about the persecution of the Jews, but Hitler's answer was this: 'There is no persecution of any sort.' Hitler said that Jews should not have taken over the industries that were supposed to be for Germans. W.R. answered back, 'I should think industries would belong to every nationality.' Then they said goodbye." W.R. arranged for his meeting with Hitler to be featured by a British newspaper, the *Manchester Guardian*, but when pressed by the media back home, W.R. refused to say anything public about it.

It was also during the German leg of the trip when W.R. learned that socialist Upton Sinclair had won the Democratic nomination for governor of California. With his expansive social reforms known as End Poverty in California (EPIC), Sinclair was seen as a favorite to bring radical change to the state. His opponent in the primary had been George Creel, Woodrow Wilson's propaganda chief during World War I. Hearst advisor and lawyer for the Hearst enterprises John Francis Neylan cabled W.R. in Europe from San Francisco:

SINCLAIR BEATS CREEL OVERWHELMINGLY. SINCLAIR SUPPORT NOT ULTRA RADICAL BUT IN LARGE PART PEOPLE DISGUSTED WITH END-LESS EXPERIMENTATION AND LACK OF JOBS....AT MOMENT SITUATION MUCH CONFUSED. TENS OF THOUSANDS OF DEMOCRATS WILL NOT SUPPORT SINCLAIR.

W.R. decided not to think about the cable. He preferred to say nothing rather than to answer hastily. For now, W.R. ignored Upton Sinclair and the contest between him and his Republican opponent, Frank Merriam.

Marion's politics were open-minded, and she took no side on the Sinclair question. She preferred to judge people by how they treated others rather than by their political leanings, a position that served her well in many situations but clouds any attempt to assess her true political feelings. She was what her future friend Stanley Flink called a "natural liberal," erring on the side of "yes" rather than "no." When approached with political questions, she judged issues from a humanitarian standpoint rather than based on any party's ideology. Up to this point, Marion had been a supporter of Democratic candidates and progressive political ideals. She was interested in politics and voted in every election, mailing her vote if she was ever going to be out of the country, but put more emphasis on defending an underdog, no matter their politics.

When the group went on to Spain, they stopped at the British territory of Gibraltar. Upon their arrival, Marion was told that Gandhi would need to be quarantined. This upset Marion so much that she began arguing with the customs official, an action very much out of character for her. They were to spend the night in Gibraltar, but because of Marion's fear of leaving Gandhi in quarantine, the itinerary changed and the group never passed through customs into Gibraltar. Instead, they spent the night on the Spanish side of the peninsula, and they liked that part of Spain so much that they ended up staying for several days. Even Gandhi seemed to know that he was the cause of their being diverted, as he allowed the hotel owner to pick him up and kiss him upon their departure. "You golden dog," said the owner.

The political climate in Spain was also reaching a fever pitch, with clashes between left- and right-wing political parties, poverty, and worker strikes dominating Spanish society. The home movies from Spain reveal a country on the brink of revolution, which would take place in October of that year. Many of the videos show the rural poverty of Spain before the Spanish Civil War, and children, barefoot and dirty, frequently follow the party around, fascinated by the camera and the well-dressed foreigners. At one point, Marion is shown giving a group of children what looks to be candy.

From Spain they were to go to England, but W.R. wanted to avoid going through France. France had since rescinded its ban on having W.R. in the country, but he still harbored resentment toward them and didn't want to stop in the country even for his regular antique shopping. The sons, however, wanted to go, so they took the cars and drove across the border. W.R., Marion, Buster Collier, and Dorothy Mackaill took one of W.R.'s chartered planes from Madrid to London, to attend a cocktail reception for the press at Claridge's Hotel. A few hours after takeoff, the atmosphere on the plane quickly turned fearful as the pilot announced that due to a mechanical problem the passengers should prepare themselves for an emergency landing. Buster Collier remembered that Marion was the only one who appeared composed, more worried about running late for the cocktail party than about the incident. "She just buckled herself in," he said, "and didn't say a word."

Marion would recall the incident as one in which she was terrified. "But when I'm frightened," she said, "I can't say anything. Unless I get really scared, in which case I let out a tremendous roar." Marion's speech problems were often triggered when she was in a state of heightened emotion, and her inability to speak at this moment due to her stutter was a fact lost on her friends. It was a rough landing, but everyone was safe, and the group made their way to Claridge's, where they finally arrived at 5:00 in the morning, exhausted from their ordeal. They had missed the press cocktail party.

Marion, W.R., and their party sailed back to New York on the *Bremen* on September 27. On Saturday, October 20, to celebrate their return from Europe, W.R. and Marion threw a large party at the Beach House, this time making Tyrolean dress its theme. Many of the usual attendees came—Norma Shearer, outfitted in a huge headdress and traditional Germanic garb, arrived with husband Irving Thalberg, whose small size was punctuated by lederhosen that made him look like a child. Many of the women were outfitted in lederhosen as well, unusual for a Marion Davies party in which women usually avoided pants. Jean Harlow was there, and a somewhat awkward photo was taken of her, Marion, Constance Bennett, and Gloria Swanson. Swanson had recently divorced from the Marquis Henri de la Falaise de la Coudraye, who days later married Bennett. Despite what was sure to have been an invitation error, the two kept things civil and the party was a success.

On the political front, the Upton Sinclair campaign was heating up. Sinclair owned a newspaper, the tabloid *EPIC News*, which served as the campaign's primary communication medium. W.R. ridiculed Sinclair in the *New York Times* as someone "whose remedies, like his writings, are pure fiction." In turn, Sinclair had written that he was sick of watching the "richest newspaper publisher keeping his movie mistress in a private city of palaces and cathedrals, furnished with shiploads of junk imported from Europe, and surrounded by vast acres reserved for zebras and giraffes." The Hearst papers responded by ignoring the attacks, depriving the Sinclair campaign of the press it needed. Sinclair wrote to W.R. about this, promising not to make "attacks on individuals" any longer, but hoped that W.R. would stop demonizing EPIC activities.

Sinclair's EPIC activities were threatening to the studios, too. Realizing how much power the movies had to sway the voting public of California, MGM head of production Irving Thalberg filmed staged propaganda newsreels to damage Sinclair. The films purported to be actual newsreels showing regular citizens who were voting for either Upton Sinclair or Frank Merriam, but they were, in fact, actors from MGM hired to portray Sinclair as the wrong choice, and Merriam as the right choice. Theaters frequently showed newsreels before a film, and these faux "newsreels" were distributed to theaters across California, free of charge. Only MGM knew that the newsreels were fictional anti-Sinclair propaganda, and public opinion of Sinclair began to erode. When it came time for the election, the newsreels had done their job. Merriam won by a quarter million votes, and Sinclair demanded a congressional investigation. "Whether or not you sympathize with me on my platform is beside the point," he wrote in a telegram to Senator David Walsh of Massachusetts, and to Congressman Wright Patman. "If the picture industry is permitted to defeat unworthy candidates it can be used to defeat worthy candidates. If it can be used to influence voters justly, it can be used to influence voters unjustly." The investigation never happened.

MGM made the decision to give both *The Barretts of Wimpole Street* and *Marie Antoinette* to Norma Shearer instead of to Marion. The evolution of the studio's politics made it so that the power and appeal that the Hearst press and Louella Parsons brought to the studio were waning, and Irving Thalberg's desires dominated W.R's. Louella Parsons was no longer an anchor by which W.R. could curry favor with Louis B. Mayer, and Mayer no longer felt that W.R. and Marion remaining at MGM was essential to promoting MGM films in the press. The symbiotic nature of the collaboration in its early days had died. When W.R. threatened to leave MGM if Marion were not cast in *Marie Antoinette* and *The Barretts of Wimpole Street*, Mayer made little effort to stop him.

After several years of exploration, the deal between Cosmopolitan and Warner Bros. finally came to fruition. Studio head Jack Warner still believed in the power of the Hearst press and Louella Parsons, and in late 1934, W.R. signed a contract with Jack Warner, and made arrangements to leave MGM, after ten years of partnership. W.R. was unwilling to leave Marion's historic

1925 bungalow, where so many studio parties had occurred, and plans were made to uproot the fourteen-room bungalow and haul it, in one piece, over to the Warner Bros. lot.

MGM had been Marion's home since 1925. The move to Warner Bros. signified the end of an era for her, and a goodbye to the friends and connections Marion had made over the past ten years. There was a sadness and sense of nostalgia to her leaving, and while Marion rarely let her true feelings show, preferring to keep a stiff upper lip, her friends recognized her emotion as she bade them farewell.

"Anyway, I didn't want a part where I just sit on my tail and recite poetry," she told Frances Marion and a group of friends upon her departure. "I love to laugh and dance and have fun." And with that, the trailer pulling the bungalow began its journey to Warner Bros. in Burbank, and Marion's era at MGM ended. Louis B. Mayer waved them off with tears in his eyes. The trailer hauling the giant bungalow finally faded from view, and as soon as they were gone, Mayer wiped the tears from his eyes, smiled at Irving Thalberg, and asked, "How did I do?"

In December 1934, Marion signed the contract to start her new work at Warner Bros. Cosmopolitan was to make twelve pictures over the span of two years, four of which were to be Marion Davies productions. As was standard procedure for Warner Bros. at the time, if Marion was not able to make one of those movies, the time of that movie would be tacked on to the end of her contract. The studio system, complete with its imbalance in power dynamics, was in full swing by this time. Marion's Warner Bros. contract was reminiscent of most at this studio in the 1930s. The practice of extending time on seven-year agreements was found illegal in 1944, when Olivia de Havilland toppled the procedures at Warner Bros. in the landmark De Havilland Decision. In this ruling, the Supreme Court of California clarified that a seven-year contract meant seven calendar years, not seven years of time worked, under California law. But for Marion, and others at the studio in the 1930s, refusal to make a movie meant extra time was added.

In early April 1935, Marion began work on her first Warner Bros. film, *Page Miss Glory*. She took to co-star Dick Powell right away, and he to her. Powell felt that Marion might be developing a crush on him, and with W.R. on the set constantly, he feared what this might mean for his career.

As with all of Marion's flirtations, it is difficult to know when the line crossed between a platonic friendship and romantic interest. She developed the same kind of crush on Leslie Howard on the set of *Five and Ten*, and of course with Charlie Chaplin a decade earlier, which seemed to amount to far more than Marion's on-set crushes. Marion was very tactile and demonstrative in her affection, hugging, kissing, and touching freely, and it was easy for many people to misinterpret this as romantic. However harmless Marion's potential crushes were, they frightened her co-stars, who were all too aware of the power that W.R. wielded over their careers.

As at MGM, elaborate lunches for the cast were held at Marion's bungalow. Much like the picnics at San Simeon, there was chicken and champagne, and W.R. kept a watchful eye on Marion throughout. At one of these lunches, given for some Hearst higher-ups from the East Coast, W.R. was busy talking to guests when Powell entered the bungalow. When Marion caught a glimpse of Powell coming through the door, she gleefully welcomed him by blowing exuberant kisses across the room, beckoning with both her arms for him to come over and sit in the seat she had saved next to her. Powell, afraid that W.R. would turn around and catch the whole scene, meekly waved to Marion and gestured to her in no uncertain terms that she should be very careful. In addition to the fear that Powell had of W.R.'s jealousy, he also knew that "the Chief" had the power to ruin his career in a single blow if Powell displeased him. "You always felt Mr. Hearst's possessive attitude toward Miss Davies," Powell recalled for the Hearst biographer W.A. Swanberg. "I remember feeling that he had a possession complex—that Miss Davies was his possession and had to be guarded."

Given W.R.'s all-encompassing need for control, Powell approached him about what was going on between Marion and himself. W.R. just laughed pleasantly at the insinuation that he was jealous of Powell, but he seemed to appreciate this gesture because from there on out, he trusted Powell with small favors and showed him a great deal of consideration. He came to like Powell so much that he began calling him "Richard" in place of "Mr. Powell," an unusual informality for the era.

To Powell, Marion was the "best-hearted woman in the world," whose interactions with him on set were endearing more than anything else. Marion, in turn, remembered Dick Powell with tenderness and love. "I really adore him," she said. "He's a darling. He's one of the sweetest persons I've ever met."

Papa Ben was now living in Los Angeles, Marion having brought him out from New York in 1931, so that the family could be closer to him as he got older. He continued to work as a lawyer in California before he felt too frail to continue. He fell ill in late April, and Ethel took on the duties of caring for Papa Ben while Reine, Rose, and Marion checked in often.

After his son Charles's death thirty-five years earlier in 1900, Papa Ben had retreated into alcohol and isolation. Regardless, Marion desperately wanted to be close to him. Unlike Mama Rose, who was always there when she needed her, Marion's father was an unreliable figure in her life. Still, she remained devoted, protective, and loving, taking him on trips to Europe, bringing him out to California, and supporting him with all her emotional and financial wealth. Papa Ben realized in his final years all he had missed in his relationship with his children. When Papa Ben's life was nearing its end in late April 1935, Marion took regular trips to Ethel's and sat with her father by his bedside, talking with him and tending to his every need. According to biographer Fred Lawrence Guiles, Papa Ben's final thoughts to Marion were that she was the one thing in his life that he had ever been proud of. He died on April 25 with Marion by his side, and was buried at the family mausoleum at Hollywood Cemetery.

Weeks later, in mid-May 1935, Marion was back at work. Normally, Marion and W.R. threw a large birthday party on the occasion of W.R.'s birthday on April 29. But owing to the death of Papa Ben, the party was cancelled, and Marion and W.R. did not make plans to go to Europe that summer. With both her parents now gone, Marion was grieving and out of sorts as she finished work on *Page Miss Glory*.

During this time, Pepi's drug habit had spiraled out of control. Prior to Papa Ben's death, Marion had convinced Pepi to return from an extended vacation in Europe to visit Reine and see Papa Ben. Pepi had been in Europe with her most recent girlfriend, Monica Morrice, and did not want to come back. Marion didn't like Morrice, and saw her as responsible for Pepi's further descent into drugs and alcohol. Pepi agreed to come home to California only if Morrice could come, and reluctantly, Marion gave her permission to get Pepi back home.

But Pepi continued to use drugs and partake in destructive behavior while home in California. Separating Pepi from this girlfriend, Marion felt, would help wean her off the drugs that had come to dominate her life. Ultimately, Marion felt that there was nothing left to do for her niece but to admit her to the psychiatric ward of the Good Samaritan Hospital in Los Angeles for treatment. In the 1930s, before widespread mental health reform, involuntary admission of adults for psychiatric treatment was widespread, and this was where Marion felt Pepi would finally be safe.

Upon arrival at the hospital, Pepi seemed calm and obliging. Two days later, a nurse, Marion Pope, came in to find her sitting in bed reading a fan magazine. She seemed nervous and agitated, Miss Pope noted. Pepi asked her to order her a salad from the cafeteria, and just as Miss Pope stepped out to order the food, she suddenly heard a loud crash. She turned, startled, to see Pepi's body tumbling out of the window of her sixth-story room. Pepi's body landed in a large patch of shrubbery below, and despite hospital attendants rushing to her aid, she was pronounced dead at the scene. She had recently turned 26 years old.

Newspaper reports were that Pepi had been suffering from "acute melancholia," a code word in those days for severe depression. "Pep was a very unhappy child," said longtime family friend Marie Glendinning. The stigma of suicide in the family was a powerful force, and several newspapers reported that Pepi had simply stumbled and fallen out the window. But when Marion heard the news, she collapsed on the floor in a heap of sadness, pain, and guilt.

Like Papa Ben less than two months earlier, Pepi was interred in the family mausoleum at Hollywood Cemetery. Her unhappiness had been informed by living in the shadow of her gifted younger brother, favored by the family, and by her sexuality and gender presentation that was not accepted in her time. Later, Louise Brooks would write about Pepi and how much she loved her, in her memoir *Lulu in Hollywood*. She also insinuated that W.R. and Marion were somehow to blame for Pepi's suicide, due to their committal of Pepi to the hospital and disapproval of Monica Morrice. But Pepi's struggles, relating to society's intolerance of her sexuality and masculine appearance, had affected her since childhood.

Shortly after Pepi's death, Marion took publicity photos to advertise *Page Miss Glory*. One photo is especially telling—she is staring, hauntingly, into the camera, with a look of weariness and exhaustion in her eyes that reveals the shock and sadness of the past few months. *Page Miss Glory* is an upbeat, positive movie, but in this photo shoot, Marion is unable to hide her private grief from the camera.

"Just Make One Good Picture a Year"

In 1935, Marion was 38 years old. The sadness of the past few years contributed to her increased drinking, and W.R. noticed. He hid Marion's alcohol at the Beach House, sending her on frantic searches to find it. When she discovered the bottles, she would hide them herself in bathrooms and cupboards, places where she thought W.R. wouldn't see them. Inevitably, he would locate them again and the game of hide-and-seek would continue. When W.R. had found a particularly good hiding place, Marion would make her way over to Anita Loos's house half a block north and throw pebbles at her window, until Anita came down and Marion would ask for some of what was in her liquor cabinet.

Friends noticed that despite her upbeat demeanor, there had always been an underlying aura of unhappiness about Marion. Now, in addition to the deaths in her family, Marion was approaching an age when most actresses faded. She confided to her friend Evelyn Wells during this period that she would be happy if she could just drink herself to death. Evelyn believed she meant it.

There were still joys and successes. In 1935, she was elected to head the Motion Picture Relief Fund for the third time. Under Marion's oversight, the fund had managed to help 9,500 individuals and families who came to them for help, and she received high praise from the executive committee for her efforts. Despite the increasing number of industry members needing the Motion Picture Relief Fund's help, the fund ended the year with a $13,437 surplus.

Page Miss Glory was released in July 1935, ahead of schedule, and got mostly positive reviews. Marion and W.R. were at Wyntoon at the time, entertaining a group of twenty-five guests. Before the picture's general release, Marion organized a preview party for locals, at the California Theatre in the neighboring town of Dunsmuir, California. "All the guests, Mr. Hearst etc., were there," wrote the electrician Louis Schallich to architect George Loorz, about the event. "The whole town was lined up before the theater to get an eye full of the movies [*sic*] people." Hundreds gathered in front of the theater to catch a glimpse of Marion, W.R., and the other celebrities who had come to their town. Guests included Mary Carlisle, Constance Talmadge, and director Raoul Walsh. When the film started, the theater was filled to capacity.

Following the preview, theater manager Walter D. Stevens introduced Marion, who came onstage wearing a yellow blouse and blue slacks. Stevens gave her a bouquet of flowers, and after thanking the people who had come to see the movie, Marion introduced Mary Carlisle as "one of the coming motion picture stars of the younger generation of actresses." Mary then came onstage and took a bow, and they were given an enthusiastic ovation by the crowd.

"This was a treat to the home folks," Schallich continued in his letter, "but to us it was just another picture."

Critics found that the story of *Page Miss Glory* was still as "engagingly fresh and amusing as it was behind the footlights," and praised Marion for performing in "admirable style," saying that the performance would "remain in your memory for a very long time."

Marion's generosity and good nature were also extolled in the press. The *Hartford Courant*, a non-Hearst paper, ran an article in late June 1935 noting Marion's positive relationships on her sets, and how she used the power she wielded for the good of others. She provided alibis for minor players who were late to the set, and took the blame when other actors flubbed their lines. "During the filming of a scene, no matter who slips, it's always the star's fault," wrote the paper. Overall, *Page Miss Glory* and the attention that came from it were a feather in Marion's cap that she needed after a hard year.

In August 1935, however, an article in *New Theatre* zeroed in on Marion's relationship with Louella Parsons as it related to W.R. The journal, published by the left-wing New Theatre League, brought Marion down along with its attempt to weaken the power of the Hearst press and W.R.'s growing hostility toward Roosevelt. "Louella's chief function," wrote Joel Faith of the New Theatre, "is to ballyhoo Marion Davies, the blond girlfriend of her boss. Willie's greatest sorrow is that with all his money and power he has not been able to convince the American people that his bosom friend is an actress. Year after year the senile Sultan of San Simeon pours out his gold on more and more lavish streams trying to buy popularity for Marion. His chief aide in that attempted fraud is Louella. Thus Willie, Marion and Louella constitute the most powerful triumvirate in Hollywood."

If the article had been written two years earlier, Joel Faith might have had a point with his claim that W.R., Marion, and Louella Parsons constituted the most powerful triumvirate in Hollywood. But Louis B. Mayer had been right when he estimated that the Hearst press was not as potent as it had been when Cosmopolitan had joined MGM in 1924. Hearst's influence in the industry had significantly weakened by the time of the article's publication. Radio was an increasingly frequent method of getting information, made even more impactful by President Roosevelt's fireside chats. Marion made a concerted effort not to read her own publicity. When she did come across something, she was self-effacing and even agreed with her negative press. This was a method of self-defense, as much as it was extreme modesty. But she had been living with these kinds of statements for upward of a decade, and the inaccuracy of the information, along with the negative statements about Marion, surely made the barb sting even more.

Marion next began work on her second movie under her Warner Bros. contract, *Hearts Divided*, co-starring once more with Dick Powell. *Hearts Divided* was set during the Napoleonic era, with Marion playing Elizabeth "Betsy" Patterson, the wife of Napoleon's brother Jêrome. With many emotional scenes and plenty of comedy, the movie appeared to be headed toward success. Marion looked young and beautiful in her Napoleonic garb and hair that seemed more platinum with every passing movie. Marion and W.R. planned to leave for San Simeon as soon as filming was finished, but those plans were held up when Dick Powell came down with laryngitis and couldn't complete his final number. After several days of inactivity on *Hearts Divided*, Powell finally consulted with doctors to see what they could do. One put a tincture of silver on his vocal cords, allowing him to sing the final number and get Marion and W.R. off to San Simeon. However, Powell said that he developed a vocal cord nodule due to the silver, and couldn't sing for four months afterward.

The reviews were not what anyone had hoped. "Marion Davies is getting old and hard-looking," wrote one reviewer in Kentucky for the *Motion Picture Herald*. Another review read: "Cosmopolitan Productions knows full well that Miss Davies is no box office draw without a strong supporting cast, but in spite of that the picture is poor." W.R. countered the negative comments about Marion by making her next productions even more lavish and expensive. This was designed to highlight what he still believed was Marion's youthful beauty and charm. But Marion's career was fading, and she knew it.

In late 1935, Walter MacEwan, the executive assistant to Hal Wallis at Warner Bros., pitched a musical, *Cain and Mabel*, to producer Bob Lord, imagining it as a film for James Cagney and Ruby Keeler. But when the script ultimately ended up at Cosmopolitan, W.R. grabbed it for Marion. *Cain and Mabel* was a story by H.C. Witwer, by way of a 1926 play by Witwer and William Le Baron. In it, a young waitress named Mabel O'Dare decides to become an actress after losing her day job. When the play flops, a cunning publicity man cooks up a romance between her and Larry Cain, the most popular boxer in town, played by Clark Gable. The film gives Marion a rare opportunity to show off her dancing. The slight weight gain due to her alcoholism did not affect Marion's abilities, and she remained quite skilled.

Marion began filming *Cain and Mabel* in June 1936, just after the release of *Hearts Divided*. Hearst had borrowed Clark Gable from MGM for the production, an expensive move. But the success of Marion's prior teaming with him in *Polly of the Circus* four years earlier, as well as Gable's superstar power that he had since attained, would hopefully ensure *Cain and Mabel*'s success. Hearst planned to exceed even his own standards in terms of sets, costumes, and scenery. *Cain and Mabel* was to be shot on Stage 7 at Warner Bros., and Hearst ordered the soundstage raised a whopping thirty-one feet in the air in order to accommodate the grand production number, "I'll Sing You a Thousand Love Songs." An employee in the grip department, Champ Milaman, was one of the workers who helped make the new stage a reality. They dug below the stage, placing hundreds of hand jacks underneath the building's foundation to crank it thirty feet toward the sky. "A guy would blow a whistle and everybody would take a turn, pull one turn on the jack," he remembered. The building rose to ninety-eight feet, and today, Stage 7 (now renamed Stage 16) is still considered to be the tallest purpose-built soundstage in the world. The seam on the side, where the new bottom from 1936 joins with the old top, is still visible.

The musical numbers were directed by Bobby Connolly, who later choreographed *Broadway Melody of 1940* and *For Me and My Gal* (1942). Connolly's signature choreography can be seen in the delightful "Coney Island" number, where Marion and Sammy White dance their way through the wax museum and encounter historical figures there.

W.R., who for a time had backed off Marion and allowed her more artistic freedom in her roles, was now reverting to his controlling ways. When *Cain and Mabel* had its preview in late 1936, W.R. wrote to Jack Warner to complain that Marion's character used what he deemed to be "unnecessary slang." Jack Warner wrote back apologetically, and the comedic tone of the movie was scaled back. To compound W.R.'s demands, the Motion Picture Production Code had been strengthened in 1934, and was at its height in 1936. A strict censorship office had emerged under Joseph Breen, Will Hays's replacement at the production office, and Hollywood was scrambling to comply. Several letters from Breen arrived at the studio, objecting to script content in *Cain and Mabel*. He also cautioned against certain scenes that might prove to be problematic to the film. The line "I'm surprised you don't speak with a lisp" was considered objectionable because of the gay implications, and Breen urged caution when filming a dressing room scene that Breen thought would have potential to expose Marion's body. Reading the letters brings to mind the kind of eye through which the censorship office had to look at these scripts—a mind perpetually thinking in double entendre, seemingly contrary to the beliefs of the Motion Picture Production Code office. But ultimately, the film was deemed acceptable.

Even after all these years, W.R. was suspicious of Marion and overly worried about her flirtatious nature. Guarding the set of *Cain and Mabel* were two policemen who had been given explicit instructions by W.R. to let only approved people onto the stage. One day Harry Warren, the composer of *Cain and Mabel*'s songs, and the lyricist Al Dubin had been called to the set but refused entry by the guards. Frustrated, they returned to Warren's bungalow and received a call from W.R. "Where are you guys? Come on over!" They returned, only to be sent back to the bungalow again. When the phone rang a second time, Warren answered angrily, "You go screw yourself! If you want us, you better tell those two cops to leave, or we're not coming any more!"

The filming took place during one of the most intense heat waves in U.S. history in the summer of 1936. The grand production number, "I'll Sing You a Thousand Love Songs," was filmed in July, the most sweltering month. Because the soundstage had been lifted thirty feet in the air, the temperature in the rafters was even higher. At one point, Marion cut the scene, and yelled to the men that they should take off their shirts to try to cool down. Thus, much of the number was orchestrated by shirtless men in the rafters.

The heat wave in the summer of 1936 exacerbated conditions in a country still suffering from the effects of the Depression. A severe drought spanned the continent, and dust covered the croplands from Texas to Nebraska, contributing to massive migration from the Dust Bowl region. Agricultural workers flocked to California, which had been spared the devastation of the Dust Bowl but suffered under the miserable heat of this unprecedented weather event.

Once *Cain and Mabel* was officially finished, in August of 1936 Marion and W.R. traveled to Europe again in grand style. They sailed with a party of family and friends that included George Hearst, Patricia, the actor Arthur Lake (of *Blondie* fame), the actress Mary Carlisle, and, as always, Gandhi the dachshund. They landed first in Naples, where they were met by the editor of the *New York Journal*, Arthur Brisbane, and by Alice Head when they reached Rome a few days later. After sightseeing for several days, they spent the night at Villa Madama, the home of Countess Dorothy di Frasso that overlooked the Tiber River. There, at Villa Madama high above the sights of Rome, they had dinner with high-ranking Italian ministers, including Mussolini's son-in-law Count Galeazzo Ciano, who was also the newly elected foreign minister.

Italy's victory in the Second Abyssinian War in May 1936 meant they occupied the territory now known as Ethiopia, and its citizens were subjugated to the rule of Mussolini. Marion's inherent pacifism was angered by the war in Ethiopia, a country with a tiny military that was no match for the vast Italian army. As Count Ciano attempted to make small talk, Marion had her mind on Italian politics.

"I would love to visit Hollywood," the count said to Marion. "I've heard so much about it."

Marion had no interest in being polite when sitting next to the person who had engineered war against the Ethiopian people. She got straight to the point. "What are you doing to the Abyssinians?" she asked. The rest of the party waited on bated breath to see how the count would respond to such a brazenly blunt question. According to Alice Head, Arthur Brisbane was especially petrified that such a question could lead to international repercussions. But Count Ciano, it seemed, had been so taken by Marion's charm throughout the evening that he engaged with her questions. The group relaxed, and Count Ciano's reaction soothed Arthur Brisbane's fears.

The group spent several days in Rome, visiting the Vatican, St. Peter's Square, the Pantheon, and the Church of Santa Maria sopra Minerva. Afternoons were spent at the Tivoli Gardens. Soon, the heat became unbearable, and they ventured north to Florence and Venice. After Italy, the group went on to Lucerne and Munich and by the time the trip ended in October, the party had been in Europe for three months. Marion was typically magnanimous throughout the trip. In a shop window in Italy, Mary Carlisle admired two handmade nightgowns that the shop didn't have in her size or in the color she wanted. The shop was closing, and there was no time to put in an order. She sadly gave up on the opportunity to have the nightgowns, but the next morning when she awoke, she found those same two nightgowns, in her size and in the color she wanted, waiting for her at the front desk of the hotel. After they had gotten back to the hotel, Marion had put in an order with the store's seamstress to sew the nightgown in Mary's size by morning, as a special gift.

"You have to have money, of course, to do things like that," Mary Carlisle recalled. "But there are lots of people who have millions, and who wouldn't give you ten cents. But Marion was a giver. I was lucky to know her."

The group became sad and nostalgic when it was time to leave, wondering when they would all see each other next. Marion, with her usual flair for cheering people up, exclaimed brightly, "Don't worry! We'll be over for the wedding. Maybe we'll be bridesmaids." Marion's casual mention of a wedding took the group by surprise. "What wedding?" asked Alice Head. There were no impending marriages in the present company, though Marion's niece Patricia was starting to become involved with Arthur Lake (they would marry at San Simeon the next year, in 1937). But there were no wedding plans yet.

It turned out that during the trip to Europe, when everyone except W.R. was blissfully ignorant of things going on in the news, King Edward had abdicated the British throne with the intent of marrying divorced American commoner Wallis Simpson. A relationship shunned by the British royal family, Edward had been faced with the choice of abdicating the throne or giving up Wallis. He chose to give up the throne and marry. W.R., for his part, was also fascinated by the story of Wallis Simpson. He spared nothing in publicizing the upcoming marriage in his papers.

Domestically, W.R. was concerned about the election. While he had disagreements with Roosevelt from the start, W.R.'s feelings had evolved to enthusiastic support by 1934, and then to outright hostility in 1935 when the National Recovery Administration wanted the publishing industry to set its own regulations on minimum wages and maximum hours. W.R. believed this action curtailed the freedom of the press, and he further balked at the "wealth tax" that came with Roosevelt's Revenue Act of 1935. This cut to the core of W.R.'s belief system—he had spent his life advocating for governmental regulation and the rights of the worker, but when it came to his own industry, he couldn't abide those stances. W.R.'s conservatism began to affect Marion's social life among politically active Democrats, many of whom she counted as close friends. One was Carole Lombard, who remained a close friend and frequent guest at San Simeon and the Beach House. Marion also liked and wanted to be close to Myrna Loy, but Loy could not bring herself to accept an invitation to San Simeon. She loved Marion and called her a "sweet soul," but "my politics and Hearst's simply didn't mix," she wrote.

Despite W.R.'s very public objections to Roosevelt's reelection, he won again in a landslide against Governor Alf Landon of Kansas. Roosevelt was inaugurated for his second term on January 20, 1937, the first time a president was inaugurated in January rather than March.

From the mid-1930s, the relationship between Roosevelt and Hearst became increasingly contentious, to the point where Secretary of the Treasury Henry Morgenthau explored looking into Hearst's taxes, as well as Marion's, to see if he could find something incriminating. While Morgenthau found that there was "plenty there" to investigate, he ultimately decided it was better for the administration not to do it. Part of the decision may have been directly related to Marion. She had developed a great fondness for the Roosevelt family personally, and became especially close with his daughter Anna in ensuing years. The Hearst newspapers ran scathing articles about Roosevelt, and prominent Hearst writer Westbrook Pegler, known for his "poison pen" and assaults on those with whom he disagreed, particularly went after Eleanor Roosevelt beginning in the early 1940s. Marion was disgusted by his writing. She would denounce Pegler's attacks on the First Lady, in which he insulted her looks and her voice, calling her "La Boca Grande" ("the big mouth"). Marion found this appalling and offensive. "What did Mrs. Roosevelt ever do to him?"

For W.R.'s seventy-fourth birthday in April 1937, five hundred guests were invited to the Beach House for a celebration in the theme of "The Greatest Show on Earth." In a sense it was fitting and symbolic—the theatrical sensibility of W.R.'s life and career in yellow journalism and the movies was perhaps best summed up by a circus, the larger-than-life magnification of real life reflecting his own unique reality.

A carousel was borrowed from Warner Bros., and Marion cleared the tennis court to accommodate the guests. Among the attendees were Irene Dunne, Carole Lombard and Clark Gable (who had recently begun dating), Claudette Colbert, and Louella Parsons. Marion had installed an air machine in the floor to blow skirts up, in the style of a boardwalk carnival. Marion's sisters and Patricia were also there, dressed in circus outfits, and Frances Marion came as a fortune teller. Marion's creativity shone in the preparation of this party—a cake was rolled out in the shape of a circus tent, and dozens of balloons fell from the ceiling along with a large banner that unfolded to read "HAPPY BIRTHDAY."

Marion's joy is palpable in photographs and footage from the party. On the carousel, Marion was photographed in a state of pure happiness, smiling and yelling with glee. W.R., too, seemed carefree as he enjoyed the celebration. It was, in some ways, the last hurrah of the life they had lived for the past decade at the Beach House.

The year 1937 was a frightening one for the Hearst enterprises. While he had been spared the ravages of the Depression, W.R. had spent himself into the ground on antiques and architecture. San Simeon was expensive and time-consuming to maintain, and he couldn't seem to stop building. He sought advice and financial counsel from trusted and high-power friends, including Joseph P. Kennedy and Judge Clarence J. Shearn, an attorney from his New York political days. Kennedy lowballed a $14 million offer for the Hearst magazines, wanting to take advantage of the situation for his own gain, but it was rejected, and the Hearst holdings remained in dire straits throughout 1937. He began selling possessions frantically and stopped all pending projects on San Simeon. The zoo was dramatically reduced in size, with animals being sold or given to other local zoos.

Compounding these financial issues was the continued slowdown of Marion's career. *Boy Meets Girl* could not be released until 1938 due to legal complications with the original play, so production on it was postponed indefinitely. Meanwhile, she was cast alongside Robert Montgomery in what looked to be another standard Marion Davies vehicle, *Ever Since Eve*. In the film, Marion plays a young secretary who is out of a job, but her beauty is a hindrance whenever she applies for one. She dresses down, and lands a job as the secretary to a novel writer (Robert Montgomery). It was standard mid-1930s fare, but it gave Marion a chance to show that she still had her beauty, her acting skills, and her knack for comedy.

It had been five years since Marion had last worked with Robert Montgomery. She enjoyed working with him, and since their last teaming, Montgomery and his wife, Elizabeth Allan, had welcomed a daughter, Elizabeth. Marion always took a special interest in her friends' children, and delighted in giving them gifts and trinkets.

In spite of the pleasant time she had during filming with Montgomery, reviews were poor when *Ever Since Eve* had its premiere in June 1937. "Marion Davies and Robert Montgomery…provide summer entertainment in a picture of no importance," noted *Picture Play* in its review. Frank S. Nugent of the *New York Times* wrote that Marion had been playing the ingenue for "more years than it would be polite to mention." He went on to say that the plot had been followed by "hacks ever since Adam wrote the first farce," and that the movie was so bad that it had to be one of the year's worst.

In the wake of the disappointing reviews for *Ever Since Eve*, Warner Bros. decided that Marion should not go through with *Boy Meets Girl*. On November 29, she got behind a microphone again to do a radio version of *Peg O' My Heart* with Brian Aherne for Lux Radio Theatre, and to discuss what was next in her career. She discusses her future in films and the possibility of doing *Pygmalion* with George Bernard Shaw. Shaw had even gone so far as to send Marion an annotated script, instructing her on how she should play the part of Eliza Doolittle. "I greatly admire George Bernard Shaw," Marion said to host Cecil B. DeMille, "and I'd love to do Pygmalion. But Warner Bros. has the first claim on my services." But, she went on to say, she was cutting back on movies. "I think that you, Mr. DeMille, have the right idea. Just make one good picture a year." With this statement, Marion acknowledges that the possibilities are dwindling for her, and that her time in films is coming to an end.

In a way, it was fortuitous timing. She enjoyed her work in films and was proud of it, but with the Hearst finances in dire straits and W.R. getting on in years, she made the conscious decision to leave her career behind. The decision to retire was made consciously, with thoughtful deliberation, and seemingly without regret. *Ever Since Eve* would be her final film. Through hard work and determination, she had survived eight years of sound while battling her stutter, and now, as the "captain of her soul" she always considered herself to be, she could retire on her own terms. W.R. moved Cosmopolitan Productions to Twentieth Century Fox, where it would continue operations for the next two years, and the bungalow was moved as well. Ultimately, when Cosmopolitan parted ways with Twentieth Century Fox for good, the bungalow ended up at 910 Benedict Canyon Drive, a new Beverly Hills home that Marion was sharing among her family members.

Marion's niece Patricia married the young *Blondie* actor Arthur Lake at San Simeon on July 25, 1937. Patricia was very young, having just turned 18 the previous month, but had already made the news with several relationships with prominent socialites in Los Angeles. She and Arthur Lake had known each other for at least a year, when they went to Europe with Marion and W.R. in 1936. At Patricia's wedding, Rose was the matron of honor and Marion was the maid of honor, reflecting Patricia's deep connection to her aunt Marion.

Between late 1937 and 1938, Marion and W.R. decided to keep costs down by splitting their time between San Simeon and Wyntoon. Wyntoon was significantly cheaper to maintain than San Simeon or the Beach House, and they would keep Wyntoon as a base for the next several years while the Hearst empire attempted to recover from its financial hardship.

In January 1938, just a few months following her quiet retirement from films, Marion received a confirmation of just how much she had meant to the filmgoing public. Clark Alvord, a former Nevada miner turned shopkeeper who had been a Marion Davies fan for years, died in Las Vegas with no heirs. He and Marion had never met, but had sent a few letters back and forth and when Marion heard of his death, she sent two floral pieces to Las Vegas with instructions that they were to be placed on Alvord's grave, attaching a note: "With deepest sympathy, Marion Davies."

When Alvord's will was read, Marion was shocked to receive notification that Alvord had written, "I give and bequeath to my beloved Marion Davies all my property, both real and personal." The sum totaled $10,000. Marion felt she couldn't keep the money, and she told newspapers she would probably give it to some charity in Alvord's name. She ultimately decided that the best way to honor Alvord's memory was to donate it to a Las Vegas charity, and in keeping with Marion's interest in medical issues, she chose to sponsor a bed in a Las Vegas hospital charity ward.

The year 1938 was a turning point in Marion and W.R.'s life together. With her retirement and his money problems, there seemed to be little need or desire for the lavish parties that defined their earlier life at the Beach House and San Simeon. The final Beach House birthday party was on April 30 of that year, with an Early American theme. Now 41 and with her working life behind her, Marion relaxed by sewing, embroidering, and quilting, and enjoyed the calm and quiet of family and close friends. She kept busy with the Marion Davies Children's Clinic and various social functions, and gave an appreciation dinner for the doctors of the clinic in December 1938.

Earlier in 1938, on February 24, Marion and W.R. were at San Simeon to host Terence Conyngham, Sixth Baron Plunket, and his wife, Dorothé Mabel Barnato, Lady Plunket and the Seventh Marquess of Londonderry, on their visit to California. Lady Plunket was the daughter of the actress Fannie Ward, whom Marion had known from her early days at the 127th Street studio in New York. W.R. had sent his plane down to Los Angeles to pick them up, and Marion was having a quiet day at San Simeon with her friend Dorothy Mackaill as they waited for the arrival of the Plunkets. She and Dorothy had bet on a horse at Santa Anita on which they wanted to check the results. They picked up the phone to dial the racetrack, when they heard a male voice on the other end: "Dammit, get off the phone!" Startled and slightly annoyed at the interruption, Dorothy and Marion instead went outside to meet the plane that they knew would be arriving any minute. When they stepped out of the house, they saw a sea of fog surrounding the plane field. All of a sudden, black smoke began billowing through it. "My god, Marion," said Dorothy Mackaill, "the plane's down!" Marion ran back inside to W.R.'s office. "The plane's down!" she screamed. W.R. leapt up. "You don't know what you're talking about!" he yelled in panic, as he rushed out of his office following Marion and Dorothy Mackaill. When they got back outside, the fog had rolled out, revealing the smoldering plane. As it turned out, the pilot had sent a trainee, who didn't know the geography or weather of the area, the short distance to pick up Lord and Lady Plunket. It was important for the plane to leave Los Angeles on time, because the fog would roll into the San Simeon area very quickly, reducing visibility, and roll back out shortly thereafter. The plane had left Los Angeles an hour late, and when Marion picked up the phone to check on the horse, the pilot had been trying to communicate to the plane to detour to Santa Maria. The pilot didn't hear the instruction in time, and upon trying to turn back, the plane crashed and burst into flames, killing Lord and Lady Plunket instantly. The pilot, T.J. "Tex" Phillips, also died in the crash. The only survivor was the Plunkets' traveling companion, Jack Lawrence, who suffered burns and a broken ankle.

Already overly sensitive to death, Marion suffered tremendously after the incident and always felt guilty, as though she had been directly responsible for the accident. She sank into a deep depression. "Marion Davies went out of her head, completely, for 48 hours," Dorothy remembered. Her near mutism returned as it did when she was in a heightened emotional state, and while Marion claimed that she made the phone call to Lady Plunket's mother Fannie Ward, Dorothy said she had been unable to.

Back at home in Beverly Hills, Reine was not doing well. Marion's eldest sister was now nearing her fifty-third birthday, and since her daughter Pepi's death three years earlier, her health had been in decline. She took to her bed in late March, and on April 2, Reine died at her home from an undisclosed illness. Funeral services were conducted three days later and Reine was interred in the family mausoleum, the third burial in as many years.

"What Difference Does It Make If You Walk Up to the Altar?"

The 1930s had been challenging for many Hollywood stars, leading to the retirement of most of Marion's co-stars from the silent era. For some, the pressures and stresses of the new era had even led to their deaths. Karl Dane, a co-star of Marion's in *The Red Mill* and a big star in silent Hollywood, spoke limited English and couldn't rid himself of his thick Danish accent, which destroyed his career when sound came in. His source of income stopped, and he spent the rest of his life living penny to penny on loans from friends, before committing suicide in 1934.

Constance and Norma Talmadge, frequent guests at San Simeon and friends of Marion's since *Zander the Great*, had invested wisely and retired when sound came in. Their voices would not have registered well onscreen, they felt, and Constance left the industry almost immediately. After some time trying to perfect the timbre of her voice to preserve her career, Norma also decided not to take the risk.

John Gilbert was a prominent, and tragic, casualty of the coming of sound. When King Vidor and Eleanor Boardman were married at Marion's Lexington Road home, it had been planned as a double wedding alongside Gilbert and Greta Garbo. According to John Gilbert's daughter, the film historian Leatrice Gilbert Fountain, at the time that the wedding was supposed to start, everyone was at the house except Greta Garbo. King and Eleanor, sympathetic to Gilbert's plight, stalled as long as they could. Champagne was served, and still no Garbo. Wedding photos were taken, and still no Garbo. Finally, the priest said that he had to get started, because he had other engagements that evening. King and Eleanor had their wedding, and John Gilbert was left in the dust.

According to Fountain, Louis B. Mayer, who had never been fond of John

Gilbert as a person, came up behind him and hit him on the back. A crude remark about Gilbert's character made all the anger boil up in him. He lost his cool, suddenly grabbing Mayer by the neck and slamming his head against the tile in the wall, sending Mayer's glasses flying into the air. Eddie Mannix heard the scuffle and ran into the room, retrieving Mayer's glasses and pushing Gilbert out into the hall. He brought a towel in to wipe Mayer's face, but Mayer pushed it away and rose from the wall like a cobra. "Gilbert," he hissed, "you're through. I'll destroy you if it costs me a million dollars."

When talkies came in, Gilbert received consistently poor scripts and experienced a steep decline in his popularity. He became anxious about his future in the industry, and his dependence on alcohol intensified. In 1933, he starred in his most successful talkie, *Queen Christina*, alongside Greta Garbo. Garbo's name appeared above the title, but Gilbert's was below. He retired in 1934 and died of alcoholism in 1936.

Charlie Chaplin stubbornly persisted in making silent films into the 1930s. They continued to bring him critical and financial success, and he held tight to the idea that silent film would become the industry standard again. In 1930, while filming *City Lights*, leading lady Virginia Cherrill made too many mistakes for the perfectionist Chaplin, and he fired her from the production when she was late to the set one afternoon. Upon hearing the news, Marion invited her to San Simeon for a vacation. She knew Chaplin too well to believe he would let Cherrill stay away for long. Cherrill celebrated her twenty-first birthday at San Simeon and Marion assuaged her fears.

"You're not really fired," Marion told her. "Charlie'll have you back because he'll never waste all that film." Eventually, Chaplin did become impatient, tracked her down at San Simeon, and accused Cherrill of intentionally missing work in an angry phone call, which she took with Marion in the room.

"You remember—you fired me," Cherrill told him.

Chaplin was adamant. "Come back down here, behave yourself, get back to work."

"Wait a minute," Marion interrupted, speaking to Cherrill. "You had your twenty-first birthday up here. Your contract's no good. You can get more money."

"How much shall I ask for?"

"At least double."

Cherrill's salary had been $75 per week. She spoke into the phone again, and explained that she was now of age and her prior contract was invalid. Cherrill demanded $150 per week for the rest of the film if she were to return.

Chaplin initially balked at the demand, but upon discussion with his lawyer, he agreed to negotiate. Cherrill soon left for Los Angeles, where she bargained a new contract and finished the film at $150 per week.

William Haines's career at MGM had ended in 1933. Louis B. Mayer had been telling him for some time that he needed to marry a woman, to quell the rumors about his sexuality. Haines refused, the relationship with Mayer deteriorated, and he left the studio for good to spend the rest of his life with his longtime companion, Jimmy Shields.

Billy was at a loss as to what he should do next, and W.R. had a suggestion. Billy had always shown a particular interest in W.R.'s antiques when he visited San Simeon, and W.R. considered him to have a natural talent.

"Why don't you try your hand at decorating?" W.R. suggested. The idea appealed to Billy, and he opened an interior design studio shortly thereafter, which turned into a fulfilling and lucrative business. He became one of the most sought-after decorators in the Los Angeles area, and he counted many A-list stars as his clients, Marion included.

In June of 1936, Billy and Jimmy Shields were targets of an anti-gay hate crime. A mob of about a hundred people attacked them on a beach outside a home they had rented in El Porto, California, as they were relaxing together. Marion was horrified and spent a great deal of time pressing the Hearst newspapers to push for prosecution of the criminals to the full extent of the law. She only relented in her crusade when Billy and Jimmy told her to stop, saying that they didn't want to give the criminals any further publicity.

Marion's friend from the chorus, Justine Johnstone, tired of the stage and changed career paths to go into medicine. Her husband, Walter Wanger, had fallen ill in 1927, and Justine decided to take some science courses at Columbia University to better understand her husband's condition. Her work awed her professors, and she became a noted researcher who revolutionized treatments for shock and discovered that cryogenic therapy could kill some cancer cells. By 1938 she had moved back to Los Angeles, and on many occasions served as a trusted personal medical advisor to Marion.

Mary Pickford also retired from the screen shortly after sound came in, despite having won an Oscar for her first talkie, *Coquette*. Because many stars felt that the silent era dated them, they barely spoke of their time in silents. Marion had been among the last holdouts from the silent era, and when she did have people over to watch something, the early films in her collection would rarely be shown, even to her own family.

During the early months of 1938, Hearst holdings had been liquidated at an astonishing rate. Auctions of art, rare books, and silver brought in several hundred thousand dollars, but still not enough to bring the organization out of the red. Building at San Simeon was ordered to stop in mid-1938. Marion was aware of all this and became increasingly concerned as the months wore on. She listened at the door to important meetings with executives, sometimes with friends who had come up to keep her company. From these closed-door meetings, Marion got the impression that the Hearst empire was on the edge of financial ruin. She learned that the Hearst enterprises were unable to pay their quarterly dividend due in June, and that several newspapers were failing and would likely fold if the money didn't appear quickly.

At this point, W.R. started working with Joseph P. Kennedy again. As a former bank examiner, Kennedy was always eager to help organize people's books, and he jumped at the opportunity to gain some personal advantage from W.R.'s troubles. He suggested that W.R. sell bonds linked to his real estate properties to bring the empire to solvency. But ironically, Kennedy's own Securities and Exchange Commission mandates, from his time as chairman of the SEC, made his recommendations illegal.

Marion wanted to help. She could afford it, she thought. Her jewelry alone would at least make a dent in the corporation's debts. Marion never particularly cared for jewelry, rarely wore it except on special occasions, and even then, just a piece or two as an accessory. Her ties to her humble roots were anathema to W.R.'s lavish living, and she felt little connection to the gifts and jewels that had been bestowed on her over the years, except for sentimental reasons. On June 24, 1938, a telegram arrived at Roach and Driver's jewelry store in Los Angeles. "Marion is returning to you by express a gold necklace mounted with rubies and diamonds," read the telegram. "Kindly acknowledge receipt and oblige." Through a series of actions like this, selling jewels and using others as collateral to obtain loans, as well as selling stocks and real estate, Marion was able to come to W.R. within forty-eight hours and hand him a check for $1 million.

W.R. was shocked and declined immediately. But when he spoke to the board about what had happened, the members urged him to accept Marion's offer. W.R. finally came around and accepted, on the condition that Marion was to be given adequate collateral and be paid back. He approached Marion with these conditions, and Marion refused. She wanted to give the money outright, no strings attached, because she felt that the Hearst enterprises were responsible for her own financial security. But the board had insisted, and while W.R. wanted to give Marion the entire Hearst Magazine group,

Marion also refused that. She was finally convinced, under pressure, to take two weak Boston papers, the *Daily Record* and the *Evening American*, as collateral, the closest she could get to making a gift of the money. The decision was made by the board that Marion would be paid back at a rate of $100,000 every four months, which ended up being far too slow for W.R. "At this rate," he wrote in a letter to Judge Clarence J. Shearn a year later, "it will take her more [than] two years to get her money back." Irritated by how slowly Marion was being repaid, he expressed his sentiment that it should be $50,000 every month. Marion was still upset that she was being paid back at all. Her contribution, combined with loans from journalist Cissy Patterson and John D. Rockefeller Jr.'s wife Abby, was enough to bring the Hearst empire to solvency.

Like many in Marion's life, W.R. had taken her selflessness for granted. In his frequent blindness to others' perspectives, he had neglected to see just how much he had let her down. The one thing she truly wanted from W.R. was something he couldn't give her. For the first time in his life, W.R. became aware of this to the point that he began to take steps to make their relationship legitimate in the eyes of society.

W.R. had been trying for years to get Millicent to agree to a divorce. Millicent was a socialite by nature, enjoying her associations with high New York society. She had established a firm footing in that world due to her marriage and was considered a hostess of the highest order. Her status as the wife of William Randolph Hearst gave her a sense of purpose and an unequaled social position. She was not about to give that up, though "he tried very hard," as Marion would say in 1953. According to Stanley Flink, who heard the story from the composer and screenwriter Harry Ruby (married to Marion's good friend Eileen Percy), around the time of Marion's contribution to the Hearst enterprises, W.R. managed to get Millicent to agree to a divorce in exchange for several Hearst newspapers and magazines. Plans came together quickly, and Marion and W.R. had to scramble to get their things together and fly down to Mexico. Divorce in Mexico was quicker and easier, and many Americans took advantage of the process. With Harry Ruby and Eileen Percy in tow to act as witnesses, Marion and W.R., along with forty other friends, flew down to W.R.'s vast Babicora Ranch in Chihuahua, Mexico. They had found a "fallen" Mexican priest, one who didn't entirely follow the teachings of the Catholic church, willing to marry them once the divorce became final, which was to happen within days.

At the last minute, a message from Millicent came through to the ranch.

She had amended the divorce agreement to include the magazine *Cosmopolitan*, and if W.R. refused to honor the amended agreement, there would be no divorce. W.R. found himself in a serious dilemma. *Cosmopolitan* was his favorite magazine. Up to now, he had been able to live with his private and public spheres entirely separate. His two-sided personality was, to this point, unchallenged; he could be one person in his business dealings, another in his private life. A choice between *Cosmopolitan* and marriage with Marion was inconceivable to him. *Cosmopolitan* existed in his public life, his relationship with Marion existed in his private life. The two were not supposed to mix, but here they were. Any decision he could make threatened to destroy the other side of his life, and both choices were equally devastating. He was unable to reconcile this dilemma, and ultimately, he chose not to honor Millicent's amended divorce agreement so he could keep *Cosmopolitan*. The divorce and subsequent marriage were called off.

Marion's heart was irreparably broken. Marion, W.R., Eileen Percy, and Harry Ruby flew home to Wyntoon, a sad and pensive trip. Shortly after their arrival, it was discovered that Marion had disappeared from the property. In those days, there were few opportunities for shelter outside of the Hearst estate in rural northern California. Where Marion went, and how she survived during her disappearance, is unknown. But when she was finally located a week later, she was discovered to have been on a severe alcoholic bender.

Despite the *entente* that existed among Marion, Millicent, and W.R., there had always been pain. When Millicent came to California to visit, Marion left for a different residence, with no outward complaint but surely experiencing pangs of emotional distress. Once, Billy Haines remembered, Marion and W.R. were entertaining a group of people for a weekend and W.R. was called to the phone during lunch. He left the group to take the call, and the guests heard his end of the conversation. It grew increasingly argumentative. "If you come here, Millicent," W.R. declared, "there won't be one servant left on the hill." With that, he slammed down the phone and returned to the table, as white as a sheet. "We are packing and leaving," he said to Marion. A caravan of automobiles arrived, and everyone on the hill got in a car, their luggage packed for them, and headed to San Luis Obispo to catch the train back to Los Angeles.

Marion's internal strength and stamina had served her well up to this point. She had been able to mask the extent of her suffering for the benefit of those around her, from the time she and W.R. first got together. But the cancellation of the marriage in Mexico caused her to snap. This event marked a turning point for Marion. She began to admit to herself that a divorce would never happen. Yet despite the impossibility of marriage, leaving was inconceivable to her. "He knew I had no intentions of ever getting married to anybody, because he knew I was in love with him," Marion remembered. Reflecting on this inevitability, she once again downplayed her feelings. "Love comes from the heart," she said. "What difference does it make if you walk up to the altar, and they say 'you are now man and wife?' Does that make love any more potent? No, it doesn't. It doesn't make any difference." But privately, her friends saw through her words, and recognized her true pain. And for the rest of Marion's life, her problems with alcohol were more severe than they had ever been.

In mid-September of 1938, still reeling from the events in Mexico and Reine's death earlier in the year, Marion managed to rally. She held a grand tea at the Beach House for the women of the American Legion, female veterans of World War I. It was their twentieth annual convention, and eight hundred women attended, as well as Marion's friends Norma Shearer, Mary Carlisle, and her niece Patricia, now 19 years old and just past her first wedding anniversary with Arthur Lake. There is a sadness evident in Marion in the footage from the party. She looks somewhat tired, nowhere near as vivacious as she had been in the past, and she moves slowly. At times, she seems distracted, even surrounded by the servicewomen and the neighbors and friends who had come for the party.

The women entered the Beach House and sat down to tea, with Marion making the rounds through the crowd talking to people and signing autographs. Afterward, Marion was presented with a certificate of appreciation for her kindness that read: "In sincere appreciation for her hospitality and generosity, in acting as our hostess and sponsor of the 20th National American Legion Convention Tea for Ex-Service Women at Santa Monica Beach." When she accepted it, Marion's speech was halted as she tried to keep her stutter as undetectable as possible. For the cameras present, Marion tried her acceptance once more, and this time managed with fewer halts and pauses. She smiled triumphantly when she made it through.

The global political situation was worsening by the day. The Anschluss occurred on March 12, 1938, establishing the German occupation of Austria. Votes had been manipulated to show that 99 percent of Austria's citizens wanted German occupation. Jews and Roma had not been allowed to vote. Adolf Hitler next set his sights on a German-speaking part of Czechoslovakia, the Sudetenland, which under the Treaty of Saint-Germain had been incorporated as part of Czechoslovakia. The Sudetenland was ceded to Hitler at the Munich Conference in September, since Britain believed it to be his final design on Europe to create a unified German-speaking state.

By October 1938, the occupation had begun. Isolationists pressed President Roosevelt to stay out of the impending conflict in Europe, and W.R. fell squarely into that camp. Parliament backbencher Winston Churchill, who still had enormous influence on British politics, was a particular target. On October 5, 1938, Churchill gave a stirring radio address to the United States, asking them to join with England and France to defeat Germany's growing aggression. Believing this to be an attempt to lure the United States into war, W.R. replied that "English propaganda is again flooding the United States," in his own radio "reply" from San Simeon.

Marion's political stance at this point was less staunch. Although she agreed that "foreign entanglements" were bad for the United States as of 1938, she busied herself more with California politics. Through her friend Irene Castle, the dancer she had known and loved since her days in *The Sunshine Girl*, Marion became interested in the fight against vivisection. Her compassion for animals had always been a driving force in Marion's life, and when she heard of the work Irene Castle was doing against animal testing in medical laboratories, she wanted to be involved. Marion's powerful microphone would be a boon to the cause if she could get W.R. on board with the movement, spreading the word through the power of the Hearst press. It was not difficult to do. W.R. shared a fondness for animals, as evidenced by the dachshunds and his private zoo at San Simeon (though caring for them appropriately was a separate matter), and Marion easily convinced W.R. to join the anti-vivisection fight. From Wyntoon, W.R. and Marion wired editors of Hearst papers around the country to write articles decrying the use of animals in medical testing. Throughout the midterm election year of 1938, articles and editorials appeared in Hearst papers enthusiastically supporting California's Proposition 2, which would allow for state regulation of animal pounds, prohibiting them from selling dogs and cats to medical laboratories. Testimonials from pet owners and animal welfare experts dominated the pages of Hearst papers in California before the election, showing graphic photos of animals in laboratories and accusing those who were against the proposition of misleading the public. Shortly before the election, *Life* magazine (a competitor of the Hearst papers) ran a scathing opinion of the Hearst papers' efforts against vivisection and showed a photo of Marion with the caption "Actress Marion Davies is the Most Powerful Anti-Vivisectionist

Through Publisher Friend William Randolph Hearst." Despite their best efforts, Proposition 2 was defeated on the 1938 ballot. It was a devastating outcome, and both Marion and W.R. remained ardent anti-vivisectionists to the end of their lives. "They should discover an easier way," Marion later said about medical testing on animals, "because I wouldn't want to be bound down like that with my mouth open and have them cut me open, even if I were a rat."

In September of 1939, Hitler invaded Poland, bringing the United Kingdom to its ally's defense, and World War II began. The following year was an election year for the United States, and by July of 1940, it was clear that Franklin D. Roosevelt was going to be the incumbent nominee once more, making history by being the only president to hold three terms in office. On July 18, he was officially nominated at the Democratic National Convention in Chicago. Those concerned about the war raging in Europe rejoiced at the nomination. If Roosevelt won, the United States would soon do its part to end the war in Europe—he had already taken steps to help the British in their fight against the Axis forces.

On the same day as Roosevelt's nomination, Marion's beloved sister Ethel died at home in Beverly Hills. She had been entertaining guests and was suddenly "stricken" with something. Ethel went upstairs, and shortly thereafter her body was discovered by Kay English, the companion and ex-Follies girl that she had been living with for several years. Her death was reported in the press as having been from a heart attack, but the true cause remains unclear.

Marion and W.R. made their way from Wyntoon to Los Angeles upon hearing the news of Ethel's death and stayed there for the funeral, which took place on the following Tuesday. Ethel had always been Marion's favorite sister, and as young women, they bore an amazing family resemblance, more than any of the sisters. In some early photos, Marion and Ethel could have passed for twins. And with her bawdy humor and flair for shocking people, Ethel delighted Marion and, in many ways, molded her own vivacious personality.

The family mausoleum now held a growing number of family members—Mama Rose, Papa Ben, Reine, Ethel, Pepi, and George Lederer's son Maitland, who had died from the effects of his Addison's disease in 1934. With Ethel gone, only Rose and Marion were left—and the sisters clung to each other while simultaneously struggling with their own difficulties. Like her sister, Rose's dependency on alcohol increased in times of stress. Where Marion was generally calm and her generosity expanded, Rose became violent and rageful. The two fought about Rose's loud and forward behavior, which Marion found distasteful. Rose would respond with attacks that cut to the bone. "You'll never have a wedding ring on your finger!" she once screamed at Marion in a rage. With the family shrinking fast, Marion's sisterly relationship with Rose became even more precious, regardless of the abuse Rose was capable of heaping on her younger sister.

In these personally and politically difficult times, Marion thrived on philanthropy. Inspired by Mary Pickford, who had sponsored a large bungalow on the property of the Jewish Home for the Aged in Boyle Heights, Marion began to take an interest in the thirty-year-old organization for elderly Jewish residents of Los Angeles. She approached Ida Mayer Cummings, sister of Louis B. Mayer and president of the Junior Auxiliary Board of the home, to see what she could do to help. Ida told her that the best thing for the organization would be for Marion to become a board member of the Junior Auxiliary. In June 1941, Marion was appointed to lifetime membership as a trustee of the Jewish Home for the Aged. In this position, she helped to drive the direction of the home and the expansion of the campus in Reseda, which broadened the home's reach in the San Fernando Valley.

In the morning of December 7, 1941, while Marion and W.R. were at Wyntoon, the naval bases at Pearl Harbor, Hawaii, were bombed by Japanese air forces. Attention turned to the California coast, and the safety of homes on the beach became a worry. Marion and W.R. were at once relieved that they had made the decision to retreat to Wyntoon and were concerned about the safety of the Beach House.

The Hearst papers had considered Japan the greatest threat to the United States since 1905, when Japan won the Russo-Japanese War and expanded their control over the Pacific. In the ensuing years and through World War I, they warned of attacks by the Japanese, who the papers frequently depicted in terms crossing into outright stereotypical depictions. Fear of Japan had driven many of W.R.'s views on foreign policy since that time, and now he felt that those fears were becoming a reality.

Following the Pearl Harbor attack, Marion's passive isolationism disappeared, and she became a vocal advocate for the United States' involvement in World War II and the California State Coast Guard in particular. Within a month, Marion put together the Marion Davies War Work Committee, an organization providing those in Hollywood with a way to contribute time and money to the war effort. Those who accepted membership and pledged to take part in the War Work Committee included Jack Warner, Claudette

Colbert, Louella Parsons, and Carole Lombard, and all were enthusiastic about Marion's commitment to the war effort. At the Beach House swimming pool, Marion installed dozens of sewing machines at which she, Norma Shearer, Merle Oberon, and countless other women from the industry gathered to make garments and clothes for hospital use. "I got so interested in sewing during the war that I gave up most of my [other] work," she recalled in later years. "I used to make quilts and shirts and hospital stuff. I got to thinking I was the best seamstress in the world."

She also saw the potential in the Marion Davies Children's Clinic buildings, and in early January 1942, she moved to have her foundation turn the hospital over to the First Medical Battalion of the California State Guard for use as a staff headquarters and military care facility. High praise for Marion's patriotism immediately poured in from the highest offices of the state. Governor Culbert Olson, upon learning the news, wrote to Marion: "As Governor of the State of California and on behalf of the people, I want to thank you for this splendid contribution in making this hospital available to the guardsmen whose sole goal and main objective is to aid and protect life and property during our present war emergency."

Also moved by Marion's generosity was the State Guard, which made her an honorary captain. "It's Captain Davies Now," read a headline on January 14, 1942, as Marion was sworn in by Colonel Rupert Hughes. The clinic continued to operate for the low-income children of West Los Angeles, and would expand to include children of Navy families, regardless of income, for the duration of the war. Marion's justification for the expansion was that the Naval Dispensary was in Long Beach, an inconvenient distance for many families in need of care. Throughout 1942, the number of requests from such families steadily increased, and by the end of that year amounted to about a hundred a month.

For the formal transfer of the clinic to the California State Guard, Marion and W.R. came down from Wyntoon and many members of the Marion Davies War Work Committee attended the ceremony. One very meaningful regret came from Carole Lombard, the day that Marion and W.R. left Wyntoon for Los Angeles: "Dear Marion and W.R.: Regret terribly cannot appear at Hospital this time as I am leaving for Indiana on a government defense rally. Please call on me anytime as I should love to serve."

Lombard never got the chance. She left for Indiana for her government defense rally and succeeded in raising upward of $2 million for the war effort. On January 16, one week to the day from when Marion and W.R. received her note, Lombard boarded TWA Flight 3 from Indiana to Los Angeles. When the plane stopped to refuel in Las Vegas and took off for its final leg of the journey, many airplane beacons were off due to wartime restrictions. This, along with other mechanical errors, caused the pilot to lose control and the plane crashed violently into Mount Potosi in the Spring Mountains surrounding Las Vegas. Carole, along with her mother, Bess, and all other passengers onboard, died in the crash. Because Carole had been in Indianapolis to raise money for the war effort, to this day she is considered a casualty of the American war effort.

The news devastated Marion. Carole Lombard was a good friend and a frequent guest at parties both at San Simeon and the Beach House, and the wife of one of Marion's favorite co-stars, Clark Gable. She was also Marion's natural comedic descendant. The type of comedy that Marion pioneered in the late 1920s was continued by Carole Lombard in the 1930s and given a name—screwball comedy—attached to Lombard for immortality. Marion felt an affinity and connection to Carole, and she and W.R. were among the few who were invited to her modest funeral at Forest Lawn Memorial Park on January 21.

In April, Marion planned to hold a grand military ball at the Hollywood Palladium to raise money for the hospital, to be known as the Marion Davies War Work Hospital for the duration of the war. It was to be a large affair, with many members of the Hollywood set to be in attendance. In breach of the usual protocol, W.R. would also appear alongside her at the event. Marion invited President Roosevelt's daughter Anna, and her husband, John Boettinger. "Dear John and Anna—," the telegram read, "We are having a big Military Ball in Los Angeles on April fifteenth. Your presence would give distinction and grace to the occasion. Will you attend as our guests? I am going to make a speech. That alone should be worth the long trip."

John Boettinger was working for one of the Hearst papers, the *Seattle Post-Intelligencer*. In November of 1936, though W.R. was vehemently against Roosevelt by that point, he had given John Boettinger editorial oversight on the *Post-Intelligencer* and Anna a women's column. Marion had become very close to Anna, and she had visited Marion on the set of *Cain and Mabel*.

Sitting at Marion's table would be Claudette Colbert, Sonia Henie, Judy Canova, Hedy Lamarr, George Montgomery, Robert Young, Gracie Allen, George Burns, Sally Eilers, Cesar Romero, along with Jack Benny and Mary Livingstone, Dorothy Lamour, and Randolph Scott. Entertainment arrangements were made with the Glenn Miller Orchestra and the Andrews Sisters, who both waived their fees in support of the War Work Hospital. Marion wore a special khaki uniform that she had been given as an honorary captain.

Helping the California State Guard in its operations at the hospital was a Merchant Marines captain by the name of Horace Brown, who had just started going out with Marion's sister Rose. Captain Brown had become acquainted with Rose through Arthur Lake, who had served in the State Guard. Marion thought a union between Rose and Horace would be a good match. Horace was attractive, which to Marion seemed to be enough to make him appeal to Rose. Not wanting to disappoint her sister, Rose went along with Marion's matchmaking, though she herself was not as enamored of Horace as he was of her. When Horace began to think seriously of marriage, Rose stalled, staving Horace off and standing him up when it came time to get a blood test before the marriage. This irritated Marion, who believed Rose to have been truthful when she told Marion she liked Horace. Frustrated though she was, Horace remained a part of their circle. He also bore a striking resemblance to W.R.

"Marion Has to Take the First Step Herself"

In late 1941, Marion's sister Rose stormed out of a Los Angeles movie theater in a rage. She drove to Marion's and thrust open the front door, seething. "I'll kill him," Rose growled.

"What's the matter?" Marion asked.

"It's against you," Rose replied. "It's terrible. Everybody knows *Citizen Kane* is supposed to be Mr. Hearst's life. They didn't paint you too good."

Frances Marion saw the final released version of *Citizen Kane* with W.R. in San Francisco. After the movie was over, there was a veritable tension in the room. "I never realized the power of silence," Frances recalled. "He said nothing. He just got up and walked out."

Based on the life of a fictional newspaper czar that bore a strong resemblance to W.R., *Citizen Kane* follows his friends after his death as they try to find the significance of his final word, "Rosebud." We then see Charles Foster Kane's life unfold as his longtime acquaintances retell it. It was directed, produced, and co-written by Orson Welles, who had made a splash three years earlier with his Mercury Theatre's "War of the Worlds" broadcast over the radio. His dramatic interpretation of an alien invasion, presented as a news program, had led to several reforms in the Federal Communications Commission (FCC), to protect the integrity of legitimate news programs. *Citizen Kane* was 25-year-old Orson Welles's first movie, and the innovations of the production alone are enough to merit its inclusion on a list of the most influential movies. The long takes made cutting nearly impossible, and the overlapping of dialogue flew in the face of established norms of filmmaking. Instead of the stand-alone sets that were typical, Welles used sets with ceilings in indoor scenes to give the audience the impression of being in a room. The film is marvelously self-aware, and Welles's first line as Charles Foster

Kane was "Don't believe everything you hear on the radio," an allusion to "War of the Worlds."

The co-writer, Herman Mankiewicz, was a good friend of Marion's nephew, Charlie Lederer, and had been a guest at San Simeon on a few occasions. Marion barely knew him. Nonetheless, one of the featured women in the film is Charles Foster Kane's love interest and eventual wife, Susan Alexander. A blonde aspiring opera singer with an alcohol problem, a love for puzzles, and no talent, Kane had thrown all his time and energy into making her a star...and had failed. To this day, many believe that Susan Alexander Kane was created to be Marion Davies, but the character is far more like Ganna Walska.

Ganna Walska was a Polish opera singer whose unsuccessful debut in Havana, Cuba, in 1918 caught the attention of a Chicago businessman by the name of Harold McCormick. McCormick was a key supporter of the Chicago Opera, and Walska met with him in the hopes of securing a singing opportunity there. Smitten with Walska, McCormick made it his personal goal to advance her career. Over the next several years, while they were both married, McCormick and Walska continued their association, both romantic and professional. McCormick divorced his wife to marry Walska, and Walska reluctantly divorced her husband to marry him. He purchased the Théâtre des Champs-Élysées in Paris for his new wife and spent a huge fortune trying to maintain her lifestyle and career, and still Walska refused to come back to Chicago to live with him. Despondent, and realizing that he was much more devoted to Walska than she was to him, McCormick filed for divorce.

In a stroke of coincidence, Marion and Ganna Walska knew each other. At the American Embassy lunch in Paris back in 1930, Walska dined with the group as the partner of Harold McCormick. Although Marion never mentioned Walska's resemblance to the character of Susan Alexander, Walska's romance with Harold McCormick is much closer to what is portrayed in *Citizen Kane* than the story of Marion Davies and William Randolph Hearst.

The mutually devoted Hearst-Davies relationship bears little resemblance to the relationship between Susan Alexander and Charles Foster Kane. But because Hearst is far more well-known than Harold McCormick to the public mind, it is commonly assumed that Kane is fully Hearst, and Susan Alexander is fully Marion Davies—when in truth, both characters were intended to be vague.

There has also been some discussion about the meaning of the term "Rosebud," and pervasive rumors have raged in the modern era that "rosebud" was the term W.R. used to describe Marion's genitalia. It is a ridiculous claim. Both W.R. and Marion were too discreet to discuss anything related to their sex life with anyone else, and the idea that something so private could have gone so far as to make it into *Citizen Kane* is laughable. However, there was a "Rosebud" in W.R.'s life—Phoebe Apperson Hearst. Their family friend Orrin Peck took to calling W.R.'s mother "Rosebud" early in their acquaintance, perhaps due to Phoebe coming from an area of Missouri near the town of Rosebud, or because of a Kentucky Derby winner by the name of "Old Rosebud" in 1914. But Orson Welles himself denied that there was any underlying meaning to the name of Charles Foster Kane's sled, and said that "Rosebud" was nothing more than a plot gimmick.

Louella Parsons and others who worked for Hearst immediately sprang into action to defend W.R. and Marion. Later, Marion said that it wasn't W.R. who went after the picture, but rather his workers who went to bat for the man they called "The Chief." Powerful figures such as Louis B. Mayer and Nelson Rockefeller offered to help quash the film for good. RKO was fearful of these forces, and delayed the release of the film until May 1, when it finally opened to stellar reviews in New York City. As good as the reviews were, the buzz had run out by the end of the year, and RKO retired it in 1942. At the Academy Awards that year, *Citizen Kane* lost to *How Green Was My Valley* for Best Picture and was never shown publicly again until the mid-1950s. By the time the film had its public rebirth, the new audience barely knew how to tell the reality from the myth, having never lived through Hearst's America.

Marion's reaction to *Citizen Kane* was nonchalant. "Who am I to step in and say 'I don't like the way you're doing your picture?'" she told Stan Flink. "No, I'm not built that way." Her general rule of not reading her own reviews, or her own publicity, was something to which she held tightly for her own sanity. She explained to Stan Flink that this was a lesson that W.R. taught her. "He said, 'Don't ever read anything that's against you or me or anybody. Any of your friends. Don't read them. Just ignore it. Because yesterday's newspapers are old news.' So I never did anything about *Citizen Kane*."

In 1975, Orson Welles was approached to write the foreword to *The Times We Had*, the posthumous assembling of Marion's autobiographical tapes. In it, he tries to correct the public's view of Susan Alexander. "To Marion Davies she bears no resemblance at all," he says of Kane's paramour. "Kane picked up Susan on a street corner—from nowhere—where the poor girl herself thought she belonged. Marion Davies was no dim shopgirl." Of the relationship between Hearst and Marion, he writes, "She was the precious treasure of his heart for more than thirty years, until his last breath of life. Theirs is truly a love story. Love is not the subject of *Citizen Kane*."

In late 1942 at age 45, Marion fell ill with a frightening and debilitating illness. She began having noticeable problems with her legs and balance, and though some people initially thought it was due to Marion's drinking, it became clear that there was something seriously wrong. Although Marion never publicly revealed what her illness was, several friends have reported that she had a mild case of polio.

From the mid-1940s, Marion seemed to feel uncomfortable in traditional shoes, appearing much of the time in house slippers. Stan Flink, who met Marion almost a decade later, noticed that the way Marion walked with her "spastic leg" was like the way another friend who had polio walked. "You would aid her in the walking," said Anne Shirley. "She would make jokes about it, she would say 'Oh, my rubber legs.' They didn't work properly."

Through September of 1942, Marion was in San Francisco with W.R., going to doctor's appointments and getting varying opinions on what should be done. Some doctors advised immediate surgery, and some advised waiting. "Marion has been very ill, and still is," wrote W.R. to John Francis Neylan, and in late September they returned to Wyntoon to think things over. W.R. wrote that likely they would "be back soon, and Marion will have her operation." W.R. mentioned that "the prospect is not pleasant. However, we got the best advice we could, and that is our conclusion."

Marion was monitored by San Francisco–based doctors for the next few months while she rested at Wyntoon. She asked Rose to come keep her company at the isolated estate, which she did. During this time, she learned that Patricia was pregnant with her first child, and this gave Marion a sense of purpose during her recovery, knitting essentials for the baby. "I am busy getting some things together for your little papoose," she wrote her niece from Wyntoon, "and I feel as excited about the coming event as you and Artie do."

In the wake of the trouble the illness gave her legs, Marion began to employ day nurses who would usually appear on her arm when she met guests. W.R. was frequently busy with work and travel, so this also gave Marion companionship during times that were often lonely. Marion kept unusual hours after her retirement from films, influenced by the nocturnal schedule the chorus girls kept in the theater. She preferred to go to sleep around 6:00 a.m., and awaken around 4:00 p.m., which meant that she was alone in many of her waking hours.

At the same time, Marion's beloved dachshund Gandhi was aging and in poor health. He was approaching the upper limit of life expectancy for dachshunds, and Marion knew that the end was near. She avoided the vet, thereby avoiding the decision to euthanize him. Over the next two years he became confused and incontinent, and Marion outfitted him with a diaper for when he lost control of his bowels in the house. Marion also adopted a second dachshund, Cuddles, possibly to give Gandhi some companionship.

Marion and W.R. went to Mexico in December 1942. The U.S. Navy needed mahogany for its ships, and due to wartime restrictions, it could not procure its regular supply from Asia. W.R. had a large amount of it at his property in Campeche, on Mexico's Yucatán Peninsula. He scheduled this rather impromptu trip to get some for the navy's use. Marion left Gandhi in the care of photographer Lee Wenzlick at Wyntoon. Because of Gandhi's age and increasing need for care, Marion didn't feel comfortable bringing him along on trips like she did in the 1930s. He would be more comfortable, Marion felt, at Wyntoon with Cuddles and Wenzlick's dachshund, Heinie. Nonetheless, she worried about her beloved companion and wrote to Wenzlick asking how he was from a train stop in Douglas, Arizona.

Following their return to the United States in the early months of 1943, Marion and W.R., along with Gandhi and Cuddles, went to southern California to avoid another cold winter at Wyntoon. Being back with her friends after such a long period away was a relief to Marion emotionally, but a disaster for her alcoholism. W.R. watched her like a hawk during these times, constantly surveilling whatever small amount of alcohol she could manage to obtain. But back at the Beach House, she was on her own turf again. Her friends came over, and they retired to the bathroom to talk and drink. Marion fell back to her old habits, and her old memories. Remembering the comfort of alcohol, she drank more and more until, by the second week of February, it was completely out of control. Although alcohol on its own normally made Marion calmer, the anxiety of the past few years created a disastrous situation. Her personality changed and she became angry and erratic, frightening the people around her with her screaming and rage. W.R. was terrified of what she was doing to herself, and managed to check her into a local hospital for her own protection.

The nurses asked for W.R. to stay away for the first few days so that they could establish a baseline for Marion's care. After a few days of rest and regaining her stability in the hospital, W.R. came to see Marion.

"Why did you put me here?" Marion asked W.R.

"Because nobody could control you outside of the hospital," W.R. answered. "Neither doctors nor nurses nor priests, nor those who love you best."

Charlie Lederer met with W.R. at the Beach House to try to come up with a solution that would help Marion. They discussed the idea of hiring a psychiatrist, but as far as can be determined, no psychiatrist ever came to pass. It was clear to everyone involved that Marion's problems were psychological, her alcoholism fueled by the long-term heartbreak of her situation, which had become painfully clear to her after the cancelled wedding in Mexico.

Her anxieties continued to worsen. In the late 1940s, W.R. was concerned for her welfare more than ever, and came up with a plan to get Marion the help she needed. He knew that Marion would not seek help of her own accord, so he told Marion they were going to go to Seattle to see a Parkinson's specialist for W.R.'s hands, which had started to tremble. His secretary hired Howard Hughes to fix up an airplane to look like a bedroom, and take Marion, W.R., and the nurses off to a treatment center in Seattle. It was hoped that upon talking with the staff at the center, she would agree to stay and be treated for her alcoholism and anxiety. Marion went along with what she thought was the plan, but before the plane could leave, she was informed of the trick, and it was called off.

At a loss, W.R. asked Adela Rogers St. Johns for advice. Adela's daughter had been in Alcoholics Anonymous and was getting good results, and W.R. wanted the same for Marion. "It was hard for him to understand that AA couldn't send a houseful of people and seven AA doctors to set this up," Adela said. She understood his concern but stated to him in no uncertain terms, "Mr. Hearst, Marion has to take the first step herself."

A lift to Marion's spirits came in June 1944, when she was honored for her dedication as a trustee of the Jewish Home for the Aged, at a ceremony at the Biltmore Bowl. Since 1941, she had served as a lifetime member on the board of directors and, at the ceremony, President Ida Mayer Cummings said of Marion's passion for the organization: "There has never been a time when I have written to or called Miss Davies...when she did not grant my wish." In recognition of her efforts, Marion was presented with a gold mezuzah. Rabbi Edgar F. Magnin explained the significance of the mezuzah: "the religious symbol which, hung on the door, dedicates the home to good." When Marion was informed that she would be receiving the honor, she wrote to Ida Mayer Cummings: "I do not think I deserve any recognition for my interest in so worthy and so appealing a cause. I am only too happy to join with you and my other good friends in support of the home for the aged." With her letter, she enclosed a $100 donation.

Marion's dachshund Gandhi continued to get sicker and sicker, and by the middle of 1944, Marion panicked. She had tried to keep W.R. away from him, because she knew that W.R. would bring the vet in to euthanize Gandhi. But she couldn't keep W.R. away forever, and when he saw the dog, he was appalled at how much his condition had deteriorated. He was angry at Marion for not calling the vet sooner, and he took it upon himself to call an emergency vet who arrived to find a terrified Marion. W.R. ushered her out of the room while he talked to the vet about putting Gandhi to sleep, but Marion was listening at the door and burst in, stating emphatically, "Over my dead body!" She was so worked up about Gandhi that she seems to have stopped breathing and passed out at the scene. When she awoke, she saw W.R. and the vet administering the shot to her beloved dog. Gandhi died on July 12, 1944.

The emotions that Marion had been avoiding all came bubbling to the surface. She began screaming in anger, grabbing items off her bureau and throwing them against the wall. She could not speak. As she screamed wordlessly, W.R. led the vet away so he would not have to witness Marion's veritable nervous breakdown. The fact that she couldn't speak, only scream in anger, added to the frightening nature of the episode, both for Marion and for the vet.

Gandhi was buried at Wyntoon. He had been Marion's crutch in many ways for thirteen years. Despite his problems with other people, being loyal only to Marion, Gandhi's unconditional love was a comfort to her. He was rarely out of her sight, and when he died, a little piece of Marion seemed to die, too.

In March of 1943, Patricia had given birth to her first child, a son whom she named Arthur Patrick. Marion was thrilled with her new great-nephew, and especially with the fact that she was named the baby's godmother. Her joy was augmented in October of 1944 when Patricia gave birth to a second child, a girl she named Marion Rose. Marion was tickled and flattered that the new baby was named for her, but Rose was furious at the name order. "I'm the grandmother!" she exclaimed. "She should be named Rose Marion!" But her protests held no ground with Patricia, whose devotion to her aunt Marion was unmatched even by her devotion to her own mother. Marion and Marion Rose would become very close, and Marion doted proudly on her great-niece, including her and Arthur Patrick in vacations, celebrations, ceremonies, and photo shoots. W.R. also took a great liking to both Marion Rose and Arthur Patrick, though in their young eyes he seemed somewhat big, frightening, and old.

The April following Marion Rose's birth, the elder Marion and W.R. were entertaining several close friends at San Simeon when suddenly, after lunch, Marion fell to the floor and began screaming in pain. W.R. rushed over and helped her to House A, which was functioning as their primary residence at the time. They called Marion's nurse, Miss Marsh, and upon her arrival and seeing Marion in such a state, Miss Marsh declared that Marion needed to be seen by a doctor immediately. A Dr. Hagen was brought in from San Luis Obispo to examine Marion, who was still in the throes of extreme pain. Upon examination, the doctor determined that the cause of Marion's pain was appendicitis. "We've got to operate," he said.

An operation was unthinkable to Marion. "No," said W.R. "I'm taking her to San Francisco." He went to the phone and telephoned a doctor he knew there, Dr. Weeks at St. Luke's Hospital. Dr. Weeks told W.R. that Marion needed to come immediately. But Marion's extreme pain made it impossible to move her.

Dr. Hagen recommended a codeine shot that would put her to sleep. Through her screams, Marion protested. But W.R. told the doctor to give the shot, and soon Marion was quiet.

She was taken by plane to St. Luke's Hospital in San Francisco, where she awoke not knowing where she was. There, she was further diagnosed with peritonitis, and placed under observation for a week. Marion was in an uncharacteristically bad mood in the hospital, and appealed to W.R. to get her out. "I'm going crazy!" she told him. Ultimately, no operation was necessary but Marion was kept under medical observation for a week.

While Marion recovered at St. Luke's Hospital, the war in Europe was coming ever closer to an end. The day after Marion entered the hospital, on April 12, President Franklin Delano Roosevelt died of a cerebral hemorrhage. Marion wrote a telegram to his daughter Anna, whom she had always adored, from her hospital bed. "Dear Anna," she wrote, "I am in St Luke's hospital in San Francisco with appendicitis. I take this first opportunity to send you heartfelt condolence over the death of your father the President. Mr. Hearst joins me in best love and sincerest sympathy." Roosevelt's death came just seventeen days before the United Nations Conference in San Francisco, set to begin on April 25.

When the Allied forces had achieved victory in Europe on May 7, the

Los Angeles Times ran the headline "EXTRA! V-E DAY! WAR IS JUST HALF OVER!" The campaign in the Pacific was looking promising, and now the question was whether to continue the island-hopping tactic to defeat Japan, or to take more drastic measures.

Marion's condition improved over the course of her weeklong hospital stay, but she was still weak upon her discharge and physicians recommended a long period of rest to make a full recovery. Marion's regular place of residence when in San Francisco was the Fairmont Hotel on Mason Street, but she found that the Fairmont was booked for the United Nations Conference on International Organization. Delegates from Saudi Arabia were occupying Marion's normal room, so instead she reserved a room at the nearby Huntington Hotel on California Street. This offered a tranquil scene as she recovered from her illness.

W.R. was busy with the editorial needs of the convention much of the time, and Marion had expressed interest in meeting the delegates who had come from other countries, particularly Russia. Her illness made that impossible, so she relied on W.R. to tell her about what everyone was like. Marion left the Huntington and went back to San Simeon before the conference was over, but on June 26, fifty countries signed the United Nations Charter in San Francisco, expanding hope for world peace. The charter was a longtime dream of President Roosevelt.

The question of how to end the war against Japan was answered on August 6 and 9, when atomic bombs were dropped on Hiroshima and Nagasaki. Despite W.R.'s long antagonism against Japan, he found himself enraged, as Marion was, by the actions of the United States against Japan. Princess Conchita Pignatelli, a Hollywood friend of W.R. and Marion's who wrote for the *Los Angeles Examiner*, came to San Simeon that day to visit. When she arrived, W.R. looked exhausted and horrified.

"What's wrong?" she asked.

"Something horrible has been done," W.R. answered. "We have just dropped an atomic bomb on Japan."

In addition to his shock at the loss of life, W.R. had another thing on his mind. The scripted dialogue in a Cosmopolitan film of 1933, *Gabriel over the White House*, included a prediction of "inconceivably devastating explosives" dropped from the air that would "destroy populations." That line, meant to evoke a dystopian future, had come to reflect reality.

By the mid-1940s, Hollywood had become unrecognizable to Marion. Since her retirement in 1937, the film industry had changed so much that movies made her uneasy. She rarely went out to see them. Marion did, however, keep copies of her own films. With her nieces and nephews she only showed the talkies—perhaps out of self-consciousness, perhaps because she thought the silents would bore the young children. She was proud of her career, but unlike Gloria Swanson or Mary Pickford, stardom was not important to her. When she retired, she didn't feel that she had lost much of a career. What she did miss were the large groups of people who surrounded her almost constantly while she was working. Those days, and that company, were mostly gone. Most of the time, it was just Marion and W.R. together at San Simeon, spending quiet time alone with the dachshunds.

The actress Colleen Moore recalled a visit to San Simeon during this period. She noticed how Marion had changed into a tranquil, domestic woman devoted to taking care of the aging W.R. The two former actresses discussed their current lives, and Colleen was flabbergasted to discover that aside from the charity boards that Marion served on, her life now consisted of sewing, washing, and ironing.

After dinner, Marion, Colleen, and W.R. retired to the theater to watch a movie, as they often did. Before the film, Colleen recalled, Marion wrapped a blanket around W.R.'s knees, then took his glasses to polish them with her handkerchief. They were holding hands when the movie began and, at that moment, Colleen recognized the simplicity of Marion's life at San Simeon. She had matured—no longer was she the carefree girl of the 1920s who thrived on dozens of guests and grand costume parties. It was just Marion and W.R. now, and Colleen believed she was happy.

. . .

The paradox of the regal grandeur of San Simeon and the disappointments in W.R.'s private life had always been evident to his closest friends. When Frances Marion's husband, Fred Thomson, had died in 1928, Marion insisted that she come spend some time at San Simeon to rest. One morning, Frances got up early and took a walk along the grounds, where she saw W.R. walking, seemingly lost in thought. He paused silently every now and then to stare at the hills and sea below. He sat on a marble bench, with his head down on his chest, in a sad, pensive pose.

Despite an empire worth millions, an extraordinary amount of power, and the love of the woman he considered to be perfect, too many of his great ambitions in life had been failures. "Was he unhappy because he had dreams of becoming the foremost producer in the picture business and had been met with nothing but defeat, brought on by his stubbornness?" Frances wrote later. "Did anyone really know this man who could be ruthless and kind, gentle and savage-tempered, calm and violent during one single story conference with him?" Compounding these failures that Frances observed as early as 1928 was perhaps the biggest disappointment of William Randolph Hearst's life—the fact that he never succeeded in obtaining a divorce so that he could marry Marion.

In late 1944, when W.R. was 81 years old and Marion 47, they began to entertain the idea of selling the Beach House. It was becoming too expensive to maintain, and they were rarely there anymore. The library at the Beach House was far too big to transport, so on December 3 and 4, an auction was held to sell off some of Marion's precious books, ones that had given her so much pleasure over the years. Included were twenty lots by Marion's favorite, Charles Dickens, sets of the Bronte sisters and Jane Austen, as well as dozens of reference books and historical works.

One day in 1946 Marion was approached by Hearst Corporation representatives Martin Huberth and Dick Berlin with some surprising information. They told her that the corporation, at the direction of W.R., had established a trust fund for Marion (without her knowledge), and had put money toward it regularly up until the failure of the Hearst organizations in the late 1930s, in the amount of $150,000 a year. The corporation owed W.R. $850,000 in dividends. After that time, they couldn't afford to keep making payments to either W.R. or Marion's trust fund, but they wanted to make good on their obligations. "If you give us the Beach House," they said, "we will pay you $850,000, or the amount that we owe you."

Since Marion didn't know that she had a trust fund anyway, she agreed to receive W.R.'s dividends of $850,000 in exchange for the Hearst Corporation taking possession of the Beach House and selling it. The Beach House would become the property of the Hearst Magazines, Inc., which eventually sold it to hotel entrepreneur Joseph Drown. It was the end of an era—the days of those magnificent gatherings at the immense house on the beach in Santa Monica, the themed birthday parties with carousels, costumes, and laughter, officially came to a close.

W.R. was now 83 years old, and his health had been declining for years. In 1946 he had been diagnosed with an irregular heartbeat, and may have had a mild heart attack. Marion took care of him as well as she knew how, but doctors worried about the physical distance of San Simeon from available hospitals in case of an emergency. The doctors disapproved of the difficult roads that an ambulance would have to negotiate, and they advised Marion and W.R. to find a home closer to a hospital so that he could have more extensive care and monitoring.

W.R. was heartbroken about leaving San Simeon. Marion looked for a permanent home for both of them in Los Angeles, and soon found one on the market—a spacious, Spanish-style mansion at 1007 North Beverly Drive in Beverly Hills. Comprising twenty-two rooms, a grand backyard garden with a large swimming pool, and an impressive library for their books, it seemed to be fit only for William Randolph Hearst. The owner, George Bruce, had set the home's value at $110,000. By the standards of Hearst and Marion, that was a relatively low price, and Marion bought the house for herself and W.R. on June 1, 1946.

They would have access to the distinguished Cedars of Lebanon Hospital and medical teams at UCLA and USC, and W.R. would also be close to the *Los Angeles Examiner* and the large community of friends that he and Marion had built in their life together. This select group of friends would be able to visit, giving him a sense of continuity and Marion some respite.

Prized possessions were packed, many of the remaining animals were given to nearby zoos, and in mid-1947, Marion and W.R. left San Simeon for good. Driving the road to and from San Simeon, the castle appeared and disappeared on the mountaintop like flashes of memory. W.R.'s eyes filled with tears as he looked back at his beloved ranch, leaving behind a land that was the culmination of a childhood dream. As they drove, Marion held W.R. and whispered, "We'll come back someday, W.R., you'll see…"

FIGURE 31. Marion and W.R. preparing for takeoff to their next European destination, 1934. From a collection of keepsake photos sent to Julia Morgan. Courtesy of California Polytechnic State University, Kennedy Library.

FIGURE 32. The 1934 traveling crew. On the left: Sir Charles Allom. Back row: a local art dealer, Harry Crocker, Buster Collier. Middle: Dorothy Mackaill, Eileen Percy. Front row: Lorna Hearst (wife of George), W.R. Hearst, Marion Davies, George Hearst.

FIGURE 33. Marion eyes the microphone before her radio debut with Gary Cooper in a production of *Operator 13* (1934). Ted Healy is seated on Marion's left. Courtesy of The Academy of Motion Picture Arts and Sciences.

Marion looking especially pensive at San Simeon.   1930.

FIGURE 34. Pensive at San Simeon. Photo by Clarence Sinclair Bull.

FIGURE 35. The Marion Davies Children's Clinic building.

FIGURE 36. During the war, Marion donated the Marion Davies Children's Clinic for use by the California State Guard. Here, she hands over the keys. Courtesy of the Los Angeles Public Library.

FIGURE 37. Relaxing with W.R. at Wyntoon. *Life* magazine, August 27, 1951.

FIGURE 38. Marion holds hands with Anne Shirley at a party in May 1951. From left: Marion Davies, Anne Shirley, Greg Bautzer, Marjorie Hartford, Hyatt Dehn, Louella Parsons, Patricia Lake, Charles Lederer. Courtesy of USC Digital Library, Los Angeles Examiner Photographs Collection.

FIGURE 39. In the garden with her great-niece, Marion Rose, at the house on North Beverly Drive. Courtesy of *Life* magazine/Shutterstock.

FIGURE 40. (right) The day of William Randolph Hearst's death, with Helena on the bed. The inscription on the portrait next to the bed is from *Romeo and Juliet*: "My bounty is as boundless as the sea, my love as deep." *Life* magazine, August 27, 1951.

FIGURE 41. Marion tried to divorce Horace Brown several times, but always went back.

FIGURE 42. At dinner with friends and family. Standing from left: Douglas Wood, Horace Brown, Arthur Lake. Seated: Patricia Lake, Marion Davies, Marjorie Hartford. Courtesy of Los Angeles Public Library.

FIGURE 43. A happy moment in the garden. Courtesy of *Life* magazine/Shutterstock.

FIGURE 44. Preparing for *Hedda Hopper's Hollywood*. Behind Marion is a painting of her nearly forty years before in *Little Old New York* (1923). Courtesy of The Academy of Motion Picture Arts and Sciences.

FIGURE 45. Marion's last public appearance, at the inauguration of John F. Kennedy in January 20, 1961. Marion is toward the top left.

"The Girl Who Lies by My Side at Night"

Oh the night is blue and the stars are bright
Like the eyes of the girl of whom I write
And the day is a glimmer of golden light
Like the locks of the girl of whom I write
And the skies are soft and the clouds are white
Like the limbs of the girl of whom I write
But no beauty of earth is so fair a sight
As the girl who lies by my side at night
Then carry me speedily over the plain
And carry me speedily back again
To the sun lit land of love and light
And the girl who lies by my side at night

WILLIAM RANDOLPH HEARST
love poem to Marion Davies, circa 1947

Due to the 1942 illness that affected Marion's legs, she needed help with her daily tasks, including someone to lean on to steady her balance, and to assist her with standing for long periods of time. Marion had a day nurse, Mrs. Davis, but given Marion's unusual sleep schedule, there was often no one around to help her when she needed it. Shortly after Marion and W.R. arrived at the house on Beverly Drive, W.R. called a staffing agency to employ a night nurse for Marion.

The nurse that the agency sent, Floretta Mauser, took over night duties after Mrs. Davis left at 3 p.m. Since Marion was rarely awake then, Mrs. Mauser was on duty during the majority of Marion's waking hours, and they became very close. Mauser recognized Marion's love of reading and remembered that she usually had a book in her hand, wherever she was. She particularly liked mysteries. Mauser sat with Marion for hours on end, talking with her about the highs and lows of her life, what she missed and what she didn't miss. Mauser noticed Marion's tendency to skip over stories about the movies, preferring to go straight back to her time as a chorus girl, seemingly the most joyous time of her life.

In 1949, Charlie Lederer brought the actress Anne Shirley to the house on Beverly Drive to introduce her to Marion. In a few weeks, they would be married, and Charlie wanted to get Marion's blessing. Anne had been acting since the age of three. She had starred in such films as *Stella Dallas* and *Anne of Green Gables*, changing her name from Dawn O'Day to Anne Shirley to reflect the role she played.

As Anne approached the door, she was terribly nervous. "I wanted her to like me," she said about meeting the woman who was more like Charlie's mother than his own. Anne entered to find Marion just as nervous. The dinner, with just the three of them, was cheery and lighthearted. Marion took to Anne immediately, and she to Marion. They found they had a lot in common and could talk at ease about the entertainment industry. "She was an extraordinary woman," Anne recalled, and though she never felt comfortable calling her "Aunt Marion" as Charlie did, she always referred to her warmly as "Marion." Anne had not been privy to most of the events that had shaped the Douras family's life and had never known Pepi, Ethel, Reine, Mama Rose, or Papa Ben. Nonetheless, she became a cherished part of Marion's family and inner circle. Marion cared for Anne unconditionally, just as she did Charlie.

Anne met W.R. only once. By 1949, he was mostly confined to the upstairs bedrooms and hallways, seeing very few people. Those he did see were always approved by Marion. Louis B. Mayer often brought him matzo ball soup, which W.R. loved. "It always made him feel better," Marion remembered. From time to time, Marion would order his preferred dish, bouillabaisse, from Romanoff's, or bring him one of his favorite desserts, a chocolate milkshake. Millicent remained in New York.

Ill though he was, having dropped to 128 pounds by 1950, W.R. continued to control the editorial policy of his newspapers. The pro-worker, pro-union philosophies that had dominated the Hearst papers in their early days had all but disappeared as the 1950s approached. As the House Un-American Activities Committee (HUAC) began their investigations of Alger Hiss and others suspected of belonging to the Communist Party, the Hearst papers took a hard pro-HUAC stance. When Senator Joseph McCarthy accused the Truman administration of placing Communists in high governmental positions, W.R. gave the order to print favorable coverage of McCarthy and his crusade.

Marion was taken slightly aback at his rigidity against Communism. "He was very, very, very... not rabid, entirely—almost so," she said after his death.

This fervor was scaled back when W.R. read that McCarthy had as much worry about "homosexuals as worry about Stalinists," and that McCarthy would "discover anything possible about Communist-led white-collar workers' outfits." This signaled to W.R. that the papers needed to stop, and that McCarthy, perhaps more than Communism, was a danger to the United States. "Now it is the time for us to halt the fight for a while," he told Raymond T. Van Ettisch, editor of the *Los Angeles Examiner*, to communicate to his editors, "and take a breathing spell until we can more fully determine the international situation." A few days later, W.R.'s son, Bill Jr., countered his father's instructions, declaring that no change was to be made to the Hearst papers' coverage of McCarthy. W.R. did not protest, and his son took charge. Though he would remain legally in charge until he died, this, essentially, ceded power to Bill Jr. as the chief communicator.

Sometime in mid-1950, Marion and W.R.'s old friend (and Rose's former boyfriend) Captain Horace Brown was a guest of Marion and W.R. at the house on Beverly Drive. Horace was an ex-stuntman, a widower with three sons, whose wife Virginia Powell had died in a car accident shortly before he had dated Rose in 1942. During World War II, he served as a captain in the Merchant Marines in Europe. Afterward, he spent some time stationed in Guam before the outbreak of the Korean War. His ship then traveled to Korea, followed by Yokohama, Japan. It was from Japan that he took leave from his military post and visited Marion and W.R. in 1950.

At W.R.'s encouragement, Marion and Horace spent a good deal of time talking alone. W.R. had always liked Horace, as had Marion, and they had been formidable partners in the cribbage games they often played before Horace left for the war. During his visit in mid-1950, W.R. often ushered Marion and Horace into private rooms, where they talked—sometimes for hours at a time. When Horace went back to Japan, he and Marion continued to have extensive conversations over the phone.

Horace's physical resemblance to W.R. was staggering. With the same large build, long face, and prominent nose, Horace could have been W.R.'s twin from certain angles. With her extroverted personality and need to be surrounded by people, no one knew how Marion would fare after W.R. was gone. By encouraging Marion to associate with Horace, W.R. seemed to be preparing her for his death.

In these waning days of W.R.'s life, friends showed a growing concern for Marion's future. W.R.'s lawyers had warned him that if he didn't make a provision for Marion in his will, the Hearst Corporation could invoke the community property law—in which half of everything Marion owned would be taken away and turned over to the corporation or the estate for use by the Hearst sons or Millicent. Joseph P. Kennedy, who had always had a true fondness for Marion, engaged W.R. in conversation about it. "I hope I'm not being too forward," he said, but "it seems to me that things...should be earmarked for her right away so any disputes might be avoided."

W.R. had become increasingly worried about Marion's emotional, financial, and legal well-being. Though she was independently wealthy and didn't need the money, the legal ramifications of three decades together without marriage were dire. He called Marion into his office sometime in the evening of November 5, 1950. In his hand W.R. held a document, a ten-page legal contract drawn up by the well-known Hollywood lawyer Greg Bautzer earlier in the week, that he handed to Marion to read. In appreciation of Marion's efforts for the Hearst Corporation in the late 1930s, W.R. was bequeathing to her the voting rights to all 100,000 shares of the common Hearst Corporation stock, as well as the remaining 170,000 shares of the preferred stock, which belonged to W.R. himself. This agreement would give Marion the power to choose all executives and directors of subsidiary corporations and would essentially make her the chief governing officer of the Hearst Corporation. Additionally, the agreement pooled the Hearst stock and set up a voting trust, for which Hearst and Marion were the sole trustees. The purpose of this was "to obtain and insure [sic] continuity of control for a definite and substantial period of years," and it stipulated that in the event of the death of either Hearst or Marion, the surviving trustee should vote the entire stock of the Hearst Corporation for his or her lifetime, giving the survivor full control. Marion would receive no pay as trustee. "You know my theories," W.R. said to her, "and I want to make you the vote." W.R.'s motives for establishing Marion in such a high position within the Hearst Corporation were evidence of a changing psyche that had for so long kept separate his private and business lives. With this provision for Marion, W.R. acknowledged, in a sense, his guilt over never having been able to marry Marion, for prioritizing his business affairs and public perception over his love for her.

To W.R., this was a way of thanking Marion for her role in bringing the Hearst Corporation into financial solvency and acknowledging her publicly. But the move puzzled Marion, who was aware of her limitations. "He could see further than I could," she remembered in 1953, "but I'm afraid he was just as shortsighted as I was." Marion, who had no experience with newspapers outside of sitting in on Hearst Corporation meetings, had never learned what a vote even meant in corporate terminology. "I thought it meant voting for president. I didn't know." On the advice of Greg Bautzer, Marion signed the agreement. In her mind, she was simply complying with W.R.'s request for her to continue the Hearst Corporation according to his wishes after his death. Little did she know the gravity of what her signature on the document meant, and how much this document would plague her in the coming months.

During this complex time, Marion became acquainted with Stanley Flink, a young Yale graduate who had recently started working for *Life* magazine. Marion and Flink had been introduced through a mutual friend, Speed Lamkin, an up-and-coming writer whom Flink had met at an artists' colony in Pacific Palisades. Lamkin saw Flink's formal style of dress and asked him cheerfully, "Yale or Harvard?" Flink was impressed with this satirical observation and engaged him in conversation. They had a good initial rapport, and suddenly Lamkin burst out with, "How would you like to meet Marion Davies?" Lamkin knew Marion through a mutual friend, Harry Crocker.

Flink was stunned by the question. "I'd like to very much," he said, "but I understand that *Time* and *Life* people are not admitted to the house." Lamkin convinced him that working for magazines that rivaled Hearst's would not be a problem and would not impede his chances of meeting Marion. "I'll take you there and introduce you," he said.

A week later, Lamkin brought Stan Flink to W.R. and Marion's house. Marion appeared on the arm of Mrs. Davis, and even in her simple attire of brown slacks and a white blouse, Flink was immediately taken with Marion's striking looks. She retained a glow in her cheeks and a youthful rosy complexion that gave credence to the old cliché of "peach skin." Paired with the enormous blue eyes that, he said, seemed to be "twice the size of ordinary human eyes" and "peered at you with a brightness and an intrigue" that was so intense as to be almost distracting, the result was a unique and alluring beauty. Her hair, Flink noticed, was different. Having been electrified and treated so many times over the years, it had become damaged and rough, an "illogical companion" to the softness of her face.

They got along well, and soon Flink proposed that they run an article entitled "*Life* Visits Marion Davies," a variation on a standard feature in which Flink would report on Marion's current social schedule and post-Hollywood activities. Marion loved the idea, and Flink began preparations for an in-depth report. For the article, Marion hosted a tea with several friends that included Gloria Vanderbilt and Gloria Swanson, a quiet affair until a rowdy

Errol Flynn arrived uninvited. Marion brought Marion Rose and Arthur Patrick, now six and eight years old, dressed in their best clothes to be photographed in the garden by the *Life* team.

In interviewing Marion's friends for the story, Flink was taken by the particular sincerity and devotion of Eileen Percy. Eileen seemed to be the one who most appreciated Marion for herself and understood the unique emotions that she experienced because of the circumstances of her life. Where others tended to see Marion in the frame of how she affected their lives, Eileen understood Marion as the person she was. "Everyone else tried to put themselves into the equation," remembers Flink. "Not Eileen."

While not able to partake in the goings-on downstairs, W.R. was kept in the loop by Marion's daily reports and his occasional gaze out the window when people were in the garden. Despite the Hearst Corporation's general objection to *Time* and *Life*, Marion had managed to convince W.R. that Flink was a reputable and trustworthy reporter. "I'd like to meet him sometime," W.R. told Marion one evening.

W.R.'s trust in Marion regarding journalistic integrity was unwavering. In healthier times, W.R. had often sought Marion's opinion on the news, having her write the anti-vivisection editorials about which they were both passionate, and sit in on important Hearst Corporation meetings. Although Marion somewhat laughed off W.R.'s practice of having her be an honorary part of the corporation, and always maintained that she knew nothing about newspapers, Marion's mind absorbed information like a sponge. She processed important Hearst Corporation business such as options, which papers were doing well, which were not, and how to communicate with top executives. In these days before W.R.'s death, Marion utilized the skills she had learned in these meetings, taking a greater role in the everyday functioning of the Hearst papers when W.R. could not. She diligently transmitted his editorials to the press offices of each of his papers, sending telegrams when she could not reach someone on the phone.

Marion's dictation of W.R.'s desires and her direction of the newspapers was not always taken well by the higher-ups at the papers or understood by those outside of the immediate Hearst-Davies circle. Louis Shainmark, former editor of the *Chicago-American*, told Hearst biographer W.A. Swanberg that he felt that Marion was "horning in" on Hearst publicity, pushing forth projects of her friends and projects that she felt important, and appointing her friends to positions within the corporation.

One such project was righting the wrong that she felt had been done to

Ingrid Bergman, who was lambasted in the presses of both the United States and her native Sweden due to a scandal that had mirrored Marion's own life.

Over the course of the past few years, Bergman had been involved in a romance with director Roberto Rossellini. They had begun a passionate love affair while he directed her in *Stromboli*, despite Bergman's marriage to Petter Lindstrom, the father of her daughter, Pia. In mid-1949, she found herself pregnant with Rossellini's child. Bergman had been known for saintly roles, in *The Bells of St. Mary's* and, just the previous year, in *Joan of Arc*. The news of her affair and pregnancy shocked the world. In February 1950, Bergman gave birth to a son, whom she named Roberto Rossellini Jr. In the wake of the child's birth, newspapers in both Sweden and the United States called Bergman a loose woman, a whore, and a "blot on the Swedish flag." She refused to deny her relationship with Rossellini or be ashamed of her son's existence. Bergman also invoked the ire of women's clubs, which aimed to reform morality and public policy. These groups had a great influence on the media and were regular contributors to the Hearst papers. News outlets across the country denounced Ingrid Bergman and promoted boycotts of her films.

When Marion heard of the treatment Bergman was receiving, she sprang into action and stood up for her publicly. This was an arena with which Marion was deeply familiar. "She was nailed to the cross," Marion said about Bergman. "If a woman of her great character has courage enough to really go ahead with her life, why should she be criticized?" They had never met, but Marion felt a kinship with Ingrid Bergman that she couldn't ignore, and she took it upon herself to make the restoration of Ingrid Bergman's character a personal goal. On the birth of Roberto Jr., Marion's congratulatory telegram was among the first messages Bergman received, and the director and the star were both moved. "Think of it," Rossellini told the *Los Angeles Times*. "This great actress of the silent films remembered us."

Taking advantage of the editorial power she enjoyed as a member of the Hearst circle, Marion then wrote an editorial about Ingrid Bergman for the *Los Angeles Examiner*. "I called up the *Examiner* to put in an article saying that I agreed perfectly with Ingrid Bergman," she recalled. "I said I thought she was entirely right."

The article made it into the first edition of the *Examiner*, but when Hearst lawyer Henry MacKay (nicknamed "Heinie") saw it, he immediately had it pulled and went to Hearst. But it was too late—the *Los Angeles Times* had seen the first edition, and the article was repeated in the *Times*, making it appear to those who read both papers that Marion had given the story to the *Times* and not the *Examiner*.

According to Marion's account, Heinie MacKay was livid about the article. "It's horrible what Miss Davies has done," he told W.R.

"Why?"

"She won't be accepted by the women's clubs."

One of the benefits for Marion no longer being in movies was her relative freedom, not having to worry about what the papers said about her. Nonetheless, W.R. was concerned about what she was saying, and about his circulation. He called Marion into his office.

"I think you've made a mistake," he told her. "Heinie MacKay said you won't be accepted by the women's clubs."

"The women's clubs?" Marion scoffed incredulously. "Don't make me laugh." Marion showed W.R. a copy of the *Los Angeles Times*.

"What happened?" he asked.

Marion explained, and W.R. recognized the mistake.

"Heinie MacKay's fired," he said. W.R. called MacKay, but instead of firing him, gave him a stern lecture over the telephone.

"How dare you do that to Miss Davies?" W.R. told MacKay. "When she gives an order, the *Examiner*'s got to go through with it and don't you dare countermand it." Warning him that if it happened again, he would be out on his ear, W.R. hung up.

"Marion was insecure, but she was also brave," Anne Shirley said of her. The combination of Marion's power, sanctioned by W.R., and her humanitarian spirit created an unintentionally tense atmosphere among the newspaper editors that never totally faded, even after W.R.'s death. In her desire to help, she overstepped bounds due to her relative naiveté about the business. Her kindnesses, on the other hand, were not forgotten by the people she helped. Ingrid Bergman, who married Roberto Rossellini after her divorce from Petter Lindstrom became final, held Marion's support very close to her heart and wrote Marion later expressing her gratitude.

On W.R.'s eighty-eighth birthday on April 29, Marion gathered a small group of friends to celebrate, including Eleanor Boardman, Eileen Percy, and China Harris. Marion had been careful to invite only women this year, because she anticipated that her gift would move him to tears. She knew W.R. well enough to know that he would not want to cry in front of a man, and in his fragile state she felt it imperative to protect his emotional well-being.

When the guests arrived, they found W.R. sitting in his room in a wheelchair. He was frail and pallid, with only the spark in his eyes reminding the women of the intimidating presence who had once been one of the most powerful forces in Hollywood. Marion presented W.R. with his gift, and he opened it slowly, revealing a painting that Marion had commissioned of him as an infant with his beloved mother, Phoebe. His cool blue eyes filled with tears, and he buried his head in his hands as he cried. At the sheer poignancy of the moment the rest of the guests began to cry as well, as Marion ran to W.R. and threw her arms around W.R.'s legs, comforting him as he cried. "She just grabbed him by the knees," recalled Eleanor Boardman. "It was the most touching scene."

Marion called on enormous reserves of strength to be there for W.R. in his final year, in spite of her own anxieties. "I think I'm getting old," W.R. would say. Calling upon their friend who was still spry at 92, Marion replied, "Now, does George Bernard Shaw think that way? You're good for at least ten or twenty more years. Nobody dies nowadays, not with science." Then she took him by the arm and led him in a Charleston, just as they had more than thirty years before, the dance now modified for W.R.'s age and Marion's weak legs. "He must have thought I was the craziest nut who ever lived," Marion said. "But it did pep him up." W.R. wrote Marion nightly notes of affection and love on small strips of yellow foolscap paper, slipping them under her door before he went to bed. Stanley Flink found this to be a remarkable relationship. "The fact that Hearst was still writing affectionate notes, and slipping them under Marion's bedroom door, when he was in his eighties is evidence of an attachment that ran very deep," he remembers.

When George Bernard Shaw died at the age of 93, Marion worried about how the news of their friend's death would affect W.R. She decided to take matters into her own hands to protect his emotional state. She rang up the staff at the *Los Angeles Examiner* to ask them a favor. "Just make a special edition for W.R.," she told the staff, "cutting out the part that George Bernard Shaw died." That morning, W.R. received a special edition of the paper with the article about George Bernard Shaw's death omitted. In the last few months of W.R.'s life, Marion did this several more times, requesting a special edition of the *Los Angeles Examiner* removing any article about a death that she felt would upset him. "I didn't want him to realize that people died, or could die," she recalled. Particularly upsetting to W.R. was any mention of cancer in the newspaper, which was a phobia of his. "Don't think about those things," Marion told him, "because you can wish them on yourself." W.R. worried that cancer was claiming the lives of an increasing number of people, and in the days before the disease was well understood, he worried that it was contagious. "Now look," Marion said, "If I counted up all the people around me, I'd have 50,000 cancers."

When W.R. became bedridden in his final month, Marion was essentially housebound. She would go out only when he was asleep, with the understanding that when he woke up, a nurse was to call her wherever she was, and Marion would get in the car and return home. One evening, she went to a cocktail party at actress Cobina Wright's house up the hill, with the same instructions to Mrs. Mauser. Marion was able to stay at Cobina Wright's until late in the evening as W.R. slept. A three-piece band played at the party, and Marion asked if she could make a request. She asked the band to play the wedding march, put a handkerchief over her head, and grabbed the nearest young man, whom she didn't know. "C-c-come on, honey," she stuttered, "we're going to be married." And she and the unknown man walked down the imaginary aisle to the tune of the wedding march.

By Sunday, August 12, 1951, W.R. had deteriorated to the point that not even the optimistic Marion, who had so encouraged him to think positively about old age, could imagine him living more than a few days longer. She stayed by his side as W.R. lay in bed, his voice barely more than a whisper as he dictated his last notes to his editors. Visitors continued to come, including their old friend Frances Marion who, for Marion and W.R., represented pleasant memories of days long past. For W.R.'s sake, Frances tried to be cheerful as she told him news from her life, including her plans for an upcoming trip to San Francisco. W.R. suddenly looked nostalgic. "Frances," he said to her, "please stop at San Simeon and look the place over. I want to make sure everything is all right there." Frances promised she would, though she, as everyone else, knew that this would most likely be their last visit. And even now, with W.R. so close to death, Frances noticed that his big blue eyes never left Marion, following her lovingly wherever she went as though afraid of losing her at any moment.

The following evening, the house was filled with editors, representatives from the Hearst Corporation, and those wishing to say their final goodbyes to "the Chief." Marion stayed by W.R.'s bedside while the visitors mingled downstairs. Distraught, afraid, and in desperate need of the sleep that she so fearfully avoided, she kept vigil by W.R.'s side in anticipation of the inevitable, to be with him to the very end. After kissing Marion good night, W.R. quietly slipped into a coma.

Kissing Marion Davies would be the last thing William Randolph Hearst ever did.

. . .

In the late hours of August 13, Marion was distressed and agitated, lack of sleep and exhaustion wreaking havoc on her mind. That night, Marie Glendinning, one of Marion's final remaining links to her childhood, came over to be with her. A friend of the family since Marion was a preteen, Marie had watched her grow up and had been there at every jubilant occasion, as well as every sorrow, since Marion was 11 years old. After W.R.'s death, Marion would write Marie a letter: "My darling Marie... You have been a great friend to me. Like a shining light in the sky that never fades. If there were more like you, the world would be a better world. All my love and devotion, affectionately, Marion." At one point during the evening, Marion and Marie went into the bathroom together, and suddenly reality hit Marion that this was the end of W.R.'s life. She was going to be all alone after tonight.

She sat down and sighed. "I think I could do with a drink."

"I think you should have a little one," said Marie. Aware of Marion's problem with alcohol, Marie was even more keenly aware of the nervousness in her friend's voice. She sat with Marion as she poured herself a drink.

W.R.'s son Randolph, known to Marion as Randy, made his way over to the two friends and put his hand on Marie's shoulder. "Marie, what are you going to do tonight?" he asked.

"I think I'll stay with Marion tonight," Marie said.

"Good," replied Randy. "I think she'll need you."

Marie stayed with Marion through the night. Finally, when Dr. Eliot Corday saw Marion in her sleep-deprived state, he became concerned about the toll that Marion's refusal to sleep was taking on her body and mind. He offered to give her a sedative to calm her, but Marion refused and insisted on keeping her spot at W.R.'s bedside until the moment came. Worried that she was doing herself harm by maintaining her vigil, and not knowing when Hearst's death would come, Dr. Corday called Charlie Lederer, whom he felt could persuade Marion to take a sedative. Charlie drove to the house and talked with Marion. Within minutes, she allowed Dr. Corday to give her the sedative, and Marion fell into the first sleep she had had in three days.

"My Bounty Is as Boundless as the Sea"

ROMEO: O, wilt thou leave me so unsatisfied?
JULIET: What satisfaction canst thou have tonight?
ROMEO: The exchange of thy love's faithful vow for mine.
JULIET: I gave thee mine before thou didst request it:
And yet I would it were to give again.
ROMEO: Wouldst thou withdraw it? for what purpose, love?
JULIET: But to be frank, and give it thee again.
And yet I wish but for the thing I have.
My bounty is as boundless as the sea,
My love as deep; the more I give to thee,
The more I have, for both are infinite.

ROMEO AND JULIET, *act 2, scene 2*

At 9:50 in the morning on August 14, 1951, Marion was still sleeping under the effects of the sedative when W.R. died in his bedroom at 1007 N. Beverly Drive. On her way up to San Francisco, Frances had honored W.R.'s wishes by stopping at San Simeon. As she stood at the top of the hill, she noticed the almost eerie stillness of her surroundings, quieter than it had ever been. She found the gates closing as she arrived up the narrow, curving hill she had traveled so often before. Frances greeted the gateman who told her solemnly, "Mr. Hearst died today."

Bill Jr. and David were summoned to Beverly Drive. Charlie Lederer, who over the course of the previous evening had gone back to his house on Bedford Drive after coaxing Marion to be sedated, was called back. Charlie rushed to the house and was met at the door by Richard "Dick" Berlin, president of the Hearst Corporation. A scuffle ensued when Berlin told Charlie that his presence was unwelcome. "This is Marion Davies' house," Charlie told him, "I'll do what I want."

News of Hearst's death spread quickly through the press, and when Stan Flink heard the report on the radio on his way to an appointment at Paramount Studios, he turned around and went immediately to Marion's home.

Upon his arrival, he found the morticians carrying Hearst's body down the gardener's staircase, wrapped in a simple army blanket. A small floral delivery truck with two vertical doors in the back was waiting at the back entrance to avoid the inevitable questions of the press, who would be expecting a hearse or a limousine. The significance of seeing the most powerful and influential journalistic power in the world relegated to a small army blanket in a delivery truck in death was an irony not lost on Flink, the sole member of the press to witness it.

He met Marion's secretary, Tom Kennington, at the door and was brought into the house, where Tom suggested that he stay in one of the storerooms adjoining the kitchen. There, he would be free of the tense atmosphere of the house and avoid interference from the guards. From that room, which he shared with more than a dozen Bissell vacuum cleaners, Flink could get a good view of the goings-on outside via the side windows at either end. Through the door he saw the kitchen where, earlier, Dick Berlin had combed his hair as he gathered the employees of the residence. As Kennington related the scene to Flink, Berlin hoisted himself up on a chair and issued an ominous statement to the staff: "You work for me now."

Flink emerged when the crowd had dispersed, and he discovered that Marion was still asleep. Shortly after 2:00 p.m., Marion finally awoke from her sedation and Dr. Corday told her that W.R. was gone. "Oh my god, no," she cried, rushing across the hall to find W.R.'s room empty. Flink was waiting downstairs for the distraught Marion, when she finally appeared on the arm of Mrs. Davis. "Oh Stan," she cried, "I had him for 32 years, and then whoosh, he was gone." Overcome with emotion, she continued: "Old W.R. was gone. Do you realize what they did? They stole a possession of mine. He was mine for 32 years."

W.R.'s body was flown to San Francisco in a World War II trainer combat plane, piloted by Paul Mantz, its owner and a renowned stunt movie pilot acquainted with the Hearst family. Later that night, Marion received a call from Bill Jr.

"You wouldn't let me say goodbye to him," Marion said. "The least you can do is tell me when the services are so I can pray for him down here."

Bill Jr.'s response was that the plans were being organized by Millicent Hearst. At that, Marion broke down, and cried, "Tell her to wear her widow's weeds," before hanging up, sobbing.

The body lay in state at Grace Cathedral in San Francisco for two days until the funeral on Thursday, August 16. The press coverage of W.R.'s death carefully made it sound like W.R. had died surrounded by family rather than at the home of Marion Davies. The first five pages of the August 15 issue of the *San Francisco Examiner* was dedicated to W.R. and his memory, with several references to "sons at his bedside" and not a single mention of Marion.

Marion was not asked to go to the funeral, nor did she ask for an invitation. "I thought I might go to church, but I'll just stay here," she told her nurse Mrs. Davis. "He knew how I felt about him, and I know how he felt about me. There's no need for dramatics." But privately, Marion retained the sadness of what could have been. This was a mask that she frequently wore, concealing the deep and unrelenting frustration that had plagued her throughout her relationship with W.R.—her longing to be a part of his family, to make their love legitimate in the eyes of the world.

On the day of the funeral, Flink received a call from Marion, asking that he come to the house to be with her. He arrived to find Eileen Percy, Justine Johnstone, and China Harris, all friends from Marion's Ziegfeld days, sitting in the breakfast room, waiting for Marion to come down in the elevator adjacent to the nearby powder room. When they heard her stirring upstairs, they moved there to meet her as she emerged from the elevator.

At 4:00 in that afternoon of August 16, 1951, W.R.'s funeral was held at Grace Cathedral in San Francisco. It was ornate and larger-than-life, with more than 1,500 attendees in the church while many more gathered outside. Some of the most prominent names in politics, finance, and entertainment served as honorary pallbearers. Millicent had flown in from New York along with their son, John, to attend the funeral of a husband who spent most of their married life in the arms of another woman. Production stopped at the Hearst newspapers around the country, as "the Chief" was honored with a minute of silence. And nearly four hundred miles away, the love of his life for more than three decades sat cross-legged on a white shag rug. Marion's fear was palpable. "She was an open wound at that point," recalls Stan Flink. "You could almost feel the terror for what her life was going to be."

In the hours following Hearst's death, all of his possessions had been cleared from his room, except for one photo of Marion Davies. The photo was inscribed "To W.R. from Marion" with a quote from *Romeo and Juliet*: "My bounty is as boundless as the sea, my love as deep." Earlier, Stan Flink had called a *Life* photographer, Alan Grant, to come to the house and photograph the scene. Flink picked up Helena, the last of W.R.'s beloved dachshunds, and placed her on Hearst's bed. She sat directly on the large monogram in the center of the white satin bedcover. With his large, old-fashioned camera, Grant snapped a photo of Helena, and in the silence of the house, the buzzing of the shutter attracted Helena's attention. The dog turned and looked directly into the camera, creating a poignant portrait of where William Randolph Hearst spent his final hours.

Downstairs, Marion took the hands of her friends. She reached out to Flink, who had been an observer up to that point, silently asking him to join them. Although Flink had been called to the house as a friend, he felt conflicted between his obligations as a journalist and the personal nature of his visit to the house. "Marion was always uncertain of her relationship with the press, because so much of it seemed to belong to Hearst," he remembers. Flink tried to treat the visit as a time to comfort Marion, but he could not completely separate himself from his perspective as a reporter. After a moment of hesitation, he joined the group. And as the lavish funeral began in San Francisco, a ray of sunlight shone through the window of 1007 N. Beverly Drive. Marion and her four friends held hands, cross-legged on the floor of the powder room, where they quietly recited the Lord's Prayer.

. . .

After the death of W.R., letters of condolence came pouring in for Marion. Included among them was a letter from Ingrid Bergman, who had not forgotten Marion's unwavering support of her during her pregnancy with Roberto Jr., who by this time was a year old. "We think of you so much!" she wrote. "My husband and I will always remember with deep gratitude how kind you were to us during our hard time."

Marion's friend Constance Moore remembered that Marion "changed entirely" in the period following W.R.'s death. The day after the funeral, Marion awoke to find that her copies of the Hearst newspapers had not arrived on her doorstep. Upon inquiry, she learned that they would not be arriving anymore. With W.R.'s death, Marion's ties with everything she shared with him were slowly being cut. Friends whose livelihoods no longer depended on being a part of the Hearst-Davies circle unceremoniously stopped contacting Marion, including people who had been fixtures for decades. Louella Parsons was among them. Marion began to feel that over all these years, Louella had been using her for her links to the Hearst papers, only to be left in the dust when she was no longer needed. Marion did not carry a grudge easily, but when Louella abandoned her after W.R.'s death, Marion never forgave her.

When Marion began recording her autobiographical tapes a few years later, she was so upset with Louella for her actions following W.R.'s death that she asked that Louella not be mentioned in any biography of her life. "Louella was a traitor," she said. Naturally, such a wish is impossible to honor. Louella Parsons is an inextricable part of the career of Marion Davies, and Marion knew it, which made her abandonment more excruciatingly painful. Marion had not only lost W.R., but she was losing many things that they shared, even some of their friends.

"*Life* Visits Marion Davies" had morphed into a large spread in *Life* focusing on the death of William Randolph Hearst. Stan Flink used his observations from the day of W.R.'s death to write a heartfelt account from Marion's perspective for the August 27, 1951 edition of *Life*. Included in the article was the photo of Helena the dog, with Marion's inscribed photo in the background, taken in W.R.'s empty room.

The story established Marion, and her relationship with W.R., in the mainstream press more than any other article written in her lifetime. She kept her private life closely guarded around journalists she didn't completely trust, and even her close friend Hedda Hopper had not earned that trust. Marion did not want Hedda to have the story that would publicly reveal the truth of her relationship with Hearst for the first time. Stan Flink was one of the few people in her life who had earned it. She wanted Flink, and only Flink, to have the story. In the article, Flink told of the hours after W.R.'s death. He described how Helena the dog had gone from door to door sniffing for scents of W.R., while Marion nervously walked up and down the downstairs hall. On the walls, towering over her, were twelve life-size paintings of Marion in silent movies, playing the roles W.R. had so loved.

When W.R.'s will was read, questions inevitably began to bubble to the surface. Reporters noticed that in the will, the only provision made for Marion was the home, "together with all furniture, furnishing, fixtures, silverware, chinaware, rugs, works of art, antiques, and other contents of said home," a codicil that was struck out "without explanation." The press whispered about a potential rift between Marion and W.R., and swarmed with the news that W.R. had included, then cut out, a provision for "the former actress Marion Davies."

The codicil was stricken out because the house was no longer his to give. At the time of W.R.'s death, their home on Beverly Drive belonged to Marion. After they moved in following their departure from San Simeon, W.R. had bought the house from her, and then gifted it back to her. When he gave it back to Marion, W.R. neglected to have the owner's name legally changed and the house was still listed as W.R.'s in county records, creating a great deal of confusion. Marion made a statement to the press via one of her lawyers, A. Laurence Mitchell, explaining the unusual history of the house, and the matter seemed to have been resolved.

Within a day of the funeral, the secret document of November 5, 1950, became public. The Hearst lawyers were presented with a copy of the agreement giving Marion Davies total voting power in the Hearst Corporation, essentially stripping the Hearst sons of any say in the company. The agreement shocked all involved, and it was immediately disputed. According to lawyers for the Hearst sons, the agreement had never been executed, despite both W.R. and Marion having signed it. The presentation of the agreement to the five Hearst sons set off a legal firestorm, with Marion in the middle. She found herself cornered on all sides by a powerful legal team intent on preserving for the Hearst sons what they felt was their rightful inheritance. In late October, Marion ceded to the sons, and gave up her rights "as voting trustee for the stock of the Hearst Corporation" for the price of $1. She maintained the rights to choose executives, and the Hearst Corporation continued to allow Marion to use the newspapers to publicize her work with the Marion Davies Children's Clinic and other activities. Marion and the Hearst Corporation announced this in a joint statement, adding that Marion had also agreed to serve "as official consultant and adviser to the Hearst Corporation."

W.R.'s fears about lawyers invoking the community property law proved prophetic. Having stated in his will that he was without resources when Marion gave him the $1 million, everything he had, by default, had been earned since that time. Half of that belonged to Millicent. Because of that wording in his will, everything W.R. had wanted Marion to have was in danger of being lost.

In the wake of all this commotion around the will, Horace Brown reached out to be of comfort. He returned from Korea and sat with Marion for hours on end, talking to her and sharing memories with her. At a time when she felt the world was abandoning her, Horace became an important part of Marion's grieving process. She was lonely, and she loved Horace as a grateful friend. He moved into a guest house on the property and lived there for several weeks following W.R.'s death. The two continued to have intimate conversations, in the same way they did when W.R. ushered them into a room alone.

Frances Marion later told W.A. Swanberg that she thought the reason Marion loved having weddings at San Simeon was because she couldn't have one herself. Whenever a film extra would get married, Frances told Swanberg,

Marion would bring the wedding to San Simeon, almost as if to live vicariously through the couple. She wanted marriage so badly, and had come to resign herself to the fact that it was not going to happen for her with W.R. In the fog of her grief, Marion felt that Horace was the person who could finally make her a married woman, in a way that W.R. never could. She would be a proper, upstanding member of society, Mrs. Horace Brown.

On October 31, 1951, two and a half months after W.R.'s death and within the same twenty-four-hour period when she gave up the Hearst Corporation vote, Marion eloped to Nevada with Horace. They arrived by plane in Las Vegas at 3:15 a.m. and made their way to the El Rancho Vegas Hotel, where they were to be married by James Down, justice of the peace. They obtained a marriage license at the hotel, and the entire wedding ceremony lasted a total of three minutes. Justice Down had to stop Marion from saying the vows before it was time. Newspaper reports of the wedding were brief, but almost universally noted that it was "Miss Davies's first marriage."

Marion and Horace had invited Stan Flink to come along on the Palm Springs honeymoon, with the hope that he could fend off the inevitable swarm of press. Even after convincing Marion and Horace that he was a reporter, not a press agent, they still wanted Flink to be there. He once again faced the dilemma of what his responsibilities were as a reporter, and what they were as a friend. He eventually went to Palm Springs, and made sure it was photographed for *Life*.

After the wedding, Marion's friend Ruth Alexander wrote to her in a letter: "You have traveled a long and rocky road, my dear. And now that you are safe in gentle harbour, you can rest."

After the wedding, Louella Parsons called the writer Gene Fowler to discuss it. "Don't you think Marion was hasty?" she asked.

"What did you want her to do," replied Gene, "wait another 32 years?"

. . .

The similarities between Horace and W.R. ended with their looks. Where W.R. was sophisticated and cultured, Horace was lowbrow and crass. W.R., while being a large man, was graceful and light on his feet. Horace was a bull in a china shop, blustering his way through the house, bellowing in his loud Southern accent. Many friends felt Horace meant well but couldn't help his nature. No matter how good his intentions were, "he was a brute," said Marion's nurse Floretta Mauser.

One explanation that Anne Shirley hypothesized was that Horace was hard of hearing. Marion's friends would gather in the home and talk about old times, the industry, or other subjects of which Horace knew nothing. He would frequently interrupt, loudly, asking something that was completely off topic. "Would you like some nuts?" he would ask at a high volume, and two minutes later point to one of Marion's portraits: "Hey! Who did this painting?" Irritated and embarrassed, Marion would lash out at Horace, telling him to go away if he had nothing to contribute. But to Anne, Horace's voice signaled that something was off, and it was more than just Horace's boorish nature.

Marion's marriage to Horace spurred predominantly negative feelings among her family and close friends. Many saw Horace as a menace and, with W.R. gone, many friends who had been connected to Marion through the Hearst empire disappeared, seemingly with no reason to maintain contact in the absence of the Chief. They were suspicious of Horace's motives and too tactful to express their concern to Marion.

Others felt differently about Marion's new husband. "I never disliked Horace," Frances Marion said, a few years after Marion's death in 1961. "He was big, blundering, ill-bred, common, from the other side of the railroad tracks, but he was very warm-hearted." She went on to compare him to a well-meaning but badly behaved dog she once had, who would jump on people just after playing in the mud. That was Horace, Frances said. His nature was not inherently malicious, and she couldn't hate him.

In contrast with what Frances Marion observed, in private, Horace was revealed to be a man with sadistic tendencies. Marion's nocturnal "theatre routine" was a lifestyle to which Horace was unaccustomed. One day, he got so frustrated with Marion's sleeping habits that he stormed out to the car, started it, and crashed it into the side of the house. He felt that Marion's friends were a bad influence, and he resented the time that Marion spent on the phone with them, even cutting the phone lines when he felt a conversation was going on too long. On another occasion, as she slept one day, Horace ran into her room with a gun. "There's someone in the garden," he said. Horace opened the window, aimed the gun, and began firing shots into the garden. Marion was horrified at guns and violence, and began to cry and scream for him to stop. Arthur and Pat Lake happened to be staying with Marion at the time, heard her screams, and ran to her rescue. Arthur managed to wrestle the gun out of Horace's hand and went to comfort the terrified Marion. There was no one in the garden.

On another occasion, Marion had rented a house on the beach while a friend of hers stayed at N. Beverly Drive. The rented home had a beautiful bar illuminated by overhead lights, where Marion liked to sit quietly by herself. One day, Marion was sitting at the bar when Horace came barging in with his gun. One by one, he shot out all the lights above the bar, then turned the gun on a mirror and shot at it several times. "It cost her a fortune to replace all that," remembered Floretta Mauser, who also said that Marion told her why Horace acted this way. "He has no respect for me, and he wants me to know how little respect he has for me."

Marion's friends were concerned for her well-being and jumped to her defense. At parties, which were as frequent with Horace as they were with W.R., Marion drank to excess, emboldened by her husband. Compared to W.R.'s strictness around alcohol, Horace's encouragement of Marion's drinking was distressing to her friends, who remembered W.R.'s fear that Marion's alcoholism would kill her.

By mid-1952, Marion's difficulties had reached a breaking point. Her correspondence with friends and staff from 1952 reveal that Marion was exhausted, upset with the Hearst Corporation and having trouble with Horace. In May she phoned Hedda Hopper to tell her that she was thinking of getting a divorce. Although Marion and Horace had been married for only seven months, to Hedda this was a long overdue piece of news.

"Give him anything he wants, but get rid of him," Hedda told her.

"He was terribly jealous," Marion confided to Hedda. "If a person really loves you, he believes in you; he kept suspecting me when there was no reason."

"I saw that he wouldn't let you have any time alone with anyone. It was like your being in prison," replied Hedda.

"I know. It got to the point finally, where I said 'All right, this is enough.'"

Marion filed for divorce in July of 1952 but retracted the legal papers soon thereafter. She had talked to Horace and "straightened everything out," as she wrote to Bobo Rockefeller the same month. Though Horace was never physically violent with Marion, as far as it is known, his cruelty was emotionally abusive. Yet she continued to characterize him as a sympathetic person, seeming to ignore all her own suffering. "He pays all the bills just the way W.R. did," Marion told Hedda Hopper in the same telephone conversation. "He has always been most gracious. It is in his makeup—you don't just pick that up out of the flowers."

The family held out hope that Marion would finally come to her senses and divorce Horace. Pat and Arthur Lake worried about the psychological effect that Horace was having on Marion, and they often stayed at the Beverly Drive house in order to keep an eye on her. As much as Marion Rose and Arthur Patrick enjoyed spending time with their doting and loving "Aunt Marion," Horace's brutal conduct disturbed the children and they became fearful of him.

On October 2, 1952, Marion and Horace threw an elaborate party, costing upward of $30,000, to celebrate singer Johnny Ray's opening at Ciro's Nightclub. Ray had also just had a wedding, to Marilyn Morrison, the daughter of the owner of the Mocambo Nightclub. When asked why Marion wanted a party on such a grand scale, she replied, "I wanted to have some fun before I die." The party rivaled any that Marion had given at the Beach House or San Simeon, with more than a thousand people in attendance. The champagne flowed freely, and Cadillacs were lined up for a mile down the block. Newspapers reported that "the guest list read like a 1952 edition of a Hollywood Who's Who."

Marion and Horace received the guests side by side at the door, putting on the pretense of a happy marriage. But in truth, the grandiosity of the Johnny Ray party masked what was a very difficult time for Marion and Horace. Later that month, those concerned about Marion found new reason to be optimistic about Marion leaving her abusive marriage. In scrawled, messy handwriting pocked with ink stains, Marion wrote a note to her upstairs maid, Faith Grant, regarding the upcoming one-year anniversary of her marriage to Horace:

> Faith—Will you please call [lawyer] Mr. Bautzer and tell him...that I am very exhausted having not slept for three days and three nights and thank him for wanting to come over and celebrate my anniversary, but there is no such a thing. I would very much like to see him when he prefers—I would sincerely like to get a divorce. I'll notify him at the proper time.
> Lots of love–
> Marion

But once again, she forgave Horace and her desire for a divorce didn't progress beyond this initial planning stage.

Marion's longtime friend Dorothy Mackaill had not wanted to contact Marion directly about her unhappy state with Horace, since "the going must be a little rough out there," but she expressed concern for Marion and her present situation to Hedda Hopper. "Please let her know that if I can do anything or take her out of S. California to Europe or h——, anywhere, I'll only be too happy as she's 'My Marianne,'" she said.

Dr. Corday, who was now Marion's primary physician, was concerned by Marion's sleeplessness and her anxiety surrounding Horace's attacks. In order to ease her symptoms, he prescribed her meprobamate, with the common brand name of Miltown, to calm her nerves and allow her to sleep. Marion took the drug, a sedative similar to Xanax, several times a day as needed and the medication made her drowsy and lethargic, effects noticed by her friends and family.

Also contributing to this anxiety were continuing issues with the Hearst sons. As tense as things were after W.R.'s death between Marion and W.R.'s children, they heated up even further in the ensuing years. Marion wrote to Hearst Corporation board chairman Martin Huberth in early 1953: "Since the time of Mr. Hearst's demise I have not received any notice of meetings, etc., of the Hearst Corporation, of which, I think, I am a vice president. Would you kindly explain why I have not been given this information?" Marion was convinced that the Hearst Corporation in general, and the Hearst sons in particular, were conspiring against her to oust her from the corporation.

In November 1952, Marion and Horace were dining at Romanoff's with Kay Spreckels, an actress and good friend of Marion's, who would later marry Clark Gable. Toward the end of their meal, Kay's expression became excited and she waved enthusiastically at someone behind Horace. "Why, there's Bill Hearst!" she exclaimed. The group turned to look, and there was W.R.'s son, at the entrance to the restaurant chatting with the maitre d'.

"Go over and invite him to join us," Marion implored Horace.

Horace had never before met Bill, and couldn't pick out which man he was in the crowded restaurant. He went to a doorman and asked which man was William Randolph Hearst Jr., and the doorman informed him that he had just stepped outside. Horace went outside, and saw him standing on the sidewalk.

"I'm Captain Horace Brown," Horace stated. "My wife, Miss Marion Davies, would like to have you join us at our table."

Bill declined. When Horace questioned him why, and brought up that none of his brothers seemed to have ill feelings toward Marion, Bill called Marion an insulting name. Despite his brutishness, Horace could be very protective of Marion. He lunged at Bill and hit him in the face. He hit back and a parking lot attendant rushed over to break up the fight. The attendant grabbed Horace as he attempted to hit Bill again, and the restraint seemed to calm Horace a bit. He followed Bill to his car, and once again asked him to join their table. The answer was still no, and Bill drove off.

Hearing of the incident afterward, Marion was extremely upset. She had always hated any kind of conflict, and to learn of this public incident between her husband and W.R.'s son, regardless of their current relationship, affected her deeply. The brawl, intended to defend Marion against defamation, only served to alienate Marion further from Horace.

. . .

In early 1953, Charlie Lederer approached Stan Flink about the prospect of helping Marion write her autobiography. Marion's reluctance to give interviews, her anxiety, and her cautiousness around strangers meant that anyone who was going to help Marion write her life story would have to be a trusted friend. Charlie felt Stan could put her at ease and give her a trustworthy and knowledgeable assistant in the project. Flink was enthusiastic about the idea of Marion's life officially appearing in print. The only thing that held him back from immediately agreeing to the project was his fear of a conflict of interest with *Life*. In talking to the higher-ups at the magazine, it was ultimately decided that something useful to *Life* might come from Stan's interviews with Marion. Thus, he was granted a sabbatical to record Marion's memories. Charlie Lederer, along with Marion's lawyer Gregson Bautzer, drafted a contract on February 18, 1953, to officially hire Stan Flink. All material recorded would be hers, material she could then use to write her story.

Gregson Bautzer, often shortened to "Greg," was a well-known Hollywood attorney notorious for being "the toughest lawyer in town." His steamy affairs with women (including, notably, Joan Crawford and Lana Turner) were as famous as his "addiction to winning," and his fierce loyalty to his clients, both personally and professionally. Marion had come to depend on him as much as she depended on her nephew Charlie Lederer, and often referred to them as a unit: "Charlie and Bautzer." In contrast to Charlie's devoted love, Bautzer's loyalty was controlling and domineering. When Stan Flink was writing "*Life* Visits Marion Davies," Bautzer told him, "Don't call me a Hollywood lawyer." After that, Stan walked away, then Bautzer called out a few seconds later. "But if you do," he said angrily, "call me a *top* Hollywood lawyer!"

In keeping with Marion's innate blindness toward anyone who might be taking advantage of her or have unwarranted control over her life, she became very attached to Bautzer. She was comfortable communicating the streak of competition she still felt with Millicent, and sometimes acted on it. "I would like to have a Rolls Royce," Marion said to him one day, "and I would like it to be black."

"But Marion," Bautzer said to her, "you already have cars, why a Rolls Royce? And why does it have to be black?"

"Well," said Marion with a twinkle in her eye, "the widow has one."

"It was not malicious at all," remembered Lea Sullivan, Bautzer's office manager. "It was said with sort of a strut."

Despite Bautzer's controlling ways, he often found himself having to draw a professional boundary with her. Several times, Marion attempted to give him munificent gifts that he, as a member of the bar, could not ethically accept. The Rolls Royce that Marion did end up purchasing became a gift to Bautzer, presented to him with a large bow on top and the pink slip in his name. Later in life, when Bautzer was helping Marion draw up her will, she tried to leave him a large plot of land. His ethical responsibility as a lawyer precluded him from being named as a beneficiary in a will he drew up. "That's very kind of you," Bautzer told her, "but that is not correct and it can't be done." Ethical obligations aside, Bautzer was a dominating force in nearly every aspect of Marion's life, and Stan Flink was witness to this firsthand.

Stan knew that Bautzer, despite having drawn up the contract himself, was fearful of anything Marion might say during her reminiscences that might incriminate her or anger the Hearst Corporation. In order to keep a highly "sanitized" environment while Marion reminisced, Bautzer set up hidden microphones that recorded Stan recording Marion. Marion knew about the setup, and was too smart to think that Stan didn't know, but the presence of the hidden microphones soured the interviews from the start. Despite her comfort with Stan, Marion's answers to probing questions about her relationship with W.R. were often glossed over, veiled, or diluted. When a question about the Hearst Corporation came up, Marion tended to respond with a simple "Can't talk about that." At times she was almost apologetic to Stan about her vague answers, and would drop him as many hints as she could get away with while Bautzer's microphones recorded everything she said.

Marion waxed nostalgic about Hearst as a man, but only intermittently, and rather tentatively, expressed anything other than friendship with him. She did admit being in love with W.R., and never being able to leave him for anyone else. "He knew I had no intentions of ever getting married to anybody, because he knew I was in love with him," Marion said, in response to a question about not being able to marry. But then, not thirty seconds later, Marion veiled her feelings again. "I'd keep saying, 'Forget it. I don't want it that way. We're fine, we have great companionship, we have an understanding...and let it stay that way. Don't worry about it. It doesn't mean anything to me, I'm not the type to say "I want to be Mrs. So-and-so."' I was never that type."

Eileen Percy and Justine Johnstone confirmed to Stan Flink what he had suspected about these statements—that in talking this way, Marion hid her true desire to be a married woman. Putting on a brave or indifferent front was typical of Marion when she was feeling vulnerable, and her regrets at never having been able to marry W.R. were still haunting her.

"Not If They Offered Me Mars
on a Silver Platter"

During the time that Marion and Stan Flink were recording the tapes, the world outside Marion's home on North Beverly Drive was changing. Residential areas of Los Angeles County were seeing exponential growth in the postwar years, as the baby boom drove more families to buy single-family dwellings instead of living in apartments toward the city's downtown. In 1953, Marion's address changed from 1007 to 1011 N. Beverly Drive, as Beverly Hills expanded and more homes were built on Marion's street to meet the demand.

The film industry changed, too, as television became its competition. New innovations tried to lure viewers out of their homes and into the theaters. Movies were filmed in 3-D, and the Cinerama technique allowed for films to be experienced on a huge, curved screen with a 146-degree arc. These sweeping changes made Marion feel even more self-conscious about her age and the era she represented. She felt as though she were from a different world, one that few in the industry recognized anymore. "I've lived too long," she said to her friends, and told her nurse Floretta Mauser that she was "cracking up," feeling that she was going crazy as the industry galloped ahead of everything she knew.

Along with the baby boom and housing growth, the 1950s saw an increase in consumerist culture, and television became mainstream as more families could afford a set. Marion had owned a television since at least April 1951, before W.R. died, but it didn't work very well in the house. Horace enjoyed watching boxing matches on the television, in spite of the poor reception, but Marion preferred to listen to the news on the radio, or read. She had an active account at Martindale's bookstore on Santa Monica Blvd., and when new titles arrived, the owner Thomas Martindale would send them to Marion, stacks at a time.

By the mid-1950s, interest piqued regarding Marion's unusual life story. Twentieth Century-Fox contacted her, and because she was in the midst of her tapes and caught up in the whirlpool of autobiography, she expressed interest in a film version made of her life. The plans fizzled, but Marion was becoming more open to talking. Up to this point, aside from run-of-the-mill star sketches in fan magazines, Marion steadfastly avoided speaking about her experiences, either on camera or off. In addition to her concern about her privacy and the secrets she guarded, Marion was self-conscious of her stutter and feared its appearance in candid television interviews. During the 1950s, many stars of Marion's era were reinventing themselves for the television cameras, making guest appearances on popular television shows such as *What's My Line?* Marion's speech, she decided, precluded her from these opportunities and she shied away from them.

Hedda Hopper knew Marion's reservations, so when Hedda approached her for a rare interview in 1954, she assured her that the questions would be gentle and the interview would be solely in print. Marion agreed and Hedda published the interview in her syndicated "Motion Pictures" column. In it, Marion claimed to have hated making movies.

"Would you do another picture if it was a good story?" asked Hedda.

"Not if they offered me Mars on a silver platter," was Marion's reply. "I was never crazy about making movies. It was such a waste of time."

This change of heart may have been a reflection of sadness at how her life had turned out, and partly a result of the gradual psychological changes due to the Miltown that she still took for anxiety. Marion's alcoholism continued to affect her, and the combination of alcohol and Miltown was a likely cause of the mental fogginess that Marion experienced during this period. However, her memory was still generally sharp and the dynamic of Marion's remaining close friendships remained as strong as ever. Her diligent correspondence with old friends continued, those who had loyally stuck by her side, and she by theirs. But regarding her unhappy marriage with Horace, few friends intervened past the point of surface-level worry. Marion's cycle of divorce proceedings, followed by short-lived reconciliation, continued.

Joseph P. Kennedy was getting ready for three family weddings within the same year, and in May 1953, Marion and Horace were invited to attend all of them. The first was the marriage of Kennedy's daughter, Eunice, to Sargent

Shriver. In September, then-Senator John F. Kennedy would be marrying Jacqueline Bouvier, and in April 1954, Joe's daughter Patricia was to marry Peter Lawford. Marion wanted to attend all three weddings, so they planned to vacation on the East Coast for six months so that they could be there for the first two weddings. Then they would go back to California and return in April for the Lawford wedding. Although Marion was a registered Republican, she remained what Stan Flink had called a "natural liberal." After W.R.'s death, her politics had drifted left, and she became a strong supporter of JFK.

Joe Kennedy remained by her side, seeing himself as a kind of protector, as he had been in the days when he had encouraged W.R. to provide for Marion in his will. Horace had taken a liking to Joe Kennedy as well, and at the wedding of "Jack" and "Jackie" on September 12, Horace and Marion were featured in the newsreel footage of the event. As Marion got out of the car on Horace's arm, her "rubber legs" were evident, as she was limping and seeming to favor her left foot.

Marion had arranged three wedding gifts for the Bouvier-Kennedy wedding—cufflinks for Jack, a bracelet for Jackie, and the Beverly Drive house to use for their honeymoon. After their wedding, Jack and Jackie made their way West to spend a week at the N. Beverly Drive home while Marion and Horace remained in the East. Jackie wrote her from the house, using Marion's stationery:

> We have just had the most perfect four days imaginable at your house—how can the rest of our lives help but be a tragic anticlimax....
>
> Jacqueline Kennedy

And then a note in Jack's handwriting:

> The house is sensational—as we say here on the Coast. Many many thanks.... You are terrific—Best to the Captain.
> All care,
> Jack

When Marion returned to California, she and Stan Flink resumed their work on her autobiography. Stan quickly realized that the story was not unfolding in the way he hoped it would. Knowing the depth of Marion's relationship with W.R., he thought that Marion's watered-down sentiments masked the true feelings she was unable to articulate. The theatrical, larger-than-life quality of the relationship between Marion and W.R. got lost in a shuffle of fear and anxiety, with an ever-present Greg Bautzer controlling what was said through his hidden microphones. As Stan's hopes for a full and honest autobiography faded, he began to explore the idea of annulling his contract.

He approached Charlie Lederer with his concerns, and Charlie agreed that the prospect of an autobiography was proving to be a lost cause. He and Bautzer drafted an agreement that formally stopped the progress on Marion's autobiography, and relieved Stan Flink of his contract. It was a friendly agreement, and all involved seemed happy with the outcome. Marion's secretary, Tom Kennington, noticed Flink's relief and wrote a P.S. at the end of the letter to Greg Bautzer informing him of the annulled contract: "I could have sworn that Stan had the biggest grin on his face."

Marion still possessed a great deal of energy. She took her first trip to Harbelle, Horace's family estate in Virginia, in May 1954, shortly after the Kennedy weddings. At the same time, Marion sought to further her business interests in New York. She bought several properties in the early 1950s that she enjoyed developing—in 1954, she purchased a building at 57th and Park, which she named the Davies Building, and a seventeen-story high-rise on Madison and 55th in New York that she named the Douras Building, in memory of her father.

Beginning in 1953, Marion's nephew Charlie Lederer had been hard at work on a musical adaptation of Edward Knoblock's 1911 play *Kismet*. Along with co-writer Luther Davis, Charlie wrote the book to a "musical Arabian night," a play set to the melodies of composer Alexander Borodin about a poet assuming the identity of a beggar, and experiencing a series of life-changing events over the course of a single day in Baghdad. *Kismet* was slated to be the highlight of the San Francisco and Los Angeles Civic Light Opera seasons that year, and following the California productions, if successful, the play was to go to New York for a Broadway run.

Following the Los Angeles premiere, *Kismet* received a front-page spread in the *Los Angeles Times* extolling its praises. Reporter Albert Goldberg wrote that the play "has all the ingredients of a genuinely popular entertainment," and that it appealed "both to an audience's imagination and its intelligence." The review specifically praised *Kismet*'s writing, and the "plot of lively and consistent interest, and characters as fantastic as they are real." Similar reviews came from Bay Area critics, with Wood Soanes of the *Oakland Tribune* calling it "one of the most satisfying musicals ever to be produced in the West." In the wake of these rave reviews, producer Edwin Lester turned the production over to Charlie Lederer to produce *Kismet*'s New York run.

As Charlie made arrangements to move the show east, Marion quietly invested $185,000 in the production, becoming *Kismet*'s chief backer. Her motive was to help Charlie, and in spite of the play's success, she thought she would probably write off a loss for her investment. Newspapers learned that Marion was the principal force behind the Broadway run of *Kismet* and Walter Winchell named her in his column. "Marion Davies, the former star, is reported *Kismet*'s top angel," he wrote on November 23, "for more than $200,000." Marion wired him a correction that appeared in his column the following week: "It was $180,000, but I am no angel, regardless of what you hear."

Kismet was sold out for weeks in advance by the time it opened at the Ziegfeld Theatre on West 54th Street in Manhattan, on December 3, 1953. Reviews continued to be stellar, and when the Tony Awards were held on March 28 of the following year, Charlie Lederer and his co-writer Luther Davis received awards for their libretto, and *Kismet* won Best Musical. Up to this point, Marion had steadfastly refused free tickets, preferring to buy them and contribute to the show's success. Only when she found that she might miss her nephew's Tony-winning show altogether did she agree to "swindle a couple from management," securing tickets in early May 1954. At its peak, *Kismet* was bringing in a $58,000 profit per week, which was a great surprise and delight to Marion.

MGM bought the rights for *Kismet* to be adapted into a movie in 1955, with Charlie writing the screenplay. The rights to the musical numbers were purchased from Marion, who owned them as the play's chief backer. Although MGM had changed a great deal since she had left the studio in 1934 (Louis B. Mayer had been pushed out, and MGM was now under the auspices of Dore Schary as president), there was a certain irony in the turning of the tables. Marion's continued involvement in show business, nearly two decades after her retirement, tickled her. *Kismet* remains a mainstay of musical theater to this day, known for the standards "Baubles, Bangles, and Beads" and "Stranger in Paradise."

Around the same time as *Kismet*'s success, Marion got to know Lea Sullivan, the young office manager of her lawyer Greg Bautzer, as a good friend. Lea was lively, spunky, and adventurous, with a heart of gold. Marion called her "Sullivan," as it seemed to fit her better than "Lea," and the two became fast friends, each having a mischievous and fearless streak in them. Sullivan tried to call her "Davies," but it felt odd to Marion. "I like Sullivan," she said. "I don't like Davies. It isn't feminine."

"She was spontaneous, she was fun, and she was smart," Sullivan remembered. She also recalled Marion's unusual way of expressing herself in language. Whenever they were together and they encountered someone Marion especially liked, Marion would say, "Oh, Sullivan, I think we ought to grab him." When a member of the household staff made her angry, instead of saying that she wanted to fire the person, she would say, "We'll miss him." This type of self-expression endeared Marion to her, and Marion's intelligence and knowledge of current events impressed her. Marion would often end conversations with "Watch out for the fallout, Sullivan," referring to the nuclear age's fear of an atomic blast and the fallout that would come from it.

As Bautzer's assistant, Sullivan would also be there when Marion bought a new building, and she witnessed Marion's real estate and business prowess firsthand. In 1955, Marion decided to shake up her real estate holdings, and expressed interest in purchasing the Desert Inn, a Palm Springs hotel that had been in operation since 1909. Marion managed to reduce the price to just under $2 million. "It'll cost a lot more by the time we get through with it," Marion told reporters. "I plan to turn it into a miniature Rockefeller Center."

Under Marion's ownership, the Desert Inn flourished. It became one of her favorite holdings, and she put a great deal of attention and effort into it. In addition, it was close enough to Los Angeles that Marion could simply go there for dinner, which she did often. She never alerted the management, preferring to just show up like anybody else, but when Lea Sullivan knew of her plans she took it upon herself to alert Bob Taliaferro, the manager, so that the kitchen could prepare something special for Marion's arrival.

Marion had a penchant for naming all her real estate, and once asked Greg Bautzer for his advice on what to name it. "Why, Marion?" asked Bautzer. "Why do you name all your buildings?"

Marion ignored the question. "Well, if you're not going to h-help me," she said, "I'll j-just name it the M-M-Marion D-D-Davies B-b-building. And," she added, "I want you to write it down exactly like I said it." At that, she burst out laughing, which became contagious and everyone else started laughing too. Sullivan appreciated Marion's ability to laugh at herself. "With that problem that she had, to be able to laugh at herself about it was wonderful. She taught me... don't sweat the small stuff. Lighten up."

Sullivan's hobbies included daredevil sports such as racecar driving and bullfighting, and Marion, knowing her love of racing, gave Sullivan a solid gold St. Christopher, adorned with rubies and presented with the admonition, "Now, the Pope tells me that this is only good under 50 miles an hour. After that, you're on your own."

As accepting as Marion was, Lea Sullivan's love of bullfighting was one thing that Marion could not support. She tried hard to be supportive and nonjudgmental. Marion bought Lea bullfighting-related gifts, and gave her some posters that had hung in the Desert Inn. But ultimately, Marion's love for animals and her crusades against vivisection rendered her unable to continue to support friend's activities. One day, she took Sullivan aside and told her of her concern. "You know, you could get hurt," Marion told her. "And even if you don't get hurt, the bull can."

"Well, yes…"

"I just wish you'd think about it," said Marion.

Marion's words took Sullivan by surprise. She had never encountered anyone who had stood up for the bulls before, and didn't know that Marion was so devoted to animals. "I knew she was crazy about dogs," recalled Sullivan later, "but a lot of people are crazy about dogs and don't mention animal rights at all." In addition, she never *had* really thought about the implications of bullfighting. And coming from Marion, a woman she had come to love and respect, it made Sullivan reconsider the sport. "If she said *anything* to me, I paid attention." Soon after her conversation with Marion, Sullivan stopped bullfighting. Taking the animal into account in bullfighting opened up a door for Sullivan that led to taking them into account in everything she did, and she became an advocate for animal rights. Over the next few years, Sullivan adopted Marion's animal rights activism—becoming an ethical vegetarian and helping at the local animal shelter.

As Marion's interest in real estate was coming to a peak, plans were made for a residence at 20 Sutton Place South so that she could be closer to her real estate interests in the city. This necessitated cutting back the staff at the house in Beverly Hills, and reluctantly, Marion had to tell her beloved Mrs. Davis that she would need to let her go. As a parting gift, in addition to her leaving pay, Marion gave Mrs. Davis $1,000 in cash. Mrs. Davis had been good to her, and it was difficult to say goodbye.

The two Lake children, Marion Rose and Arthur Patrick, grew up spending much of their time with their great-aunt Marion. In the summer of 1954, Marion sponsored a new television series starring Arthur Lake, Patricia, and their children. Known as "Meet the Family," it capitalized on Arthur's "Dagwood" character from the *Blondie* series. The first episode was filmed in Guatemala, with the goal to show Americans a country most had never been to. With "Meet the Family," the children were often on the road, but when they were home, they accompanied Marion and Horace on trips to New York to check on Marion's real estate. To entertain them, Marion and Horace would take the children to matinees of the latest shows on Broadway, which by 1956 included *My Fair Lady*, starring Julie Andrews and Rex Harrison. They held the memories of going to see *My Fair Lady* very dearly, and recalled later the way they, along with their aunt Marion, would get on a boat on the Hudson River following the show and sing the entire score of the musical, acting out all the parts.

Marion continued to give seemingly endlessly to her friends, family, and charities. The Jewish Home for the Aged, of which Marion still served as a lifetime trustee, announced in December 1956 that Marion and Horace would be donating a $25,000 elevator to the Mary Pickford wing of the home. It would be the second such elevator in the building, one that was "much needed," and the donation would be made in memory of Marion's parents, Bernard and Rose Douras.

Comedian Joe Frisco, an acquaintance of Marion's during her early days as a chorus girl, was down on his luck and couldn't pay his taxes. Marion read about his situation in the newspapers, and decided to send him money regularly. She didn't know him very well, but there was a double closeness she felt to him—they had both been on Broadway at the same time, and they both stuttered. After a while, she heard that Joe was using the money to feed his gambling and drinking habit. Friends chided her for continuing to give him money, but Marion refused to stop. "It's Joe's money," Marion would say, "and he can do what he wants with it."

Around the same time, Marion learned that Eleanor Boardman was looking for a new home. She had been living in Europe for the past several years, having married a Frenchman, Harry d'Abbadie d'Arrast, but had always rented a home in California to come back to. Her children, Belinda and Antonia, were in school in the United States and she wanted to be near them. When her rented California house was sold by the owner, Marion wrote a note to Cleo, one of her butlers at N. Beverly Drive. She asked Cleo to get the living quarters prepared in the Gate House, a small guest house on Marion's property, that Marion had never used. Eleanor would be moving in.

Eleanor wanted to pay Marion rent for the use of the house. Marion refused, but Eleanor knew how much Marion loved presents. Every month, she would take her daughter Belinda down to the shops and buy Marion a gift. When Eleanor was in California, she continued to live in the house for the rest of Marion's life, and even until well after Marion's death in 1961.

Although her new buildings and Eleanor's presence gave her pleasure, Marion continued to show the psychological strain of living with Horace. She filed for divorce once again in October 1954, citing the mental cruelty that Horace was so wont to display, and Horace moved out of the house on Beverly Drive to relocate to San Francisco for three months. Less than a week after filing the suit, Marion and Horace reconciled once again. Horace moved back into the house on North Beverly Drive, and the cycle of dysfunction and reconciliation continued.

One summer evening in July 1956, Horace rushed Marion to the Cedars of Lebanon Hospital after becoming concerned that she might be having a stroke. Upon arrival at Cedars of Lebanon, Horace's suspicions were confirmed. The papers quickly picked up on the story and upon questioning the hospital staff, the news outlets reported that despite her stroke, which was minor, Marion was in "very good condition." Marion's secretary, "Bill" Williams, disclosed to the papers that she had been in a state of exhaustion, and Marion remained at the hospital for four days, going home on July 23. Marion wrote Hedda Hopper on July 27: "I am feeling better but have to rest for three months. Seems a long time. I think the doctor underestimated [sic] my ability to relax that long."

Fortunately for Marion, she was on the road to recovery, and she purchased a new property in Rancho Mirage, southeast of Palm Springs, where she could recuperate and rest. W.R.'s eldest son, George Hearst, who was still very close to Marion, was also recovering from surgery at that time, and when Marion moved in, he moved in as well. The house was near the Tamarisk Country Club, and close enough to Los Angeles that she could go back and forth as she wished, often on weekends with her nieces and nephews. Occasionally driven by her youngest stepson Russell, Marion Rose and Arthur Patrick could ride horses and spend time at Tamarisk while Marion recovered.

In 1957, Marion and Horace threw a large party at the house on Beverly Drive, inviting upwards of seven hundred guests. Some of Marion's oldest and most loyal friends, including Frances Marion, were not invited. It seemed odd to Marion's friends that certain important people in Marion's life were left off the guest list. Perhaps this was due to Horace's belief that Marion's friends were a bad influence, and in order to avoid another fight, Marion didn't protest.

Frances Marion wrote a scathing letter to Hedda Hopper describing what she had heard of the occasion from actor David Wayne and his wife:

> All agreed it was a disappointment—no fights—no nudes descending the staircase or leaping into the pool—and Marion being able to stand on her two feet until long after midnight. Almost 700 partook of excellent champagne and lousy food .... The most touching speech was made by the host—and Jane said everyone gasped when he took the spotlight, mouthed a lot of squashy sentiment about Marion and ended up by saying 'I love her. I love her more than anybody in the whole world has ever loved her. Except Mr. Hearst, of course.' Thus ends the saga which we have followed throughout these many years and I wonder if WR's dust stirred slightly when he heard about those brave bold words spoken by the ex-stuntman who now sleeps in his bed.

Frances's recounting of the story to Hedda Hopper in such a tone is undoubtedly the result of bruised emotions at not having been invited to the party. But it speaks to an almost undisputed sentiment regarding the character of Marion's husband, and how Marion's life changed after her marriage to Horace. Like so many, Frances had run out of patience.

"I Don't Think She Was Afraid of Death"

As the 1950s progressed, Lea Sullivan began to notice the same changes that Constance Moore had noticed earlier in Marion. Her behavior and the way she carried herself, always having been extraordinarily graceful and elegant, were now less so. She put less effort into her appearance and carriage. Marion's eyes, always large and full of life, had become bulgy and sometimes glazed over. Lea noticed that sometimes she wouldn't get into street clothes for a week, or more, at a time. She relied more and more on her nurses and friends to help her walk.

Regardless, Marion continued to devote her time to the things that gave her pleasure. The tiny children's clinic that had been founded on Beloit Avenue to care for the low-income children of West Los Angeles had become bigger than Marion ever thought it would, now serving 600–800 children every month. Even the larger, five-acre Julia Morgan property from the initial clinic expansion in 1928 seemed too small. In May 1952, Marion and the Marion Davies Foundation proposed a merger between the Children's Clinic and the UCLA Medical Center. The new clinic would expand beyond outpatient services and provide a comprehensive inpatient hospital. Marion and the foundation had been wanting to expand the clinic for some time, but an inpatient hospital in conjunction with the outpatient clinic proved too costly. The merger with UCLA would allow the foundation to have financial support from the UCLA Medical Center, while still maintaining control of the clinic's oversight.

The UCLA regents debated the proposal, and ultimately decided to accept. The Marion Davies Children's Clinic officially became a part of UCLA, and the specialty departments founded in the wake of the merger included a clinic for children with cerebral palsy, a neurology center, and a support group for parents and children with developmental delays. The new clinic also featured a full-fledged speech-language pathology department, a relatively new and rare specialty. When Marion was a child struggling with her stutter, no such clinic was available to her. For that reason, this new department was particularly meaningful.

In 1957, Marion began to think about dissolving the Marion Davies Foundation. Its initial purpose had been to oversee the clinic, and now with its day-to-day operations run almost exclusively by UCLA, Marion felt that the best way to serve the future interests of the clinic would be to officially hand control to UCLA. She would liquidate the Marion Davies Foundation, putting the money left in the foundation account toward funding a new clinic building. The clinic had been a vital and important part of Marion's life, and she had seen it grow from the tiny project that served a hundred children in 1926 to the successful and multidisciplinary system that now served tens of thousands of children every year.

She petitioned the California Superior Court to allow the foundation to dissolve. There was $1.5 million in the foundation account, money that Marion was ready to hand to UCLA for a new clinic, but during meetings and discussions with both UCLA and the trustee of the foundation, Bank of America, it was decided that instead of a new clinic, it would be more financially efficient and beneficial to all parties to have the money go toward a new hospital wing. The wing would be a four-story, stand-alone building, serving "400–500 children a month for everything from psychiatry to measles," explained Horace in his statement to the court, and it "fulfills a lifelong desire of Miss Davies."

On March 28, 1958, UCLA sold the clinic building to a group of psychiatrists for the price of $426,000, and the money from the sale went to augment the Marion Davies Foundation's initial gift. The total amount given to UCLA, then, was nearly $2 million.

"I'll probably be remembered more for the parties I gave at the Beach House," Marion mused in 1960, "but the clinic is the real joy of my life."

. . .

Remember how we laughed even when we were crying? How we danced the shimmy and the Charleston...tossed our petticoats over the windmill...
Then the thirties...those fabulous excursions to San Simeon...a lot of us wilder than the flowers but just as pretty...

All this was ours to enjoy and be grateful for the rest of our lives. And none of these memories could have graced our past if it hadn't been for you and your loving kindness.

(Letter from Frances Marion to Marion Davies, 1961)

By the time construction on the new clinic began in 1960, Marion was 63 years old and seriously ill.

She was having trouble with Horace again, and Charlie Lederer had arranged for her to temporarily move into the home of Charlie's friend Ben Hecht. Following the routine extraction of a tooth while living with Hecht, Marion developed an infection in her jaw. That infection turned into osteomyelitis, and then quickly into a painful, devastating jaw cancer. Marion was given the option to have that portion of her jaw removed, but doctors told her she would be disfigured for the rest of her life. She declined.

As Marion's disease progressed, her pain increased until it was nearly constant. Her nurses remembered that they had to watch her body language for signs of the intense pain in her jaw, since Marion never complained about being in pain and rarely asked for anything. She seemed to be suffering in silence for the benefit of those around her, not wanting to be a burden on anyone, even her nurses.

As Marion's illness worsened, Hedda Hopper asked her to be part of the television special based on her newspaper column, *Hedda Hopper's Hollywood*. Marion's cancer was beginning to affect her appearance—her body was becoming weaker, and she had become rail thin. According to Hedda Hopper, word got out that she had asked Marion to participate in the show, and her friends expressed concern for how Marion would look onscreen. "She can't possibly do it," Kay Gable, the former Kay Spreckels, who had been close to Marion, told Hedda. "She's not well enough."

"Why do you think I asked her?" said Hedda. "For one reason only—to lift her morale."

"But she looks so ill," Kay persisted.

"Take it from me, she'll look beautiful."

Marion agreed to appear on the show, and returned to N. Beverly Drive to get ready for the shoot. Horace remained at the house, but stayed out of the way of the production. Gene Hibbs, a makeup artist who specialized in recreating youthful appearances, was called in to prepare her for the camera. Hibbs had done Hedda's makeup the same day, and when Marion complimented Hedda on her appearance, she brushed it off. "Wait until you see what he does for you."

Marion's nurse Floretta Mauser helped Marion downstairs to the dressing room, where Hibbs and George Masters, a hairstylist, were waiting to make Marion camera-ready. "I went off to the bottom of her garden to shoot some scenes there," wrote Hedda. "When I came back, the transformation had worked. It was as if a magic wand had waved lovingly over her. She looked thirty years younger than when I'd left her not more than an hour before."

It instantly brightened Marion's mood. She proudly put on a blue satin gown, now much too large for her thin figure, and Hedda recommended that Marion wear a mink stole to fill out her thin shoulders. Marion looked at herself in the mirror.

"You look beautiful," Hedda told her.

Marion smiled, and nodded in agreement. Hedda called Charlie Lederer, wanting him to see his beloved aunt. When Charlie came over and saw Marion, "with her age and sickness erased," he burst into tears and had to leave the room.

Marion's part in *Hedda Hopper's Hollywood* consisted of one simple line: "It's so nice to have you here. Welcome to my home." Her mouth shows a slight droop on the left side, evidence of the stroke she had suffered in 1956. The camera then pans around the room, showing paintings that had been done by Federico Beltrán-Masses in Europe many years earlier, scenes from *Little Old New York*, and souvenirs from a life well lived.

Hedda stated that the simplicity of Marion's appearance, and her short line, was purposeful in order to reduce the chances of Marion stuttering, and to minimize her exhaustion. But, ever the hard worker even while battling cancer, Marion wanted to continue. "Is this all I get to do?" she asked. "I want more." Hedda stuck with her convictions and Marion acquiesced, changing her insistence from wanting more lines to showing her friends how young she looked. She visited Pickfair to show Mary Pickford, then drove to see people all over town until midnight. When Marion finally returned home, she couldn't manage to get the makeup off and phoned Hedda. "How do I get this stuff off my face?"

In July of 1960, the Democratic National Convention was held in Los Angeles to nominate John F. Kennedy for the Democratic presidential ticket. Jack and Jackie were staying in an apartment on N. Rossmore Avenue, by the Wilshire Country Club, but just as she had when Jack and Jackie got married, Marion wanted to offer her home to the campaign. With the bevy of staff, a pool, and multiple telephone lines, the house was ideal for a campaign headquarters. Although the security was not tight enough for Jack and Jackie, it was the perfect place for Joe, where he could lay low and yet be as well-connected as needed. Marion and Horace temporarily moved to a rented house in Santa Monica while they lent the house to Joe for the convention.

While the newspapers initially had been hesitant in reporting Marion's condition, by 1960 they disclosed that she had indeed suffered from osteomyelitis, but they insisted that the prognosis was good. They did not disclose that the osteomyelitis was now cancer and that Marion had very little time left.

Marion's approach to death seemed thoughtful and accepting. "I don't think she was afraid of death. I don't think she was afraid of much of anything, except the fallout," recalled her friend Lea Sullivan, remembering the funny way that Marion used to end conversations by telling her to watch out for the fallout. Upon her realization that this cancer would be terminal, Marion began to reach out to old friends. She called Alice Head, the managing director of Hearst's National Magazine Company, to come over from London to see her one last time. "She was very fond of Marion," recalled Eleanor Boardman, who was called to accompany Alice on an outing to Palm Springs. The three of them reminisced about old times, and about St. Donat's, where they had all been together and which had recently been sold by the Hearst Corporation.

After John F. Kennedy was elected president in November, Marion and Horace together were invited to his inauguration. It was a thank you from Joe for her devotion to the campaign and their long friendship. She made the trip to Washington, DC, with Horace, despite her quickly failing health. A few weeks before they left, Hedda Hopper threw a farewell party for Marion at Hedda's home and wrote to Frances Marion, who was on the East Coast and couldn't attend, that it was "the most nostalgic thing I have ever given."

From the right side of the president's box, Marion and Horace watched while the thirty-fifth president of the United States was inaugurated, on the morning of January 20, 1961. It was a very cold day in the nation's capital, and Marion kept a handkerchief over her mouth to protect her sensitive jaw from the frigid air. The Kennedy inauguration was Marion's last public appearance.

Marion and Horace were treated as special guests throughout the inaugural festivities. Joe had arranged for them to stay in the presidential suite of the Sheridan Park Hotel in Washington, DC. Uncomplaining though Marion was, Joe Kennedy noticed that she was in pain. On May 17, 1961, when Marion and Horace had returned to Los Angeles, Marion was rehospitalized at Cedars of Lebanon Hospital, and doctors approached her once again with the prospect of surgery. Joe Kennedy, concerned about Marion's welfare, sent his own specialists from New York's Memorial Hospital for consultation at Cedars of Lebanon, and on their recommendation, Marion agreed to have the cancerous portion of her jaw removed. She underwent surgery on June 7.

Marion had a difficult recovery. On June 19, as she was "resting comfortably" at the hospital, Marion attempted to get out of bed and fell, fracturing a bone in her left leg. This shock to Marion's system, along with her late-stage cancer and the stress of her surgery, was one that her body couldn't take.

"I have loved Marion since she was a beautiful young girl in New York," wrote Grace Dawley, an acquaintance from Marion's New York days, to Horace. "Although I have scarcely seen her in recent years, I have never ceased to love her and have spoken her name in every prayer." Frances Marion vowed in a July 1961 letter that she would come to the hospital, "so I can peek in on one I have cared deeply for ever since Elsie Janis said to me—many, many years ago—'I want you to meet the most beautiful girl in America. And the sweetest.'"

As Marion lay in her hospital bed at Cedars of Lebanon, letters came pouring in from appreciative and concerned fans around the world. Some of these letters came from people who wanted to share their own experiences with osteomyelitis, while others simply wanted to thank Marion for her contributions to their lives as one who brought them so much joy in those bygone days. A fan in Ohio wrote: "In my mind, you represent the leading facet in a jewel of entertainment that can never be replaced, no TV or rock 'n roll, method system or juvenile ingenue can hold an audience as well as you."

One particularly moving and nostalgic note came from Frank Irvine in Hampstead, New York, who, after wishing Marion a speedy recovery, mentioned that he had been the chief accountant at the old 127th Street studio in New York. The letter flooded Marion with memories of her days at the 127th Street studio, filming *When Knighthood Was in Flower* and *Little Old New York*, learning fencing, and dressing in lavish period costumes. Now close to death, with this letter, Marion was transported back to her early days in New York that seemed a lifetime ago and had set the stage for all that had happened since.

After she broke her leg, Marion's condition declined rapidly and in the early autumn, at the age of 64, she slipped into a coma. News traveled quickly around Marion's extended circles, and friends and family rallied around her. On September 22, 1961, Marion was given her last rites in her room at Cedars of Lebanon Hospital. Horace, Rose, Patricia, Arthur, Marion Rose, and Arthur Patrick sat at her bedside all day and into the evening. Shortly before 7:00 p.m., the machines keeping her alive started beeping rapidly. The rose in her cheeks and her peach complexion, gracing her face until the end, began to fade as the vibrancy of her life drained out of her. Marion died at 7:00 p.m. that evening, surrounded by love.

Her funeral, held on September 26 at the Beverly Hills Immaculate Heart of Mary Church, was modest. Around two hundred mourners were in attendance, including Mary Pickford and Buddy Rogers, Kay Gable, Harold Lloyd and Mildred Davis. There was no eulogy. George Hearst, W.R.'s eldest son and a friend to Marion to the very end, was one of the pallbearers.

When the will was opened a week later, she had divided the majority of her estate equally among her sister Rose, her niece Patricia, and her nephew Charlie, and their children. A trust fund was set up for the children, paying their tuition at any university of their choosing, anywhere in the world. To Horace, she left half a million dollars in trust to pay out at a rate of $3,000 a month, as well as the houses on Beverly Drive and in Palm Springs.

In their remembrances of Marion, newspapers pointed to her accomplishments with nearly one hundred charities, including acknowledgments from the Jewish Home for the Aged and the Marion Davies Children's Clinic— "the greatest joy of my life," as Marion had put it a few years before.

Due to Hedda Hopper's long personal friendship with Marion, she soon began work on a book project about Marion's life. She planned to base it around letters that she claimed to have, written by W.R. to Marion. But when she received a letter from Bill Hearst Jr., threatening her with a lawsuit if she published any of those letters, her plans were derailed, and the publishing deal fell through.

In his bedroom in his home at Hyannis Port, Massachusetts, Joseph P. Kennedy had only one picture, despite having a wife and nine children. The picture on Joe's nightstand at Hyannis Port was of Marion Davies, young and smiling. "She was a wonderful woman, she was a great friend," he told his chauffeur upon hearing of Marion's death. "She was a woman who understood men. She understood men who wanted great things. She understood me."

Five years later, in late December 1966, a letter arrived in Hedda Hopper's mailbox. It was from Madelaine Lundy, a parent of two children who had been treated at the Marion Davies Children's Clinic during the Depression. Mrs. Lundy had read Hedda Hopper's tribute to Marion in her Christmas column, remembering Marion on her favorite holiday. "In your column you spoke of Marion Davies, and although I am not gifted in writing, decided to let you know how I feel about that very wonderful person."

She wrote of what the Marion Davies Children's Clinic had meant to her family during a very difficult time in their life. "The kindness we received there I can never forget, and the medical help the children needed was graciously given," wrote Mrs. Lundy in a handwritten letter. "My children of course are now all grown, and I have 6 grandchildren and 2 great-grandchildren. My eldest son would have died I am sure without the Marion Davies Clinic help."

"Yes," she closed her letter, "it's knowing folks like her, that makes life worth living for folks like me."

Epilogue

More than sixty years after Marion Davies's death, her presence is still keenly felt in the places important in her life.

W.R. had expressed the desire for the ranch at San Simeon to go to the University of California as a gift upon his death. The University of California rejected the property, and the question arose as to what to do with it. Shortly after Marion's marriage to Horace Brown in 1951, she sent Horace and his son, Russell, up to San Simeon to see the property. The caretaker took them around the estate, which had become overgrown with weeds and with algae growing in the pools. Few staff remained on the hilltop, and the task of maintaining the estate had overwhelmed them in the years since Marion and W.R.'s departure in 1947. Horace and Russell sat in the refectory and ate lunch, as Horace pondered what to do. Upon his return to Beverly Hills, he told Marion that he felt the place would indeed be too costly for the Hearst Corporation to keep, and that Marion should advise the Hearst sons to give it to the State of California. In 1957, the Hearst Corporation donated the hilltop property to the State of California in memory of W.R.'s mother, Phoebe Apperson Hearst. The state embraced the land and its history, restoring Casa Grande, the guest cottages, the pools, and W.R.'s cherished landscaping. The property was formally named Hearst Castle, and it opened to the public in June 1958.

Hearst Castle is now one of California's most popular tourist attractions, accommodating as many as 850,000 visitors per year. On guided tours, guests learn about the history of the land, and the storied guests who stayed there as guests of Marion and W.R. For many years, Marion Davies's history at Hearst Castle was ignored. But in recent years, as the relationship between Marion and W.R. has become more accepted, Marion's history is embraced and recounted by the guides as an integral part of Hearst Castle. In recent years, there has been a push to restore the gardens to the way they were when Marion and W.R. were there. With a much smaller budget than Hearst had, this has been a difficult task. But with the help of the Olmsted Center for Landscape Preservation, a garden restoration plan has been implemented and visitors can now see the gardens as Hearst saw them, though on a somewhat smaller scale. The land surrounding Casa Grande remains the domain of the Hearst family, and several enterprises are run from its grounds, including Hearst Ranch Beef and Hearst Ranch Winery.

Marion and W.R. never returned to Wyntoon after 1944. Under a Hearst Corporation reorganization plan in 1943, profit-minded Dick Berlin was made president, and he saw Wyntoon as a potential financial asset. While W.R. was alive, no wild animal was allowed to be killed and no tree was allowed to be felled. But Berlin turned the property into a profitable logging business, with new trees planted and felled on vast stretches of the 67,000 acres of land, providing a financial return of about $2 million annually. Today, the estate remains the property of the Hearst family and is not open to the public, but kayakers on the upper stretch of the McCloud River pass through Wyntoon, and can still see the Bavarian Village and many other buildings from the water.

Soon after Marion sold the Beach House to Hearst Magazines, Inc., the property was in turn sold to the real estate developer Joseph Drown. For a short time, Drown used the main house as a hotel he called Ocean House, while using the other, smaller guest houses and servants' quarters as a private beach club. The hotel proved too costly, and Drown obtained a permit to demolish the main house in 1956. Demolition occurred in 1957, and he used the old property as a nine-hundred-car parking lot for the beach club.

The home's demolition devastated Marion. "It should never have been torn down," she said in 1960. "It could have been kept open for the public to see. It was an artistic and historic masterpiece." The beach club expanded and came to be known as the Sand and Sea Club, one of the few limited membership clubs in the area to embrace members from all races and religions. In 1959, the property was sold to the state, then leased back to the city of Santa Monica. The Sand and Sea Club remained until 1990, and in 1994 the effects of the Northridge earthquake rendered nearly all the remaining buildings unsafe. The property lay in ruin until 2005, as the city debated what to do with it. It was then that Wallis Annenberg, the daughter of media tycoon Walter Annenberg, stepped in. Annenberg had spent summers at the Sand

and Sea Club as a child, and pledged $27.5 million to save the property and turn it into a community beach facility.

Today, the property is the vibrant Annenberg Community Beach House, a community recreation center offering a range of classes, activities, and events for residents of Santa Monica. The joy of children fills the outdoor area, as they play in the fountains and swim in the marble and mosaic pool that still remains. It is difficult to think of a more fitting purpose for a former property of Marion's than a community center catering to the children she so loved.

At the far end of the property, a white Georgian Revival building stands, the last architectural remnant of Marion Davies's Beach House. The structure is now called the Marion Davies Guest House, and it operates as a museum devoted to Marion Davies, operated by passionate and knowledgeable volunteers from the Santa Monica Conservancy.

The home at 331 Riverside Drive that W.R. purchased for Marion and her family was sold to George Jephson, a wealthy food manufacturer, after Marion moved to California. Jephson occupied the home until he died in 1951. Shortly thereafter, the New American Buddhist Academy bought the property, and it remains the New York Buddhist Church to this day. The clergy are passionate about the history of the building, and have kept the interior largely unchanged, with spaces repurposed to serve the needs of the church. The dining room is now a meditation room, and the annex next door, where Marion's father Bernard Douras lived, is now split in two. The main sanctuary of the New York Buddhist Church occupies most of the annex, while the Kokushi Budo Institute, the oldest dojo in New York City, occupies the rest.

The Marion Davies Children's Clinic was fully incorporated into the medical center of the University of California at Los Angeles when Marion transferred the clinic to the hospital's control. The new wing in Marion's name broke ground in 1960, and was ready to see children in 1962 as the Marion Davies Children's Health Center. The center was folded into the general pediatrics department for maximum reach, and today it operates as a part of the UCLA Department of Pediatrics. In recent years, pediatricians and researchers working at the Marion Davies Children's Health Center have contributed to substantial scholarship on pediatric AIDS and the effects of the Zika virus on the fetus during pregnancy.

After Marion's death, Rose Davies had taken control of her alcoholism and became sober for an extended period of time. As complicated as Rose's relationship was with her daughter, Patricia, she was always close to Patricia's daughter, Marion Rose. In the year following Marion's death, Rose took her granddaughter on an extended trip to Europe along with Rose's best friend, the Princess Nina Mdivani. In France, Rose became extremely sad and depressed. She was reminded of her tragic love affair with the Marquis Roland de Brissac in the late 1920s, in which his family had refused to let him marry "the sister of the actress." The marquis died in 1936 at the age of 37, from undisclosed causes. Rose's depression triggered a relapse of her alcoholism, and she returned to the United States where she died in 1963 at the age of 68, from complications of cirrhosis of the liver.

Patricia (Van Cleve) Lake's kidnapping in 1928 had a lasting effect on her, and amid her conflicted feelings toward her parents, she clung tightly to the unconditional love and care of her aunt Marion. When Marion died, Patricia became so intensely emotional that she slashed a painting of Marion in her home in her despair. In later years, she experienced renewed anger against her mother, Rose, and her father, George Van Cleve, for the pain and trouble of her childhood, and became convinced of the idea that Marion and W.R. were her biological parents. This, she said, was based on a comment that W.R. made to her on her wedding day to Arthur Lake in 1937, a comment that appears to have been misinterpreted. Despite no suspicion of Patricia's parentage during Marion's lifetime and little useful evidence, Patricia's claim was written in her obituary when she died in 1993, leading to much confusion to this day.

Arthur Patrick Lake's childhood experiences, filming "Meet the Family" with his parents and sister, piqued his interest in the film industry and he remained an active member of the Screen Actors Guild for forty-five years, performing work as a stuntman. Although Arthur Patrick ran into trouble with the law as early as 1961 and led a frequently difficult life, those who knew him remembered him as a talented actor and writer. He died from injuries sustained in an accident in 1994, leaving behind his children and nine grandchildren.

Marion Rose Lake was still in Europe with Nina Mdivani when received the news of her grandmother Rose's death. "There is nothing left in Hollywood for you," Nina Mdivani told her. "You should stay here in Europe." Marion Rose decided to take Nina Mdivani's advice, and did not return to the United States. With the fund established for her by her great-aunt Marion, she enrolled at the Sorbonne, where she got a master's in literature and met and married a Corsican couturier. They had two daughters in Paris, and the family ultimately moved to the south of France. She now resides in Provence, close to her daughter, her granddaughter, and her great-granddaughter.

Charlie Lederer remained married to Anne Shirley until the end of his life. With Anne, he had a son, Daniel Lederer, and he was also a devoted step-father to Julie Payne, Anne's daughter from her previous marriage to actor John Payne. Charlie collaborated on the screenplay of the original *Oceans 11* (1960) and *Mutiny on the Bounty* (1962). The latter was his final hit. Charlie stopped writing shortly after Marion's death, seeing his final film credit as co-writer of *A Global Affair*, released in 1964. Charlie developed debilitating arthritis in the late 1960s, leading to an addiction to various prescription drugs and, as the disease progressed, heroin. Much of the money and many of the possessions he inherited from Marion were sold for money to fuel his habit, and he died of his addiction in 1976, at the age of 65. He was cremated, and there were no services.

The Motion Picture Relief Fund continued to provide help to industry members through the Depression and beyond. In 1940, actor Jean Hersholt found seven acres of land in Woodland Hills, near Calabasas, that could serve as a specialized care facility for industry members who needed a place to live in retirement. Those seven acres became the Motion Picture Country House and Hospital, and, along with the Jewish Home for the Aged (now known as the Los Angeles Jewish Home), another of Marion's favorite causes, it continues to operate to this day as a premier senior care facility in Los Angeles County. In 2021, the Motion Picture Relief Fund, now the Motion Picture and Television Fund, celebrated its hundredth anniversary.

Frances Marion continued to work at MGM until the mid-1940s. She found her work as a script doctor unrewarding, and when her contract was up, she left and shifted her focus to visual art, enrolling in sculpting classes at USC and spending more time on her lifelong love of painting. Frances split her time between coasts for the next several decades and continued to support writers, fervently defending them against society's devaluation of their work. She died of a brain aneurysm in Los Angeles in 1973 at age 84, leaving behind her two sons, Dick and Fred Jr., and four grandchildren.

Stanley Flink continued his work as a correspondent for Time Inc., the corporation that owned *Life* magazine, until 1958. During his time as a correspondent in California, he came to know many key figures in 1950s Los Angeles intimately, including Marilyn Monroe, whom he profiled for *Life* in 1953. He transferred to television news in 1958, becoming an associate producer at CBS and a producer and writer at NBC. In 1963, he moved to London to work as a consultant on public affairs and in theatrical productions, before returning to his alma mater Yale to serve as the first director of the Office of Public Information and Alumni Services. For thirty years, between 1980 and 2010, Flink taught the undergraduate course "Ethics in the Media" at Yale, and was awarded the Yale Medal in 1994. He is the author of many books and articles, including the novel *But Will They Get It in Des Moines?* and *Sentinel Under Siege,* an analysis of freedom of the press in America. He celebrated his ninety-seventh birthday in 2021, and lives in Connecticut with his wife of nearly fifty years.

Greg Bautzer continued to be involved with his law practice for the rest of his life. In 1972, he married his fourth wife, Niki Schenck Dantine, twenty-three years his junior and the daughter of one of his old clients, Nick Schenck. Bautzer struggled with alcohol and deteriorating health for many years, and his wife Niki was with him when he suffered a fatal heart attack at home in 1987. After his death, the law firm of Wyman Bautzer dissolved following a heated power struggle, and the remaining attorneys joined the Chicago-based firm of Katten Muchin & Zavis.

After Marion's death, Horace Brown continued to live in the house on Beverly Drive. Horace offered to sell the property to the city of Beverly Hills, but the city was still recovering from the cost of having bought the Greystone Manor, and declined Horace's offer. Following the rejection by the city, Horace finally sold the property in 1966 and moved to take up residence on his yacht, *Destiny*, in Newport Beach. His demeanor calmed, and he enjoyed hosting Marion Rose, her husband Jean, and their two young children when they came to visit Los Angeles from France. Despite their marital problems, Horace always spoke fondly of his marriage to Marion, and kept her mementos prominently displayed on the *Destiny*. He died in 1972 at the age of 67.

In 1976, attorney Leonard M. Ross bought the house at 1011 N. Beverly Drive. Several attempts were made to sell the property, but heavy taxes prohibited a sale until 2021, when it sold for $63 million to Nicolas Berggruen. Over the years, the house's exterior has attracted film crews looking for shots of a lavish estate, and 1011 N. Beverly Drive is seen in such films as *The Godfather, The Bodyguard,* and *The Jerk*. It has come to be called "The Beverly House," though no such name was used during Marion's lifetime.

W.R.'s eldest son, George Randolph Hearst, served as vice president of the *Los Angeles Examiner* until 1953. He was a man of varied interests, including aviation and photography, and worked closely with the Hearst papers' photographers. Among Hearst journalists, he was known as "the friend of the guy with the camera." During World War II George was a naval reserve intelligence officer who flew anti-submarine patrols for the California Coast Guard. George married six times and had two children, twins Phoebe Millicent Hearst and George Randolph Hearst Jr., the latter of whom took over publishing the *Los Angeles Examiner* after his father's retirement. George Sr. remained active in his father's legacy, serving as the vice president of the Hearst Corporation, president of the Hearst Foundation, Inc., and as a member of the San Simeon Historical Monument Society. He died at the age of 67 in 1972, leaving behind his children and his wife, Rosalie.

During World War II, W.R.'s second son, William Randolph Hearst Jr., served as a war correspondent in Europe and North Africa, where he wrote dispatches that soon established him as a bona fide newspaperman in the eyes of his father. Bill Jr., who had always been motivated to lead the Hearst empire, became editor-in-chief after his father's death in 1951. He won a Pulitzer Prize in 1956 for his interview with Nikita Khrushchev, and briefed President Dwight D. Eisenhower on Khrushchev's political power. The irony of winning the Pulitzer Prize, named for his father's main rival, was not lost on Bill Jr. He married three times, and with his wife Austine had two sons, William Randolph Hearst III and Austin Hearst. Bill Jr. remained editor-in-chief of the Hearst media empire until his death from a heart attack in 1993. His son William Randolph Hearst III is currently the chairman of the Hearst Corporation as well as the editor and publisher of *Alta* magazine.

John Randolph Hearst, W.R.'s third son, was the only one of the Hearst sons whom Marion never got to know well. Out of loyalty to Millicent, John spent much of his time on the East Coast with his mother and visited California far less than his four brothers. After their father's death, John became the president of Harper's Bazaar–Cosmopolitan Book Corp., and general manager of both the International Magazine Corp. and the Hearst radio operations. In spite of his relative distance from his father's influence, John was considered to be an extremely talented executive. He married three times, with the first marriage to Dorothy Hart ending in divorce for "extreme cruelty," which John denied. He had four children: Joanne, John Randolph Hearst Jr., William Randolph Hearst II, and Deborah. In 1958, with his third wife, Fanne Wade Hearst, John went on vacation to the Virgin Islands and while there, he suffered a sudden heart attack and died at the age of 49. His son John Jr., known to the family as "Bunky," represented John's side of the family as a trustee of the Hearst Corporation until his own death in 2011.

Known to most as "Randy," Randolph Apperson Hearst enjoyed the internal business sphere of the Hearst Corporation more than the editorial side. He served as chairman of the board between 1973 and 1996, before retiring and giving his seat to his nephew George Randolph Hearst Jr. In his early years as chairman of the board, he was also serving as the editor and president of the *San Francisco Examiner* when his daughter Patricia (a name inspired, family lore says, by Marion's niece Patricia) was kidnapped by the Symbionese Liberation Army. The SLA was a domestic terrorist organization with a hideout near Patricia's residence at UC Berkeley. As a captive of the SLA, Patricia was radicalized, sexually assaulted, brainwashed, and coerced to commit several illegal acts—including robbing a San Francisco bank and helping to make explosive devices. She was arrested and, after a long and complex hearing and trial, sentenced to thirty-five years in prison for bank robbery. President Jimmy Carter commuted her sentence after twenty-two months.

As the editor of the *San Francisco Examiner* during the time of the "Patty Hearst kidnapping," Randy was obliged to publish all the distressing news stories emerging about his own daughter. The psychological toll put an unbearable strain on his marriage to Patricia's mother, Catherine, and they divorced in 1976. He married twice more, and died of a stroke in 2000 at the age of 85. In addition to Patricia, he had four other daughters: Catherine, Virginia, Anne, and Victoria. Following his death, Randy's daughter Virginia took his seat as a trustee of the Hearst Corporation. Patricia Hearst lives a quiet life in Connecticut and in 1996 wrote *Murder at San Simeon*, a fictional reimagining of Thomas Ince's death.

David Whitmire Hearst began his career as a reporter at the *New York Journal-American*, then went to the *Baltimore News-Post*, where he became city editor. He joined the advertising department of the *Los Angeles Evening Herald-Express* in 1938, became executive publisher in 1947, and in 1950, he succeeded Frank Barham as the paper's head publisher. David retired in 1960, but remained vice president and a member of the board of directors of the Hearst Corporation. He was diagnosed with cancer and died in 1986, leaving behind his wife, Hope, and his two children, Millicent and David Jr.

Millicent Veronica Willson Hearst outlived her husband by twenty-three years. Although she struggled with deafness as she reached her 70s, she remained generous with interviewers and gave several hours of her time to W.A. Swanberg, who at the time was writing *Citizen Hearst*. "I was impressed by her apparent admiration for Hearst, although he had left her for Marion Davies," wrote Swanberg in his notes. She lived at 4 East 66th Street, in a home she shared with her sister Anita. After Anita died in November 1974,

Millicent, then 92 years old, had a steep decline in health and she died three weeks later on December 5. W.R. was buried at Cypress Lawn Memorial Park in Colma, California, but Millicent chose not to be interred beside him. Instead, she was buried at her family's mausoleum at Woodlawn Cemetery in The Bronx, New York.

FILMOGRAPHY

1917

Runaway Romany

Dir. George Lederer. Ardsley Art Film Corp., released by Pathé. Written by staff writers of the *Pittsburgh Post-Gazette* (Marion Davies credited as writer). Cast: Marion Davies, W.W. Bitner, Boyce Combe, Pedro de Cordoba, Ormi Hawley, Gladden James, Joseph Kilgour, Matt Moore. 5 reels.

1918

Cecilia of the Pink Roses

Dir. Julius Steger. Marion Davies Film Corp., released by Select. Written by S.M. Weller, based on the book by Katherine Haviland-Taylor. Cast: Marion Davies, Harry Benham, Edward O'Connor, Willette Kershaw, Charles Jackson, George LeGuere, Danny Sullivan, John Charles, Eva Campbell, Joseph Burke. 6 reels.

The Burden of Proof

Dir. John G. Adolfi and Julius Steger. Marion Davies Film Corp., released by Select. Written by S.M. Weller. Cast: Marion Davies, Mary Richards, Eloise Clement, John Merkyl, L. Rogers Lytton, Willard Cooley, Fred Hearn, Fred Lenox, Maude Lowe. 5 reels.

1919

The Belle of New York

Dir. Julius Steger. Marion Davies Film Corp., released by Select. Written by Eugene Walter. Cast: Marion Davies, Etienne Girardot, L. Rogers Lytton, Franklyn Hanna, Raymond Bloomer, Christian Rub, Barbara Sabin, Nick Thompson. 5 reels.

Getting Mary Married

Dir. Allan Dwan. Cosmopolitan Productions and Marion Davies Film Corp., released by Select. Written by Anita Loos and John Emerson. Cast: Marion Davies, Norman Kerry, Matt Moore, Frederick Burton, Amelia Summerville, Constance Beaumar, Elmer Grandin, Helen Lindroth. 5 reels.

The Dark Star

Dir. Allan Dwan. Cosmopolitan Productions and International Film Service, released by Famous Players-Lasky, A Paramount Artcraft Special. Written by Frances Marion. Cast: Marion Davies, Dorothy Green, Norman Kerry, Matt Moore, Ward Crane, George Cooper, Arthur Earle, Gustav von Seyffertitz, Emil Hoch, Fred Hearn, James Laffey, William Brotherhood, Eddie Sturgis. 7 reels.

The Cinema Murder

Dir. George D. Baker. Cosmopolitan Productions and International Film Service, released by Famous Players-Lasky and Paramount Artcraft Pictures. Written by Frances Marion. Cast: Marion Davies, Peggy Parr, Eulalie Jensen, Nigel Barrie, W. Scott Moore, Anders Randolf, Reginald Barlow. 6 reels.

1920

April Folly

Dir. Robert Z. Leonard. Cosmopolitan Productions and International Film Service. Written by Adrian Johnson. Cast: Marion Davies, Madeline Marshall, Hattie Delaro, Amelia Summerville, Conway Tearle, J. Herbert Frank, Warren Cook, Spencer Charters, Charles Peyton, Agnes Nielson. 5 reels.

The Restless Sex

Dir. Leonard D'Usseau and Robert Z. Leonard. Cosmopolitan Productions and International Film Service, released by Famous Players-Lasky and Paramount Pictures. Written by Robert Z. Leonard. Cast: Marion Davies, Ralph Kellard, Carlyle Blackwell, Charles Lane, Robert Vivian, Etna Ross, Stephen Carr, Vivienne Osborne, Corinne Barker, Jane Darwell. 7 reels.

1921

Buried Treasure

Dir. George D. Baker. Cosmopolitan Productions, released by Paramount Pictures. Written by George D. Baker, based on a short story by F. Britten Austin. Cast:

Marion Davies, Norman Kerry, Anders Randolf, Edith Shayne, Earl Schenck, John Charles, Thomas Findley. 7 reels.

Enchantment

Dir. Robert G. Vignola. Cosmopolitan Productions, released by Paramount Pictures. Written by Luther Reed, based on the story "Manhandling Ethel" by Frank R. Adams. Cast: Marion Davies, Forrest Stanley, Edith Shayne, Tom Lewis, Arthur Rankin, Corinne Barker, Maude Turner Gordon, Edith Lyle, Huntley Gordon, Emmet Foy, Julia Hurley, Gilbert Rooney. 7 reels.

1922

The Bride's Play

Dir. George Terwilliger. Cosmopolitan Productions, released by Paramount Pictures. Written by Mildred Considine. Cast: Marion Davies, John O'Brien, Frank Shannon, Wyndham Standing, Carl Miller, Richard Cummings, Eleanor Middleton, Thea Talbot, John P. Wade, Julia Hurley, George Spink, Louise Emmons. 7 reels.

Beauty's Worth

Dir. Robert G. Vignola. Cosmopolitan Productions, released by Famous Players-Lasky and Paramount Pictures. Written by Luther Reed. Cast: Marion Davies, Forrest Stanley, June Elvidge, Truly Shattuck, Lydia Yeamans Titus, Hallam Cooley, Antrim Short, Thomas Jefferson, Martha Mattox, Aileen Manning, Gordon Dooley, Johnny Dooley. 7 reels.

The Young Diana

Dir. Albert Capellani and Robert G. Vignola. Cosmopolitan Productions, released by Paramount Pictures. Written by Luther Reed. Cast: Marion Davies, Macklyn Arbuckle, Forrest Stanley, Gypsy O'Brien, Pedro de Cordoba. 7 reels.

When Knighthood Was in Flower

Dir. Robert G. Vignola. Cosmopolitan Productions, released by Paramount Pictures. Written by Luther Reed. Cast: Marion Davies, Forrest Stanley, Lyn Harding, Theresa Maxwell Conover, Pedro de Cordoba, Ruth Shepley, Ernest Glendinning, Arthur Forrest, Johnny Dooley, William Kent, Charles K. Gerrard, Arthur Donaldson, Downing Clarke, William Norris, Macey Harlam, William Powell, George Nash, Gustav von Seyffertitz. 12 reels.

1923

Adam and Eva

Dir. Robert G. Vignola. Cosmopolitan Productions, released by Paramount Pictures. Written by Luther Reed. Cast: Marion Davies, T. Roy Barnes, Tom Lewis, William Norris, Percy Ames, Leon Gordon, Luella Gear, William B. Davidson, Edward Douglas, Bradley Barker, John Powers, Horace James, Dorothy Portingall. 8 reels.

Little Old New York

Dir. Sidney Olcott. Cosmopolitan Productions, released by Goldwyn-Cosmopolitan Distributing Corp. Written by Luther Reed. Cast: Marion Davies, Stephen Carr, J.M. Kerrigan, Harrison Ford, Courtenay Foote, Mahlon Hamilton, Norval Keedwell, George Barraud, Sam Hardy, Andrew Dillon, Riley Hatch, Charles Kennedy, Spencer Charters, Harry Watson, Louis Wolheim, Charles Judels, Gypsy O'Brien, Mary Kennedy. 11 reels.

1924

Yolanda

Dir. Robert G. Vignola. Cosmopolitan Pictures, released by Metro-Goldwyn Distributing Corp. Written by Luther Reed. Cast: Marion Davies, Lyn Harding, Macklyn Arbuckle, Holbrook Blinn, Johnny Dooley, Arthur Donaldson, Ralph Graves, Ian Maclaren, Gustav von Seyffertitz, Theresa Maxwell Conover, Martin Faust, Thomas Findley, Paul McAllister, Leon Errol, Mary Kennedy, Roy Applegate, Arthur Tovey, Kit Wain. 11 reels.

Janice Meredith

Dir. E. Mason Hopper. Cosmopolitan Pictures, released by Metro-Goldwyn Distributing Corp. Written by Lillie Hayward. Cast: Marion Davies, Holbrook Blinn, Harrison Ford, Macklyn Arbuckle, Hattie Delaro, Olin Howland, Spencer Charters, May Vokes, Mildred Arden, Joseph Kilgour, Douglas Stevenson, George Nash, W.C. Fields, George Siegmann, Helen Lee Worthing, Tyrone Power Sr., Princess Marie de Bourbon, Lionel Adams, Florence Turner. 11 reels.

1925

Zander the Great

Dir. George Hill. Cosmopolitan Pictures, released by Metro-Goldwyn Distributing Corp. Written by Frances Marion. Cast: Marion Davies, Holbrook Blinn, Harrison Ford, Harry Watson, Harry Myers, George Siegmann, Emily Fitzroy, Hobart Bosworth, Richard Carle, Hedda Hopper, Olin Howland, Jack Huff, Josephine Crowell, Betsy Ann Hisle, Carmencita Johnson, Dick Sutherland, Pat Wing, Toby Wing. 8 reels.

Lights of Old Broadway

Dir. Monta Bell. Cosmopolitan Pictures, released by Metro-Goldwyn Distributing Corp. Written by Carey Wilson and Joseph W. Farnham. Cast: Marion Davies, Conrad Nagel, Frank Currier, George K. Arthur, Charles McHugh, Eleanor Lawson, Julia Swayne Gordon, Matthew Betz, Wilbur Higby, Bodil Rosing, George Bunny, George Harris, Bernard Berger, J. Frank Glendon, Buck Black, Karl Dane, William De Vaull, Mary Gordon. 7 reels.

1926

Beverly of Graustark

Dir. Sidney Franklin. Cosmopolitan Productions, released by Metro-Goldwyn-Mayer Distributing Corp. Written by Agnes Christine Johnston and Joseph W. Farnham. Cast: Marion Davies, Antonio Moreno, Creighton Hale, Roy D'Arcy, Albert Gran, Paulette Duval, Max Barwyn, Charles Clary, Sidney Bracey, Lou Duello, Edward Scarpa. 7 reels.

1927

The Red Mill

Dir. William Goodrich aka Roscoe "Fatty" Arbuckle. Cosmopolitan Productions, released by Metro-Goldwyn-Mayer Distributing Corp. Written by Frances Marion and J.W. Farnham. Cast: Marion Davies, Owen Moore, Louise Fazenda, George Siegmann, Karl Dane, Russ Powell, Snitz Edwards, William Orlamond, William White, Fred Bloss, John D. Bloss, Roy Bloss, Micky Delano, Kay Deslys, Caroline Dine, Sally Eilers, Fred Gamble, Carl Roup, "Ignatz" the mouse. 7 reels.

Tillie the Toiler

Dir. Hobart Henley. Cosmopolitan Productions, released by Metro-Goldwyn-Mayer Distributing Corp. Written by A.P. Younger, Agnes Christine Johnston, Edward T. Lowe, Ralph Spence. Cast: Marion Davies, Matt Moore, Harry Crocker, George Fawcett, George K. Arthur, Estelle Clark, Bert Roach, Gertrude Short, Claire McDowell, Arthur Hoyt, Mary Forbes, Ida May, James Murray, Russ Powell, Turner Savage. 7 reels.

The Fair Co-Ed

Dir. Sam Wood. Metro-Goldwyn-Mayer Corp. Written by Byron Morgan, Joseph W. Farnham. Cast: Marion Davies, Johnny Mack Brown, Jane Winton, Thelma Hill, Lillian Leighton, Gene Stone, James Bradbury, Sr., Dean Harrell, Joel McCrea, Jacques Tourneur, Coy Watson. 7 reels.

Quality Street

Dir. Sidney Franklin. Cosmopolitan Productions, released by Metro-Goldwyn-Mayer Distributing Corp. Written by Hans Kraly, Albert Lewin, Marian Ainslee, Ruth Cummings. Cast: Marion Davies, Conrad Nagel, Helen Jerome Eddy, Flora Finch, Margaret Seddon, Marcelle Corday, Kate Price, Vondell Darr, Audrey Howell, Leon Janney, Austen Jewell, Mickey McBan, Harry Murray, Coy Watson, Walter Wilkinson. 8 reels.

1928

The Patsy

Dir. King Vidor. Metro-Goldwyn-Mayer Corp. Written by Agnes Christine Johnston and Ralph Spence. Cast: Marion Davies, Orville Caldwell, Marie Dressler, Lawrence Gray, Dell Henderson, Jane Winton, William A. Broadway, Dick Gordon, William H. O'Brien. 8 reels.

The Cardboard Lover

Dir. Robert Z. Leonard. Cosmopolitan Productions, released by Metro-Goldwyn-Mayer Distributing Corp. Written by F. Hugh Herbert, Carey Wilson, Lucille Newmark. Cast: Marion Davies, Jetta Goudal, Nils Asther, Andrés de Segurola, Tenen Holtz, Pepi Lederer, Carrie Daumery. 8 reels.

Show People

Dir. King Vidor. Metro-Goldwyn-Mayer Corp. Written by Agnes Christine Johnston, Laurence Stallings, Wanda Tuchock, Ralph Spence. Cast: Marion Davies, William Haines, Dell Henderson, Paul Ralli, Tenen Holtz, Harry Gribbon, Sidney Bracey, Polly Moran, Albert Conti, Renée Adorée, George K. Arthur, Gordon Avil, Eleanor Boardman, Symona Boniface, Charles Chaplin, Lew Cody, Ray Cooke, Harry Crocker. 9 reels.

1929

The Hollywood Revue of 1929

Dir. Charles Reisner, Christy Cabanne, Norman Houston. Metro-Goldwyn-Mayer

Corp. Written by J.W. Farnham, Al Boasberg, Robert E. Hopkins. Cast: Conrad Nagel, Jack Benny, John Gilbert, Norma Shearer, Joan Crawford, Bessie Love, Cliff Edwards, Stan Laurel, Oliver Hardy, Anita Page, Nils Asther. 13 reels.

Marianne (silent)

Dir. Robert Z. Leonard. Cosmopolitan Productions, released by Metro-Goldwyn-Mayer Distributing Corp. Written by Dale Van Every, J.W. Farnham. Cast: Marion Davies, Oscar Shaw, Fred Solm, Robert Ames, Scott Kolk, Emile Chautard, Mack Swain, Oscar Apfel. 7 reels.

Marianne (talkie)

Dir. Robert Z. Leonard. Metro-Goldwyn Mayer Corp. Written by Dale Van Every, Laurence Stallings, Gladys Unger. Cast: Marion Davies, George Baxter, Lawrence Gray, Cliff Edwards, Benny Rubin, Scott Kolk, Robert Edeson, Emile Chautard. 12 reels.

1930

Not So Dumb

Dir. King Vidor. Metro-Goldwyn-Mayer Corp. Written by Wanda Tuchock, Edwin Justus Mayer, Lucille Newmark. Cast: Marion Davies, Elliott Nugent, Raymond Hackett, Franklin Pangborn, Julia Faye, William Holden, Donald Ogden Stewart, Sally Starr, George Davis, George Irving. 9 reels.

The Florodora Girl

Dir. Harry Beaumont. Metro-Goldwyn-Mayer Corp. Written by Gene Markey, Ralph Spence, Al Boasberg, Robert E. Hopkins. Cast: Marion Davies, Lawrence Gray, Walter Catlett, Louis John Bartels, Ilka Chase, Vivien Oakland, Jed Prouty, Claud Allister, Sam Hardy, Nance O'Neil, Robert Bolder, Jane Keithley, Maude Turner Gordon, George Chandler, Anita Louise, Mary Jane Irving. 9 reels.

1931

The Bachelor Father

Dir. Robert Z. Leonard. Cosmopolitan Productions, released by Metro-Goldwyn-Mayer Distributing Corp. Cast: Marion Davies, Ralph Forbes, C. Aubrey Smith, Ray Milland, Guinn "Big Boy" Williams, David Torrence, Doris Lloyd, Edgar Norton, Nina Quartero, Hallowell Hobbes, Elizabeth Murray, James Gordon, Harry Allen. 10 reels.

It's a Wise Child

Dir. Robert Z. Leonard. Cosmopolitan Productions, released by Metro-Goldwyn-Mayer Distributing Corp. Cast: Marion Davies, Sidney Blackmer, James Gleason, Polly Moran, Lester Vail, Marie Prevost, Clara Blandick, Robert McWade, Johnny Arthur, Hilda Vaughn, Ben Alexander, Emily Fitzroy. 9 reels.

Five and Ten

Dir. Robert Z. Leonard. Cosmopolitan Productions, released by Metro-Goldwyn-Mayer Distributing Corp. Written by Andrew Percival Younger, from the book by Fannie Hurst. Cast: Marion Davies, Leslie Howard, Richard Bennett, Irene Rich, Douglass Montgomery, Mary Duncan. 10 reels.

The Christmas Party (short)

Dir. Charles Reisner. Metro-Goldwyn-Mayer Corp. Written by Robert E. Hopkins. Cast: Lionel Barrymore, Wallace Beery, Jackie Cooper, Marion Davies, Dorothy DeBorba, Reginald Denny, Marie Dressler, Jimmy Durante, Cliff Edwards, Clark Gable, Charlotte Greenwood, Donald Haines, Allen "Farina" Hoskins, Bobby "Wheezer" Hutchins, Leila Hyams, Mary Ann Jackson, Carmencita Johnson, Jerry Madden. 1 reel.

1932

Polly of the Circus

Dir. Alfred Santell. Metro-Goldwyn-Mayer Corp. Written by Carey Wilson. Cast: Marion Davies, Clark Gable, C. Aubrey Smith, Raymond Hatton, David Landau, Ruth Selwyn, Maude Eburne, Little Billy, Guinn "Big Boy" Williams, Clark Marshall. 8 reels.

Blondie of the Follies

Dir. Edmund Goulding. Metro-Goldwyn-Mayer Corp. Written by Frances Marion, Anita Loos, Ralph Spence. Cast: Marion Davies, Robert Montgomery, Billie Dove, Jimmy Durante, James Gleason, ZaSu Pitts, Sidney Toler, Douglass Dumbrille, Sarah Padden, Louise Carter. 9 reels.

1933

Peg O' My Heart

Dir. Robert Z. Leonard. Metro-Goldwyn-Mayer Corp. Written by Frank R. Adams, Frances Marion. Cast: Marion Davies, Onslow Stevens, J. Farrell MacDonald,

Juliette Compton, Irene Browne, Tyrell Davis, Alan Mowbray, Doris Lloyd, Robert Greig, Nora Cecil. 9 reels.

Going Hollywood

Dir. Raoul Walsh. Metro-Goldwyn-Mayer Corp. Written by Donald Ogden Stewart, Frances Marion. Cast: Marion Davies, Bing Crosby, Fifi D'Orsay, Stuart Erwin, Ned Sparks, Patsy Kelly, Bobby Watson, Three Radio Rogues, Sam McDaniel, Fred Toones. 9 reels.

1934

Operator 13

Dir. Richard Boleslawski. Metro-Goldwyn-Mayer Corp., distributed by Loew's Inc. Written by Harvey Thew, Zelda Sears, Eve Green. Cast: Marion Davies, Gary Cooper, Jean Parker, Katharine Alexander, Ted Healy, Russell Hardie, Henry Wadsworth, Douglass Dumbrille, Willard Robertson, Fuzzy Knight. 9 reels.

1935

Page Miss Glory

Dir. Mervyn LeRoy. Warner Bros. Productions Corp., distributed by Warner Bros. Pictures, Inc. and The Vitaphone Corp. Written by Delmer Daves and Robert Lord. Cast: Marion Davies, Pat O'Brien, Dick Powell, Mary Astor, Frank McHugh, Lyle Talbot, Allen Jenkins, Barton MacLane, Patsy Kelly, Hobart Cavanaugh. 10 reels.

Pirate Party on Catalina Isle (short)

Dir. Gene Burdette (uncredited). Louis Lewyn Productions, distributed by Metro-Goldwyn-Mayer Corp. Written by Alexander Van Dorn and Gene Burdette (uncredited). Cast: Charles "Buddy" Rogers, Sterling Young, the Fanchonettes, Robert Armstrong, Vince Barnett, Jack Duffy, Blanche Mehaffey, Bill Casper, Rue Tyler's Banjo Band. Marion Davies has a brief cameo. 2 reels.

1936

Hearts Divided

Dir. Frank Borzage. First National Productions Corp. and Cosmopolitan Productions, distributed by Warner Bros. Pictures, Inc. and The Vitaphone Corp. Written by Laird Doyle, Casey Robinson. Cast: Marion Davies, Dick Powell, Charlie Ruggles, Claude Rains, Edward Everett Horton, Arthur Treacher, Henry Stephenson, Clara Blandick, John Larkin, Walter Kingsford. 9 reels.

Cain and Mabel

Dir. Lloyd Bacon. First National Productions Corp. and Cosmopolitan Productions, distributed by Warner Bros. Pictures, Inc. and The Vitaphone Corp. Written by Laird Doyle, H.C. Witwer, Earl Baldwin. Cast: Marion Davies, Clark Gable, Allen Jenkins, Roscoe Karns, Walter Catlett, Robert Paige, Hobart Cavanaugh, Ruth Donnelly, Pert Kelton, William Collier Sr. 9 reels.

1937

Ever Since Eve

Dir. Lloyd Bacon. First National Productions Corp. and Cosmopolitan Productions, distributed by Warner Bros. Pictures Inc. Written by Lawrence Riley, Earl Baldwin, Lillie Hayward, Margaret Lee, Gene Baker. Special material by Brown Holmes, Joseph Shrank, Delmer Daves, Jerry Wald. Cast: Marion Davies, Robert Montgomery, Frank McHugh, Patsy Kelly, Allen Jenkins, Louise Fazenda, Barton MacLane, Marcia Ralston, Frederick Clarke, Arthur Hoyt. 8 reels.

1960

Hedda Hopper's Hollywood

Dir. William Corrigan. Rexall TV Special, NBC. Produced by Talent Associates in association with Paramount Television Productions. Written by Sumner Locke Elliott. Guests: Lucille Ball, Anne Bauchens, Stephen Boyd, Francis X. Bushman, John Cassavetes, Gary Cooper, Ricardo Cortez, Robert Cummings, Wiliam H. Daniels, Marion Davies, Walt Disney, Bob Hope, Hedda Hopper, Hope Lange, Harold Lloyd, Jody McCrea, Liza Minnelli, Don Murray, Ramon Novarro, Anthony Perkins, Debbie Reynolds, Teddy Rooney, Venetia Stevenson, James Stewart, Gloria Swanson, King Vidor, The Westmore Brothers. 60 minutes.

NOTES

INTRODUCTION

Page

1   **Twice a week:** Stanley Flink to author, 2014.
     She wore a blouse: Ibid.
     rest her feet: Ibid.
2   **underlying sadness:** Ibid.
     "inventor, purveyor": *Life*, August 27, 1951.
     "You wrote my story, and damn well": Stanley Flink to author, 2014.
3   **"I'm the captain of my soul":** Marion Davies autobiographical tapes, tape 1.

BEGINNINGS

5   **The winter of 1896–97:** Report from *Brooklyn Eagle*, January 3, 1897.
6   **County Tyrone:** Genealogy from Skibbereen Heritage Centre, Skibbereen, County Cork, Ireland.
     Daniel and Catherine came to the United States through Liverpool: Ship passage list from Liverpool to New York, September 1852.
     "Oh, my ass for a banjo string!": Marie Glendinning to Fred Lawrence Guiles, 1969.
     She started violin lessons: Marion Lake Canessa to author, 2014.
     problems with her legs: Marion's biographer Fred Lawrence Guiles asserts that a nanny was hired to watch the children, who ended up being abusive to Rosie and damaging her legs. This is refuted by family members who knew Rosie.
7   **on January 3, 1897:** Marion Douras birth certificate, New York Department of Vital Records.
     "I don't like the name Cecilia": Marion Davies autobiographical tape transcript, Marion Davies papers, box 11.

Affectionately nicknamed "Mardie" within the family: *Lincoln Star*, February 4, 1930.

"How can a baby stand in bed?": Marion Davies autobiographical tape transcript, Marion Davies papers.

"mother complex": Marion Davies autobiographical tape transcript, Marion Davies papers.

8   the Douras family moved: In her autobiographical tapes, Marion claimed the move occurred because Charles had been playing with matches and burned the house down. There is little evidence for this story.

"the closet treatment": Marion Davies autobiographical tape transcript, Marion Davies papers.

she emerged from it with a lifelong phobia of horses: Davies, *The Times We Had*, chap. 8.

A few days after their arrival: Marion Davies autobiographical tape transcript, Marion Davies papers.

Finally, on September 7: "Brooklyn Boy Drowned," *Brooklyn Daily Eagle*, September 7, 1900, 1.

9   Ben checked into the Clarendon Hotel: Hotel arrivals, *Brooklyn Daily Eagle*, December 29, 1900, 5.

In the days before World War I: Packman et al., "Sibling Bereavement and Continuing Bonds."

"I shall not forget Charles": Letter from Rose Douras to Marion Davies, 1953.

One day, after receiving $1,500 in payment: Marie Glendinning to Fred Lawrence Guiles, 1969.

10 "I used to see these things": Marion Davies autobiographical tapes, tape 1.

"I'd say, 'Forget it...'": Ibid.

Marion was beginning to stutter: Siblings of people who stutter have a significantly higher chance of developing a stutter than they would have otherwise, and Marion likely had a genetic predisposition to stuttering that simply emerged in the high stress time following her brother's death, and the time of the growing indifference of her parents to one another. Dr. Gerald Maguire to author, 2014.

"I'm not going to go around": Marion Davies autobiographical tape transcript, Marion Davies papers.

"Marion had great intelligence": Anne Shirley to Fred Lawrence Guiles, 1969.

11 a talented athlete: *Harrisburg Telegraph*, September 29, 1937, 5.

"Marion would freeze with fear": *Screenland* profile, April 1924, 30.

"I'll read them all": "Galatea on Riverside Drive," *Photoplay*, October 1919, 62.

a secondary outlet for her energy and frustration: *Screenland* profile, April 1924, 30; Marion Lake Canessa to author, 2014.

12 "Gigi tradition": This is all according to Anita Loos. Frances Marion, who knew Mama Rose well, had a different idea. The Mama Rose she knew was a timid, introverted woman, who lived in the past and doted on her daughters. She rarely acknowledged her two youngest as grown women, and instead

focused on the time when they were little girls, never seeming to want them to be adults in their own right. Frances Marion's concept of Mama Rose was of a mother who worried about the lives that her girls were living. This speaks to a certain intimidation with the life that her daughter came to live.

In 1941, Marion would win a prize: *San Francisco Examiner,* September 21, 1941, 7.

When she saw a sign: Marion Davies autobiographical tape transcript, Marion Davies papers.

13   **Marion spent the majority:** "Galatea on Riverside Drive," *Photoplay,* October 1919, 62.

"I would like to be a toe-dancer": Autobiography in *New York Graphic,* August 2, 1925, 7-M.

in March 1909: Pepi Lederer birth announcement, *Wilkes-Barre Times Leader,* March 31, 1909, 14.

Marion was thrilled with her new niece: Letter from Marion Douras (Davies) to Kate Cushing, undated, 1909, Bob Board collection.

"She had all the things, all of the characteristics I didn't have": Autobiography in *New York Graphic,* August 2, 1925, 7-M.

Sacred Heart, a small convent school: Marion maintained in her autobiographical tapes that the convent school had been in France, but her first trip out of the country was not until 1921. The school, now defunct, was in the area of Hastings-on-Hudson, New York.

14   **hit her on the knuckles:** Marion Davies to Clare Boothe Luce, 1948, Clare Boothe Luce papers, Library of Congress, box 777.

was hesitant about her youngest daughter: Marion Davies autobiographical tape transcript, Marion Davies papers.

"ONE OF THE MOST POPULAR GIRLS IN TOWN"

15   **"whom her sister was going with":** Anne Shirley to Fred Lawrence Guiles, 1969.

Marion returned home in the early morning hours: Marion Davies autobiographical tape transcript, Marion Davies papers.

The two girls found support: Marie Glendinning to Fred Lawrence Guiles, 1969.

16   **an upcoming production, The Sunshine Girl:** In recording her autobiographical tapes, Marion would mistakenly remember this show as being 1910's *The Blue Bird,* which was indeed a 1910 Maeterlinck production as she cites. But the details she gives about the show she calls *The Blue Bird* are the same details she had given in a 1925 autobiographical piece for the *New York Graphic,* in which she names the show as *The Sunshine Girl.* Additionally, she specifically cites

the Claridge Hotel in both her autobiographical tapes and the 1925 *New York Graphic* piece. The hotel had been called the Hotel Rector until a name change in 1913, the same year as *The Sunshine Girl*.

the famous dance team: Vernon and Irene Castle later became the inspiration for a movie version of their life, *The Story of Vernon and Irene Castle,* starring Fred Astaire and Ginger Rogers.

"my ambition at that time": Autobiography in *New York Graphic*, August 2, 1925, 7-M.

Backstage at the Knickerbocker one evening: Ibid.

moved in together at 920 West End Avenue: 1915 New York census.

Marion and Rose were each earning a respectable $15 per week: Autobiography in *New York Graphic*, August 2, 1925, 7-M.

17 **"the most generous in the world":** Marion Davies autobiographical tape transcript, Marion Davies papers, box 11.

When she received her first week's pay: *Photoplay*, February 1932, 68.

"I've never met such an unselfish girl": Marie Glendinning to Fred Lawrence Guiles, 1969.

"an incredible beauty": Mary Anita Loos to Hugh Munro Neely and Elaina Archer (Friedrichsen).

"one of the most popular girls in town": Beauchamp, *Without Lying Down*, 108.

"the Christmas lady": Bob Board to author, 2014.

18 **images of Marion in Chin-Chin:** Photos of *Chin-Chin* at New York Public Library, Billy Rose Theatre Division.

"dazzling show, with a world of fun in it": *Brooklyn Daily Eagle*, October 21, 1914, 6.

Nonetheless, it was not without its technical problems: "Graustark of Beverly Hills," *Motion Picture Magazine*, June 1926, 37.

19 **She familiarized herself with intricate details:** Marion Davies autobiographical tape transcription, Marion Davies papers.

"She used to keep everyone giggling all the time": Ina Claire in *Picture Play*, December 1930, 19.

20 **Ned Wayburn:** "Mysteries of the Chorus," *New York Tribune*, May 7, 1916, 2.

"who imagine that theatrical folk go into hotels": Ibid.

another young cast member: Justine Johnstone became Justine Wanger (wife of producer Walter Wanger), a respected Columbia-educated pathologist, endocrinologist, and cancer researcher. Marion often asked Justine for medical advice, and she examined Marion on several occasions as her personal doctor.

found Ziegfeld's mistress Lillian Lorraine haughty: Larry Russell to author, 2014.

the Follies of 1916 had a Shakespearean theme: Ann Van der Merwe to author, 2015.

21 **"My Shakespeare Girls":** Ziegfeld Follies of 1916 script, Ole Olsen collection, University of Southern California.

At the dress rehearsal, she stuttered: Marion Davies autobiographical tape transcriptions, Marion Davies papers.

Marion's evenings were filled with the fun: Anita Loos to Fred Lawrence Guiles, 1969.

"It's all right until it hurts somebody": Marion Davies autobiographical tape transcriptions, Marion Davies papers.

According to Anita Loos, during one of these sessions at Anita's house: Loos, *A Girl Like I*, 210.

22 "We didn't know what alcoholism was": Anita Loos to Fred Lawrence Guiles, 1969.

Marion's first taste of alcohol: This may have been in *Oh, Boy!* An unverified story exists in *Bring Out the Girls*, the semi-truthful book by P.G. Woodhouse and Guy Bolton, stating that Justine Johnstone and Marion came up with a plan: if Marion stuttered on her line during *Oh, Boy!*, Marion would mouth the words, and Justine would speak the line for her, alternating her voice between Justine's natural speaking tone and her impression of Marion's.

champagne: Marion Davies autobiographical tape transcriptions, Marion Davies papers.

23 playful kitten: Anita Loos to Fred Lawrence Guiles, 1969.

Paul Block: Brady, *The Publisher*, 120.

Block's introduction to Marion: Ibid., 186.

24 the public was starting to take an interest in the stars: Ibid., 188.

Still, many producers were hesitant about the costs and risks: Ibid., 188.

25 beer and sandwiches: Ibid., 185.

eager to try new things: *Film Fun Magazine*, January 1918, 5–7.

The filming of *Runaway Romany*": Ibid.

Laws in Westchester County: Ibid.

26 Overcome and filled with emotion: Brady, *The Publisher*, 187.

"We run our paper": Carlson and Bates, *Hearst, Lord of San Simeon*, 49.

"a great failure": Anne Apperson Flint to W.A. Swanberg, 1958, W.A. Swanberg papers, box 8.

"A sad man": Marion, "Hollywood," unpublished manuscript.

27 "There's nobody in the world like him": Marion Davies autobiographical tapes, tape 1.

Phoebe had possessed an insatiable curiosity: Lesko, *Phoebe Elizabeth Apperson Hearst, 1842–1919*.

Following the marriage of Phoebe and George Hearst in 1862: Ibid.

"From neither father nor mother": Carlson and Bates, *Hearst: Lord of San Simeon*, 37.

28 W.R.'s passion for publishing quickly outweighed his interest in his studies: Nasaw, *The Chief*, 33.

"Nastiness is not born in him": Ibid., 35.

W.R. failed several classes, was "rusticated": Procter, *William Randolph Hearst: The Early Years*, 35.

moved photos and text with his toes: Pizzitola, *Hearst over Hollywood*, 39.

"It wasn't idle buying, only": Anne Apperson Flint to W.A. Swanberg, 1958, W.A. Swanberg papers, box 8.

29 Phoebe, the matriarch of the family, was unimpressed: W.A. Swanberg interview with Anne Apperson Flint, 1959, W.A. Swanberg papers, box 8.

"He was a great showman": Millicent Hearst to W.A. Swanberg, 1959, W.A. Swanberg papers, box 8.

W.R. saw the new medium of motion pictures: Pizzitola, *Hearst over Hollywood*, 60.

30 The partisan nature of W.R.'s reporting: Nasaw, *The Chief*, 153–54.

He continued to produce short film versions: Pizzitola, *Hearst over Hollywood*, 171.

Marion herself claimed that in childhood: Davies, *The Times We Had*, 4.

vomited on the couch cushions: Loos, *A Girl Like I*, 210.

Marion recalled little gifts: Marion Davies autobiographical tape transcriptions, Marion Davies papers.

31 "I love a girl named Marion": Ibid.

wringing his hands over his attraction: Brady, *The Publisher*, 183.

In 1918, Hearst signed a new contract with Select Pictures: Pizzitola, *Hearst over Hollywood*, 207.

pre-production began on *Cecilia of the Pink Roses*: Ibid., 276.

32 The story…was told in installments: *New York Evening Journal*, June 1–3, 1918.

signed her to a six-picture deal: Ibid.

When *Cecilia of the Pink Roses* premiered: Pizzitola, *Hearst over Hollywood*, 277.

"UNUSUAL BOX OFFICE ATTRACTION"

33 "only a marble heart": *New York American*, June 3, 1918.

"clear-cut face": *New York Journal*, June 3, 1918.

"The whole trouble": Aronson et al., *Architect of Dreams*, 49.

"Have signed up Marion Davies": *Variety*, June 7, 1918.

"a gorgeous creature in a sable coat": Barbas, *First Lady of Hollywood*, 79.

34 Louella Parsons: Ibid., 100.

Louella…at the Telegraph: Ibid., 80.

35 "A shimmering white palace": *Philadelphia Inquirer*, February 17, 1918

she recalled trying to escape out the back: Marion Davies autobiographical tape transcript, Marion Davies papers, box 11.

36 "first literary hero": Older, *William Randolph Hearst, American*, 40.

W.R. spoke with Papa Ben: Marion Davies autobiographical tape transcript, Marion Davies papers.

37 made a plea for retiring magistrates: "Douras Asks Pension for Magistrates," *New York Times*, May 3, 1930, 3.

previously the property of William Ahnelt: *Brooklyn Daily Eagle*, December 2, 1913, 10.

bruises and dirt covering her entire body: "Galatea on Riverside Drive," *Photoplay*, October 1919, 62.

"She never could be brought": Anita Loos to Fred Lawrence Guiles, 1969.

38 "She is like a child": *Morning Telegraph*, March 9, 1919.

Even in utero: Marie Glendinning to Fred Lawrence Guiles, 1969.

"I felt like I was going to die": Marion Lake Canessa to author, 2014.

"She worshiped him": Anne Shirley to Fred Lawrence Guiles, 1969.

39 Phoebe had written him out of both her Pleasanton estate and Wyntoon: Coffman, *Julia Morgan: Wyntoon and Other Hearst Projects*, 2–3.

40 Julia Morgan: Coffman, *415 Ocean Front*, introduction.

"When do you plan to complete this?": C.B. Stratton to W.A. Swanberg, 1960, W.A. Swanberg papers, box 8.

41 Marion's childlike naughtiness: Allan Dwan interview with Peter Bogdanovich, 1971, in Bogdanovich, *Allan Dwan: The Last Pioneer*, 49.

"had a sense of humor": Ibid.

"more like Mabel Normand": Anita Loos to Fred Lawrence Guiles, 1969.

42 Cosmopolitan's home: Koszarski, *Hollywood on the Hudson*, 124.

Marion Davies Baseball Team: "Reintroducing Miss Davies," *Photoplay*, April 1922, 48.

Massachusetts delegation had allotted him one vote for president: Coffman, *Hearst as Collector*, 121.

La Paz Hotel: Montecito Association History Committee, 2016, in Myrick, *Montecito and Santa Barbara*, 202.

43 "This new place is a gem": Letter from Rose Douras to daughter Rose, September 1920, Marion Lake Canessa papers.

"Would you consider": Beauchamp, *Without Lying Down*, 106.

"Everyone in his employ showed him the most awed respect": Marion, "Hollywood," unpublished manuscript.

Frances Marion: Beauchamp, *Without Lying Down*, 106.

44 teach W.R. how to shimmy: Frances Marion to Fred Lawrence Guiles, 1969.

"Come in, Fran-Frances": Beauchamp, *Without Lying Down*, 106.

"Pick-Pickford stories": Marion, "Hollywood."

Frances was dejected: Ibid.

"Lavishness doesn't guarantee a good picture": Ibid.

45 "the background was too colorless": Marion, "Hollywood."

"a beautiful bonnet on": Cari Beauchamp interview, to Hugh Munro Neely and Elaina Archer (Friedrichsen), 2000.

Frances got a phone call: Frances Marion to W.A. Swanberg, 1960, W.A. Swanberg papers, box 8.

47 He controls aspects as minute as what the first intertitle should be: William Randolph Hearst to Luther Reed, May 8, 1921, William Randolph Hearst papers, box 38.
Joseph Urban: "Joseph Urban and the Birth of American Film Design," in Aronson et al., *Architect of Dreams.*

48 Urban's first year at Cosmopolitan: Ibid.
go on to Mexico for an extended vacation: Swanberg, *Citizen Hearst,* 401.
"produce a motion picture": Marion Davies passport application, 1921.
Marion and W.R. took the opportunity: Swanberg, *Citizen Hearst,* 401.

49 In W.R.'s absence, Millicent had been talking: Joseph A. Moore papers, Library of Congress, box 7.
When W.R. saw that his directions had been discarded: Ibid.

50 *Beauty's Worth*: Basinger, *Silent Stars,* 318.
"Dancing and singing are two of the things I miss in pictures": *Scranton Republican,* July 31, 1922.
"She has had more in the way": *New York Times,* March 27, 1922, 17.

51 Although the shoot itself: *When Knighthood Was in Flower* theater program, 1922.
Mary Pickford tried several times: *Photoplay,* March 22, 1922.
"the largest set ever constructed": *When Knighthood Was in Flower* theater program, 1922.

52 Marion was ahead of her time in this way: Basinger, *Silent Stars,* 328.
Arbuckle case: *San Francisco Examiner,* September 11, 1921, 2.

53 Along with many in the industry: Marion Lake Canessa to author, 2015.
Hollywood was again rocked: Beauchamp, *Joseph P. Kennedy Presents,* 47.
Marion went to Paris: *Variety,* June 23, 1922, 156.

54 Reine gave testimony: "Not a Screen Star," *New York Times,* July 28, 1922, 7.

55 Marion was petrified: Davies, *The Times We Had,* backed up by the *New York Times,* "Marion Davies Suit Not of Her Seeking," July 27, 1922, 5.
"You've certainly upset the apple cart": Davies, *The Times We Had,* 27.

56 "it has been conclusively established": *New York Daily News,* August 3, 1922, 27.

"A GOOD ACTRESS, A BEAUTY, AND A COMEDY STARRING BET"

57 the ad campaign: Barbas, *First Lady of Hollywood,* 82.
"When Electric Light Was in Power": Louella Parsons papers, box 7.
"When Knighthood Was in Flower, the Greatest Picture Ever Filmed": *Washington Times,* August 27, 1922, 6D.
In preparation for the premiere: *New York American,* September 10, 1922.

58 she wiggles her toes: *New York American,* September 15, 1922.

"rich in educational and artistic merit": *Motion Picture News*, January 1923, 5.

Marion called Louella: Barbas, *First Lady of Hollywood*, 83.

Originally slated to be directed by... Frank Borzage: *Exhibitor's Herald*, July 29, 1922.

59 Somerset Maugham: Marion, "Hollywood," 170.

On the evening of February 18, 1923: "Cosmopolitan Studio Destroyed by Fire," *Brooklyn Daily Eagle*, February 19, 1923, 1.

60 By 1923: Stenn, *Bombshell: The Life and Death of Jean Harlow*, 14.

Cosmopolitan... executives scrambled: Koszarski, *Hollywood on the Hudson*, 123.

congratulatory telegrams: Dunlap, *The Hearst Saga*, 458.

"[It] has done a great deal to add to the glories of Marion Davies": *Morning Telegraph*, Louella Parsons scrapbook #7, October 11, 1923.

61 "vowed to rebuild": *Film Daily*, February 25, 1923, 1.

In mid-February: *Motion Picture Magazine*, August 1924, 53; *Los Angeles Evening Post-Record*, September 9, 1930, 5.

62 She had never been particularly attached to New York: Marion Davies autobiographical tapes, author's transcription, 3.

she was involved in a minor car crash: *Los Angeles Times*, September 9, 1924, 19.

63 Fallon came before the court: "Nine Jurors Picked for Fallon Trial," *New York Times*, July 23, 1924, 17.

A key part of Fallon's red herring defense: *Brooklyn Daily Eagle*, August 7, 1924, 1.

64 Photos from that trip: Photos from Marion Lake Canessa scrapbook, Marion Lake Canessa collection.

"If she had one child with Hearst": Evelyn Wells to W.A. Swanberg, September 23, 1959, W.A. Swanberg papers.

Janice Meredith premiered on August 5: Holston, *Movie Roadshows*, 38.

A great deal of building: Loe, *Hearst Castle*, 67.

$10,000 per week: *Detroit Saturday Night*, May 9, 1925.

"up from the top": *Picture Play*, May 1930, 34.

65 "I think Marion had more talent than she knew": Anne Shirley to Fred Lawrence Guiles, 1969.

"She will give the clothes off her back": Head, *It Could Never Have Happened*, 96.

"Just your friendship": Frances Marion to Fred Lawrence Guiles, 1969.

"you've got to learn": Ibid.

"IT'S VERY CONVENIENT TO HAVE A DOUBLE"

66 The atmosphere of 1920s Los Angeles: Ryan, *Angel's Flight*, 63.

In 1924, six thousand cars a day: Starr, *Material Dreams*, 173.

Egyptian Theatre: Ibid.

The outward urban growth of Los Angeles: Ibid.

The home was bought by George S. Jephson: *New York City Telegram*, April 22, 1925.

67 "like inheriting an annuity": Hopper, *From under My Hat*, 155.

Due to space constraints at the new MGM studio: Marion Davies autobiographical tapes, tape 6.

"Daisies never tell": Marion Lake Canessa to author, 2015.

Vera Burnett: Vera Burnett to Fred Lawrence Guiles, 1969.

68 A telegram from Glyn read: Chaplin, *My Autobiography*, 303.

"Marion's blonde beauty": Grace Kingsley, *New York Daily News*, November 16, 1924, 22.

Chaplin was also frequently on the set: Vera Burnett to Fred Lawrence Guiles, 1969.

Chaplin had known Millicent Hearst since the 1910s: Chaplin, *My Autobiography*, 304.

69 "we all pretend to believe him": Ibid.

During much of the filming of *Zander the Great*: Pizzitola, *Hearst over Hollywood*, 356.

70 "The important question": William Randolph Hearst to Marion Davies, September 1924. Author's collection.

"always had a book": Marion Davies autobiographical tapes, tape 6.

"It was a beautiful boat": Marion Davies autobiographical tapes, tape 7.

consulted with doctors about this yacht trip: Taves, *Thomas Ince*, 257.

The group included: Marion Davies autobiographical tapes, tape 6.

Unaware of Ince's dietary restrictions: Taves, *Thomas Ince*, 257.

71 "DYING MAN TOLD OF YACHT BOOZE": *New York Daily News*, December 10, 1924, 39.

"Louella Parsons was already working for Hearst": Barbas, *The First Lady of Hollywood*, 88.

The only time that W.R. was known to shoot a gun: Louis Shainmark to W.A. Swanberg, 1958, W.A. Swanberg papers.

"Who would shoot him?": Marion Davies autobiographical tapes, author's transcription, tape 1.

72 Nell Ince: Letter from Elinor Ince to George Pratt, July 7, 1966.

"visa to both establishments": Chaplin, *My Autobiography*, 305.

W.R. became upset: Ibid.

73 W.R. was often away from Marion in 1925: Dunlap, *The Hearst Saga*, 483–84.

Following the premiere: Barbas, *The First Lady of Hollywood*, 76.

Marion and Louella left for California: Ibid.

74 making too much noise: Fred Lawrence Guiles to Hugh Munro Neely and Elaina Archer (Friedrichsen).

Sometimes Mama Rose came downstairs: Frances Marion to Fred Lawrence Guiles, 1969.

75 **His jealousy became so severe:** Dunlap, *The Hearst Saga*, 483–84.
76 **In later years:** Marion Lake Canessa to author, 2014.

"DRINKING CHAMPAGNE OUT OF A TIN CUP"

77 **"Ninety years from now":** Beverly of Graustark profile, *Screenland*, July 1926, 46.
    "Don't try it unless you are very beautiful": *Photoplay*, January 1926, 40.
    Marion caught a bad flu: "Graustark of Beverly Hills," *Motion Picture Magazine*, 37.
    He was fascinated by exotic animals: Coffman, *Hearst and Marion*, 114.
78 **Stranded on the hillside when a moose:** Louella Parsons to W.A. Swanberg, W.A. Swanberg papers, box 8.
    large kennel of dachshunds: Anita Loos to Fred Lawrence Guiles, 1969.
    The journey would start in downtown Los Angeles or Glendale: Eleanor Boardman, Oral History San Simeon, archives at the Hearst San Simeon State Historical Monument.
    As Anita ascended the hill: Anita Loos to Fred Lawrence Guiles, 1969.
79 **"drinking champagne out of a tin cup":** William Haines to Fred Lawrence Guiles, 1969
    "If you were lucky": Anita Loos to Fred Lawrence Guiles, 1969.
    Marion's drinking needed to be controlled: Evelyn Wells to W.A. Swanberg, 1958, W.A. Swanberg papers.
    "we were all brats": Anita Loos to Fred Lawrence Guiles, 1969.
    "Why don't you just stay in there all night?": Cari Beauchamp to Hugh Munro Neely and Elaina Archer (Friedrichsen), 1999.
80 **condiments:** William Haines to Fred Lawrence Guiles, 1969.
    Parties were filled with Marion's generous spirit: Eleanor Boardman to Fred Lawrence Guiles, 1969.
    lavish western-style picnics: Jim Simpson to author, January 2016; Eleanor Boardman 1982 and King Vidor 1980, both at Oral History San Simeon, archives at the Hearst San Simeon State Historical Monument.
    Friends invited to the picnics: Ibid.
81 **"the best marriage in Hollywood":** Frances Marion to Fred Lawrence Guiles, 1969.
    Joseph P. Kennedy and Gloria Swanson: Beauchamp, *Joseph P. Kennedy Presents*, 270–71.
    Gloria, by contrast: Ibid.
82 **"The ones without wings":** "Graustark of Beverly Hills," *Motion Picture Magazine*, June 1926, 37.
83 **Not a single photo of his mother:** Julie Payne to author, 2014.
    Marion…Elaine St. Johns: Cari Beauchamp to Hugh Munro Neely and Elaina Archer (Friedrichsen), 2000.

"They're your flesh and blood": Marion Davies autobiographical tapes, tape 1.

purchase the land for a children's clinic: Marion Davies Children's Clinic documents, Pediatrics Department, UCLA.

underwrote the activities: *Santa Monica Outlook*, August 5, 1926.

84 In order to secure: Marion Davies Children's Clinic documents, Pediatrics Department, UCLA.

In view of the strain: Ibid.

At the Tivoli Theater in Sawtelle: *Santa Monica Outlook*, December 18, 1927

"You're going to make *The Red Mill*": Keaton and Sweeney, *Buster Keaton: Interviews*, 193.

85 W.R. invited Arbuckle to San Simeon: Bailey and Chermak, *Famous American Crimes and Trials*, 59.

Vidor was a frequent guest at San Simeon: Vidor, *A Tree Is a Tree*, 159.

"Mr. Hearst never gave up until he had me directing Miss Davies": King Vidor to Fred Lawrence Guiles, 1970.

86 "owners of moist brows": *Film Daily*, July 11, 1926, 12.

Carl Roup: Carl Roup to Hugh Munro Neely and Elaina Archer (Friedrichsen), 2000.

ammonia gas: "Acres of Ice for Film Frozen under July Sun," *New York Times*, February 13, 1927, 162.

87 so upset: Davies, *The Times We Had*, 81.

permanently stopped menstruating: Marion Lake Canessa to author, 2014.

"WHY DON'T WE FORGET THE PLAY THAT'S WRITTEN AND LET MARION DO WHAT SHE DOES?"

88 The large new hospital for the Marion Davies Children's Clinic: *Santa Monica Evening Outlook*, January 18, 1928.

Lupe Herrera, who grew up in the Mexican American community of West Los Angeles: Interview notes with Daniel Cano, 2000.

89 leased back to W.R.: Coffman, *Hearst and Marion*, 168.

The architect... William Flannery: Ibid., 19.

The Beach House project: Taking a chance on Flannery paid off. He was responsible for much of the Beach House's early construction, though he didn't continue with architecture as a permanent career. He later turned to set decoration, and won an Academy Award for his work on *Picnic* (1955).

W.R. envisioned a grand property: Coffman, *Hearst and Marion*, unpublished afterword, "The Hearst-Heyn Feature, 1949," 3.

The main house had about twenty rooms: Ibid., 616–19.

W.R. conducted a massive search for amenities: Associated Press, January 3, 1960.

90   "Marion Davies will soon move into her beach home": Louella Parsons column, September 9, 1926.

April 15: Coffman, *Hearst and Marion*, 26.

91   One day Anita spoke of a party to Marion: Beauchamp, *Without Lying Down*, 187.

Marion Davies productions: Louella Parsons, October 22, 1927.

reminiscent of a Lucille Ball routine: While she cannot be found in the film, Ball later claimed that she made her film debut in the background of *Tillie the Toiler*.

"I have worked very hard": Undated telegram to Irving Thalberg, February 1927, William Randolph Hearst papers, box 38.

92   "Gentle and refreshing": *New York Times*, November 2, 1927

"She gives a performance": Gene Gerhard, *New York Evening World*, quoted in the *San Francisco Examiner*, December 18, 1927, 101.

"a modern girl": Irving Thalberg to William Randolph Hearst, July 1927, William Randolph Hearst papers, box 38.

93   Mary Pickford: *Photoplay*, December 1927, 98.

W.R. walked over to the actress Marie Dressler: Adela Rogers St. Johns to W.A. Swanberg, 1959, W.A. Swanberg papers, box 8.

"It isn't the lights": *Photoplay*, December 1927, 98.

photo of Lindbergh: Hedda Hopper column, May 9, 1954.

94   combination housewarming and July Fourth party: Marion, "Hollywood," 201.

"natural born comedienne": *Photoplay*, December 1927, 55.

"I do not see that it adds materially": William Randolph Hearst to Irving Thalberg, William Randolph Hearst papers, box 38.

"I will never be wholly enamored": Ibid.

95   W.R. had approved of King Vidor's work: King Vidor to Fred Lawrence Guiles, 1970.

"Why don't we forget the play": Ibid.

"We just put those things": Ibid.

"It was not hard work": Ibid.

"Have you heard the music?": Ibid.

96   "Of all the varied Cinderellas": *New York Times*, April 23, 1928, 20.

The Patsy was also a box office success: The Patsy ledger, Marion Davies papers.

One night in late September 1927: Baltimore City Court affidavit, October 21, 1927.

On January 25, 1928: *Spokesman-Review*, January 26, 1928, 2.

97   her sensitive nose: Davies, *The Times We Had*, 112.

"When we got to the house": Ibid.

"May I be a mother to you?": Ibid.

"It was more like a father/daughter relationship": Anita Loos to Fred Lawrence Guiles, 1969.

98 **The funeral was a large affair:** Dorothy Mackaill to Fred Lawrence Guiles, 1969.

"I CANNOT DO SOUND PICTURES"

99 **"The script of a film called *Polly Preferred*:** *Show People* production notes, USC.

100 **Marion's leading man in Show People was to be James Murray:** King Vidor to Fred Lawrence Guiles, 1969.
  "unable to locate Mr. Murray": *Show People* production notes, USC.
  "I didn't need her": William Haines to Fred Lawrence Guiles, 1969.

101 **King Vidor, still in his twenties:** King Vidor to Fred Lawrence Guiles, 1969.

102 **"simmering in a delightful fashion":** *New York Times*, November 12, 1927, 27.
  "filmdom's most hilarious comedienne": *New York Daily News*, November 12, 1928.
  "Patricia had come back to the United States from France": Letter from governess Godfrey to Rose Van Cleve, June 19, 1928, Marion Lake Canessa collection.
  "I do not think it a good idea to let him have a strange governess for Pat": Undated letter, Marion Lake Canessa collection.

103 **Marion continued to bring Patricia to San Simeon frequently:** Marion Lake Canessa to author, 2014.
  In the early 1890s: Rogoff, "Edison's Dream," 60.

104 **"appalled":** Marion Davies autobiographical tapes, tape 6.
  "I am leaving for Europe": Marion Davies to Louis B. Mayer, July 20, 1928, William Randolph Hearst papers, box 38.
  "If I don't get radios from you": Dunlap, *The Hearst Saga*, 533.
  They arrived in Paris and cabled Alice Head: Head, *It Could Never Have Happened*, 113.

105 **In later years, a small group of friends came to San Simeon for a weekend:** St. Johns, *Love, Laughter, and Tears*, 87.
  "We're *much* the most important people": Head, *It Could Never Have Happened*, 114.

106 **"Never once a curse. Everything was adulation":** Marion Davies autobiographical tapes, tape 1.
  "Be sure to pay for all of Betty's meals": March 7–22, 1927, William Randolph Hearst papers, box 7.

107 **W.R.'s telegrams to Pepi when she was traveling are warm, loving, and paternal:** September 8, 1927, William Randolph Hearst papers, box 7.
  Marion and the rest of the group ventured down the Italian coast to Viareggio: Head, *It Could Never Have Happened*, 113.
  she had struck up a love affair with Roland de Cassé, the Marquis de Bris-

sac: Letters between Rose Davies and Marquis de Brissac, Marion Lake Canessa collection.

St. Donat's, a medieval castle: Royal Commission, *An Inventory of the Ancient Monuments in Glamorgan, Volume III*, 305–7.

In 1930, W.R. planned an elaborate firework display: Head, *It Could Never Have Happened*, 114.

108 sixteen trunks: *Screenland*, January 1928, 58.

One evening while staying at the Ritz Towers: Marion Davies autobiographical tapes transcript, Marion Davies papers.

With a stroke of a pencil: Marion, "Hollywood," unpublished manuscript.

109 "I didn't want to go back": Marion Davies autobiographical tapes, tape 6.

When the day came for Marion's screen test: Davies, *The Times We Had*, 72.

"A BUTTERFLY WITH GLUE ON HER WINGS"

110 "Will she retain her stutter": *Picture Play*, January 1929, 45.

"Some days she would come roaring in": Nasaw, *The Chief*, 409.

111 "McCrea had started": "Behind the Scenes in Hollywood," *Carbondale Free Press*, December 31, 1928, 5.

The reason seems to be multifold: Telegrams between William Randolph Hearst and Irving Thalberg, William Randolph Hearst papers, box 8.

Shooting of the silent version of *Marianne*: *Exhibitor's Herald World*, March 16, 1929, 46.

Marion recalled that she had heard Lawrence Gray: "Larry Comes Back," *Screenland*, December 1929, 111.

112 Marion had awakened with a sore throat: *Hollywood Revue* production notes, Cinematic Arts Library, USC.

Hollywood Revue of 1929 had a quick release: *Hollywood Filmograph*, June 15, 1929, 38.

Marion kept a tight schedule: Head, *It Could Never Have Happened*, 152.

113 letter to Robert L. Ripley: Dunlap, *The Hearst Saga*, 546.

"her own playhouse": *San Francisco Examiner*, April 1, 1929, 12.

The practice was so unknown: *San Francisco Examiner*, May 15, 1929, 16.

114 The premiere at the Mayan Theater: "Marianne Promises Surprises," *Los Angeles Times*, August 25, 1929, 36.

"sound out of sync": "The Girl with the Seven Voices," *Screenland*, March 1930, 113.

W.R. had finally admitted: William Randolph Hearst telegrams to Irving Thalberg, William Randolph Hearst papers, box 8.

"a butterfly with glue on her wings": Beauchamp, *Without Lying Down*, 133.

"vested interest in euphoria": "The 1929 Parallel," *The Atlantic*, January 1987.

115 **"Marion stuttered like mad"**: Dorothy MacKaill to Fred Lawrence Guiles, 1970.
"Once Marion got before the camera": William Haines to Fred Lawrence Guiles, 1969.
In February 1930: Dunlap, *The Hearst Saga*, 553–54.
Grace Coolidge got an unexpected taste of the "new": Marion Davies autobiographical tape transcript, Marion Davies papers.

116 **Movie theater at San Simeon**: Coffman, *Hearst and Marion*, 98.

117 **The Technicolor process**: "Two Color Process," George Eastman House, 2015.
"again the screen colony": *New York Times*, June 15, 1930.

119 **Another European holiday had been planned**: Head, *It Could Never Have Happened*, 114.
While resting in his room one day in early September: "Chicago Day Fete by Governor," *San Francisco Examiner*, October 1, 1930, 2.
Marion later claimed to have been responsible: Marion Davies autobiographical tapes, tape 6.
"If being a competent journalist": *Windsor Star*, September 2, 1930, 2.

120 **"Never pro-German"**: Marion Davies autobiographical tapes, tape 1.
The group went to the Savoy: Dunlap, *The Hearst Saga*, 560.
"I never heard of Marion Davies": Patch, *Thirty Years with George Bernard Shaw*, 187.
"I didn't think you were smart enough to read them": Dunlap, *The Hearst Saga*, 560.
a married one named Ned McLean: "McLean to Wed Sister of Screen Actress," *Post Crescent*, November 17, 1931, 4.

121 **As it turned out, McLean never got the divorce**: "Her Husband Left Rose Davies $300,000," *Pottstown Mercury*, July 29, 1941, 2.
Marion learned that a customer: Davies, *The Times We Had*, 61.
"I don't know why the nicest people always have the most horrible animals": William Haines to Fred Lawrence Guiles, 1969.

122 **a party was given for Marion at the Ambassador Hotel**: Dunlap, *The Hearst Saga,* 538.
kiddie party: "The Stars Make Merry in Rompers and Hair Ribbons," *New Movie Magazine*, April 1932, 74.
As the end of the year approached: Dunlap, *The Hearst Saga*, 581.

123 **Marion co-sponsored a massive benefit**: *Movie Classics*, January 1933, 49.

"I DIDN'T WANT A PART WHERE I JUST SIT ON MY TAIL
AND RECITE POETRY"

125 **"never had a role"**: *Brooklyn Times Union*, March 19, 1932, 58.
"curb your inclination towards humor": Beauchamp, *Without Lying Down*, 287.

126 "It hasn't the feeling of life": Ibid., 288.

When Franklin D. Roosevelt began his campaign: Carlisle, *Hearst and the New Deal*, 32–51.

127 *Going Hollywood* was originally written: Beauchamp, *Without Lying Down*, 308.

128 "Let her be older": Frances Marion to Fred Lawrence Guiles, 1969.

Peg O' My Heart began filming: Vera Burnett to Fred Lawrence Guiles, 1969.

129 "It is evidently a part": *New York Times*, May 20, 1933, 11.

The same month, Marion was elected president: *San Francisco Examiner*, June 28, 1934, 34.

130 grocery orders: *Los Angeles Times*, April 16, 1933, 40.

Christmas baskets: *Pittsburgh Sun Telegraph*, December 20, 1934, 2.

"Tonsils, boy, were coming out left and right": Lupe Herrera to Daniel Cano, 2000.

Bertram G. Knowles: *Picture Play*, December 1933, 10.

131 Future director George Sidney: George Sidney to Hugh Munro Neely and Elaina Archer (Friedrichsen), 2000.

beauty and health tips: Transcript of Lux Radio Theatre *Operator 13* broadcast, Louella Parsons papers.

132 "Mr. Hearst wants a break": Telegram from Louella Parson to Eugene Inge, Louella Parsons papers.

In late May 1934, just a few days after her successful radio debut: William "Buster" Collier papers, scrapbook.

133 Home movies from the 1934 trip to Europe: Collection of author.

"This is the best Rhine wine I have ever tasted": Buster Collier to Fred Lawrence Guiles, 1969.

a fascinating and chilling scrapbook: William "Buster" Collier papers, scrapbook.

134 Carl Laemmle... wrote to Hearst: Quoted in Nasaw, *The Chief*, 476.

135 "W.R. was not impressed by him": Davies, *The Times We Had*, 148.

Sinclair had won the Democratic nomination: Muscio, *Hollywood's New Deal*, 41; *Boston Globe*, October 29, 1934; Sinclair, *I, Candidate for Governor*.

Neylan cabled W.R. in Europe: Quoted in Mitchell, *Campaign of the Century*, 5.

136 British territory of Gibraltar: Jim Forney letter to Bertha Forney, October 14, 1935.

137 a mechanical problem: Buster Collier to Fred Lawrence Guiles, 1969.

On the political front, the Upton Sinclair campaign was heating up: Mitchell, *Campaign of the Century*, 54; *New York Times*, September 2, 1934.

139 "I didn't want a part": Marion, "Hollywood," unpublished manuscript.

140 "You always felt": Dick Powell to W.A. Swanberg, 1959, W.A. Swanberg papers.

"I really adore him": Marion Davies autobiographical tapes, tape 4.

He fell ill in late April: *Atlanta Constitution*, April 27, 1935, 20.

141 He died on April 25: Ibid.

Upon arrival at the hospital: *Los Angeles Times*, June 12, 1935, 1.

142 **"Pep was a very unhappy child"**: Marie Glendinning to Fred Lawrence Guiles, 1969.

Louise Brooks would write about Pepi: Brooks, *Lulu in Hollywood*, 55.

"JUST MAKE ONE GOOD PICTURE A YEAR"

143 **Anita Loos's house**: The 1940 census, erroneously it seems, lists Anita Loos's address as 506 Montana. Her address was 506 Ocean Front, half a block from Marion's home.

throw pebbles: Anita Loos to Fred Lawrence Guiles, 1969.

underlying aura of unhappiness: Frances Marion to Fred Lawrence Guiles, 1969.

She confided to her friend Evelyn Wells: Evelyn Wells to W.A. Swanberg, 1959, W.A. Swanberg papers, box 8.

9,500 individuals and families: "Film Charity Reviewed," *Pittsburgh Sun Telegraph*, June 26, 1935, 20.

144 **Marion organized a preview party for locals**: *Dunsmuir News*, July 12, 1935, 1.

"a treat to the home folks": Louis Schallich to George Loor, quoted in Coffman, *Building for Hearst and Morgan*, 197.

The story of *Page Miss Glory*: *Birmingham News*, October 3, 1935, 29.

Marion's positive relationships on her sets: "Miss Davies Takes Blame for Others," *Hartford Courant*, June 30, 1935, 15.

145 **"ballyhoo Marion Davies"**: *New Theatre*, August 1935.

Dick Powell came down with laryngitis: Dick Powell to W.A. Swanberg, 1958, W.A. Swanberg papers, box 8.

"Marion is getting old": *Motion Picture Herald*, August 15, 1936.

"Cosmopolitan Productions knows full well": *Motion Picture Herald*, August 1, 1936.

146 **A film for James Cagney and Ruby Keeler**: Inter-office memo between Walter MacEwen and Bob Lord, October 16, 1935, Warner Bros. Archives, USC.

soundstage raised: Bingen and Wanamaker, *Warner Bros.*, 122.

147 **"unnecessary slang"**: Letters between William Randolph Hearst and Jack Warner, Jack Warner collection, Cinematic Arts Library, USC.

Several letters from Breen arrived at the studio: *Cain and Mabel* file, Warner Bros. Archives, USC.

One day Harry Warren: Wilk, *They're Playing Our Song*, 127.

Filming took place: Vera Burnett interview, Oral History San Simeon, archives at the Hearst San Simeon State Historical Monument, 1980.

148 **in August of 1936 Marion and W.R. traveled to Europe**: Head, *It Could Never Have Happened*, 216–20.

149 **"I was lucky to know her"**: Mary Carlisle to author, 2014.

Wallis Simpson: Head, *It Could Never Have Happened*, 222.

While he had disagreements with Roosevelt from the start: Coffman, *Hearst and Marion*, 166.

150 "my politics and Hearst's simply didn't mix": Loy and Kotsilibas-Davis, *Being and Becoming*, 81.

Henry Morgenthau: Nasaw, *The Chief*, 468.

She would denounce Pegler's attacks: Marion Davies autobiographical tapes, tape 6.

A carousel was borrowed from Warner Bros.: Home movie footage, 1937, Academy of Motion Picture Arts and Sciences, Pickford Center for Motion Picture Study.

151 Joseph P. Kennedy lowballed: Beauchamp, *Joseph P. Kennedy Presents*, 345.

Compounding these financial issues: *Harrison's Reports*, August 6, 1938; *Motion Picture Daily*, July 7, 1937.

152 "provide summer entertainment": *Picture Play*, September 1937, 95.

Marion had been playing the ingenue: *New York Times*, June 25, 1937.

radio version of *Peg O' My Heart*: Lux Radio Theater, *Peg O' My Heart*, November 29, 1937, CBS Radio.

153 Clark Alvord: "Dead Admirer Wins Marion's Attention," *Daily News*, January 16, 1938, 4.

154 The plane crashed...killing Lord and Lady Plunket: Dorothy Mackaill to Fred Lawrence Guiles, 1969.

155 Reine died at her home: *Montclair Times*, April 5, 1938, 2.

"WHAT DIFFERENCE DOES IT MAKE IF YOU
WALK UP TO THE ALTAR?"

156 Karl Dane: Balogh, *Denmark's Forgotten Film Star, Karl Dane*, 67.

157 John Gilbert: Leatrice Gilbert Fountain to Hugh Munro Neely and Elaina Archer (Friedrichsen), 2000.

leading lady Virginia Cherrill: Brownlow, *The Search for Charlie Chaplin*, 744 (Kindle).

158 Billy Haines: William Haines to Fred Lawrence Guiles, 1969.

Billy and Jimmy Shields were targets: *Pittsburgh Post-Gazette*, June 3, 1936, 1.

159 He suggested that W.R. sell bonds: Beauchamp, *Joseph P. Kennedy Presents*, 345.

"Marion is returning to you": Telegram from Bill Williams to Roach and Driver's, June 24, 1938, William Randolph Hearst papers, carton 38.

160 $100,000 every four months: Dunlap, *The Hearst Saga*, 739.

"he tried very hard": Marion Davies autobiographical tapes, tape 6.

161 The divorce and subsequent marriage were called off: Stanley Flink to author, 2014.

"If you come here, Millicent": William Haines to Fred Lawrence Guiles, 1969.

162 "Love comes from the heart": Marion Davies autobiographical tapes, author's transcription, tape 1.

In mid-September: *Pittsburgh Sun-Telegraph*, September 19, 1938, 16.

The women entered the Beach House: Home movie footage of servicewomen tea, UCLA Film and TV Archive.

163 Churchill: "Hearst Lambasts Britain for Propagandizing U.S.," *Fort Myers News-Press*, October 23, 1938, 1.

From Wyntoon, W.R. and Marion wired editors: *San Francisco Examiner*, November 6, 1938, 17; November 7, 1938, 11.

"Most Powerful Anti-Vivisectionist": *Life*, October 24, 1938.

164 "even if I were a rat": Marion Davies to Stanley Flink, 1953.

Her death was reported in the press: "Ethel Davies Dies from Heart Attack," *San Bernardino County Sun*, July 20, 1940, 7.

165 "You'll never have a wedding ring on your finger": Dorothy Mackaill to Fred Lawrence Guiles, 1970.

Inspired by Mary Pickford: "Marion Davies Lauded," *Morning Post*, 21, 1942, 12.

The Hearst papers had considered Japan the greatest threat: Nasaw, *The Chief*, 242.

166 Marion installed dozens of sewing machines: Tebbel, *The Life and Good Times of William Randolph Hearst*, 17.

"quilts and shirts": Marion Davies autobiographical tape transcriptions, Marion Davies papers.

"As Governor of the State of California": "Leaders Acclaim Marion Davies Offer of Hospital for War Work," *San Francisco Examiner*, January 12, 1942, 5.

"It's Captain Davies Now": *Times Tribune*, January 14, 1942, 15.

Navy families: Marion Davies Children's Clinic documents, Pediatrics Department, UCLA.

meaningful regret came from Carole Lombard: Coffman, *Hearst and Marion*, 420.

167 Carole...died in the crash: Matzen, *Fireball: Carole Lombard and the Mystery of Flight 3*, 330.

Anna Roosevelt/John Boettinger telegram: Coffman, *Hearst and Marion*, 421.

168 Rose and Horace Brown: Floretta Mauser to Fred Lawrence Guiles, 1970.

"MARION HAS TO TAKE THE FIRST STEP HERSELF"

169 "I'll kill him": Marion Davies autobiographical tapes, tape 1.

"I never realized the power of silence": Frances Marion to Fred Lawrence Guiles, 1969.

170 **Ganna Walska:** Crawford, Ganna Walska Lotusland, 13.
Marion and Ganna Walska knew each other: Marion Davies autobiographical tapes, tape 6.

171 *Citizen Kane*: Lebo, *Citizen Kane*, 222; Rosebud plot gimmick: Carringer, *The Making of Citizen Kane*, 19.
barely knew how to tell the reality from the myth: Nasaw, *The Chief*, 572–73.
reaction to *Citizen Kane* **was nonchalant:** Marion Davies autobiographical tapes, tape 1.
Orson Welles was approached to write the foreword: Davies, *The Times We Had*, introduction.

172 **"spastic leg":** Stanley Flink to author, 2015.
"You would aid her in the walking": Anne Shirley to Fred Lawrence Guiles, 1969.
"Marion has been very ill": Letter from William Randolph Hearst to John Francis Neylan, September 26, 1942, William Randolph Hearst papers, carton 38.
"I am busy": Letter from Marion Davies to Patricia Lake, October 16, 1942, Marion Lake Canessa collection.
Marion kept unusual hours: Floretta Mauser to Fred Lawrence Guiles, 1969.

173 **Gandhi aging and in poor health:** Nasaw, *The Chief*, 563.
Marion wrote to Lee Wenzlick: Marion Davies to Lee Wenzlick, December 4, 1942, Taylor Coffman collection.
Remembering the comfort of alcohol: Undated letter from William Randolph Hearst to Rose Davies, 1943, quoted in Dunlap, *The Hearst Saga*, 812.

174 **Howard Hughes:** Stanley Flink notes, undated.
"Marion has to take the first step herself": Dunlap, *The Hearst Saga*, 812.
presented with a gold mezuzah: *Pittsburgh Sun-Telegraph*, June 10, 1944, 3.

175 **Gandhi died:** Nasaw, *The Chief*, 563.
"I'm the grandmother": Marion Lake Canessa to author, 2014.

176 **Marion fell to the floor:** Marion Davies autobiographical tapes, tape 1.
"Dear Anna": Telegram from Marion Davies to Anna Roosevelt, April 1945.

177 **V-E DAY:** *Los Angeles Times*, May 7, 1945, 1.
reserved a room at the nearby Huntington Hotel: Marion Davies autobiographical tapes, tape 1.
W.R. was busy: Ibid.
"Something horrible has been done": Dunlap, *The Hearst Saga*, 829.
Hollywood had become unrecognizable to Marion: Marion Davies to Hedda Hopper, Hedda Hopper column, May 9, 1954.

178 **only showed the talkies:** Marion Lake Canessa to author, 2014.
Colleen Moore: Colleen Moore interview, Oral History San Simeon, Hearst San Simeon State Historical Monument, 1972.
The paradox…of San Simeon: Frances Marion interview, Oral History San Simeon, Hearst San Simeon State Historical Monument, 1981.
"Was he unhappy": Marion, "Hollywood," unpublished manuscript.

179 selling the Beach House: Coffman, *Hearst and Marion*, 560.
trust fund…and dividends: Letter from Marion Davies to attorney Arnold Grant, May 2, 1957, Marion Davies papers.
his health had been declining: Marion Davies autobiographical tapes, tape 1.
180 George Bruce: "Hearst Died in Home Owned by Marion Davies," *Miami News*, August 17, 1951, 12.
"We'll come back someday": Nasaw, *The Chief*, 587.

"THE GIRL WHO LIES BY MY SIDE AT NIGHT"

181 Mrs. Mauser: Floretta Mauser to Fred Lawrence Guiles, 1969.
182 Anne Shirley: Anne Shirley to Fred Lawrence Guiles, 1969.
"It always made him feel better": Marion Davies autobiographical tapes, tape 6.
128 pounds: Nasaw, *The Chief*, 598.
House Un-American Activities Committee: Ibid., 596.
"rabid": Marion Davies autobiographical tapes, tape 1.
183 ceding power to Bill Jr.: Nasaw, *The Chief*, 598.
Horace returned from Japan: Russell Brown to author, 2014.
ushered Marion and Horace into private rooms: Ibid.
184 "I hope I'm not being too forward": Beauchamp, *Joseph P. Kennedy Presents*, 390.
voting rights: Nasaw, *The Chief*, 601.
"You know my theories": Marion Davies autobiographical tapes, author's transcriptions, tape 4.
"He could see further": Ibid.
185 "I thought it meant voting for president": Ibid.
On the advice of Greg Bautzer: Gladstone, *The Man Who Seduced Hollywood*, 212.
186 Stanley Flink and "*Life* Visits Marion Davies": Stanley Flink to author, 2014.
"I'd like to meet him sometime": Marion Davies autobiographical tapes, author's transcriptions, tape 5.
Louis Shainmark: Louis Shainmark to W.A. Swanberg, 1959, W.A. Swanberg papers.
187 "a blot on the Swedish flag": *Pittsburgh Post-Gazette*, August 10, 1949, 6.
Ingrid Bergman: Marion Davies autobiographical tapes, author's transcription, tape 1.
"Think of it": *Los Angeles Times*, February 6, 1950, 24.
"I called up the Examiner": Marion Davies autobiographical tapes, author's transcription, tape 1.
188 "Heinie MacKay's fired": Marion Davies autobiographical tapes, author's transcription, tape 1.
"insecure, but…brave": Anne Shirley to Fred Lawrence Guiles, 1969.

small group of friends: Eleanor Boardman to Fred Lawrence Guiles, 1969.

189 "I think I'm getting old": Marion Davies autobiographical tapes, author's transcription, tape 5

"an attachment that ran very deep": Stanley Flink to author, 2021.

special edition: Marion Davies autobiographical tapes, author's transcription, tape 5.

190 Cobina Wright: Eleanor Boardman to Fred Lawrence Guiles, 1969.

Frances Marion promised to go to San Simeon: Beauchamp, *Without Lying Down*, 363.

191 Marie Glendinning: Marie Glendinning to Fred Lawrence Guiles, 1969.

"I think I'll stay with Marion tonight": Ibid.

"MY BOUNTY IS AS BOUNDLESS AS THE SEA"

192 Frances had honored W.R.'s wishes: Beauchamp, *Without Lying Down*, 363.

"This is Marion Davies' house": Stanley Flink notes.

193 "I had him for 32 years": *Life*, August 27, 1951, 24.

Paul Mantz: Stanley Flink to author, 2014.

Marion received a call: Stanley Flink notes.

194 First five pages: *San Francisco Examiner*, August 15, 1951, 1–5.

"I thought I might go to church": *Life*, August 27, 1951, 24.

On the day of the funeral: Stanley Flink to author, 2014.

195 a letter from Ingrid Bergman: Letter from Ingrid Bergman to Marion Davies, September 10, 1951, Marion Davies papers, box 5.

Marion "changed entirely": Constance Moore to Hugh Munro Neely and Elaina Archer (Friedrichsen), 1999.

Louella Parsons: William Haines to Fred Lawrence Guiles, 1969.

196 "Louella was a traitor": Marion Davies autobiographical tapes, author's transcription, tape 4.

"*Life* Visits Marion Davies" had morphed: *Life*, August 27, 1951.

"together with all furniture": *The Mirror*, August 15, 1951, 16.

The codicil was stricken out: Tebbel, *The Life and Good Times of William Randolph Hearst*, 16.

197 Within a day of the funeral: Nasaw, *The Chief*, 601.

loved having weddings at San Simeon: Frances Marion to W.A. Swanberg, 1958, W.A. Swanberg papers, box 8.

198 Marion eloped to Nevada with Horace: "Marion Davies, Ship Captain Wed in Surprise Las Vegas Ceremony," *Fort Worth Star Telegram*, October 31, 1951, 1.

Stanley Flink along on honeymoon: Stanley Flink to author, 2014.

"You have traveled a long and rocky road": Ruth Alexander to Marion Davies, 1951, Marion Davies papers, box 5.

"Don't you think Marion was hasty": Letter from Hedda Hopper to Maryland McCormick, November 21, 1951, Hedda Hopper papers, box 71.

"he was a brute": Floretta Mauser to Fred Lawrence Guiles, 1970.

199 **He would frequently interrupt**: Anne Shirley to Fred Lawrence Guiles, 1969.

"I never disliked Horace": Frances Marion to Fred Lawrence Guiles, 1970.

Marion's nocturnal "theatre routine": Anne Shirley to Fred Lawrence Guiles, 1970.

as she slept one day: Marion Lake Canessa to author, 2015.

200 **"It cost her a fortune"**: Floretta Mauser to Fred Lawrence Guiles, 1970

"Give him anything he wants": Hedda Hopper and Marion Davies phone conversation transcript, Hedda Hopper papers, box 44.

"straightened everything out": Marion Davies to Bobo Rockefeller, 1952, Marion Davies papers, box 11.

201 **Johnny Ray party**: "1000 Hollywoodites Holding Heads after Davies Blowout," *Knoxville News-Sentinel,* October 3, 1952, 9.

note to … Faith Grant: Handwritten note to Faith Grant, undated. Marion Davies papers, box 5.

"Please let her know": Dorothy Mackaill to Hedda Hopper, May 6, 1952, Hedda Hopper papers, box 44.

202 **Miltown**: Marion Lake Canessa to author, 2014.

"Since the time of Mr. Hearst's demise": Marion Davies to Martin Huberth, 1953, Marion Davies papers, box 9.

"Why, there's Bill Hearst": "Two Blow-by-Blow Accounts," *Los Angeles Times,* November 13, 1952, 1.

203 **Stanley Flink sabbatical**: Stanley Flink to author, 2021.

"toughest lawyer in town": Gladstone, *The Man Who Seduced Hollywood*, 4.

"Charlie and Bautzer": Marion Davies autobiographical tapes 1–6.

204 **"Rolls Royce"**: Lea Sullivan to Hugh Munro Neely and Elaina Archer (Friedrichsen), 2000.

gift to Bautzer: Gladstone, *The Man Who Seduced Hollywood*, 215.

Bautzer set up hidden microphones: Stanley Flink to author, 2014; Marion Davies autobiographical tapes, tape 6.

"He knew": Marion Davies autobiographical tapes, author's transcription, tape 1.

205 **Eileen Percy**: Stanley Flink to author, 2014.

"NOT IF THEY OFFERED ME MARS ON A SILVER PLATTER"

206 **exponential growth in the postwar years**: Starr, *Golden Dreams*, 1–8.

"I've lived too long": Floretta Mauser to Fred Lawrence Guiles, 1969.

Marion had owned a television: Ibid.

207 **hated making movies**: Marion Davies to Hedda Hopper, in *Los Angeles Times,* May 9, 1954, 130.

"Would you do another picture": Marion Davies to Hedda Hopper, "Motion Pictures," *Spokesman-Review*, May 9, 1954.

208 Notes from Jacqueline and John F. Kennedy: September 26, 1953, Marion Davies papers, box 9.

209 annulling his contract: Stanley Flink to author, 2014.
"Stan had the biggest grin": Letter from Tom Kennington to Greg Bautzer, February 16, 1954. Marion Davies papers, box 9.
"musical Arabian night": *Brooklyn Daily Eagle*, November 29, 1953.
Kismet review: *Los Angeles Times*, August 18, 1953.
Bay Area *Kismet* review: *Oakland Tribune*, September 15, 1953.

210 Marion quietly invested $185,000 in the production: *Miami Herald*, December 8, 1953.
Walter Winchell named her in his column: *Chillicothe Gazette*, November 25, 1953, 6.
Marion wired him a correction: *Terre Haute Tribune*, December 1, 1953, 4.
"swindle a couple from management": Hedda Hopper column, *Charlotte Observer*, April 27, 1954, 19.
Marion got to know Lea Sullivan: Lea Sullivan to Hugh Munro Neely and Elaina Archer (Friedrichsen), 2000.

211 "I plan to turn it into a miniature Rockefeller Center": *The Times*, July 14, 1955, 22.
a penchant for naming all her real estate: Lea Sullivan to Hugh Munro Neely and Elaina Archer (Friedrichsen), 2000.

212 bullfighting was one thing that Marion could not support: Lea Sullivan to author, 2014.

213 *My Fair Lady*: Marion Lake Canessa to author, 2014.
donating a $25,000 elevator: *Los Angeles Times*, December 22, 1956, 9.
"much needed": *Mirror News*, December 24, 1956, 7.
Joe Frisco: Fred Lawrence Guiles in an interview with Dorothy Mackaill, 1970.
buy Marion a gift: Belinda Vidor Holliday to author, 2014.

214 Marion stroke: "Marion Davies Ailing," *Fort Worth Star-Telegram*, July 20, 1956, 117.
"feeling better": Marion Davies to Hedda Hopper, July 27, 1956, Hedda Hopper papers.
George Hearst moved in: Eleanor Boardman to Fred Lawrence Guiles, 1970.

215 "a scathing letter": Letter from Frances Marion to Hedda Hopper, October 10, [1957?], Hedda Hopper papers, box 70.

"I DON'T THINK SHE WAS AFRAID OF DEATH"

216 Lea Sullivan: Lea Sullivan to Hugh Munro Neely and Elaina Archer (Friedrichsen), 2000.

The new clinic would expand: Clinic notes, Louise M. Darling Biomedical Library, UCLA.

217 dissolving the Marion Davies Foundation: Ibid.

"psychiatry to measles": "Marion Davies Gift for UCLA Clinic Approved," *Los Angeles Times*, July 16, 1957, 5.

A group of psychiatrists: "UC Will Sell Site for New Health Center," *Van Nuys News and Valley Green Sheet*, March 27, 1958, 7.

"I'll probably be remembered more": Associated Press, January 3, 1960.

"Remember how we laughed": Letter from Frances Marion to Marion Davies, July 4, 1961, Marion Davies papers, box 7.

218 move into the home of Charlie's friend Ben Hecht: Stanley Flink to author, 2021.

"Marion never complained": Mrs. Davis to Fred Lawrence Guiles, 1969.

Hedda Hopper's Hollywood: Hopper and Brough, *The Whole Truth and Nothing But*, 196–98.

219 "In July of 1960": Beauchamp, *Joseph P. Kennedy Presents*, 394.

220 "I don't think she was afraid of death": Lea Sullivan to Hugh Munro Neely and Elaina Archer (Friedrichsen), 2000.

"She was very fond of Marion": Eleanor Boardman to Fred Lawrence Guiles, 1969.

"The most nostalgic thing I have ever given": Letter from Hedda Hopper to Frances Marion, January 11, 1961, Hedda Hopper papers, box 70.

Marion and Horace were treated: Beauchamp, *Joseph P. Kennedy Presents*, 395.

221 Marion underwent surgery: *Yuma Daily Sun*, June 12, 1961, 11.

fracturing a bone: "Ailing Marion Davies Breaks Leg," *Lancaster Eagle-Gazette*, June 20, 1961, 2.

Grace Dawley: Letter from Grace Dawley to Horace Brown, August 11, 1961, Marion Davies papers, box 44.

"one I have cared deeply for": Letter from Frances Marion to Marion Davies, July 4, 1961, Marion Davies papers, box 7.

A fan in Ohio: Ibid.

One particularly moving and nostalgic note: Frank Irvine to Marion Davies, April 1961. Marion Davies papers, box 8.

222 last rites: Marion Lake Canessa to author, 2014.

223 "She understood me": Beauchamp, *Joseph P. Kennedy Presents*, 396.

Madelaine Lundy: Letter from Madelaine Lundy to Hedda Hopper, Hedda Hopper papers, box 44.

BIBLIOGRAPHY

NEWSPAPERS

Algona Upper Des Moines, Algona, Iowa
Atlanta Constitution, Atlanta, Georgia
Atlanta Daily World, Atlanta, Georgia
Brooklyn Daily Eagle, Brooklyn, New York
Brooklyn Times-Union, Brooklyn, New York
Carbondale Free Press, Carbondale, Illinois
Chicago Tribune, Chicago, Illinois
Chillicothe Gazette, Chillicothe, Ohio
Daily Herald, Provo, Utah
Daily Inter Lake, Kalispell, Montana
Desert Sun, Palm Springs, California
Detroit Saturday Night (defunct), Detroit, Michigan
Dunkirk Evening Observer, Dunkirk, New York
Dunsmuir News, Dunsmuir, California
Exhibitor's Herald & Motion Picture World (defunct), Chicago, Illinois
Film Daily (defunct), New York, New York
Fort Worth Star-Telegram, Fort Worth, Texas
Gettysburg Times, Gettysburg, Pennsylvania
Harrisburg Telegraph, Harrisburg, Pennsylvania
Independent Press Telegram, Long Beach, California
Lancaster Eagle-Gazette, Lancaster, Ohio
Lincoln Star, Lincoln, Nebraska
Los Angeles Examiner, Los Angeles, California
Los Angeles Times, Los Angeles, California
Miami News, Miami, Florida
Middletown Times Herald, Middletown, New York
Minneapolis Star, Minneapolis, Minnesota
Montclair Times, Montclair, New Jersey

Morning Post, Camden, New Jersey
Morning Telegraph, New York, New York
Motion Picture Herald, Chicago, Illinois
Motion Picture News (defunct), New York, New York
New York American, New York, New York
New York City Telegram & Evening Mail (defunct), New York, New York
New York Daily News, New York, New York
New York Graphic (defunct), New York, New York
New York Journal, New York, New York
New York Times, New York, New York
New York Tribune, New York, New York
Newport Daily News, Newport, Rhode Island
Oakland Tribune, Oakland, California
Ogden Standard-Examiner, Ogden, Utah
Philadelphia Inquirer, Philadelphia, Pennsylvania
Pittsburgh Daily Post, Pittsburgh, Pennsylvania
Pittsburgh Post-Gazette, Pittsburgh, Pennsylvania
Pittsburgh Sun-Telegraph, Pittsburgh, Pennsylvania
Post-Crescent, Appleton, Wisconsin
Pottstown Mercury, Pottstown, Pennsylvania
Progress Index, Petersburg, Virginia
Quad City Times, Davenport, Iowa
Redlands Daily Facts, Redlands, California
Sacramento Bee, Sacramento, California
San Bernardino County Sun, San Bernardino, California
San Francisco Examiner, San Francisco, California
Santa Monica Evening Outlook, Santa Monica, California
Scranton Republican, Scranton, Pennsylvania
Shamokin News Dispatch, Shamokin, Pennsylvania
Spokesman-Review, Spokane, Washington
Terre Haute Tribune, Terre Haute, Indiana
Times-Tribune, Scranton, Pennsylvania
Van Nuys and Valley Green Sheet, Van Nuys, California
Waco News Tribune, Waco, Texas
Windsor Star, Windsor, Ontario, Canada
Yuma Daily Sun, Yuma, Arizona

ARCHIVES

Kevin Brownlow papers and photographs, private archive.
Marion Lake Canessa collection, papers and photographs, private archive.

William "Buster" Collier papers, 1909–1992, Margaret Herrick Library, Academy of Motion Picture Arts and Sciences, Los Angeles, CA.

Marion Davies film collection, 1915–1961, Moving Image section, Library of Congress, Washington, DC.

Marion Davies papers, 1906–1961, Margaret Herrick Library, Academy of Motion Picture Arts and Sciences, Los Angeles, CA.

Marion Davies Children's Clinic documentation, Louise M. Darling Biomedical Library, University of California–Los Angeles, Los Angeles, CA.

William Randolph Hearst papers, 1874–1951, Bancroft Library, University of California– Berkeley, Berkeley, CA.

Hedda Hopper papers, 1901–1966, Margaret Herrick Library, Academy of Motion Picture Arts and Sciences, Los Angeles, CA.

Clare Boothe Luce papers, 1862–1987, Manuscript Division, Library of Congress, Washington, DC.

Louella Parsons papers, Cinematic Arts Library, University of Southern California, Los Angeles, CA.

Louella Parsons scrapbooks and photographs, 1915–1961, Special Collections, Margaret Herrick Library, Academy of Motion Picture Arts and Sciences, Los Angeles, CA.

Oral History San Simeon, archives at the Hearst San Simeon State Historical Monument.

W.A. Swanberg papers, 1927–1992, Rare Book and Manuscript Library, Columbia University, New York, NY.

UCLA Film and TV Archives, Archive Research and Study Center, University of California–Los Angeles, Los Angeles, CA.

Warner Bros. Archives, 1923–1968, USC Cinematic Arts Library, University of Southern California, Los Angeles, CA.

PRINT BOOKS AND ARTICLES

Aronson, Arnold, Derek Ostergard, and Matthew Wilson Smith. *Architect of Dreams: The Theatrical Vision of Joseph Urban.* New York: Miriam and Ira D. Wallach Art Gallery, Columbia University of New York, 2000.

Bailey, Frankie Y., and Stephen M. Chermak. *Famous American Crimes and Trials.* Westport, CT: Praeger, 2004.

Ball, Lucille. *Love, Lucy.* New York: Boulevard Books, 1996.

Balogh, Laura Peterson. "Denmark's Forgotten Film Star, Karl Dane." *The Bridge* 30, no. 1 (2007): article 9.

Barbas, Samantha. *First Lady of Hollywood: A Biography of Louella Parsons.* Berkeley: University of California Press, 2006.

Basinger, Jeanine. *Silent Stars.* Middletown, CT: Wesleyan University Press, 2000.

———. *The Star Machine.* New York: Knopf, 2007.

Beauchamp, Cari. *Without Lying Down.* New York: Scribner, 1997.

———. *Joseph P. Kennedy Presents.* New York: Alfred A. Knopf, 2009.

Bergman, Ingrid, and Alan Burgess. *My Story.* New York: Dell, 1981.

Bingen, Steve, and Marc Wanamaker. *Warner Bros.: Hollywood's Ultimate Backlot.* Lanham, MD: Taylor Trade, [2014].

Bogdanovich, Peter. *Allan Dwan: The Last Pioneer.* New York: Praeger, 1971.

Brady, Frank. *The Publisher.* Lanham, MD: University Press of America, 2000.

Brooks, Louise. *Lulu in Hollywood.* New York: Limelight Editions, 1989.

Brownlow, Kevin. *The Parade's Gone By.* New York: Alfred A. Knopf, 1969.

———. *The Search for Charlie Chaplin.* London: UKA Press, 2010.

Carlisle, Rodney P. *Hearst and the New Deal: The Progressive as Reactionary.* New York: Garland, 1979.

Carlson, Oliver, and Ernest Sutherland Bates. *Hearst, Lord of San Simeon.* New York: Viking, 1936.

Carringer, Robert L. *The Making of Citizen Kane.* Berkeley: University of California Press, 1996.

Chaplin, Charles. *My Autobiography.* New York: Simon and Schuster, 1964.

Chase, Ilka. *Past Imperfect.* Garden City, NY: Doubleday, Doran, 1942.

Coffman, Taylor. *Hearst's Dream.* San Luis Obispo, CA: EZ Nature Books, 1989.

———. *The Builders behind the Castles: George Loorz & the F. C. Stolte Co.* San Luis Obispo, CA: San Luis Obispo County Historical Society, 1990.

———. *Building for Hearst and Morgan: Voices from the George Loorz Papers.* Berkeley: Berkeley Hills Books, 2003.

———. *Hearst as Collector.* Summerland, CA: Coastal Heritage Press, 2003.

———. *415 Ocean Front: The Grand Mansion That Was.* Summerland, CA: Coastal Heritage Press, 2009 (25 copies printed for private circulation).

———. *The Annotated Marion.* Privately published, 2010.

———. *Hearst and Marion: The Santa Monica Connection.* Privately published, 2010.

———. *Hearst and Pearl Harbor.* Privately published, 2013.

———. *Julia Morgan: Wyntoon and Other Hearst Projects, 1933–1946.* http://www.coffmanbooks.com/articles/MorganWyntoon-j3.pdf

Coffman, Taylor, ed. *The Unknown Hearst, 1941.* San Marino: Huntington–USC Institute on California and the West, 2008.

Coffman, Taylor, and Lynn Forney McMurray, eds. *Julia Morgan, William Randolph Hearst and Their Circle: The Morgan-Forney Bethel Island Collection, Volume I: 1928 to 1930.* Ventura, CA: Publications in Hearst Studies, 2017. Revised 2018.

Crawford, Sharon. *Ganna Walska Lotusland: The Garden and Its Creators.* Santa Barbara, CA: Ganna Walska Lotusland Foundation, 1996.

Davies, Betty. *Shadows in the Sun: The Experiences of Sibling Bereavement in Childhood.* New York: Brunner/Mazel, 1999.

Davies, Marion. *The Times We Had.* Edited by Pamela Pfau and Kenneth S. Marx. Indianapolis: Bobbs-Merrill, 1975.

Dunlap, John F. *The Hearst Saga: The Way It Really Was.* [Medford, OR:] Privately Published, 2002.

Durgnat, Raymond, and Scott Simmons. *King Vidor: American.* Berkeley: University of California Press, 1988.

Eells, George. *Hedda and Louella.* London: Allen, 1972.

Fields, Armond. *Fred Stone: Circus Performer and Musical Comedy Star.* Jefferson, NC: McFarland, 2002.

Flamini, Roland. *Thalberg, The Last Tycoon of MGM.* London: André Deutsch, 1994.

Galbraith, John Kenneth. *The Great Crash, 1929.* Boston: Houghton Mifflin, 1955.

Gilbert Fountain, Leatrice. *Dark Star: The Untold Story of the Meteoric Rise and Fall of the Legendary John Gilbert.* New York: St. Martin's Press, 1985.

Gladstone, James B. *The Man Who Seduced Hollywood: The Life and Loves of Greg Bautzer, Tinseltown's Most Powerful Lawyer.* Chicago: Chicago Review Press, 2013.

Guiles, Fred Lawrence. *Marion Davies: A Biography.* New York: Bantam Books, 1973.

Head, Alice. *It Could Never Have Happened.* London: W. Heinemann, [1939].

Hearst, William Randolph, Jr. *The Hearsts: Father and Son.* San Luis Obispo, CA: Central Coast Press, 2015.

Holston, Kim R. *Movie Roadshows: A History and Filmography of Reserved-Seat Limited Showings, 1911–1973.* Jefferson, NC: McFarland, 2013.

Hopper, Hedda. *From under My Hat.* New York: Macfadden Books, 1952.

Hopper, Hedda, and James Brough. *The Whole Truth and Nothing But.* New York: Doubleday, 1963.

Huxley, Aldous. *After Many a Summer Dies the Swan.* New York: Harper & Brothers, 1939.

Janis, Elsie. *So Far, So Good!* London: Long John, 1933.

Keaton, Buster, and Kevin W. Sweeney. *Buster Keaton: Interviews.* Jackson: University Press of Mississippi, 2007.

Koszarski, Richard. *Hollywood on the Hudson.* New Brunswick, NJ: Rutgers University Press, 2008.

Lebo, Harlan. *Citizen Kane: A Filmmaker's Journey.* New York: Thomas Dunne Books, 2016.

Lesko, Barbara S. *Phoebe Elizabeth Apperson Hearst, 1842–1919.* https://www.brown.edu/Research/Breaking_Ground/bios/Hearst_Phoebe%20Appserson.pdf

Loe, Nancy E. *Hearst Castle: An Interpretive History of W.R. Hearst's San Simeon Estate.* Santa Barbara, CA: Companion Press, 1994.

Loos, Anita. *A Girl Like I.* New York: Ballantine Books, 1975.

———. *Kiss Hollywood Goodbye.* Harmondsworth, UK: Penguin, 1979.

Loy, Myrna, and James Kotsilibas-Davis. *Being and Becoming.* New York: Knopf, 1987.

MacAdams, William. *Ben Hecht: The Man behind the Legend.* New York: Scribner, 1990.

Mann, William J. *Wisecracker: The Life and Times of William Haines, Hollywood's First Openly Gay Star.* New York: Viking, 1998.

Marion, Frances. "Hollywood." Unpublished manuscript.

Matzen, Robert. *Fireball: Carole Lombard and the Mystery of Flight 3.* Pittsburgh: GoodKnight Books, 2014.

Mitchell, Greg. *Campaign of the Century.* New York: Random House, 1992.

Muscio, Giuliana. *Hollywood's New Deal.* Philadelphia: Temple University Press, 1997.

Myrick, David F. *Montecito and Santa Barbara, Vol. 1.* Glendale: Trans-Anglo Books, 1987.

Nasaw, David. *The Chief.* Boston: Houghton Mifflin, 2001.

Older, Cora. *William Randolph Hearst, American.* New York: New York Appleton-Century, 1936.

Packman, Wendy, Heidi Horsley, Betty Davies, and Robin Kramer. "Sibling Bereavement and Continued Bonds." *Death Studies* 30 (2006): 817–41.

Patch, Blanche. *Thirty Years with George Bernard Shaw.* London: Victor Gollancz, 1951.

Pizzitola, Louis. *Hearst over Hollywood.* New York: Columbia University Press, 2002.

Procter, Ben. *William Randolph Hearst: The Early Years, 1863–1910.* New York: Oxford University Press, 1998.

———. *William Randolph Hearst: The Later Years, 1911–1951.* New York: Oxford University Press, 2007.

Rogoff, Rosalind. "Edison's Dream: A Brief History of the Kinetophone." *Cinema Journal* 15, no. 2, American Film History (Spring 1976): 58–68.

Royal Commission on the Ancient and Historical Monuments in Wales. *St. Donat's: An Inventory of the Ancient Monuments in Glamorgan Volume III.* London: Royal Commission on the Ancient and Historical Monuments in Wales, 2000.

Ryan, Don. *Angel's Flight.* New York: Boni & Liveright, 1927.

Rybczynski, Witold, and Laurie Olin. *Vizcaya: An American Villa and Its Masters.* Philadelphia: University of Pennsylvania Press, 2007.

Sinclair, Upton. *I, Candidate for Governor and How I Got Licked.* Pasadena, CA: Published by the author [1934–35].

Smith-Rosenberg, Carroll. *Disorderly Conduct: Visions of Gender in Victorian America.* New York: Oxford University Press, 1986.

St. Johns, Adela Rogers. *The Honeycomb.* Garden City, NY: Doubleday, 1969.

———. *Love, Laughter and Tears: My Hollywood Story.* New York: New American Library, 1978.

Starr, Kevin. *Material Dreams.* New York: Oxford University Press, 1990.

———. *Inventing the Dream: California through the Progressive Era.* New York: Oxford University Press, 1995.

———. *Endangered Dreams: The Great Depression in California*. New York: Oxford University Press, 1996.

———. *The Dream Endures*. Oxford: Oxford University Press, 1997.

———. *Golden Dreams: California in an Age of Abundance*. New York: Oxford University Press, 2009.

Stenn, David. *Bombshell: The Life and Death of Jean Harlow*. Raleigh, NC: Lightning Bug Press, 2000.

Swanberg, W.A. *Citizen Hearst*. New York: Scribner, 1961.

Taves, Brian. *Thomas Ince: Hollywood's Independent Pioneer*. Lexington: University Press of Kentucky, 2012.

Tebbel, John. *The Life and Good Times of William Randolph Hearst*. London: V. Gollancz, 1953.

Vidor, King. *A Tree Is a Tree*. New York: Harcourt, Brace, [1953].

Wilk, Max. *They're Playing Our Song*. Westport, CT: Easton Studio Press, 2008.

Williamson, Alice. *Alice in Movieland*. New York: D. Appleton, 1928.

Wodehouse, P.G., and Guy Bolton. *Bring on the Girls: Our Improbable Story of Our Life in Musical Comedy, with Pictures to Prove It*. New York: Limelight Editions, 1984.

INDEX

Note: page numbers followed by n refer to notes, with note number.

national Film Service, 69; Hearst's construction of, 69; move to Twentieth Century Fox, 152; move to Warner Brothers, 138–39

The Burden of Proof (1918 film), 233

Buried Treasure (1921 film), 234–35

Burke, Billy, 18–19

Burnett, Carol, 3, 95

Burnett, Vera, 67–68, 70, 74

Burns, George, 167

Cagney, James, 146

Cain and Mabel (1936 film), 146–47; Anna Roosevelt's visit to set, 167; Hearst's input on, 146–47; Hearst's spending on, 146; Hearst's tight security on set, 147; heat wave during filming of, 147–48; musical numbers in, 146; Production Code problems with, 147; production details, 242; story of, 146

California: Davies and family in, for filming of *The Bride's Play*, 42–43; Davies and family's move to, 61–62; Long Beach earthquake of 1933, 128. *See also* Los Angeles

The Cardboard Lover (1928 film), 102; Davies's rest following, 102; production details, 238; story of, 102

Carlisle, Mary, 144, 148, 149, 162

Castle, Irene, 16, 163

The Cat's Meow (Peros), 72

Cecilia of the Pink Roses (1918 film): filming of, 31–32; Hearst's publicity campaign for, 32, 33; premiere, Hearst's lavish spending on, 32; production details, 233

celebrity journalism, Parsons as pioneer of, 74

Chaplin, Charlie: and *City Lights*, Cherrill's role in, 157–58; as friend of Millicent Hearst, 68–69, 72; and Hearst, volatile relationship with, 72–73; on Hearst's yacht for Ince birthday party, 70; making of silent films into sound era, 157

Chaplin, Charlie, and Davies: on Davies's knowledge of art, 105; on Davies's publicity, 68; first meeting, 68; friendship, 68; Hearst's jealousy of, 73, 75–76, 118;

as pallbearer for Davies's mother, 98; at premier of *The Florodora Girl*, 118, *figure 28*; romantic involvement with, 68, 72, 73, 76, 139–40; at welcome home party for Davies, 109

character of Davies, 2; ability to talk intelligently with powerful men, 23; affectionate demeanor, 72, 76, 140; anxiety, 3; bravery, 188; as child, 7; and death, strong fear of, 9, 96; determination and strong work ethic, 3; Dick Powell on, 141; discomfort with rich friends, 3; and fame, lack of interest in, 178; fear of socializing with strangers, 90–91; friendliness, 1; general admiration for, 4; generosity, 17–18, 65, 80, 86, 149, 213–14; gentleness, 2; insecurity, 188; in later life, 211; mischievous sense of humor, 21–22; newspaper articles lauding, 144; and popularity as chorus girl, 17, 19; special affection for children and animals, 13, 48–49, 71, 82–83, 151; underlying sadness, 2; as vibrant and energetic, 4

charitable spending by Davies, 83–84, 88–89. *See also* Marion Davies Children's Clinic

Cherrill, Virginia, 157–58

Chicago World's Fair, 132

childhood of Davies: at Catholic boarding school, 13–14; death of brother, 8–9; and family financial worries, 7; as happy, 8; and Irish identity, 11; move to Chicago, 12–13; needlework as special interest, 12; nickname (Mardie), 7; parents' estrangement after son's death, 9–10; playing with Irish children, 11; schooling, 11; shaping of views on marriage, 10; and show business, desire to follow sisters into, 13–14; stuttering and, 10–11, 13; training in household skills, 12; visits to maternal grandparents, 8; voracious reading, 11

children, Davies's special affection for, 13, 48–49, 82–83, 151

children's clinic. *See* Marion Davies Children's Clinic

Chin-Chin (stage show), 18

chorus girl, Davies as, 15–19, *figures 4–5*; and attention from "stage-door johnnies," 17; Davies's beauty and, 17, 181–82; Davies's happy memories of, 15; first appearance in program, 18; first job, 15–16; gift of car to mother, 17; growth in confidence, 18; and Irene Castle as role model, 16; long-time friends from, 3; mother's backstage support, 17; popularity among cast members, 17, 19; residence with sisters and mother, 16–17; shows, 16, 18, 19, 245–46n16; success of, 19; unusual sleep schedule, 15. *See also* Ziegfeld Follies

The Christmas Party (1931 film), 240

Churchill, Winston, 163

The Cinema Murder (1919 film): production details, 234; screenplay for, 45

Citizen Hearst (Swanberg), 231

Citizen Kane (film), 169–72; Davies's reaction to, 171; debate on allusive meaning of "Rosebud," 170–71; efforts to suppress, 171; Hearst's reaction to, 169; identification of film's blonde singer with Davies, 1–2, 171–72

The Cocoanuts (film), 111

Colbert, Claudette, 150, 165–66, 167

Collier, Buster, 132, 133–34, 137, *figure 32*

Coolidge, Calvin, 2, 115–16

Coolidge, Grace, 115–16

Cooper, Gary, *figure 33*

Coquette (film), 158

Corday, Eliot, 191, 202

Cosmopolitan magazine, Millicent's demand for, as price of divorce, 161

Cosmopolitan Productions: baseball team, Davies as catcher for, 42; and boosting of Davies's career, 41; Hearst's founding of, 41–42; hiring of Frances Marion as screenwriter, 43–45; merger with MGM, 64; move from MGM to Warner Brothers, 138–39; move from New York to California, 60, 61; move from Warner Brothers to Twentieth Century Fox, 152; partnership with Goldwyn Pictures, 61; rumors of split with MGM, 91, 131; signing of Florence Turner, 61

Cosmopolitan Studio (Manhattan): construction of, 41–42; fire at (1923), 59–60; rebuilding of, 61

County Democracy, 5

Crawford, Joan, 112, 122, 203

Crocker, Harry, 132, 185

Crosby, Bing, 127

cross-dressing by Davies, 51–52, 58–59, 77

The Crowd (film), 100

Cuddles (Davies's dachshund), 173

Currie, George, 110, 112

dachshunds: Cuddles (Davies's second dachshund), 173; *Life* photo of Hearst's deathbed with pet dachshund, 194–95, 196, *figure 40*; at San Simeon, 78. *See also* Gandhi (Davies's dachshund)

The Dark Star (1919 film): production details, 234; screenplay for, 45

Davies, Marion: athleticism of, 11, 93; birth of, 7; business acumen of, 70; as captain of her own soul, 3, 152; care for nieces and nephews, 38–39, 82, 102–3; change of name to Davies, 12; "Daisy" as nickname of, 67, 116; and death of mother, 96–97; depictions in literature and film, 1–2; described (1953), 1; family vacation in Europe funded by Hearst (1922), 53–54; and father's final illness and death, 140–41; favorite movie of, 85; financial support of cook's orphaned child, 63; guarded privacy of, 3–4; and Hearst's inability to marry, as lifelong source of pain, 36, 161–62, 197–98; on Hearst's uniqueness, 27; on her response to fear, 137; impressions, talent for, 95, 99–100, 125, 127; infertility following illness at age thirty, 87; legal name of, 7; move to Beverly Hills with Hearst to be near hospital, 179–80; and new free attitude of 1920s vs. traditional women's roles, 90; similarities to Hearst's wife, 29; small group of close friends from early years, 3; as stage name, 12; support for less-fortunate actors, 61–62; and trial stemming from shooting at sister Reine's house, 55–56. *See also* alcoholism of Davies; character of Davies; child-

Douras, Rose "Rosie" (sister), *figure 1, figure 6*; affair with married man, 120–21; alcoholism of, 164–65, 226, 227; beauty of, 6; childhood, 7; as chorus girl, 15–17; on *Citizen Kane*, 169; Davies's relationship with, 121, 164–65; in Davies's will, 222; death of, 227; and death of Davies, 222; and death of mother, 96–97; European trip with granddaughter, 227; and father's final illness, 140; first marriage to Kernell, 38; fondness for granddaughter, 227; at Hearst's seventy-fourth birthday party, 151; hip problems, 6–7, 243n6; jealously of Davies's success, 38; limited interest in her children, 38, 82, 103, 226–27; love affair with Marquis de Brissac, 107, 227; musical talent of, 6; at Patricia Van Cleve's wedding, 153; second marriage to Van Cleve, 38, 42, 82, 96; six marriages of, 121; trips to Europe with Davies and Hearst, 53–54, 107; wartime romance, 168

Douras family: burial in Hollywood Cemetery mausoleum, 98, 141, 142, 155, 164; Davies's pride in, 5; financial worries, 7; Hearst's boosting of social standing, 36–37; involvement in New York City politics, 5; move to California, 61–62; move to Chicago, 12–13; move to new New York home (352 47th Street), 8, 244n8; origin of name, 6; parents and grandparents, 5–6; parents' estrangement after son's death, 9–10; siblings, 6–7. *See also* Hearst, William Randolph, and Davies's family; home of Douras family in New York

Dressler, Marie, 93, 127

dual roles, as trend in 1920s movies, 50–51

Dunne, Irene, 150

Durante, Jimmy, 125

Dust Bowl, 147–48

d'Utassy, George, 33, 47

Dwan, Allan, 41, 44

earthquake in Long Beach (1933), 128

Edison, Thomas, 103–4

Edward (king of Britain), 149

The Enchanted Isle (film), 69

Enchantment (1921 film): Davies's and Hearst's vacation to Mexico following, 48–49, 53; Millicent Hearst's effort to have Davies removed from publicity for, 49; production details, 235; writing of, 47

End Poverty in California (EPIC), 135, 137–38

Europe, Davies-Hearst tour of (1928), 104–8; Davies's claim to have stolen a document from U.S. embassy during, 119; Davies's interest in shopping, 105, 108; and Davies's knowledge about art, 105; in France, 105–6; in Germany, 107; at Hearst's castle in Wales, 107–8; Hearst's interest in cultural sites, 105; Hearst's payment for all guests' expenses, 105; in Italy, 106, 107, *figures 24–25*; large group of friends and family accompanying, 104; meeting of George Bernard Shaw, 120; public's interest in Davies, 105–6, 108; return to U.S., 108; travel on separate boats to avoid attention, 104; trunks of clothing brought back by Davies, 108; welcome home party, 109

Europe, Davies-Hearst tour of (1930), 119–20; and Hearst's expulsion from France, 119

Europe, Davies-Hearst tour of (1931): and acquisition of Gandhi the dachshund, 121; welcome home party at Cocoanut Grove, 122

Europe, Davies-Hearst tour of (1934), 132–37, *figures 31–32*; emergency landing of flight to England, 137; family and friends accompanying, 132; in Germany, 133–35; and Hearst's avoidance of France, 136–37; Hearst's oldest sons as members of party, 132; and Hitler, Hearst's effort to moderate antisemitism of, 134–35; home movies of, 133, 136; and Mussolini, Hearst's effort to meet, 132–33; return, party to celebrate, 137; in Spain, 136

Europe, Davies-Hearst tour of (1936), 148–49; friends and family accompanying, 148; in Italy, 148

Europe, Hearst's vacation with wife in (1922), 53; funding of parallel trip for Davies and family, 53

Ever Since Eve (1937 film), 151–52; as Davies's final film, 152; production details, 242; reviews of, 152; story of, 151

The Exploits of Elaine series, 30

The Fair Co-Ed (1927 film), 92–93; basketball scene in, 93; Davies's exercise on set, *figure 20*; Hearst's editing of, 94; Lindbergh's visit to set, 93; production details, 238; reviews of, 94; screenplay for, 92; story of, 92; Winton in, 110

The Fair Co-Ed (Ade) (play), 92

Fall, Albert B., 49–50

Fallon, William J., 62–63

Famous Players-Lasky studio, deal with Hearst to create studio in Manhattan, 41

Fields, W. C., 20

film industry, changes in 1950s, 206

filmography, 233–42

Five and Ten (1931 film), 118; and Davies's flirtations with co-stars, 139; Davies's role in, 118; as pre-Code movie, 118; production details, 240; release of, 120

The Five O'Clock Girl (film): canceling of project, 111; as planned first sound picture for Davies, 110–11

Flannery, William, 89, 117, 254n89

Flink, Stanley: and Davies's autobiographical tapes, 1, 21, 203; on Davies's character, 3; and Davies's guarded privacy, 4; and Davies's marriage to Brown, 198; on Davies's polio, 172; on Davies's politics, 136, 208; on Davies's reaction to *Citizen Kane*, 171; on Davies's reaction to Hearst's death, 194; on Davies's relationship with press, 195; Davies's trust of, 196; first meeting with Davies, 185; on Hearst divorce terms, 160; Hearst's death and, 192–94; life after Davies's death, 228–29; *Life* article on Davies, 2,

185–86, 196; and planned Davies autobiography, scrapping of, 4, 208–9

Flint, Anne Apperson, 26, 28

The Florodora Girl (1930 film): Coolidges' visit to set, 116; filming in two-strip Technicolor, 116–17; premiere of, 117–18, *figure 28*; production details, 239; story of, 116; use of Davies's Santa Monica beachfront in, 117

Flying High (Broadway show), 111

Flynn, Errol, 185–86

The Front Page (film), 38

Gable, Clark, 125, 146, 150, 167

Gable, Kay Spreckels, 202, 218, 222

Gabriel over the White House (film), 177

Gandhi (Davies's dachshund), *figure 29*; acquisition of, 121; bad-temper of, 121; as Davies's constant companion, 121–22; with Davies on trips to Europe, 132, 133, 136, 148; death of, Marian's breakdown following, 175; failing health of, 173

Garbo, Greta, 156, 157

Gesamtkunstwerk, Urban set designs and, 47

Getting Mary Married (1919 film): Davies's practical jokes with cast, 41; filming of, 40–41; production details, 234

Gilbert, John, 112, 156–57

Glendinning, Marie, 9, 15–16, 17, 142, 191

Glen Miller Orchestra, 167–68

Glyn, Elinor, 68, 70–71, 77

Going Hollywood (1933 film), 127; Davies's alcoholism and, 127; production details, 241; story of, 127; writing of screenplay, 127

Goldwyn, Sam, 24

Goldwyn family, as Davies's neighbors, 3

Goodman, Daniel Carson, 70, 71

Grauman's Chinese Theater, Davies's foot and hand prints in cement at, 113–14, *figure 27*

Gray, Lawrence, 111–12

Great Depression: Dust Bowl and, 147–48; government responses to, 129; Hearst and, 114–15, 123; and Motion Picture Relief Fund, 130, 143

Green, Alfred E., 110–11
Guiles, Fred Lawrence, 7, 141

Haines, William "Billy," *figure 26*; anti-gay
attack on, 158; on Davies's dachshund,
121; on Davies's stutter, 115; decorating
business after movie career, 158; end of
MGM career, 158; at *Florodora Girl* pre-
miere, 118; as frequent San Simeon visi-
tor, 80–81; on Hearst's balancing of wife
and Davies, 161; as openly gay, 81, 158; on
San Simeon, 79; in *Show People*, 100; at
welcome home party for Davies, 109
Hall, Mordaunt, 96, 129
Hanfstaengl, Ernst Franz Sedgwick
"Putzi," 134–35
Harding, Warren G., 49–50, 116
Harlow, Jean, 137
Harris, China, 3, 188, 194
Hays, William, 53, 118, 147
Head, Alice: Davies's final trip with, 220;
with Davies-Hearst party in Europe
(1928), 104–5, 107; with Davies-Hearst
party in Europe (1936), 148, 149; on generosity of Davies, 65; and purchase of St.
Donat's Castle, 107
health of Davies: appendicitis/peritonitis
attack (1945), 176, 177; decline in 1950s,
216; infertility following illness at age
thirty, 87; jaw cancer, 218, 221; marriage
to Brown and, 202; Miltown tranquil-
izers and, 202, 207; minor stroke (1956),
214, 219; newspaper reports on final illness, 220; nursing care, due to leg weakness, 172, 176, 181, 185; osteomyelitis,
218; polio attack (1942), leg weakness
following, 1, 172, 181, 208; refusal of surgery to remove jaw cancer, 218. *See also*
alcoholism of Davies; death of Davies
Hearst, Elbert Whitmire "David" (son of
W. R. Hearst): birth of, 29; Hearst's
death and, 192
Hearst, George (father of W. R. Hearst), 27
Hearst, George Randolph (son of W. R.
Hearst), *figure 9, figure 32*; birth of, 29;
at Davies's funeral, 222; with Davies-
Hearst party in Europe (1934), 132, 133;
with Davies-Hearst party in Europe

(1936), 148; with Davies in Ran-
cho Mirage, 214; life and career after
Hearst's death, 229–30
Hearst, John Randolph (son of W. R.
Hearst), *figure 9*; birth of, 29; with
Davies-Hearst party in Europe (1934),
132, 133; and Hearst's funeral, 194; life
and career after Hearst's death, 230
Hearst, Lorna, *figure 32*
Hearst, Millicent Willson (wife of W. R.
Hearst), *figures 8–9*; beauty and intel-
ligence of, 29; career as chorus girl, 28;
Chaplin and, 68–69, 72; children with
Hearst, 29; and Christmas of 1925, 77;
Davies's competitiveness with, 204;
death and burial of, 232; and divorce,
terms for, 160–61; estrangement from
Hearst, 29, 49; at Hearst residence in
Clarendon building, 35; and Hearst's
affair with Davies, resignation toward,
35, 69, 161; Hearst's courtship and marriage, 28–29; and Hearst's funeral, 193,
194; Hearst's marriage to, as mere pretense by 1918, 29; on Hearst's personality, 29; high society life of, 29, 35; life
after Hearst's death, 231–32; and publicity for *Enchantment*, effort to have
Davies removed from, 49; similarities
to Davies, 29; vacation with Hearst and
children in Europe (1922), 53
Hearst, Patricia "Patty," kidnapping by
Symbionese Liberation Army, 231
Hearst, Phoebe Apperson (mother of W. R.
Hearst): background of, 27; death in
Spanish flu epidemic, 39; European
travel with young W. R., 27; Hearst's
affair with Davies and, 35–36; and
Hearst's affair with young waitress,
28; and Hearst's wife, disapproval of,
29; Morgan's remodeling of Pleasanton house for, 40; as philanthropist, 27;
portrait of, as Davies's gift to Hearst on
eighty-eighth birthday, 188; and "Rosebud" in *Citizen Kane*, 171; thirst for
knowledge passed on to W. R., 27; will,
properties denied to Hearst in, 39
Hearst, Randolph Apperson "Randy" (son
of W. R. Hearst): birth of, 29; as father

of Patty Hearst (kidnapping victim),
231; Hearst's death and, 191; life and
career after Hearst's death, 230–31

Hearst, William Randolph, *figures 8–9, figures 31–32, figure 37*; appearance of, 27;
Arbuckle and, 85; as art collector, 28;
BB gun shot at pigeons, 71; book collecting with Davies, 11, 36, 179; brief
college career at Harvard, 28; business
meetings, Davies's frequent presence at,
70; at Carole Lombard's funeral, 167;
and Chaplin, awkwardness over Davies,
68–69; childhood of, 27; and *Citizen
Kane*, 169; and Dick Powell, 141; eighty-
eighth birthday party, 188–89; financial problems, and Davies's loan of $1
million, 159–60; financial problems of
late 1930s, 151, 153, 158–59; and Great
Depression, 114–15, 123; high, thin voice
of, 27; and journalists, trust in Davies's
judgment about, 186; move to California, 61; negotiations with Parsons for
columnist position, 58, 60; parents and
upbringing of, 27; and Patricia Lake's
children, fondness for, 176; romance
with Tessie Powers, 28; Roosevelt and,
126–27; seventy-fifth birthday party,
153; seventy-fourth birthday party, 150–
51; turn to newspaper business, 28; W.R.
as friends' nickname for, 27–28. *See also*
San Simeon; Wyntoon

Hearst, William Randolph, character of: as
childlike in some ways, 45; complexity
of, 26–27; drive to succeed, 31; limited
empathy for others, 45–46, 160

Hearst, William Randolph, children of, 29;
battle with Davies over Hearst's estate,
197, 202–3; Hearst's harshness toward,
83; lives after his death, 229–31; relations with Davies, 67, 83, 133

Hearst, William Randolph, and Davies's
family: boosting of social standing,
36–37; and Davies's mother, death of,
97, 98; Davies's mother's affection for,
36, 97; purchase of home for (331 Riverside Drive), 37, 55; travel with Hearst
and Davies, 35, 42, 104, 132, 148

Hearst, William Randolph, and Davies's

movie career: control over every detail
of, 33, 47, 69, 72–73, 100–102, 111, 126,
132, 146–47; and Davies's turn to comedy, 45, 52, 92, 94, 101, 114, 125; launching of, 24, 31–32; lavish sets funded by,
33, 48, 61

Hearst, William Randolph, death of: and
Brown's comforting of Davies, 197;
Davies's activities on day of funeral, 194,
195; Davies's battle with Hearst's children over estate, 197, 202–3; Davies's
bedside vigil, 2, 190–91; Davies's reaction to, 193, 194; and friends' abandonment of Davies, 195–96; funeral, 193,
194; and Hearst corporation's severing
of ties with Davies, 195, 200, 202; *Life*
article on Davies following, 2, 185–86,
196; *Life* photograph of deathbed,
194–95, 196, *figure 40*; press coverage of,
193–94; removal of body from Davies's
home, 193; sedative administered to
Davies on death watch, 191, 192; transport of body to San Francisco, 193

Hearst, William Randolph, in later life:
and cancer, great fear of, 189–90; control of newspapers' policies, 182; declining health, 179–80; final departure from
San Simeon, 179–80; move to Beverly
Hills to be near hospital, 179–80; sadness of, 178–79; setup of trust assuring
Davies's control of Hearst Corporation after his death, 183–85, 197. *See also*
home on Beverly Drive

Hearst, William Randolph, and marriage
to Davies: aborted marriage plans, 160–
61; Davies's views on marriage and, 10,
162, 205; devastating effect of aborted
marriage plans on Davies, 161–62, 194;
impossibility of marriage as painful
issue, 36, 161–62, 197–98, 205

Hearst, William Randolph, marriage to
Millicent Willson, 28–29; divorce
efforts, 160–61; estrangement from, 29,
49; as mere pretense by 1918, 35. *See also*
Hearst, Millicent Willson

Hearst, William Randolph, and movie
industry: antiques provided for film
sets, 33, 48; building of studio in

Hearst, William Randolph, and movie industry (continued)
Manhatttan, 41–42; creation of Marion Davies Film Company, 31–32; deal with Pathé to produce *Perils of Pauline* series, 30; deal with Pathé to publicize Pathé pictures, 24, 30; deal with Select Pictures to back Davies's films, 31–32, 33; deal with Selig studios for newsreel production, 30; decline of influence, 138, 145; founding of Cosmopolitan Productions, 41–42; hiring of Frances Marion as screenwriter, 43–45; launching of Davies's career, 24, 31–32; making "super pictures" as goal, 33, 47; and newsreels, investment in, 29, 30; and synergistic ties with his newspapers, 29, 30. See also Cosmopolitan Productions

Hearst, William Randolph, politics of: as anti-Communist, 182–83; and ban from entering France, 119, 136; conservatism in later life, and shunning by Hollywood liberals, 150; post–World War I reputation as pro-German, 119–20; presidential bid, 30; run for governor of New York, 30; service in Congress, 30; and Treaty of Versailles, criticism of, 119, 134

Hearst, William Randolph, romance with Davies: as both father figure and love interest, 36, 97; Davies's appeal for Hearst, 31; Davies's inexperience in love and, 36; and Davies's meeting of famous figures, 2; development of, 35; early rumors of, 35; and false rumors of hidden love child, 63–64; and fear of scandal, 49, 53; fierce defense of Davies's reputation, 53; first encounters, 23, 30–31; frequent visits to Davies's family, 36; gifts of expensive books, 36; as great love story, 2; hiding of, from Hearst's mother, 35–36; international trips, 48; and jealousy, 73, 75–76, 118; large age difference and, 36, 76; *Life* article on Davies and, 196; love poems to Davies, 30–31, 181; Millicent Hearst's resignation toward, 35, 69, 161; newspaper articles attacking, 137, 144–45; romantic interest in Davies, origin of, 26; and

Santa Monica beach house for Davies, 89–90; single case of expressing anger with Davies in front of others, 79; trial of William Fallon and, 62–63; and trial stemming from shooting at Davies's sister's house, 54–56; two-story bungalow built for Davies on MGM lot, 69; and wealth showered on Davies, 37–38

Hearst, William Randolph, will of: and community property laws threatening Davies's property, 183–84, 197; Davies's home as issue in, 196–97; Hearst's sons' legal battle with Davies over, 197, 202–3

Hearst, William Randolph Jr. (son of W. R. Hearst), *figure 9*; birth of, 29; with Davies-Hearst party in Europe (1934), 132, 133; fistfight with Horace Brown at Romanoff's, 202–3; Hearst's death and, 192, 193; life and career after Hearst's death, 230; shunning of Davies after Hearst's death, 202–3; shutting down of Hopper's book on Davies, 222; takeover of Hearst editorial policy, 183

Hearst Corporation: business meetings, Davies's frequent presence at, 70; Davies's absorption of information about, 186; Davies's aid in managing, and defense of Ingrid Bergman, 186–88; Davies's aid in managing, in Hearst's waning days, 186; employees' resentment of Davies's interference, 186; severing of ties with Davies after Hearst's death, 195, 200, 202; *Time* and *Life* as hated rivals of, 185, 186; trust set up by Hearst to assure Davies's control of, 183–85, 197

Hearst International Film Service: creation of, 30; Davies's MGM bungalow as headquarters of, 69

Hearst newspapers: and Arbuckle trial, 52–53; decline in influence, 138, 145; entertainment as focus of, 26; Hearst's control of editorial policies in later life, 182; Hearst's death and, 194; Hearst's turnover of editorial policy to son, 183; on Japanese threat to U.S., 165; and MGM publicity, 64; prank motto accidentally printed by *Los Angeles Examiner*, 122; progressive, working-class posture of, 29–30; publicity campaign for Davies's *When Knighthood Was in Flower*, 57–58; publicity campaigns for Davies's *Cecilia of the Pink Roses*, 32, 33; and Roosevelt, attacks on, 150; support for HUAC investigations, 182–83; and yellow journalism, 28

Hearts Divided (1936 film), 145; production details, 241; reviews of, 145

Hecht, Ben, 38, 218

Hedda Hopper's Hollywood (1960 TV special): Davies's appearance on, 218–19, *figure 44*; production details, 242

Henie, Sonia, 167

Herrera, Lupe, 88, 130

Herrick, Lee, 15–16

His Girl Friday (film), screenplay for, 38

Hitler, Adolf: and events leading to World War II, 163, 164; as former columnist for Hearst newspapers, 134; Hearst's effort to moderate antisemitism of, 134–35

The Hollywood Review of 1929 (1929 film), 111–13; filming of, 111–12; production details, 238–39; stars appearing in, 112

home of Davies and family in Beverly Hills (1700 Lexington Road), *figures 11–12*; architect for, 89; Hearst's purchase of, 62; parties and gatherings at, 62, 67, 74–75; titling in mother's name, 62

home of Douras family in New York (331 Riverside Drive): as gift from Hearst, 37, 55; history of, after sale, 226; sale of, after family move to California, 66–67

home on Beverly Drive (1011 North Beverly Drive): Boardman as tenant at, 213–14; cutback in staff, with frequent stays in New York, 212; described, 3; filming of *Hedda Hopper's Hollywood* segment on Davies at, 218–19; history of, after Davies's death, 229; hosting of Joseph Kennedy during Democratic National Convention, 220; JFK's honeymoon at, 208; neighborhood changes in 1950s, 206; use in Hollywood films, 3, 229; visitors to, 182, 183

home on Beverly Drive, Davies's care for Hearst at, 182, 189–91; Davies's sleepless vigil in final days, 2, 190–91; encouragement of optimism in Hearst, 189; and final month, 190; Hearst and Davies's move to, to be near hospital, 179–80; Hearst's confinement to upstairs bedrooms, 182, 186; and Hearst's eighty-eighth birthday party, 188–89; Hearst's love notes written to Davies, 189; kissing of Davies as final act, 190–91; sedative administered to Davies on death watch, 191, 192; specially-printed newspapers for Hearst with upsetting death notices removed, 189; vetting of Hearst's visitors, 182; visitors in final days, 190

Home Owners' Loan Act, 129

Hoover, Herbert, 116

Hopper, Hedda, *figure 44*; career as gossip columnist, Davies's aid in, 67; as co-star in *Zander the Great*, 67; and Davies's generosity, 65; and Davies's marriage to Brown, 200, 201–2; on Davies's personality, 67; Davies's refusal to discuss Hearst romance with, 196; *Hedda Hopper's Hollywood* TV show, Davies's appearance on, 218–19, *figure 44*; interview of Davies (1954), 207; letter from mother helped by Marion Davies Children's Clinic, 223; *Life* profile of Davies and, 2; Lindbergh and, 93; party for Davies, before her trip to Kennedy's inauguration, 220; planned book about Davies, 222

horses, Davies's fear of, 8, 67–68, 80

House Un-American Activities Committee (HUAC), Hearst newspapers' support for, 182–83

HUAC. *See* House Un-American Activities Committee

Huberth, Martin, 179, 202

Hughes, Howard, 174

immigration, National Origins Act of 1924, 50

Ince, Thomas: cruise aboard *Oneida*, fatal consequences of, 70–71; Hearst's negotiations with, 69; rumors surrounding death of, 71–72; wife's letter relating facts of death, 72

Davies's death, impact of, 227; with
Davies-Hearst party in Europe (1936),
148; Davies's hiring of governess for,
103; at Davies's tea for American Legion
women, 162; in Davies's will, 222; and
death of Davies, 222; father's abduction of, 96; father's abduction of, long
term effects of, 227; marriage of, 152–53;
and "Meet the Family" TV series, 212–
13; and parent's marital problems, 82;
rumors identifying her as Hearst-Davies
love child, 63–64; at San Simeon, 82,
103; unstable home life after parents'
divorce, 102–3
Lamarr, Hedy, 167
Lamour, Dorothy, 167
Laurel and Hardy, 112
Lawford, Peter, 208
Lawrence, Florence, 73–74
Lederer, Anne Shirley (niece-in-law), *figure 38*; on Davies's attentions to Charlie
Lederer, 38–39; on Davies's character,
187–88; on Davies family togetherness,
17; on Davies's humor about polio-
damaged legs, 172; on Davies's intelligence, 10–11; on Davies's modesty, 65;
easy integration into Davies's circle, 182;
film career of, 182; on Horace Brown,
199; introduction to Davies, 182; life
after Davies's death, 228
Lederer, Charles "Charlie" (nephew), 10–11;
attendance of Davies's early performances, 16; career as writer, 38; care for
Davies in later life, 203; and Davies's
alcoholism, 174; and Davies's autobiographical tapes, 203; Davies's care for, as
child, 38–39, 82–83; with Davies-Hearst
party in Europe, 105; and Davies's marriage to Brown, 218; and filming of
Hedda Hopper's Hollywood segment
on Davies, 219; as gifted child, 38–39;
Hearst's death and, 192; introduction of
fiancee to Davies, 182; and *Kismet* musical, 209–10; life after Davies's death,
228; Mankiewicz and, 170; and planned
Davies autobiography, 209; rumors
identifying him as Hearst-Davies love
child, 63; at San Simeon, 82; wife of, 17

Lederer, George (brother-in-law): attendance of Davies's early performances,
16; as director, 25, 26; marriage to
Davies's sister Irene, 12–13, 25
Lederer, Josephine Rose "Pepi" (niece), *figures 16–17*; birth of, 13; Davies's care for,
as child, 38, 39, 82; Davies's concerns
about her influence on, 106–7; Davies's
efforts to rehabilitate, 141; with Davies-
Hearst party in Europe, 105, 106; death
by suicide in psychiatric hospital, 141–
42; drug use and partying, as concern
to Davies, 106, 141; Hearst's support
for, 107; on Hearst yacht with Davies,
70; as lesbian, 39, 106; as neighborhood
troublemaker, 37; reasons for unhappiness, 142; resentment of attention given
to brother, 39; at San Simeon, 82; small
part in *The Cardboard Lover*, 102; visit
to New York for Davies show, 16
Lederer, Maitland (nephew), 13, 19
Leonard, Robert Z., 118
Lester, Edwin, 209–10
Life magazine: article on Davies following
Hearst's death, 2, 185–86, 196; article
on Davies's marriage to Brown, 198;
and Davies's autobiographical tapes, 1,
21, 203
The Lights of Old Broadway (1925 film):
Davies's dual role in, 74; early color-
ization techniques in, 74; production
details, 237; story of, 74
Lindbergh, Charles: celebrity status of,
92–93; Davies's tea for, at Ambassador
Hotel, 93; fascination with Davies, 93;
later-life politics of, 93; visit to set of *The
Fair Co-Ed*, 93
Lindstrom, Petter, 187, 188
The Little Cafe (stage show), 16
Little Old New York (1923 film), 58–59;
Davies's cross-dressing in, 58–59;
Davies's mother's delight with, 60; dra-
matic coach for Davies, 119; first at Cos-
mopolitan Studio and, 59–60; Louella
Parson's review of, 60; production
details, 236; reviews of, 60; social issues
addressed in, 58–59; story of, 58
Livingstone, Mary, 167

171; and Davies's departure from MGM, 139; and end of Haines' career, 158; and Hearst's departure from MGM, 138–39, 144–45; Hearst's power over, 131; and Hitler's antisemitism, 134; and Metro-Goldwyn-Mayer, founding of, 64; as neighbor of Davies's in Santa Monica, 89; and *Show People*, 101; visits to Hearst during final illness, 182; and wrecking of John Gilbert's career, 156–57

McCarthy, Joseph, 182–83
McCrea, Joel, 110–11
McLean, Ned, 120–21
McPherson, Aimee Semple, 66
"Meet the Family" TV series, 212–13
Merriam, Frank, 136, 138
Metro-Goldwyn-Meyer. *See* MGM
Mexico: Davies and Hearst in (1942), 173; Davies's and Hearst's vacation to (1921), 48–49, 53; Hearst property in Campeche, 173
MGM (Metro-Goldwyn-Meyer): Cosmopolitan Productions' move to Warner Brothers from, 138–39; culling of stars unsuitable for sound movies, 108–9; Davies's departure from, 139; Davies's sound test for, 109; Davies's two-story bungalow at, 69; decline of Hearst's influence at, 138, 145; film adaptation of *Kismet* musical, 210; founding of, 64; and Hearst newspapers' publicity, 64; move of Davies's bungalow from, 138–39; as one of top three Los Angeles studios, 66; rumors of Cosmopolitan Studio's separation from, 91, 131
MGM, Davies's contract with: large salary and other income from, 64; and oversight power over roles, 64; renewal (1926), generous terms of, 91; signing of, *figure 13*
MGM, newspaper boy at: Davies's funding of education, 86; Davies's hiring of, for *The Red Mill*, 86
Miss Information (stage show), 19
Monroe, Marilyn, 228
Montgomery, Robert, 125, 126, 151–52
Moore, Colleen, 85, 178

Morgan, Julia: as architect for San Simeon, 40, 77; career of, 40; and Davies's Santa Monica beach house, 89, 117; design of Douras family mausoleum, 98, 216; and design of Marian Davies Children's Clinic, 88, 89; design of structures for Hearst's Wyntoon retreat, 81–82; diminutive stature of, 40; work for Hearst family, 40
Morrice, Monica, 141, 142
Morrisey, Betty, 106, *figure 17*
Motion Picture Country House and Hospital, 228
Motion Picture Producers and Distributors Association (MPPDA): banning of Arbuckle, 53; defending movie industry reputation as goal of, 53, 118; shooting at Davies's sister's house and, 54
Motion Picture Production Code: and *Cain and Mabel*, 147; and pre-Code era films, 118–19; tightening of, in 1934, 147
Motion Picture Relief Fund: benefit for (1932), 123–24; Davies as president of, 129–30, 143; founding and mission of, 130; Great Depression and, 130, 143; history of, 228; renaming of, 228
movie industry: backlash in 1920s against misbehavior in, 52–53; creation of MPPDA to defend reputation of, 53; early colorization processes, introduction of, 74; Goldwyn articles on, for *Pictorial Review*, 24; shift from New York to California, 60; television and, 206; turn to feature-length films, 24
movies starring Davies. *See The Barretts of Wimpole Street*; *Beauty's Worth*; *The Belle of New York*; *Beverly of Graustark*; *Blondie of the Follies*; *Boy Meets Girl*; *The Bride's Play*; *Cain and Mabel*; *The Cardboard Lover*; *Cecilia of the Pink Roses*; *The Cinema Murder*; *The Dark Star*; *Enchantment*; *Ever Since Eve*; *The Fair Co-Ed*; *Five and Ten*; *The Five O'Clock Girl*; *The Florodora Girl*; *Getting Mary Married*; *Going Hollywood*; *Hearts Divided*; *The Hollywood Review of 1929*; *Janice Meredith*; *The Lights of Old Broadway*; *Little Old New York*;

movies starring Davies *(continued)*
    Marianne; *Not So Dumb*; *Operator 13*;
    Page Miss Glory; *The Patsy*; *Peg O' My*
    Heart; *Polly of the Circus*; *Quality Street*;
    The Red Mill; *The Restless Sex*; *Runaway*
    Romany; *Show People*; *Tillie the Toiler*;
    When Knighthood Was in Flower; *The*
    Young Diana; *Zander the Great*
movie star, Davies as: appealing quali-
    ties suitable for, 23–24; cast and crew's
    affection for, 41; concerns about over-
    exposure, 60–61; concerns about types
    of roles played, 60–61; Cosmopoli-
    tan Productions and, 41; and Davies's
    determination and strong work ethic,
    3, 25; Davies's frequent purchases of
    lunch for everyone on set, 68, 140;
    desire for more substantial roles, 126,
    127; dual roles, 50–51, 58–59, 74, 91–92;
    fan willing entire estate to Davies, 153;
    first film, 25–26; and flirtations with
    co-stars, 139–40; frequent cross-dress-
    ing, 51–52; hair styles, change in, 50,
    77, 92; Hearst's control over, 33, 47, 69,
    72–73, 100–102, 111, 126, 132, 146–47;
    Hearst's promotion of, 31–32; later-life
    reflection on, 207; launching of career,
    23–26; lavish sets funded by Hearst, 33,
    48, 61; lighting techniques, advanced,
    47–48; and lineage of female comedi-
    ans, 3, 95–96; and male co-stars' fear
    of Hearst's jealousy, 140; and Marion
    Davies productions, 91; move from
    silent to sound films, 3; negotiation of
    own contracts, 3; newspaper articles
    about her on-set thoughtfulness, 144;
    newspaper articles attacking, 144–45;
    on-set string quartet during filming, 95;
    ready-made stardom given to her, psy-
    chological effects of, 64–65; retirement,
    152; and reviews, avoidance of, 145; set
    designer for, 47; six-picture deal with
    Selznick, 32, 33; waning of career, in her
    late 30s, 143, 146, 151. *See also* Hearst,
    William Randolph, and Davies's movie
    career; MGM, Davies's contract with
movie star, Davies as, and turn to comedy:
    critics' positive response to, 94; Fran-

ces Marion's push for, 44–45; Hearst's
    views on, 45, 52, 94, 101, 114, 125; and
    potential as comedic actress, Loos on,
    41; and screwball comedy, pioneering
    of, 95–96, 167; *Tillie the Toiler* and, 91,
    92
movie stars: and celebrity journalism, 74; as
    new concept in 1910s, 24; of silent era,
    fate of, 108–9, 156–58
MPPDA. *See* Motion Picture Producers
    and Distributors Association
Mussolini, Benito, Hearst's efforts to meet,
    132–33

National Origins Act of 1924, 50
National Recovery Administration, 149
needlework, Davies's lifelong interest in, 12
Neighborhood House Association (Los
    Angeles), Davies's support of, 83
New Theater League, 144–45
New York City, social ills of early twentieth
    century, 19
Neylan, John Francis, 135, 172
Nineteenth Amendment, 50
1920s: and airplanes, public interest in,
    92–93; backlash against film industry
    misbehavior in, 52–53; celebrity culture
    of, *figure 22*; dual roles as trend in mov-
    ies of, 50–51; increased religiosity in, 50,
    52, 66; Los Angeles in, 66; political and
    economic life in, 49–50; social divide
    in, 50, 52
Normand, Mabel, 41, 53
Not So Dumb (1930 film), 115; Davies's
    speaking part in, 115; moderate success
    of, 115; production details, 239
nuclear fallout, Davies's concern about,
    211, 220

Oberon, Merle, 166
Oh, Boy! (stage show), 25, 247n22
Oneida (Hearst yacht): and Davies's
    and Hearst's vacation to Mexico, 48;
    described, 70; Ince's cruise on, with
    fatal consequences, 70–71
Operator 13 (1934 film), 131; Davies's appear-
    ance on radio to advertise, 131–32; and
    incident with boom operator, 131; pro-

duction details, 241; radio version of, *figure 33*

Page Miss Glory (1935 film), 139–40; Davies's flirtation with co-star Powell, 139–40; Davies's personal tragedies during filming of, 141–42; preview party for, 143–44; production details, 241; publicity photos for, 142; reviews of, 143, 144

Parsons, John, 34, 78

Parsons, Louella "Lolly": abandonment of Davies after Hearst's death, 195–96; ambition to be Hearst's society columnist, 34; and boosting of Davies's career, 34, 58; career of, 34; and *Citizen Kane*, 171; Davies as guest on radio show of, 131–32; Davies's help in negotiations with Hearst, 58; on Davies's marriage to Brown, 198; on Davies's Santa Monica beach house, 90; on Davies's wealth, 38; decline of influence over movie industry, 138; friendship with Davies, 34; at Hearst's seventy-fourth birthday party, 150; Hearst's use of, to spy on Davies, 73, 75; interview of Davies, 33–34; and Marion Davies War Work Committee, 165–66; marriage and child, 34; negotiations with Hearst for columnist's job, 58, 60; newspaper article attacking, 144–45; as pioneer of celebrity journalism, 74; review of *Little Old New York*, 60; review of *When Knighthood Was in Flower*, 58; and rumors surrounding death of Ince, 71; at San Simeon, 78; travel from New York to Los Angeles with Davies, 73

Pathé, Hearst's deal with: and *Perils of Pauline* series, 30; to publicize Pathé pictures, 24, 30; and *Runaway Romany* filming, 25

The Patsy (1928 film), 94–96; Davies's imitations in, 95; Davies's rest following, 99; and Davies's turn to comedy, 95; and lineage of female comedians, 95–96; production details, 238; profit from, 96; reviews of, 96; story of, 94–95; Vidor's direction of, 95; Winton in, 110

Peck, Orrin, 28, 171

Peg O' My Heart (1933 film), 127–29; Davies's accent in, 11; Davies's age as issue in, 127; as Davies's last role as young girl, 128–29; filming of, 128; Hearst's influence on, 128; interruption of filming by Long Beach earthquake, 128; production details, 240–41; radio version of, 132, 152; reviews of, 128–29

Peg O' My Heart (Manners) (play), 128

Percy, Eileen: and Davies's aborted marriage to Hearst, 160, 161; on Davies's desire to marry Hearst, 205; and Davies-Hearst trip to Europe (1934), 132, *figure 32*; at Davies's "kiddie" party, 122; on Davies's underlying sadness, 2; Flink on, 186; Hearst's death and, 194; and Hearst's eighty-eighth birthday party, 188; as longtime friend of Davies, 2, 3

Perils of Pauline series, as Hearst and Pathé joint venture, 30

Pickford, Mary: at benefit for Marion Davies Foundation, 123; Davies's visit to, in final illness, 219; and death of Davies, 222; and founding of Motion Picture Relief Fund, 130; Frances Marion as writer for, 43–44; interest in *When Knighthood Was in Flower*, 51; Lindbergh and, 93; philanthropy of, as model for Davies, 165; retirement, 158; screening of films at home of, 68; and United Artists, establishment of, 43–44

Pictorial Review: Block and, 23, 24; and celebrity journalism, 24; founding of, 37

Pirate Party on Catalina Isle (1935 short film), 241

Plunket, Baron and Lady, fatal plane crash, 153–54

politics and current events: Davies's interest in, 19, 53, 163; Davies's leftward drift after death of Hearst, 208; Davies's tolerance for Communism, 182; Davies's views on, 136. *See also* Hearst, William Randolph, politics of

Polly of the Circus (1932 film), 125–27; Davies's complex role in, 126; production details, 240; reviews of, 125, 127

Powell, Dick, 140–41, 145

Pre-Code era, 118–19
production code. *See* Motion Picture Production Code
Prohibition, 42, 50
Pygmalion, as potential Davies project, 152

Quality Street (1927 film), 91–92; Davies's dual role in, 91–92; production details, 238; reviews of, 92; story of, 91–92
Queen Christina (film), 157

radio: Davies's debut on, 131–32; Davies in *Operator 13* radio version, *figure 33*; Davies in *Peg O' My Heart* radio version, 132, 152; and declining influence of Hearst newspapers, 145
real estate investments by Davies: naming of buildings, 211; in New York City, 209; purchase of Desert Inn, 211; purchase of New York residence as base of operations, 212; purchase of Rancho Mirage home, 214; talent for, 211
Reconstruction Finance Corporation (RFC), 128
The Red Mill (1927 film), 84–85; casting of children for, 86; filming of, 86–87, *figure 21*; hiring of Arbuckle as director for, 84–85, 87; hiring of Vidor to oversee Arbuckle, 85, 95; production details, 237; retakes for, 91
Reilly, Charles (maternal grandfather), 5, 8
Reilly, Mary Cushing (maternal grandmother), 5, 8
Reilly, Rose (mother). *See* Douras, Rose Reilly
The Restless Sex (1920 film): filming of, 45; production details, 234; screenplay for, 45
retirement of Davies, 152; depression following plane crash at San Simeon, 154; and loss of large circle of friends, 178; love of reading and, 181, 206–7; and new film releases, Davies's lack of interest in, 177–78; and philanthropy, 165; polio attack (1942), leg weakness following, 1, 172, 181, 208; quiet life with Hearst at San Simeon, 178; return to chorus girl

sleep schedule, 15, 172; typical activities in, 153, 178. *See also* health of Davies; home on Beverly Drive; investments by Davies in later life
Revenue Act of 1935, 149
RFC. *See* Reconstruction Finance Corporation
Rialto Theater (San Francisco), renaming as Marion Davis Theater, 113
Ripley, Robert L., 113
Rockefeller, Nelson, 171
Rogers, Will, 123
Rolls Royce automobile, Davies's purchase of model identical to Hearst's widow, 204
Romero, Cesar, 167
Roosevelt, Anna: as columnist for Hearst newspapers, 167; Davies's friendship with, 150, 167; at Davies's wartime fundraiser, 167–68; and death of father, 176
Roosevelt, Eleanor, 150
Roosevelt, Franklin D.: at benefit for Marion Davies Foundation, 123; campaign for president, 126–27; death of, 176; and election of 1936, 149, 150; and election of 1940, 164; and Great Depression, 129; Hearst's views on, 127, 144, 149–50; political use of IRS, 150; and radio's influence, 145; and World War II, 163
Roosevelt family, Davies's fondness for, 150
Rossellini, Roberto, 187, 188
Ruby, Harry, 160, 161
Runaway Romany (1917 film), *figure 7*; filming of, 25–26; and Hearst's romantic interest in Davies, 26; poor reviews of, 26; production details, 233
Ruth, Babe, *figure 22*

San Simeon, *figure 19*; construction at, Hearst's financial crisis of late 1930s and, 159; Coolidges' stay at, 115–16; as coveted Hollywood destination, 77, 78; dachshund kennels at, 78; Davies's and Hearst's final departure from, 179–80; and Davies as outsider among educated guests, 80; Davies's family as guests at, 82; Davies's hosting of party to mark completion of, 77; Davies's love of hosting weddings at, 197–98; Davies's quiet life with Hearst after retirement, 178; dining room in, 80; donation to state of California as tourist attraction, 224–25; exotic animals roaming free on grounds, 78; frequent guests at, 80–81; gardens, 77; Great Depression and, 123; guest houses, 79; guests' travel to, 78; Hearst's conduct of business from, 64; Hearst's continual construction at, 64, 151; Hearst's efforts to control Davies's drinking at, 79; Hearst's father's purchase of property, 27; Heart's fussiness about construction details, 40; Hearst's hope for perpetual construction, 40; Hearst's inheritance of property, 39; Hearst's long-time dream of building castle at, 39–40; high cost of maintaining, 151; horseriding at, 80; land around, as still Hearst property, 225; lavish picnics and excursions for guests, 80; and long stays in California, 42; main house (Casa Grande), 78, 79; Morgan as architect for, 40; movie theater built at, 116; music piped throughout grounds, 78–79; parties hosted by Davies at, 80; plane crash killing Baron and Lady Plunket, 153–54; private zoo, 77–78, 151, 180; range of guests at, 80; restoration of gardens, 225; rules for guests, 79; schedule of activities for guests, 79

Santa Monica, as trendy spot for Hollywood elite, 66. *See also* beach house at Santa Monica

Scott, Randolph, 167

Select Pictures, Hearst's deal with, to back Davies's films, 31–32, 33

Selig studios, Hearst's deal with, for newsreel production, 30

Selznick, David O., 31

Selznick, Lewis J.: children's success in film industry, 31; Hearst's deal with, to back Davies's films, 31–32, 33; six-picture deal for Davies, 32, 33

Selznick, Myron, 31

Shanahan, R. J., 63

Shaw, George Bernard: Davies's meeting with, 2, 120; death of, 189; Hearst's final illness and, 189; interest in film version of *Pygmalion* with Davies, 152

Shearer, Norma: and *Barretts of Wimpole Street*, 129; at Davies's tea for American Legion women, 162; in *Hollywood Revue of 1929*, 112; and Marion Davies War Work Committee, 166; marriage to Thalberg, 129; as neighbor of Davies's beach house, 89; replacement of Davies in *Barretts of Wimpole Street* and *Marie Antoinette*, 138; and welcome home parties for Davies, 109, 137

Shearn, Clarence J., 151

Shields, Jimmy, 81, 109, 158

Shirley, Anne (niece-in-law). *See* Lederer, Anne Shirley

shooting at homecoming party at Davies's sister's home (1922), 54; anti-Hearst newspapers' sensationalizing of link to Davies, 54; defamation lawsuit filed by Davies's brother-in-law, 54–56; occasion for party, 53–54

Show People (1928 film), 99–102; casting of Murray as co-star, 100; comedy scenes in, 100; Davies's naturalness in, 95; Haines as co-star, 100; Hearst's cutting of pie-in-the-face scene, 100–102; previous titles of, 99; production details, 238; promotion still for, *figure 26*; reviews of, 102; as satire based on Gloria Swanson's career, 99; screenplay, writing of, 99

Shriver, Sargent, 207–8

Simpson, Wallace, 149

Sinclair, Upton: as California gubernatorial candidate, 135–36, 137–38; MGM newsreel campaign against, 138; as tabloid owner, 137

The Singing Fool (film), 108, 113

Sonny Boy (film), 113

sound movies, introduction of: Davies's anxiety about, 94, 97, 99, 104, 108; Davies's control of stutter, 112–13, 115; Davies's first onscreen words, 112; Davies's first sound movies, 110–12, 114, 115; and Davies's MGM sound

sound movies, introduction of *(continued)*
test, 109; Davies's stiffer screen presence, 113; Davies's use of improvisation
to avoid stutter triggers, 109; Davies's
voice quality and, 109; development
of technology for, 103–4; *Don Juan*
and, 104; *The Jazz Singer* and, 94, 103;
MGM culling of stars with poor voices,
108–9; and pre-Code era, 118–19; press's
speculation about Davies and, 110;
silent movie actors' careers destroyed by,
156–57; and *The Singing Fool* (film), 108;
as threat to silent film stars with voice
issues, 94, 103; voice coaches hired for
Davies, 110; work to overcome stutter,
3, 112–13
Spanish-American War, Hearst's newsreels
on, 29
Spanish flu, deaths from, 39
Spreckels, Kay. *See* Gable, Kay Spreckels
State Guard: Davies as honorary captain of,
166; use of Marion Davies Children's
Clinic in World War II, 166, *figure 36*
St. Donat's Castle (Wales), 107–8, 119
St. Johns, Adela Rogers, 43, 83, 105, 110, 174
stock market: crash of 1929, 114–15; Davies's
withdrawal from, before crash of 1929,
104
Stop! Look! Listen! (stage show), 19
studio system, and contract extensions, 139
stutter of Davies: and avoidance of interviews in later life, 207; and childhood
teasing, lifelong effect of, 113; Davies's
sense of humor about, 211; first occur-
rences of, 10, 244n10; lack of treatment for, 10–11; in later life, 1, 2–3, 211;
meeting with Maugham and, 59; radio
appearances and, 132; school and, 10–11,
13; singing unaffected by, 21; speaking
parts onstage and, 21, 22–23, 247n22;
and television, avoidance of work on,
207; and trial stemming from shooting at sister Reine's house, 55–56; use of
alcohol to treat, 22–23; willingness to
speak despite, 22; and work at Ziegfeld
Follies, 20, 21, 22–23, 247n22; worsening in times of stress, 10
stutter of Davies, and sound movies, intro-

duction of: Davies's anxiety about, 94,
97, 99, 104, 108; Davies's control of stutter, 112–13, 115; Davies's MGM sound
test, 109; Davies's stiffer screen presence, 113; Davies's use of improvisation
to avoid stutter triggers, 109; press's
speculation about, 110; voice coaches
hired to help, 110; work to overcome
stutter, 3, 112–13
Sullivan, Lea: bullfighting as hobby, 211–12;
Davies's conversion to animal rights
activism, 212; on Davies's death, 220;
on Davies's odd expressions, 211; and
Davies's trips to Desert Inn, 211; friendship with Davies, 210–12
The Sunshine Girl (stage show), 16,
245–46n16
Swanberg, W. A., 141, 231
Swanson, Gloria: affair with Joseph Kennedy, 81, 99; Davies's dislike of, 81,
99–100; divorce from Marquis de la
Coudraye, 137; as frequent guest at San
Simeon, 81; *Show People* and, 99–100;
tea with Davies for *Life* profile, 185–86;
at welcome home party for Davies, 109
Symbionese Liberation Army (SLA), 231

Talmadge, Constance, 67, 122, 144, 156
Talmadge, Norma, 67, 93, 122, 156
Tammany Hall, 5. 7, 62
Teapot Dome scandal, 49–50
Technicolor, two-strip, 74, 116–17
television: Davies's avoidance of work on,
207; in Davies's home, 206; effect on
movie industry, 206; movie stars' move
into, 207
Thalberg, Irving: and *Barretts of Wimpole
Street*, 130–31; and *Blondie of the Follies*,
125–26; and Davies's turn to comedy, 92,
114; and *The Five O'Clock Girl*, 111; marriage to Shearer, 129; and MGM newsreel campaign against Sinclair, 138; as
neighbor of Davies in Santa Monica, 89;
and *Quality Street*, 91; at San Simeon,
77; and *Show People*, 100; and welcome
home parties for Davies, 109, 137
Tillie the Toiler (1927 film): Davies's need
for rest following, 91; Davies's role as

modern girl in, 91; production details, 237

The Times We Had (Davies), 4; Welles's foreword to, 171

Treaty of Versailles, Hearst's criticism of, 119, 134

Turner, Florence, 24, 61

Turner, Lana, 203

Twentieth Century (film), 95–96

Twentieth Century Fox: Cosmopolitan Productions move to, 152; interest in filming Davies's life story, 207; move of Davies's bungalow to, 152

United Artists: establishment of, 43–44; Hearst and, 41

United Nations Charter, signing of, 177

United Nations Conference on International Organization, 177

University of California, Berkeley, Hearst's donation of Greek Theatre to, 40

Urban, Joseph: battles with Hearst over set design, 48; career of, 47; design of Davies's bungalow on MGM lot, 69; lighting techniques, advanced, 47–48; and Maugham's meeting with Davies, 59; resignation and return, 48; set design for *Zander the Great*, 69; set designs for Cosmopolitan studio, 47–48

Van Cleve, George: and Hearst's suspicions about Davies's infidelity, 76; marriage to Rose Douras, 38, 42, 82, 96; and shooting at Davies's sister's house, 54–55

Van Cleve, Patricia. *See* Lake, Patricia Van Cleve

Vanderbilt, Gloria, 185–86

Vidor, King: and filming of *The Red Mill*, 85; at *Florodora Girl* premiere, 118; as guest at San Simeon, 77, 85–86; Hearst's confidence in, 95; James Murray and, 100; marriage to Boardman, 156; and *Not So Dumb*, 115; on pleasure of working with Davies, 95; romance with Boardman, 85–86; and *Show People*, 101

vivisection, Davies and Hearst's campaign against, 163–64, 186

voting rights for women, 50

Wanger, Walter, 53, 158, 246n20

Warner, Jack: and Hearst's move to Warner Brothers, 138–39; and Marion Davies War Work Committee, 165–66

Warner Brothers: Cosmopolitan Productions' move from, 152; Cosmopolitan Productions' move to, 138–39; Davies's contract with, 139; Davies's hosting of lunches for cast, 140; Davies's move to, 139; move of Davies's MGM bungalow from, 152; move of Davies's MGM bungalow to, 138–39

Wayburn, Ned, 19–20

Welles, Orson: and *Citizen Kane*, 1–2, 169; and foreword to *The Times We Had*, 171; and "War of the Worlds," 169. *See also Citizen Kane*

Wells, Evelyn, 63–64, 79, 143

When Knighthood Was in Flower (Major) (book), 51

When Knighthood Was in Flower (1922 film), 52–53; Davies's comedy in, 52, 57–58; Davies's cross-dressing in, 51–52; Davies's fencing scene in, 51; dramatic coach for Davies, 110; extensive research for, 51; filming of, 51; Hearst's purchase of rights for, 51; lobby card for, *figure 10*; Louella Parsons' review of, 58; Mary Pickford's private screening of, 68; massive publicity campaign for, 57–58; as million-dollar epic of Tudor England, 51; premiere, Hearst's remodeling of Criterion Theater for, 57; production details, 235; songs specially written for, 57; story of, 51

When Knighthood Was in Flower (play), 51

will, of Davies, 222

will, of Hearst: and community property laws threatening Davies's property, 183–84, 197; Davies's home as issue in, 196–97; Hearst's sons' legal battle with Davies over, 197, 202–3

Williams, Ella "Bill," 96, 214

Willson, Millicent. *See* Hearst, Millicent Willson

Winchell, Walter, 210

women: in Hearst organization, equal treatment of, 43; and new attitudes of

women *(continued)*
1920s vs. traditional roles, 90; voting rights for, 50
Wood, Sam, 92, 93
World War I, and death of Maitland Lederer, 19
World War II: atomic bombing of Japan, Hearst and Davies's views on, 177; Davies's fundraiser for Hospital at Hollywood Palladium, 167–68; Davies's views on, 163; events leading to, 162–63; Hearst's supply of mahogany to the Navy, 173; Hearst's views on, 163; Marion Davies Children's Clinic and, 166, 167–68, *figure 36*; and Marion Davies War Work Committee, 165–66; Pearl Harbor attack, 165; U.S. isolationists and, 163; victory in Europe, 176–77
Wyntoon (Hearst retreat): burial of Gandhi (Davies's dachshund) at, 175; commercial logging on, after Hearst's death, 225; as Davies's and Hearst's base in late 1930s, 153; Davies's and Hearst's visits to, 81, 82, 143–44, 153, 161, 165, 172, *figure 37*; Hearst's construction at, 81–82; Hearst's mother's willing to cousin, 39, 81; Hearst's purchase of, from cousin, 81; size of, 225; as still owned by Hearst family, 225

yacht of Hearst. See *Oneida*
yellow journalism, Hearst and, 28
Yolanda (1924 film), 236
Young, Robert, 167
The Young Diana (1922 film): Davies's dual role in, 50–51; production details, 235

Zander the Great (1925 film), 67–69, *figures 14–15*; filming of, 67; as first Davies film made in California, 67; Hearst's complete overhaul of, 69; Hedda Hopper as co-star in, 67; mix of genres in, 67; premiere of, 73; production details, 236–37; story of, 67; stunt double for Davies in, 67–68; writing of, 67
Ziegfeld, Florenz, 18
Ziegfeld Follies: as escapist entertainment, 18–19; as path to success, 18; respect for dancers in, 20; stars of, 18, 20
Ziegfeld Follies, Davies's work for: and attention from "stage-door johnnies," 23; audition, 18, 19–20; dating of Paul Block, 23–24, 36; Davies's stutter and, 20, 21, 22–23, 247n22; Florida Red Cross benefit, 35; hiring, 20; meeting of Hearst, 23; off hours fun with other cast members, 21–22; shows, 20–21; and treatment of anxiety with alcohol, 22–23
Zukor, Adolph, 41, 61

Founded in 1893,
UNIVERSITY OF CALIFORNIA PRESS
publishes bold, progressive books and journals
on topics in the arts, humanities, social sciences,
and natural sciences—with a focus on social
justice issues—that inspire thought and action
among readers worldwide.

The UC PRESS FOUNDATION
raises funds to uphold the press's vital role
as an independent, nonprofit publisher, and
receives philanthropic support from a wide
range of individuals and institutions—and from
committed readers like you. To learn more, visit
ucpress.edu/supportus.